THE CONSTRUCTION LAW TITLES FROM ASPEN LAW & BUSINESS

ALTERNATIVE CLAUSES TO STANDARD CONSTRUCTION CONTRACTS
James E. Stephenson, Editor

ALTERNATIVE DISPUTE RESOLUTION IN THE CONSTRUCTION INDUSTRY
Robert F. Cushman, G. Christian Hedemann, and Avram S. Tucker, Editors

ARBITRATION OF CONSTRUCTION DISPUTES
Michael T. Callahan, Barry B. Bramble, and Paul M. Lurie

ARCHITECT AND ENGINEER LIABILITY: CLAIMS AGAINST DESIGN PROFESSIONALS
Robert F. Cushman and Thomas G. Bottum, Editors

CALCULATING CONSTRUCTION DAMAGES
William Schwartzkopf, John J. McNamara, and Julian F. Hoffar

CALIFORNIA CONSTRUCTION LAW (FIFTEENTH EDITION)
Kenneth C. Gibbs and Gordon Hunt

CONSTRUCTION AND ENVIRONMENTAL INSURANCE CASE DIGESTS
Wiley Law Publications, Editors

CONSTRUCTION BIDDING LAW
Robert F. Cushman and William J. Doyle, Editors

CONSTRUCTION CLAIMS AND LIABILITY
Michael S. Simon

CONSTRUCTION CONTRACTOR'S HANDBOOK OF BUSINESS AND LAW
Robert F. Cushman, G. Christian Hedemann, and Peter J. King, Editors

CONSTRUCTION DEFAULTS: RIGHTS, DUTIES, AND LIABILITIES
Robert F. Cushman and Charles A. Meeker, Editors

CONSTRUCTION DELAY CLAIMS (SECOND EDITION)
Barry B. Bramble and Michael T. Callahan

CONSTRUCTION ENGINEERING EVIDENCE
Loren W. Peters

CONSTRUCTION FAILURES
Robert F. Cushman, Irvin E. Richter, and Lester E. Rivelis, Editors

CONSTRUCTION INDUSTRY CONTRACTS: LEGAL CITATOR AND CASE DIGEST
Wiley Law Publications Editorial Staff

CONSTRUCTION INDUSTRY FORMS (TWO VOLUMES)
Robert F. Cushman and George L. Blick, Editors

CONSTRUCTION INDUSTRY INSURANCE HANDBOOK
Deutsch, Kerrigan & Stiles

CONSTRUCTION LITIGATION FORMBOOK
David M. Buoncristiani, John D. Carter, and Robert F. Cushman

CONSTRUCTION LITIGATION: REPRESENTING THE CONTRACTOR (SECOND EDITION)
John D. Carter, Robert F. Cushman, and William J. Palmer, Editors

CONSTRUCTION LITIGATION: REPRESENTING THE OWNER (SECOND EDITION)
Robert F. Cushman, Kenneth M. Cushman, and Stephen B. Cook, Editors

CONSTRUCTION LITIGATION: STRATEGIES AND TECHNIQUES
Barry B. Bramble and Albert E. Phillips, Editors

CONSTRUCTION RENOVATION FORMBOOK
Robert F. Cushman and John W. DiNicola, Editors

CONSTRUCTION SCHEDULING: PREPARATION, LIABILITY, AND CLAIMS
Jon M. Wickwire, Thomas J. Driscoll, and Stephen B. Hurlbut

CONSTRUCTION SUBCONTRACTING: A LEGAL GUIDE FOR INDUSTRY PROFESSIONALS
Overton A. Currie, Neal J. Sweeney, and Randall F. Hafer, Editors

DESIGN-BUILD CONTRACTING HANDBOOK
Robert F. Cushman and Kathy Sperling Taub, Editors

DESIGN PROFESSIONAL'S HANDBOOK OF BUSINESS AND LAW
Robert F. Cushman and James C. Dobbs, Editors

DRAFTING CONSTRUCTION CONTRACTS: STRATEGY AND FORMS FOR CONTRACTORS
Samuel F. Schoninger

FEDERAL CONSTRUCTION CONTRACTING
James F. Nagle

HAZARDOUS WASTE DISPOSAL AND UNDERGROUND CONSTRUCTION LAW
Robert F. Cushman and Bruce W. Ficken, Editors

LEGAL GUIDE TO AIA DOCUMENTS (THIRD EDITION)
Werner Sabo

1992 DIRECTORY OF CONSTRUCTION INDUSTRY CONSULTANTS
Wiley Law Publications, Editors

1992 WILEY CONSTRUCTION LAW UPDATE
Overton A. Currie and Neal J. Sweeney, Editors

PROVING AND PRICING CONSTRUCTION CLAIMS
Robert F. Cushman and David A. Carpenter, Editors

SWEET ON CONSTRUCTION INDUSTRY CONTRACTS (SECOND EDITION)
Justin Sweet

TROUBLED CONSTRUCTION LOANS: LAW AND PRACTICE
Stanley P. Sklar, Editor

DESIGN-BUILD CONTRACTING HANDBOOK

SUBSCRIPTION NOTICE

This Aspen Law & Business product is updated on a periodic basis with supplements to reflect important changes in the subject matter. If you purchased this product directly from Aspen Law & Business, we have already recorded your subscription for the update service.

If, however, you purchased this product from a bookstore and wish to receive future updates and revised or related volumes billed separately with a 30-day examination review, please contact our Customer Service Department at 1-800-234-1660, or send your name, company name (if applicable), address, and the title of the product to:

ASPEN LAW & BUSINESS
A Division of Aspen Publishers, Inc.
7201 McKinney Circle
Frederick, MD 21701

DESIGN-BUILD CONTRACTING HANDBOOK

ROBERT F. CUSHMAN, Esquire

KATHY SPERLING TAUB, Esquire

Editors

ASPEN LAW & BUSINESS

In recognition of the importance of preserving what has been written, it is a policy of John Wiley & Sons, Inc., to have books of enduring value published in the United States printed on acid-free paper, and we exert our best efforts to that end.

This publication is designed to provide accurate and authoritative information in regard to the subject matter covered. It is sold with the understanding that the publisher is not engaged in rendering legal, accounting, or other professional services. If legal advice or other expert assistance is required, the services of a competent professional person should be sought. *From a Declaration of Principles jointly adopted by a Committee of the American Bar Association and a Committee of Publishers.*

Library of Congress Cataloging-in-Publication Data

Published by Aspen Law & Business
Formerly published by John Wiley & Sons, Inc.

ISBN 0-7355-1265-5

Printed in the United States of America

10

PREFACE

The most prominent trend in today's construction environment is toward design-build. This book is devoted exclusively to an examination of the design-build project delivery system.

Proponents of design-build view with concern the disadvantages of the traditional design-bid-build method of project development. First, because it places the owner/developer in the middle between designers and contractors, conflicts between designers and contractors can create financial exposure to the owner/developer. Design-build, on the other hand, eliminates the owner/developer from designer-contractor conflicts because the owner/developer is entitled to a complete project. In addition, traditional project development requires the design to be substantially completed before construction begins, but design-build projects can proceed on a fast track because a single entity is responsible for design, construction, and the coordination of both.

Although much has been written about the traditional method of development, and experience has taught us methods of resolving common issues, design-build is a relatively new undertaking for commercial projects and offers few guideposts to aid us in fashioning solutions to novel issues. The reader will find this book to be a road map through the thicket of licensing statutes that never contemplated design-build, insurance programs that are only beginning to address the risks inherent in this new relationship, and contractual provisions necessary to allocate risks among the parties fairly. The chapters discussing form of organization, bonding considerations, environmental issues, and use of design-build in high technology projects will give the reader an insight into creative ways to utilize design-build to save time and money in an era where such concerns are paramount.

We believe this handbook offers the reader the unique opportunity to learn about this exciting new business opportunity from preeminent scholars in the design and construction field.

February 1992

ROBERT F. CUSHMAN
Philadelphia, Pennsylvania

KATHY SPERLING TAUB
Bethesda, Maryland

ABOUT THE EDITORS

Robert F. Cushman is a partner in the international law firm of Pepper, Hamilton & Scheetz in Philadelphia, Pennsylvania, and is a recognized specialist and lecturer on all phases of construction and real estate law. He serves as legal counsel to numerous trade associations and construction, development, and bonding companies. Mr. Cushman is the editor and co-author of several books about construction, including the following John Wiley & Sons publications: *Construction Litigation: Representing the Owner (2d ed.); Construction Defaults; Rights, Duties, and Liabilities; Construction Failures; Proving and Pricing Construction Claims;* and *Alternative Dispute Resolution in the Construction Industry.* A member of the Pennsylvania bar, he is admitted to practice before the United States Supreme Court and the Court of Appeals for the Federal Circuit. Mr. Cushman has served as executive vice president and general counsel to the Construction Industry Foundation, as counsel to the American Construction Owners Association, and as regional chairman of the Public Contract Law Section of the American Bar Association. He is permanent chairman of the Andrews Conference Group's Construction Litigation and Hazardous Waste superconferences, and is a charter member of the American College of Construction Lawyers.

Kathy Sperling Taub is general counsel of The Clark Construction Group, Inc., a nationwide general contractor headquartered in Bethesda, Maryland. She is responsible for managing all corporate legal matters, advising on contract administration and negotiations, directing corporate and real estate transactions, and engaging and supervising outside counsel. She received a bachelor's degree in sociology and political science from Duke University and a law degree from the University of Maryland School of Law. Ms. Taub joined Clark Construction Group in April 1984. Prior to that she practiced with the firm of Shapiro and Olander, where she specialized in real estate and corporate matters. Her professional affiliations include the Maryland and American Bar Associations, and she is a member of the Board of Trustees of the Baltimore City Life Museums.

SUMMARY CONTENTS

DETAILED CONTENTS

CHAPTER 1

SINGLE POINT RESPONSIBILITY IN DESIGN-BUILD CONTRACTING

Michael C. Loulakis

Michael C. Loulakis is a shareholder in the law firm of Wickwire Gavin, P.C., which has offices in Vienna, Virginia, Washington, D.C., and Madison, Wisconsin. His legal practice is exclusively devoted to representing parties in the construction industry on a national and international basis. He has represented several clients in the drafting and negotiation of design-build contracts, particularly in the power generation industry. He received his civil engineering degree from Tufts University and his J.D. from Boston University School of Law. Mr. Loulakis has also published and lectured extensively on issues relating to design-build construction, architect-engineer liability, and other construction law topics. He serves as a member of the national panel of the American Arbitration Association and is actively involved in numerous trade associations related to the construction industry.

INTRODUCTION

§ 1.1 General Considerations

Design-build contracting has assumed an increasingly prominent role in the construction industry, particularly over the past 25 years.[1] *Engineering*

---

[1] *See generally* Loulakis & Love, *Exploring the Design-Build Contract,* Construction Briefings No. 86-13 (Fed. Publications, Inc.), Dec. 1986, at 445–465.

News Record recently reported that contractors on its Top 400 list had performed design-build contracts totalling over $50 billion in 1989, a significant increase over 1988's record year.[2]

Construction owners appreciate the design-build concept because it allows them to contract with a single source for the planning, design, construction, and start-up of their facilities.[3] This avoids many of the conflicts that arise between separate design and construction firms. Similarly, construction and design firms find that design-build contracting gives them the opportunity to (1) obtain higher gross margins than traditional contracting, (2) access to unique projects with less competition, and (3) minimize the potential for cost overruns due to disputes among the construction team.

Although design-build contracting is perceived to have a number of advantages over more traditional contracting schemes, it also has some potential drawbacks, depending on the party evaluating the procurement. One of the most significant drawbacks to the owner is that the integration of the designer and the contractor into a single entity destroys many of the checks and balances inherent in the traditional contracting method, which checks and balances serve to protect the owner and the public from an inferior design. Consequently, an owner must carefully consider whether the pluses outweigh the minuses of design-build for a particular project.

This chapter will provide an overview of the design-build project delivery method, focusing upon (1) the differences between traditional project delivery methods and design-build, (2) the risks and benefits of design-build, (3) the appropriate design-build project, (4) important considerations in drafting a design-build contract, (5) special liability issues, and (6) special licensing and insurance concerns. Design-build is clearly the wave of the future and will afford both owners and prospective design-builders the opportunity to obtain or perform quality construction services on commercial terms that are beneficial to the project. However, it is critical to note that this form of contracting is not right for everyone or for every project, and its risks and rewards must be balanced on a case-by-case basis.

§ 1.2 Contracting Alternatives

In order to understand the advantages and disadvantages of the design-build method of project delivery, it is critical to have a strong understanding of other contracting arrangements that do not use a single point of

---

[2] Lawson, *Owners Warming Up to Design-Construct,* Engineering News Rec., May 24, 1990, at 77.

[3] *See generally* Note, *Design-Build Contracts in Virginia,* 14 U. Rich. L. Rev. 791, 798 (1980).

responsibility. Two of the most common contracting alternatives are the so-called traditional and construction management methods of contracting.

§ 1.3 —Traditional Contracting

Under the traditional method of contracting, design and construction of a project are performed by separate entities.[4] Typically, the owner hires a design professional, either an architect or an engineer (A/E), to design the project. Once the design is at or near completion, the owner retains a contractor to construct the project according to the A/E's design. The contractor, in turn, usually subcontracts part of the work to various trade subcontractors. During the course of construction, the owner, with the assistance of a design professional, monitors the work to determine if the contractor is complying with the plans and specifications.

There are several important dynamics at work in a traditional contracting scheme involving the architect/engineer and the contractor. The design professional seeks to design a project that meets the owner's budgetary and functional needs and attempts to obtain from the contractor full compliance with the express and implied intent of the plans and specifications. On the other hand, although the contractor is obligated to comply with the letter of the specifications, it is not required to second-guess the design and determine whether the A/E has made errors or omissions. In addition, the contractor's primary goal is typically to complete the project as quickly and efficiently as possible, in order to meet its cost objectives. As a result, the designer and the contractor often find themselves working at cross purposes, particularly in issues relating to ambiguities over scope of work and design intent.

Another important dynamic deals with the standards of liability to which designers and contractors are held. Under the traditional contracting scheme, the designer is held to the standard of professional negligence, absent any express warranties to the contrary. Thus, the design need not be perfect; it must merely meet the standard of care for the industry. The contractor, on the other hand, is responsible for strictly meeting the requirements of the plans and specifications. A problem can occur when the contractor demonstrates that it met the plans and specifications, and the construction project has problems, as might be the case if the HVAC system for the project did not adequately cool the facility. Unless the owner can demonstrate that the designer failed to live up to industry standards with regard to the HVAC design, the owner has no remedy and must bear the costs of correction itself.

---

[4] Loulakis & Love, *Exploring the Design-Build Contract,* Construction Briefings No. 86-13 (Fed. Publications, Inc.), Dec. 1986, at 445–465 [hereinafter Loulakis & Love].

It is also critical to note that as between the owner and the contractor, the owner is the party held responsible for the adequacy of the specifications. It impliedly warrants that, if followed, the specifications will produce the desired result. This warranty shields the contractor in the event that the project fails to meet the owner's expectations.[5] The owner will also be held responsible for the engineer's representations of subsurface conditions.[6]

§ 1.4 —Construction Management

A construction manager (CM) is a professional retained by the owner to interface with the design professional and trade contractors on various aspects of the work. There are many different variations of construction management contracts, including (1) one in which the CM is a pure agent for the owner and does not hold trade contracts, and (2) one in which the CM provides a guaranteed maximum price for the work and retains all subcontractors. The common thread running throughout these types of contracts is that the CM will be actively involved in reviewing the design for constructability and cost effectiveness. Value engineering efforts can result in a substantial savings to the owner in terms of both time to construct and total construction costs.

During construction, the CM plays a major role in project scheduling, payment requisition review, and change order analysis. The latter responsibility is particularly important, because the CM may look more objectively at the design and potential ambiguities in it than would the design professional on the project.

Projects that use a CM approach can provide a more cost-effective product to the owner than the traditional method of project delivery. However, the fundamental relationship among the parties remain the same because the design and construction functions are being performed by separate entities, even though there is more of a preconstruction review of the design with a CM than under the traditional method of contracting.

§ 1.5 Overview of Design-Build

The overall effect of design-build is to create a single entity with whom the owner deals, thus easing coordination between the contracting parties.

---

[5] United States v. Spearin, 248 U.S. 132 (1918); 2 R. Nash & J. Cibinic, Federal Procurement Law 1015–26 (3d ed. 1980).

[6] *See, e.g.*, Acchione & Canuso, Inc. v. Commonwealth, 461 A.2d 765 (Pa. 1983) (owner held liable on a constructive fraud theory for inaccurate representations made by engineer, even though he had no knowledge that the representations were inaccurate).

When the designer and the contractor are members of the same team, design decisions can be made quickly and in a more congenial atmosphere, even after construction has commenced. Likewise, construction decisions can be made early in the design process, thus minimizing delays and cost overruns. The owner may lose some of its input into the design and construction processes, but it gains the advantage of a single point of contact.

Although the design-builder has the responsibility for both the design and construction of a project, owners can become actively involved in the design process. Some owners participate in the design phase of the project so actively that each phase of the design must be completely approved before construction commences. This may take away some of the benefits of design-build, because it may slow down the overall project development. In addition, the extent to which the owner monitors the work can have important legal ramifications, because the owner may be assuming the risk that it approved a deficient design and thus could be precluded from claiming that the design-builder is responsible for the associated financial consequences. What is gained, however, is that the owner is assured of obtaining a quality project.

Another important point to recognize is that design-build applies not only to entire projects but also to portions of projects. For example, some specialty subcontractors perform design-build work on fire protection systems, sheeting and shoring designs, and automated environmental controls. Their work is simply integrated into the overall project by the general contractor, with the design's being reviewed by the A/E and appropriate testing or governmental agencies.

Although design-build differs from traditional contracting in terms of risk allocation and the relationships between the contracting parties, the elements essential to successful completion of the project remain unchanged. These elements are: (1) direct interaction between the designer and the owner, (2) strong and knowledgeable management of a project through all of its phases, and (3) short and direct lines of communication between the designer, the owner, and the construction team.[7]

§ 1.6 Implications of Using the Terms "Design-Build" and "Turnkey"

The term *design-build* is often used interchangeably with the terms *turnkey* and *EPC* (engineer, procure, and construct). There are some minor differences among these project delivery forms as they are used in the trade. For

[7] A Committee of 100 Report: The Pendulum Swings Toward Design-Construction 74 (Oct. 1984).

example, turnkey often is applied in situations in which the owner is not only receiving design and construction services from the same entity but also is receiving financing for the facility, as well as operation and maintenance services, from the turnkey contractor. Nevertheless, despite some trade differences, it does not appear that any judicial distinctions are made among these terms, inasmuch as they all require single point contracting authority for all or part of a project.

It is critical for parties entering into construction contracts to understand that the mere use in a contract of the terms "design-build" or "turnkey" will not, in and of itself, shift all the risks from one party to another or create a single point of responsibility. Courts will look carefully at all of the other terms in the contract and determine the true intent of the parties on risk allocation.

For example, consider *Glassman Construction Co. v. Maryland City Plaza, Inc.,*[8] which involved the construction of a shopping center. The dispute centered around the degree of completion required by the contract documents. In its pertinent part, the contract read:

> The Contractor agrees to construct the entire shopping center on a turn-key job basis; that is, the stores to be constructed by the Contractor shall be accepted by the tenants thereof and the requirements of the tenants in accordance with their leases shall be met.

The owner's intention was that all work requisite to getting the tenants in their space, including changes and additions subsequent to the contract date, should fall within the scope of the turnkey contract and require no adjustment to the contract price. The plaintiff contractor, who did not design the original plans and specifications, sought to finish the work in accordance with the plans and specifications and contended that it should not be bound to meet lease requirements unless they were shown on the plans and specifications. The court looked at the plain meaning of the term turnkey and found for the owner.

In a recent case involving the construction of a container yard in Texas, the appellate court in *Chapman & Cole v. Itel Container International, B.V.,*[9] held that even though (1) "turn-key" was used in the contract documents and (2) the contractor recognized that it had an obligation to build a facility capable of meeting the owner's intended use, the owner and the contractor had not agreed to a traditional turnkey situation. Itel, which is in the business of owning, leasing, storing, and moving large aluminum and steel containers worldwide, made a corporate decision to establish a container yard in Houston. Chapman was retained by Itel to purchase property

---

[8] 371 F. Supp. 1154 (D. Md. 1974).

[9] 865 F.2d 676 (5th Cir. 1989).

for the site, develop it pursuant to plans approved by both Chapman and Itel, and lease the property back to Itel for a 10-year term.

The only written agreements between Itel and Chapman were a standardized industrial/commercial lease and addendum. The addendum contained a provision that "expressly required Chapman to construct the Itel facility on a 'turn-key condition upon occupancy' basis so that Itel 'would have the capacity to immediately commence [its] normal operations.'"[10]

The facts showed that during the planning stage of the project, Itel advised Chapman that the maximum weight to be used on the yard would be 30,000 pounds, and that the containers would be stacked on timber rails to allow for proper drainage and to prevent damage to the flexible pavement. It was also demonstrated that Itel had met with Chapman on numerous occasions to review the plan and design of the facility.

After completion of the facility, Itel used forklifts that weighed about 48,000 pounds and exerted as much as 80,000 pounds of weight on any given location. During the first month of operation, cracks began appearing in the surface. Chapman initially repaired such cracks. However, when it learned of the weight of the forklifts, it refused to perform any additional corrective work. Itel ceased making rent payments and eventually vacated the property. Chapman successfully brought an action against Itel for its misuse of the facility and breaches of the lease.

On appeal, Itel argued that the district court misapprehended the turnkey nature of the contract between the parties. The appellate court disagreed. It noted that a turnkey contract has a well-defined meaning in law and in fact:

> A "turn-key" job is defined as "a job or contract in which the contractor agrees to complete the work of the building and installation to the point of readiness for operation or occupancy." *Hawaiian Independent Refinery, Inc. v. United States,* 697 F.2d 1063, 1065 n.4 (Fed. Cir.), *cert. denied,* 464 U.S. 816 . . . (1984) . . . The developer "assumes all risks incident to the creation of a fully completed facility," *Securities & Exchange Commission v. Senex Corp.,* 399 F. Supp. 497, 500 n.1 (E.D. Ky. 1975), *aff'd,* 534 F.2d 1240 (6th Cir. 1976), and must bear "the risk for all loss and damage to the work until its completion and acceptance." *Chemical & Industrial Corp. v. State Tax Com.,* 11 Utah 2d 406, 360 P.2d 819, 820 (1961).[11]

Although Chapman admitted its obligation to build a facility capable of Itel's intended use, it did not believe that this contract was a typical turnkey arrangement. The appellate court agreed with the reasoning of the district court and found, after looking at the entire agreement between the parties,

---

[10] *Id.* at 681.

[11] *Id.*

that the business deal was not intended to impose turnkey obligations onto Chapman.

The court cited two factors in support of its decision. First, Itel had agreed to accept the premises in their condition existing as of the date of the lease and acknowledged in the lease that Chapman had not represented or warranted that the facility was suitable to the conduct of Itel's business. Itel had also agreed in the lease that Chapman would not be liable for injury due to the conditions of the premises. In reviewing these contract terms, the appellate court noted that "[if] Itel had wished to make Chapman liable under a turn-key contract, it would not have prepared and executed an instrument expressly relieving Chapman of liability to Itel and expressly disclaiming warranty as to the suitability of the premises to Itel's business."[12]

The court also found that Chapman did present Itel with a facility that conformed to the specifications that both parties had agreed could handle Itel's normal business operations. The appellate court agreed with the district court that the destruction of the property was created by Itel's misrepresentation of what constituted normal business operations.

ASSESSING THE SUITABILITY OF DESIGN-BUILD

§ 1.7 The Appropriate Design-Build Project

Like any other contracting scheme, design-build is best suited for certain situations. The factors in §§ **1.8** through **1.11** should be considered in determining whether the design-build method is appropriate for a particular project.

§ 1.8 Nature of the Project

The nature of a project should be carefully considered in determining whether it is appropriate for design-build. Projects with aspects that are repetitive in nature or that do not require detailed owner input into design and construction tend to be well-suited to the design-build method. Good examples of such projects are fast-food restaurants and tract housing.[13] Design-build is also suitable for complex projects in which the owner lacks the experience for meaningful participation and must rely on a contractor

---

[12] *Id.* at 682.

[13] Nash & Love, *Innovations In Federal Construction Contracting,* Geo. Wash. L. Rev. 309, 356–365 (1977).

with the experience and expertise to meet the state of the art. Hence, design-build has been used successfully in the construction of petrochemical facilities,[14] hydroelectric plants,[15] and steel mills.[16]

Design-build has particularly strong application in the development of so-called high technology projects. These projects, such as clean rooms and "smart buildings," often are constructed on a design-build basis because of the necessity to protect trade secrets and the limited number of contractors who are expert in these types of construction projects.[17]

§ 1.9 Capabilities of Available Firms

The availability of experienced firms is another factor to be taken into account in considering the design-build alternative. If the available firms lack the capability or expertise to undertake a design-build project and cannot acquire that capability through subcontracting or joint venture, then design-build may not be a feasible alternative. If, on the other hand, firms that have successfully completed similar projects on a design-build basis are available, design-build may be the method of choice.

This issue is particularly important with regard to subcontracts that are undertaken on a design-build basis. Specialty trade subcontractors, such as those in the mechanical, fire protection, and sheeting and shoring areas, may have particular knowledge of equipment needs, licensing and permit issues, and other facets of performance that make them valuable members in designing aspects of the work. It is critical for such subcontractors to look carefully at the specifications to determine precisely what their role will be with regard to the design.[18]

§ 1.10 Financial Resources

One of the advantages to an owner who chooses a design-build or turnkey contractual arrangement is that the financial resources available for project

---

[14] *See, e.g.*, Hawaiian Indep. Refinery Inc. v. United States, 697 F.2d 1063 (Fed. Cir. 1983) (design-build used successfully in construction of an oil refinery).

[15] Ebasco Servs., Inc. v. Pennsylvania P. & L. Co., 460 F. Supp. 163 (E.D. Pa. 1978).

[16] Koppers Co. v. Inland Steel Co., 498 N.E.2d 1247 (Ind. Ct. App. 1986).

[17] *See generally* Richelo, *Legal Implications of Design-Build Method in High Technology Projects, in* Design/Build: Issues for the 90's and Beyond, A.B.A. Forum on Construction Industry (1990).

[18] *See generally* Siegfried, *The Covert Design/Build Package: Use of Design/Build Subcontractors, in* Design/Build: Issues for the 90's and Beyond, A.B.A. Forum on Construction Industry (1990).

construction may be available from the design builder. Examples of this include facilities that will be constructed and leased back to the user, such as warehouse space, power generation facilities, or commercial office buildings, with the user's taking full ownership of the facility at the end of the lease term.

§ 1.11 Statutory Constraints

Public owners face a number of constraints in their procurement of design and construction services. The Brooks Architects-Engineers Act (the Brooks Bill),[19] for example, requires public owners to procure design services on all federal projects without price competition.[20] Under the Brooks Bill, the government is to select the best offeror on the basis of demonstrated competence and qualifications and then, if possible, to negotiate a fair and reasonable price with the offeror.

Despite the problems created by the Brooks Bill, many federal agencies have not only used design-build but have found that design-build contracting creates significant benefits to the government. For example, the Corps of Engineers has used design-build on military housing projects with great success, through a specific statutory amendment allowing this type of contracting.[21] Many states have enacted their own versions of the Brooks Bill and have made the use of design-build quite difficult. In Florida, for example, a court struck down the city of Lynn Haven's procurement procedures for public housing projects. Those procedures allowed a contractor who supplied the lowest bid to select and hire a design professional for the project (in effect, design-build contract for the project). The court found the procurement procedures to be contrary to public policy because they did not assure that the design fees the city paid were competitive or fair and did not assure that the design services were performed by the most highly qualified entities.[22]

It should be noted, however, that some states have allowed design-build contracting for certain procurement. This may be accompanied by certain restrictions, such as preplanning studies[23] or requirements that the design

---

[19] 40 U.S.C. § 541 (1988).

[20] *See* 2 J. Cibinic & R. Nash, Formation of Government Contracts 88-297 (2d ed. 1986) (discussion of changes made by the Competition in Contracting Act, Pub. L. No. 98-369).

[21] *See generally* Jennings, *Government Experience with Design/Build: A View From the Corps of Engineers, in* Design/Build: Issues for the 90's and Beyond, A.B.A. Forum on Construction Industry (1990).

[22] Lynn Haven v. Bay County Council, 528 So. 2d 1244 (Fla. Dist. Ct. App. 1988).

[23] *See, e.g.,* Va. Code Ann. § 11-41.2.

work be approved by a licensed architect.[24] Other jurisdictions have passed laws making the state's version of the Brooks Bill inapplicable to situations in which design-build packages are solicited.[25]

PARTIES' RISKS AND BENEFITS

§ 1.12 The Design-Builder

One of the greatest attractions of design-build to the prospective design-builder is the efficiency of having the designer and the builder on the same team.[26] As a team, the designer and the builder can focus their attention on the successful completion of the project, without the adversarial posturing that often comes when contractors and architects or engineers interface.

Unfortunately, this team aspect is the very feature that poses the greatest risk to the design-builder. The design-builder occupies the position that the owner would hold between the designer and the contractor under the traditional method of contacting. To the extent that the plans and specifications contain errors, the design-builder, rather than the owner, must absorb the costs of the mistakes.

Consider, for example, the case of *Mobile Housing Environments v. Barton & Barton,*[27] which involved an action to recover damages for the improper construction of a mobile home park in Colorado. The district court noted that use of the term "turn-key" in a construction contract imposed on the contractor the responsibility for providing the design of the project. The court therefore held the contractor responsible for all of the defects and deficiencies in the design, beyond those that were specifically waived or limited by the contract document.

This is not to suggest that the design-builder is entirely without recourse if the design it furnishes is defective. For example, in *Mudgett v. Marshall,*[28] a design-builder who had been awarded a contract for the design and fabrication of the structural steel of a storage facility subcontracted the design of the steel members to an engineer. The steel frame subsequently collapsed, killing one construction worker and causing injuries to others. It was later discovered that the collapse was due to miscalculations on the part of the engineer.

---

[24] *See, e.g.,* Cal. Pub. Cont. Code §§ 10503, 10708.

[25] *See, e.g.,* Alaska Stat. § 36.30.270(e).

[26] *See* Loulakis & Love.

[27] 432 F. Supp. 1343 (D. Colo. 1977).

[28] 574 A.2d 867 (Me. 1990).

The court held that the engineer was responsible for the injuries to the construction workers, despite the lack of privity. It found that the engineer's status as designer of the steel erection imposed on him the duty to create a design that would not pose unreasonable danger to those implementing it. The court granted a directed verdict in favor of the design-builder, because it found no duty on the part of the design-builder to review the engineer's calculations to detect mathematical errors.

The design-builder assumes greater liability for errors in the specifications than the general contractor does under the traditional contracting method. Under the design-build approach, the owner is no longer supplying the specifications for the contractor to follow in constructing the project. Therefore, the design-builder may no longer invoke, as did the contractor, the implied warranty of the specifications if the project goes awry despite the fact that the specifications were followed.[29]

The design-builder may also be liable to trade subcontractors under an implied warranty for errors in the specifications, and it will have to absorb the costs from errors in the construction and from overruns resulting when the equipment or materials specified in the plans prove to be unsuitable for the project. In a recent case in Texas, for example, an architect was found liable under an implied warranty theory for specifying the wrong type of flooring tile for a shopping center. The architect had failed to adequately investigate the properties of the tile before recommending it, thereby causing extensive cost overruns when a significant number of the tiles had to be replaced.[30]

Design-builders also may suffer risk exposure in some jurisdictions because of their inability to maintain certain mechanic's liens. Recently, in *Miller Construction Co. v. First Industrial Technology Corp.*,[31] a Florida court ruled that a design-builder could not maintain a mechanic's lien for design services it had subcontracted to a licensed architect. A provision of the Florida mechanic's lien statute allows any person who performs services as an architect to maintain a lien if the design documents result in improvements to the property. In this case, however, the court found that the design documents had been used merely to obtain project financing, so that the provision was inapplicable. Noting that the design-builder was not itself a licensed architect, the court refused to apply another provision of

[29] J. Ray McDermott & Co. v. Vessell Morning Star, 431 F.2d 714 (5th Cir. 1979) (owner-ordered changes do not relieve a design builder of its design responsibilities); Louisiana Molasses Co. v. LeSassier, 28 So. 2d 697 (La. 1900); Barraque v. Neff, 11 So. 2d 697 (La. 1942); Lincoln Stone & Supply Co. v. Ludwig, 144 N.W. 782 (Neb. 1913); Rosell v. Silver Crest Enters., 436 P.2d 915 (Ariz. 1968).

[30] White Budd Van Ness Partnership v. Major-Gladys Drive Joint Venture, 798 S.W.2d 805 (Tex. Ct. App. 1990).

[31] 576 So. 2d 748 (Fla. Dist. Ct. App. 1991).

the statute allowing architects to maintain liens in their own right, even when the design documents did not result in physical improvements to the property.

§ 1.13 The Owner

One of the most appealing aspects of design-build from the owner's perspective is the single point responsibility of the design-builder. Under the design-build scheme, the owner may hold one party accountable for the design and construction of the entire project. This is an excellent way to obtain performance guarantees from a prospective design-builder, which is quite difficult in situations in which the design and construction functions are performed by separate entities.

Another advantage is that when an entity is given the authority to perform all of the work necessary for the completion of a project, it is often willing to have lower margins than the combined fees of several parties working under the traditional contracting scheme. Moreover, design-build is highly compatible with fast-track construction, under which construction is started before the design is complete. This enables the owner to obtain its project earlier than under a traditional approach.

One of the disadvantages to design-build is that the owner must rely solely on the design-builder for compensation if something goes wrong.[32] Litigants often prefer to have liability spread over multiple parties, thereby creating a pool of funds if something should go wrong. This is particularly useful if the design-builder does not have the financial means of paying an award.

One further risk to the owner is that design-build eliminates some of the checks and balances inherent in the traditional method. In the traditional method, the A/E regularly examines the contractor's work to determine whether payment is justified and the work is proceeding in accordance with the design. One way to avoid this problem is for the owner to (1) insist that a detailed set of plans be developed prior to the start of construction, and (2) retain the services of a consulting engineer to evaluate the design-builder's payment applications and compliance with the design.

§ 1.14 The Surety

Design-build poses several unique problems for the surety. As a result, many sureties are unwilling to write performance and payment bonds for

---

[32] *See* Loulakis & Love, at 5–6.

design-build projects, despite the fact that they could charge higher premiums for doing so.[33]

One problem is that design-build is often used with fast-track construction, wherein construction begins before the scope of the work has been fully determined. Consequently, the surety will not always be able to determine the size of the bond needed for a project. The surety may reduce its risk by underwriting the design-build project incrementally. Under this approach, the surety would write bonds only for those portions of the project that have been fully designed and will be completed in the near future. Of course, the surety can always choose not to write additional bonds, even in the middle of construction. This is particularly likely to happen when the project has incurred significant losses, making it difficult for the owner to find another surety willing to underwrite the rest of the project.[34]

Another problem facing the surety stems from the fact that the designer is no longer an independent entity in a design-build situation. Under the traditional contracting method, the design professional reviews the work of the contractor. In the design-build scheme, however, there is no longer an independent architect to oversee progress payment requests. This creates a problem if the surety's principal, the design-builder, is overpaid and then defaults.[35] The surety can minimize this risk by hiring an independent architect or engineer to review certificates of payment to ensure that the design-builder is not being overpaid. Even if the design-builder is overpaid, such overpayment may reduce some of the surety's responsibilities under the bond.

§ 1.15 Subcontractors

Subcontractors of design-builders are typically in the same relative position that they would be in under traditional contracting mechanisms. Thus, they look to the party with whom they have contracted (that is, the design-builder) for payment, scope of work, and coordination of their activities with others. Nevertheless, there are some subtleties that should be considered in the design-build context.

For example, in some jurisdictions contractors and designers who subcontract to a design-builder do not have all the lien rights they would have by contracting directly to the owner.[36] Thus, in such jurisdictions, the

---

[33] Foster, *Construction Management and Design-Build/Fast Track Construction: A Solution Which Uncovers a Problem for the Surety,* 46 Law & Contemp. Probs. 95, 120 (Winter 1983).

[34] *Id.* at 121.

[35] *Id.* at 123.

[36] Miller Constr. Co. v. First Indus. Technology Corp., 576 So. 2d 748 (Fla. Dist. Ct. App. 1991).

subcontractor will not have the property as an asset to look to in recovering for the value of its services. Consequently, subcontractors in these jurisdictions should carefully assess the credit-worthiness and expertise of the design-builder before entering into a contractual agreement on the project.

It is also important to note that entities who perform design services on a subcontract basis may face more liability than under a traditional approach. As noted in § **1.12**, a design professional does not typically guarantee that its design will meet certain performance requirements or achieve specific results. On the other hand, in a design-build context, a designer, even if operating on a subcontract basis, may be held to the guarantee standard.[37]

§ 1.16 Lenders

Lenders may be exposed to greater risk in a design-build setting than in the traditional setting, particularly if the owner seeks a loan commitment on an incomplete design. The situation differs from that of the surety in that the risk may be balanced by the benefit to the lender in having all of the responsibility for design and construction vested in a single entity.[38] However, the lender should consider hiring an independent party to review the performance of the design-builder, particularly to ensure that it is not being overpaid.

DESIGN-BUILD CONTRACT TERMS

§ 1.17 General Contract Drafting Issues

Most traditional construction contracts are based on standard form contracts developed by trade associations such as the American Institute of Architects (AIA), the Associated General Contractors of America (AGC), and the Engineer's Joint Contract Committee.[39] Unfortunately, design-build projects tend to be project specific, and the contours of the design-build approach are not as well established as those of the traditional contracting method. These factors make it difficult to establish a standard form contract for design-build projects.

---

[37] *See, e.g.,* Arkansas Rice Growers Coop. Ass'n v. Alchemy Indus., Inc., 797 F.2d 565 (8th Cir. 1986).

[38] Coulson, *Dispute Management Under Modern Construction Systems,* 46 Law & Contemp. Probs. 127, 130 (Winter 1983).

[39] *See* Smith, Loulakis, & McGrath, *Recent Developments in Standard Form Contracts,* Construction Briefings No. 85-4 (Fed. Publications, Inc.), Apr. 1985, at 69–86.

It should also be noted that the law is not settled regarding many aspects of design-build, as there are few cases that discuss these projects. It is therefore crucial that the agreement between the owner and the design-builder accurately reflect the degree of risk that each party is willing to assume. The agreement should specify performance requirements as well as any foreseeable contingencies that could arise during performance.

§ 1.18 Payment

There are three common methods of providing payment to the design-builder.[40] First, payment may be made for the construction and the design work in its entirety based on a straight cost-plus-fee arrangement. Under this arrangement, the owner assumes the risk of the entire cost of the project. Second, the parties may agree to a lump sum price for the entire contract, with the design-builder's focusing on performance requirements expected of him in developing a price, because the final design may not be complete. In this situation, it is critical for both the owner and design-builder to have a strong understanding of what the final product will be, in order to avoid issues relative to whether the scope of work is complete.

A third pricing alternative is to compensate the design-builder for its design efforts on a cost-plus-fixed-fee basis, with a lump sum price's being established as soon as the design is sufficiently complete to allow a reliable estimate to be made.[41] This is a hybrid of the lump sum and cost-plus-fixed-fee approaches and was developed as an attempt to do away with the risk allocation problem by deferring the final price until the plans and specifications are sufficiently definite. This option allows the design-builder to fill in the details of the design in enough detail to estimate the project's cost, thus alleviating the need for a final, biddable set of plans.

However, even the hybrid approach leaves most of the burden of the risk on the owner. After the design phase is complete, the owner still has the choice either to accept the design-builder's price or to begin construction on the finalized set of plans with a new construction contractor. If the owner begins construction with a new party, however, he faces remobilization costs, loss of learning curve, and assumption of the additional risk of having a construction contractor build according to the plans of the original design-builder.[42]

When a lump sum price is used, the design-builder bears the risk for the cost of the entire project—absent equitable adjustments and changes

---

[40] *See* Loulakis & Love, at 5–6.

[41] *See* Foster, *Construction Management and Design-Build/Fast Track Construction: A Solution Which Uncovers a Problem for the Surety,* 46 Law & Contemp. Probs. 95, 118 (Winter 1983).

[42] *Id.*

allowed by the contract—regardless of what the actual cost turns out to be. However, even in a cost-plus arrangement, the estimates used by the design-builder will be carefully analyzed by a court in determining whether such costs should be reimbursed.

Consider, for example, *Koppers Co. v. Inland Steel Co.*[43] In this case, Inland Steel, the owner of a blast furnace and coke facility, brought suit against Koppers, the design-builder, for time and cost overruns. The contract between Koppers and Inland had established a series of target prices for engineering and construction costs, with overruns to be reimbursable to Koppers under certain criteria in the contract. The original estimate for the project was $267 million, with an estimate of 44,000 man-days for engineering time. The actual project cost was $444 million, with Koppers' billing over 100,000 man-days for engineering.

The evidence showed that Koppers had internal information at the time of contract indicating that a much higher number of man-days would be required to perform the original design. There was also evidence from Inland's expert witness that apart from design changes, Koppers needed in excess of 72,000 man-days to perform the engineering on the project. The Indiana Court of Appeals found that these factors justified a verdict in favor of Inland for $3.8 million in excess engineering charges.

As noted in § **1.13**, an owner should carefully consider its ability to handle payment requisitions before undertaking a design-build project. One approach that is successfully used is to have the parties agree to payment milestones for specific aspects of the work. This not only makes the determination of progress more objectively determined during construction, but it also allows the owner to understand its cashflow needs.

§ 1.19 Changes

In any large construction project, changes almost inevitably will occur because of (1) field conditions, (2) changes in the owner's needs, (3) errors in the plans and specifications, or (4) changes in technology. Most contracts allow for changes through a *changes clause,* such as that found in AIA Document A201-1976, Article 12.1.2. This type of clause allows the contractor additional time and money under the contract yet gives the owner the flexibility to make changes as it deems necessary.

One of the problems with design-build is that pricing is generally based upon performance requirements of the owner. In a typical design-build setting, the owner establishes certain broad performance specifications for the project and allows the design-builder some discretion in meeting these specifications. This can create a misunderstanding between the owner

---

[43] 498 N.E.2d 1247 (Ind. Ct. App. 1986).

and the design-builder as to whether or not a compensable change has occurred.[44] The situation may be worse in a fast-track setting, in which changes in the design of later phases of the project may have an adverse effect on earlier phases of the project that have already been constructed.

It is in the best interests of both the owner and the design-builder to tie the changes clause to some specific benchmark so that compensable changes are easily recognizable. For instance, if the contracting parties intend to have schematic drawings converted into full-scale construction drawings, the point at which the owner approves of the full-scale construction drawings could serve as a convenient benchmark. After that point, it is reasonable for the design-builder to be compensated for any changes arising through no fault of its own.

It is also crucial that both the owner and design-builder identify and agree upon all performance requirements of the project at the time of contracting, so as to establish this baseline for changes. For example, depending upon the type of project being constructed, specifications might include the approximate area of the project, the type and function of the structure, and details regarding the types, sizes, and approximate locations of materials and equipment.

In the event that the project is a production facility such as a hydroelectric or petrochemical plant, the performance output of the facility will certainly be specified. However, the parties should also address such items as testing criteria, ambient temperature corrections, and remedies in the event the testing fails.

Some owners have the philosophy that no changes will be allowed unless there is a complete agreement on price and the time impact of the change. This puts the owner in a precarious position, essentially allowing the design-builder to hold the owner hostage to the terms the design-builder wants. Consider, for example, a change to a cooling tower on a cogeneration project that is mandated by the municipality after construction starts. If the design-builder seeks an unreasonable price adjustment for such change, the only choices that the owner would have are (1) to accept the terms or (2) to obtain the services of another contractor. In light of the above, the progressive owner would retain the flexibility to order changes to the work unilaterally and to reimburse the contractor for the reasonable actual costs of such work.

§ 1.20 Differing Site Conditions

Differing site conditions or *changed conditions clauses* are contract clauses through which the owner agrees to bear the risk of certain unanticipated

---

[44] *See, e.g.,* Aiken County v. BSP Div. of Envirotech Corp., 866 F.2d 661 (4th Cir. 1989).

site conditions.[45] Use of such clauses encourages the contractor to submit bids that do not include amounts for unexpected contingencies.[46] The owner benefits by receiving the lowest bid possible, and the design-builder has the assurance that it will be compensated if unexpected conditions are encountered. Ideally, the owner should pay the same through a differing site conditions clause as if the actual conditions were known at the time of contracting.[47]

Differing site conditions clauses assume that the owner will accumulate adequate information during the design phase regarding subsurface conditions to permit design of the project. The reality, however, is that owners often tend to cut back on subsurface investigations during the design phase in an effort to minimize costs. When the design-builder is the party responsible for conducting the site investigation, there are some interesting problems that can arise.

§ 1.21 —Site Investigation

Some owners argue that the design-builder has an obligation to conduct an appropriate site investigation prior to bidding, and if the design-builder's analysis fails to uncover the true subsurface conditions, then the design-builder bears the risk. Owners also argue that design-builders have no incentive to conduct a pre-bid site investigation when the contract contains a differing site conditions clause, because the design-builder can simply rely on the clause for compensation for any site condition.

Perhaps the best remedy for this situation is for the design-builder and the owner to agree at the time of contracting on a reasonable and prudent site investigation program. The design-builder could reasonably rely on the information generated from this program and could claim a differing site condition in the event that conditions differed materially from those indicated by the investigation. This scheme also enables the design-builder to lower its overall price in the event that it already possesses sufficient information about the design of the project and the likely range of subsurface conditions to be encountered.

From the owner's perspective, agreement beforehand on a site investigation program provides assurance that a reasonable site investigation has

---

[45] *See, e.g.,* AIA A201-1976, art. 12.2.1.

[46] J. Cibinic & R. Nash, Administration of Government Contracts (2d ed. 1985). *See also* Currie, Abernathy, & Chambers, *Changed Conditions,* Construction Briefings No. 84-12 (Fed. Publications, Inc.), Dec. 1984, at 489–507.

[47] *See* Cagne v. Bertran, 275 P.2d 15 (Cal. 1954); Wendward Corp. v. Group Design, Inc., 428 A.2d 54 (Me. 1980); Progressive Survey, Inc. v. Pearson, 410 A.2d 1123 (N.H. 1980); Valley Inland Pac. Constructors, Inc. v. Clackamas Water Dist., 603 P.2d 1381 (Or. 1979).

been undertaken to allow the design-builder to economically fulfill its duties. It also gives the owner the option of lessening its risk through a more highly detailed pre-design site investigation.

§ 1.22 Liability Limitations

Design-builders often attempt to limit their liability for design or construction deficiencies through *limitations of liability clauses.* These claims may limit damages by:

1. Excluding all implied warranties[48]
2. Excluding actions of certain third parties
3. Requiring the owner to maintain a builder's risk insurance policy
4. Excluding liability for consequential damages[49]
5. Limiting the design-builder's liability for defective work to the cost of redesign or repair
6. Setting a cap on the amount of damages for which the design-builder will be responsible.[50]

The courts will normally uphold limitations of liability provisions if they are unambiguous and not against public policy. In *Ebasco Services, Inc. v. Pennsylvania Power & Light Co.,*[51] a subcontractor who supplied turbines to a power plant project brought an action to recover payments withheld. The utility counterclaimed for the cost of replacement power it was forced to purchase because of the subcontractor's delays in the construction of the facility. In answering the counterclaim, the subcontractor relied on a limitations of liability clause negotiated between itself and the design-builder. In relevant part, that provision stated:

> The seller warrants to the Purchaser and Owner that the Equipment to be delivered hereunder will be free from defects in material, workmanship and title and will meet the specifications contained in the contract. The foregoing warranty is exclusive and in lieu of all other warranties whether written, oral or implied, including any warrant of merchant ability or fitness for purpose.[52]

The court held that the design-builder acted within the scope of its powers in issuing the limitation of liability provision and that the provision was

---

[48] Ebasco Servs., Inc. v. Pennsylvania Power & Light Co., 460 F. Supp. 163 (E.D. Pa. 1978).

[49] Adams Labs. v. Jacobs Eng'g Co., 761 F.2d 1218 (7th Cir. 1985).

[50] *Id.* at 1219.

[51] 460 F. Supp. 163 (E.D. Pa. 1978).

[52] *Id.* at 168 n.2.

valid. The court also noted that the cost of the replacement power incurred by the utility was a consequential damage arising from the subcontractor's alleged breach of warranty and was therefore excluded by the limitations of liability provision.[53]

When a contracting party attempts to limit its liability through a limitations of liability clause, the clause will be strictly construed against its drafter. This was illustrated in *William Graham, Inc. v. City of Cave City,*[54] which involved an action for breach of contract brought against the designer of a wastewater treatment facility. Both parties to the contract were aware that late submission of the plans to a certain government agency would result in reduction of project funding from 75 percent to 55 percent. The appellant designer contracted to meet the deadline but failed to do so, resulting in a reduction in project funding amounting to $338,935.

In its pertinent part, the contract specified:

> The OWNER [appellee] agrees to limit the ENGINEER'S [appellant's] liability to the OWNER and to all Construction Contractors and Subcontractors on the Project, due to the ENGINEER'S professional negligent acts, errors or omissions, such that the total aggregate liability of the ENGINEER to those named shall not exceed $50,000 or the ENGINEER'S total fee for services rendered on the project, whichever is greater.

The appellant's fee for its services was $99,214. The appellant contended that this amount acted as a cap to its liability under the limitations of liability provision.

Although it did not dispute the validity of the limitations of liability clause, the court refused to apply it to damages for breach of contract. The court noted that the clause cited only damages based upon professional negligent acts, errors, or omissions; no mention was made of liability for breach of contract or for the damages accompanying such a breach. The court reasoned that because the appellant had the opportunity to unambiguously limit its liability for breach of contract and failed to do so, the clause should not now be read to reach that contingency.[55]

It should also be noted that many state legislatures have prohibited contracting parties from excluding themselves from liability for injuries or damages arising out of their own negligence.[56]

---

[53] *Id.* at 168; *but see* Hawaiian Tel. Co. v. Microform Data Sys., 829 F.2d 919 (9th Cir. 1987) (court ignored a similar provision and awarded consequential damages because defendant had not performed at all).

[54] 289 Ark. 105, 709 S.W.2d 94 (1986); *see also* Koppers, Co. v. Inland Steel Co., 498 N.E.2d 1247 (Ind. Ct. App. 1986).

[55] *See also* Waldor Pump & Equip. Co. v. Orr-Schelen-Mayeron & Assoc., 386 N.W.2d 375 (Minn. 1986); Harbor Ins. Co. v. Omni Constr., Inc., 912 F.2d 1520 (D.C. Cir. 1990).

[56] *See, e.g.,* Wis. Stat. Ann. § 895.49.

POTENTIAL LIABILITY

§ 1.23 Overview of Potential Liability

As noted at the outset, liability under a design-build contract is different from that in a traditional contract setting. Traditionally, the owner is held liable for breaches of express and implied duties through its contract with the builder. The designer, on the other hand, is generally liable in negligence arising from professional malpractice.[57] To prove negligence, the owner must demonstrate that the design professional failed to perform with the same degree of skill and professional care commonly employed by other professionals working in the same area.[58] This often leaves the owner in the middle of contract disputes between the contractor and the designer for design deficiencies.

In a design-build setting, the design-builder, rather than the owner, generally absorbs the costs of such design deficiencies. Moreover, it is typical that a design-builder will face liability for performance guarantees, which imposes upon it a guarantee of design. This is far greater liability than would be the case under a typical owner-designer relationship.

§ 1.24 Liability of Owner to Design-Builder

The potential liability of the owner is limited in the design-build context by the fact that the owner is not coordinating the work of or resolving disputes between the designer and the contractor. However, the owner's liability can be significantly affected by its degree of participation in the design-build project. If the owner is involved intimately in the everyday decisions of the project or acts in some supervisory role, its liability to the design-builder may be comparable to its liability to the contractor in a traditional contract setting.[59]

Consider, for example, *Armour & Company v. Scott,*[60] which involved the design and construction of a meat packing plant. The owner became so actively involved in the design process, increasing the size of the facility and modifying the mechanical and electrical systems, that the court found the

---

[57] *See generally* Note, *Architectural Malpractice: A Contract Based Approach,* 92 Harv. L. Rev. 1075 (1975).

[58] *See generally* A.F. Blair Co. v. Mason, 406 So. 2d 6 (La. Ct. App. 1981), *cert. denied,* 410 So. 2d 1132 (La. 1982).

[59] Pierce Assoc., Inc., GSBCA No. 4163, 77-2 BCA (CCH) ¶ 12,476 (1977); *but see* Broadway Maintenance Corp. v. Rutgers State Univ., 447 A.2d 906 (N.J. 1982).

[60] 360 F. Supp. 319 (W.D. Pa. 1972), *aff'd,* 480 F.2d 611 (3d Cir. 1973).

relationship to be a de facto partnership. These interferences were determined to be a breach of contract by the owner.

§ 1.25 Design-Builder's Liability to Owner

The standard of care to which a design-builder is held is largely determined by its contractual obligations to the owner. In traditional contracting, the contractor is liable to the owner for any deviations from the contract requirements. This liability is mitigated only by the doctrine of substantial performance, under which the owner must pay for work that is substantially complete even if it is not strictly in conformance with the contract requirements. Even under this doctrine, however, the contractor may be liable for money damages amounting to either (1) the cost of completing the project in accordance with the specifications, or (2) the difference between the value of the project as completed and the value of the project had it been completed according to the specifications.

In contrast, design-builders are usually hired to achieve certain goals set forth in the contract. In one action brought by an electric cooperative against a boiler manufacturer, for example, the court noted:

> This was a "design-and-build" contract. That is, the Technical Specifications described and defined only the general parameters of the boiler, leaving the specifics of design, fabrication, and erection to the expertise of the boiler manufacturers.[61]

The design-builder usually warrants that these goals will be met, thus greatly increasing its exposure to liability.

The design-builder's liability to the owner can be based upon: (1) strict contractual liability, (2) professional negligence or malpractice, (3) breach of warranty, or (4) strict liability. If a court views the design-builder as providing a product, it may hold the design-builder to a standard of strict liability.[62] That is, the design-builder will be held liable for providing a defective product even if that product was produced according to someone else's specifications.[63] Some jurisdictions have been unwilling, however, to extend strict liability to construction projects.[64] In any case, the design-builder can protect itself contractually through provisions limiting its strict

---

[61] *In re* Cajun Elec. Power Coop., 791 F.2d 353, 354 (5th Cir. 1986).

[62] Abdulwarith v. Arthur G. McKee & Co., 488 F. Supp. 306 (E.D. Pa. 1980); La Rosa v. Scientific Design Co., 403 F.2d 937 (3d Cir. 1968).

[63] Del Mar Beach Club v. Imperial Contracting Co., 123 Cal. App. 3d 898, 176 Cal. Rptr. 886 (1981).

[64] *Id.* at 894.

liability, though such provisions will be interpreted in light of trade usage and past dealings between the parties.[65]

§ 1.26 —Design Responsibility

The design-builder owes all of the duties and obligations to the owner that the architect-engineer owes under the traditional contracting method. In general, the design-builder is responsible for designing a project that will serve its intended purpose.[66] This is particularly true when faced with the failure of the project to meet performance specifications.

For example, in *Aiken County v. BSP Division of Envirotech Corp.*,[67] an action for fraud and breach of contract was brought by Aiken County, South Carolina against a design-build subcontractor. The subcontractor had contracted to supply a heat treatment system for a wastewater treatment plant in Aiken County. The contract specified that "systems furnished . . . shall be placed in operation ready to operate on a 24-hour per day basis with not more than 15% of total time required for maintenance and repairs."[68] However, the repair and maintenance time required for the system consistently exceeded this level, ranging between 36 percent and 42 percent of the total operating time over a three-month period. The appellate court upheld a lower court's assessment of compensatory damages against the subcontractor.

§ 1.27 —Warranty

The design-builder will be held liable for any express warranties it makes about the capabilities a project will have when it is complete.[69] In fact, one of the attractions of design-build is that the design-builder has either built this type of project before or is certain enough of success to be able to make such a warranty.

---

[65] Ebasco Servs., Inc. v. Pennsylvania Power & Light Co., 460 F. Supp. 163 (E.D. Pa. 1978).

[66] Rosell v. Silver Crest Enters., 436 P.2d 915 (Ariz. 1968). *See* Brandywine Sch. Auth. v. Van Cor, Inc., 57 Pa. D. & C.2d 606 (1971). *See also* Air Heaters, Inc. v. Johnson Elec. Inc., 258 N.W.2d 649 (N.D. 1977); Aced v. Hobbs-Sesack Plumbing Co., 360 P.2d 897 (Cal. 1961); Vernali v. Centrella, 266 A.2d 200 (Conn. Super. Ct. 1970); Grable v. Silver, 285 So. 2d 11 (Fla. Dist. Ct. App.), *aff'd,* 264 So. 2d 418 (Fla. 1972); INA v. Radiant Elec. Co., 222 N.W.2d 323 (Mich. 1974).

[67] 866 F.2d 661 (4th Cir. 1989).

[68] *Id.* at 670. *See also* Omaha Pollution Control Corp. v. Carver-Greenfield, 413 F. Supp. 1069 (D. Neb. 1976) (court reached a similar ruling on a similar fact pattern).

[69] *See* Gurney Indus., Inc. v. St. Paul Fire & Marine Ins. Co., 467 F.2d 588 (4th Cir. 1972).

In *Fort Howard Paper Co. v. Standard Havens, Inc.,*[70] a paper company brought suit against a firm that designed, built, and installed a pollution control device in the company's plant. The device was designed to remove fly ash from the flue gases of the plant prior to their emission into the atmosphere. Build-up of fly ash on the filters of such devices can lead to higher operating costs, due to the greater power required to move the flue gases through the filter system. Consequently, the filter manufacturer warranted the device against filter cloggage, as measured by the pressure drop of the flue gases across the surface of the device. Under this warranty, the maximum allowable pressure drop was not to exceed six inches of water. The paper company successfully sued when the pressure drop consistently exceeded this level.

§ 1.28 —Impossibility as a Defense

Because design-build is used in performance guarantee situations, the question often arises as to what liability the design-builder has if it finds that it is impossible to meet the performance guarantee. Two basic factors are generally considered in addressing this issue: (1) the precise contract terms agreed upon by the design-builder, and (2) the relative knowledge of the owner and design-builder regarding the "impossible specification."[71]

In *Colorado-Ute Electric Association v. Envirotech Corp.,*[72] Envirotech, the contractor, agreed to provide a hot-side electrostatic precipitator at a coal-fired electric power plant for Colorado-Ute, an electric utility. Envirotech agreed to meet certain performance requirements that were tied into state air quality standards, specifically warranting that it would bear the cost of all corrective measures and field tests until continuous compliance could be achieved. Envirotech attempted but failed to achieve compliance with the specifications and ultimately asserted that the owner had failed to provide the design temperature and flue-gas volume required by the contract.

The court held that Envirotech had made an express warranty that it could provide the utility with a satisfactory precipitator and thus assumed the risk of impossibility. The court also found the product to be a sale of goods under the Uniform Commercial Code in reaching its decision.

Another case is instructive in this area. In *J.C. Penney Company v. Davis & Davis, Inc.,*[73] an issue arose as to the workmanship of a sheet metal

---

[70] 901 F.2d 1373 (7th Cir. 1990).

[71] *See generally* Richelo, *Legal Implications of Design-Build Method in High Technology Projects, in* Design/Build: Issues for the 90's and Beyond, A.B.A. Forum on Construction Industry (1990).

[72] 524 F. Supp. 1152 (D. Colo. 1981).

[73] 158 Ga. App. 169, 279 S.E.2d 461 (1981).

assembly and coping work. The specifications provided that the work was to "be true to line, without buckling, creasing, warp or wind in finished surfaces."[74] The design-builder acknowledged that the work did not comply with the specifications, but contended that it was impossible to meet the specifications.

The court found that impossibility would not allow the design-builder to recover additional costs from the owner in attempting to comply with the specifications, under a Georgia statute which stated that "impossible, immoral and illegal conditions are void and are binding upon no one."[75] This case is particularly significant in the area of liability from the design-builder to the owner, because the owner should also be precluded from recovery if the design-builder fails to meet performance guarantees that are impossible to meet.

§ 1.29 Design-Builder's Liability to Third Parties

The design-builder may be liable to third parties, such as the ultimate users of the project, for defects in the design and construction of the project. It may be easier for a third party to demonstrate culpability on the part of a design-builder than in the traditional contract setting, because there is only one party to "point the finger at." Because the standard of care owed to third parties, absent strict liability, is negligence, the plaintiff must establish the standard of care in the industry for the design and construction of the particular project. This may be difficult if the design-builder complied with the performance guarantees stated in its contract with the owner, regardless of the perceived industry standard.

Design-builders may be more likely than traditional contractors to be held strictly liable to third parties for defects in design or construction, particularly when they are mass producers of a facility, such as might occur with a mass-home builder.[76] Most design-builders differ from mass-home builders in that they build only one or a few projects of a particular type at any time and lack the ability to properly apportion the risk over their customer base.

§ 1.30 Design-Builder's Liability to Subcontractors

The design-builder's liability to subcontractors or trade contractors is usually greater in the design-build setting than the liability of either the

---

[74] 279 S.E.2d at 463.

[75] Ga. Code Ann. § 20-111.

[76] *See also* Tasher, *Liabilities of California Building Contractors & Construction Professionals: The Need For Equality In Legal Responsibilities,* 15 Cal. W. L. Rev. 305 (1979).

designer or contractor under the traditional method. This is because the owner's involvement is minimized in the design-build setting and the design-builder is directly liable for design problems.

SPECIAL PROBLEM AREAS

§ 1.31 Licensing Problems

In most states, it is illegal for an individual or business entity to practice architecture or engineering without a license.[77] This can create severe problems for design-build contractors, because some courts have found that even when design services are performed by a licensed design professional, the design-build contract is unenforceable.[78] Therefore, a design-builder must carefully review the laws of each state to determine what the licensing requirements are and whether design-build is legal.

There are numerous decisions which review the question of licensing and validity of design-build.[79] Many of the cases seem to draw a distinction between contracts which call for the design-builder to "furnish" a design versus those that call for the design-builder to "provide" a design. The former contemplates that a registered design professional will design the project and is often considered to be acceptable by the courts. The latter language is often construed as improperly practicing architecture or engineering, and may be a problem for the enforceability of the contract.

Consider, for example, *Seaview Hospital, Inc. v. Medicenter of America.*[80] In this case, a turnkey contractor subcontracted the design of the facility to a licensed architect. When the contractor sued to enforce the agreement, the owner defended by claiming that the contract was void under Texas law, because neither the contractor nor its employees were licensed architects or engineers. In upholding the contract, the court found that a general contractor was not precluded from entering into a contract under which it agreed to "engage or hire architects and engineers who are duly licensed in Texas."[81] The court distinguished the contract from situations in which the

---

[77] *See, e.g.,* Lunch, *New Construction Methods & New Roles For Engineers,* 46 Law & Contemp. Probs 83 (Winter 1983).

[78] American Store Equip. & Constr. Corp. v. Jack Dempsey's Punch Bowl, 21 N.Y.S.2d 117, *aff'd* 258 A.D. 794 (1939); Arkansas State Bd. v. Bank Bldg. & Equip. Co., 286 S.W.2d 323 (Ark. 1956).

[79] *See, e.g.,* Quatman, *Validity of Design/Build under State and Federal Law, in* Design/Build: Issues for the 90's and Beyond, A.B.A. Forum on Construction Industry (1990).

[80] 570 S.W.2d 35 (Tex. Ct. App. 1978).

[81] *Id.* at 40.

contractor was to "perform" such design services, which would be violative of the statute.

As a result of the importance of this issue, it is critical for parties contemplating a design-build contract to have a clear understanding of the applicable state licensing laws and views toward design-build.

§ 1.32 Insurance

Design-build raises special issues regarding insurance. The errors and omissions insurance typically obtained by design professionals does not cover construction errors. Similarly, most commercial general liability (CGL) insurance policies obtained by general contractors do not have provisions for errors or omissions in design. When both entities are merged in the design-build situation, neither type of policy will be sufficient. It is crucial, therefore, for the design-builder to have insurance policies that cover both design and construction areas. As an added precaution, the design-builder may wish to obtain a builder's risk policy and a difference-in-conditions policy to cover any potential gaps in the other policies.

§ 1.33 Conflict for the Architect/Engineer

One of the potential drawbacks of design-build is that it places the architect/engineer in a conflict of interest situation.[82] In the traditional contracting scheme, design professionals are obligated to exercise their professional judgment so as to give the owner the best product at the most reasonable price. Because there are no ties between the designer and the contractor, design professionals are free to exercise their judgment independent of the wishes of the contractor.

In the design-build scheme, however, the architect/engineer is no longer isolated from the contractor. Instead, the contractor is in a position to directly influence design decisions. Design professionals may find that the impartial performance of their duties is threatened by pressure to make the construction as cost-effective and easy as possible, regardless of the owner's needs. This could create issues of premature obsolescence or inferior materials being used on the project. Because of the licensing statutes affecting design professionals, it is critical for the designer to balance its relationship with the contractor with its duties to the ultimate user and the public.

---

[82] *See* Loulakis & Love, at 3.

CHAPTER 2

APPLICATION OF DESIGN-BUILD TO AGE OF TECHNOLOGICAL ADVANCEMENT

Thomas Richelo

Thomas Richelo received an A.B. degree, magna cum laude, in political science from Duke University in 1978 and a J.D., with distinction, from Duke University School of Law in 1981. He has practiced in the construction law field since then, with Peterson Dillard Young Self & Asselin (formerly Peterson Young Self & Asselin) from 1981 to 1991, and formed the Law Offices of Thomas Richelo on March 1, 1991 in Atlanta, Georgia. Mr. Richelo has represented general contractors, subcontractors, suppliers, designers, owners, sureties, and all categories of participants in the construction process, handling cases in state and federal courts, boards of contract appeals, and arbitrations throughout the United States. He is a member of the American Bar Association's sections and committees dealing with the construction industry, litigation, and environmental law, and serves as an arbitrator of construction disputes for the American Arbitration Association. He has spoken and written for national and local audiences on construction law, use of the design-build method, suretyship, arbitration, and dispute-avoidance techniques.

§ 2.1 Introduction

Since World War II there have been tremendous advances in the technology of construction, manufacturing, and other industries. Advanced technology not only creates new ways to build traditional things but also creates new things to build. The increased use of the design-build method has paralleled the development of high technology construction projects. *High technology,* as used in this chapter, means technology on the forefront or cutting edge. It sometimes involves advanced methods or products that frequently have not yet been proven to work at the time they are conceived or specified for a project. High technology projects, and particularly those involving the design-build approach, have given rise to numerous legal issues which are themselves on the cutting edge of the law's evolution.

This chapter identifies reasons why the design-build method has gained popularity in high technology fields, touching on the general advantages that are, at least theoretically, available for owners. Some key legal issues presented by high technology projects are examined. Owners and design-builders contemplating using this method to perform high technology projects must be sensitive to these legal issues as well as the business considerations.

The law relating to high technology design-build projects is developing along with technology itself. As a result, there often is not a lengthy history of case law for researching these issues and predicting how courts, boards, and arbitrators will decide similar disputes in the future. Therefore, the most analogous legal developments in other areas of construction law and the common law must be examined for comparison. In this arena, courts, boards, and arbitrators are likely to adapt equitable principles to the resolution of these emerging issues. This chapter recommends some methods for users of design-build in high technology applications to deal with those legal issues, principally through awareness of general trends in the developing law, as the best predictor of which way the law is headed. Also, understanding the risk allocation opportunities presented at the contract drafting stage of high technology projects is critical to avoiding the typical pitfalls of such projects. Because numerous legal principles in this area are in a formative stage, design-builders, owners, and their attorneys face an exciting and challenging future as their experiences contribute to the law's development.

DESIGN-BUILD'S PREVALENCE IN TECHNOLOGICALLY ADVANCED PROJECTS

§ 2.2 Defining the High Technology Project

One definition of technology is "the totality of the means employed to provide objects necessary for human sustenance and comfort."[1] High technology is a term in common usage today, but it may not have a readily available dictionary definition. The term has two distinct connotations for most users. First, it indicates new, advanced, or recent technology; second, there appears to be a quantitative element to the term, suggesting that the technology involved is of major significance in the end product itself. By way of comparison, a concrete block used today in typical residential foundation construction may be the end product of brand new, highly advanced technological manufacturing processes. But the product itself is still a concrete block. Most users of the term are unlikely to think of such a concrete block as a "high tech" product. In contrast, a newly developed computer chip or surveying instrument would readily earn the high technology label. The product itself embodies and displays its technological advancement.

A focus on high technology in a construction or procurement context calls to mind products and processes that have gone through significant states of development in approximately the last 30 years. Numerous important societal and scientific advances coincide with this time frame. These advances have been so significant that in many ways they define this time period; for example, the terms "computer age" and "space age" are recognizable labels for this modern era. Great impacts on the construction industry have been experienced as a result of these technological advancements.

Technologically advanced applications to the construction industry take two forms: (1) high technology in the method of construction of finished products which themselves are not technologically advanced, or (2) the delivery of a product which itself embodies and utilizes technological advances. This chapter emphasizes the latter for a specific reason. Advanced methods of producing traditional construction products or projects are not as likely to present new or unique legal challenges as do advanced products

---

[1] Webster's New Collegiate Dictionary 1197 (8th ed. 1974).

or projects themselves. This is so, primarily, because high technology products of the construction industry are generally expected in some way to out-perform the products they replace. As a result, the most likely legal concerns relating to the new product pertain to evaluating the benefits of the new product's alleged superior performance, determining whether that performance is actually being achieved, and supplying legal remedies to the disappointed owner when the performance falls short of its advertised objectives.

This discussion of high technology developments may appear, in some respects, to be more pertinent to the manufacturing industry than to construction. That perspective can arise, for example, when looking at advanced computer, control, and security systems. The great technological advances of those types of equipment may seem more a function of developments in the factory than in the field. However, the parties involved in the construction industry face legal responsibilities and problems that are inseparable from those of the manufacturers of products that contractors install. After all, the design-builder is called upon to specify such products; to build structures for them; to furnish and install them; to supply power to them; to maintain appropriate environmental conditions for the operations of them; and, usually, to warranty the continued successful operation of such equipment for a period of years after substantial completion. Engineering principles of the manufacturing and construction industries are also common to one another, being based upon the same mathematics, physics, and chemistry principles that govern the physical world. For purposes of describing the design-build contractor's responsibilities, therefore, this chapter treats the terms *product* (which is more closely associated with manufacturing) and *project* (more closely associated with construction) interchangeably. That usage consciously reflects that the design-build responsibility in the high technology area induces a contractor to be as focused upon the performance aspect of its assignment as a manufacturer traditionally would be.

§ 2.3 Why Design-Build Is Preferred in Advanced Technology Projects

Evidence is abundant that the design-build method of project delivery is being used with increased frequency in high technology areas. The 1991 survey of the top 400 contractors in *Engineering News Record* lists the 50 largest design-build contractors in the United States.[2] A clear majority of the top 20 contractors on this list identified power plant and industrial plant projects—clearly advanced technology ventures—among the types of

[2] Engineering News Record, May 27, 1991, at 68.

projects they perform. Six of the top 10 indicated more than one billion dollars in foreign design/build work. This latter statistic evidences the spread of American technology to developing nations.

In May 1990, *Engineering News Record* reported that contractors on its top 400 list had acquired design-build contracts totalling $54.1 billion in 1989, an increase of 21% over the previous year's level.[3] In May 1991, the same survey reported $57.3 billion of such contracts for 1990, an increase of 5.6 percent.[4] At a time when recession was affecting much of the construction industry, these growth figures reveal a significant swing in favor of design-build. The trend is toward greater acceptance of the method by public owners and an expansion of its use into broader areas than the traditional industrial markets.

Numerical totals alone do not reveal the reasons why high technology work is being performed under a design-build approach with increasing frequency. In the simplest analysis, the trend is explained by the coincidental growth in the use of the design-build method for all types of projects and the rapid increase in the high technology projects which the marketplace is demanding.

The design-build method's growing use must mean that its theoretical advantages are being realized to some degree by its users. The design-build method traditionally has been cited as a technique for delivering a customized project to an owner. Such a project, it is believed, matches more closely the owner's ideals than a shelf project would. The customizing of the project can be achieved when design professionals analyze the owner's needs and prepare performance specifications. In fact, the contractor who constructs a project, or any aspect of a project, from performance specifications is necessarily engaging in a design-build function, even if the contractor does not think of itself as a design-builder.

The performance specification has the obvious advantage of defining the project on the basis of what the owner wants the project to achieve, that is, its performance. To use a comparison from the consumer context, consider the way people shop for a new automobile. Most people likely shop for cars by matching their self-image with the image they perceive to be associated with a particular make and model, limited, of course, by what they can afford. A consumer who instead follows a "performance specification" approach to the search for a new automobile defines the size, power, gas mileage, comfort, and options the consumer desires. By systematically surveying available automobiles, the consumer is then more likely to choose the car which best suits the person's needs and desires, if not ego. In a

---

[3] Lawson, *Owners Warming Up to Design-Construct,* Engineering News Record, May 24, 1990, at 77.

[4] Grogan, Design-Constructors Boost Awards 5.6%, Engineering News Record, May 27, 1991, at 68.

similar fashion, defining desired performance criteria and presenting them as an assignment to a design-builder creates an enhanced likelihood of producing the product that the owner truly wants and needs.

Another significant advantage of the design-build alternative is the increased accountability of the design-builder. In the traditional approach, in which one entity designs and another entity constructs for the owner, there is always the risk that an unsatisfactory result or performance will lead to those two parties' blaming each other for the failure. The owner, lacking the technical expertise of either the design or construction disciplines, is hard pressed to determine where fault really lies. When both hats are worn by the same party, there is clearly no available scapegoat; the design-builder alone must answer for the resultant deficiency. It would require extensive survey data to prove that the dual responsibility of a design-builder actually leads to less design errors and less construction errors, or a greater willingness by the design-builder to correct them, but the design-build approach certainly creates added incentives for the design-builder to avoid or correct deficient performance in comparison to projects with separate designers and builders. For example, the construction arm of a design-build entity should be more willing to call attention to an apparent problem, knowing that responsibility, one way or another, lies within its own company. In contrast, a construct-only builder is often reluctant to identify the same problem because it anticipates a dispute with the design professional over who is responsible for the error.

Whether these advantages of the design-build method are truly being realized by public and private owners or are merely perceived to exist, they have clearly fueled design-build's growing popularity. At the same time, several major societal and scientific trends have heightened the demand for high technology construction in the last 30 years and can be expected to increase that demand even further:

Space age spinoffs. Soviet and American space programs began in earnest in the late 1950s. The frontier in that field has shifted from a race to put a man on the moon to satellite communications, potential military applications, and sending probes to the far reaches of the universe. The aerospace industry is not only a consumer of construction services itself but has also been a catalyst in producing scientific advances impacting many other areas of construction. In large part, the American space program has been the proving ground for most advances in the science of rocketry for the last 30 years, for example. The experience of the Patriot missile in the Persian Gulf War shows that such technological advances should continue to be exploited in the defense contracting industry and thus continue to spill over into other applications as well.

Growing environmental awareness and regulations. In the United States, ecological awareness became heightened in the late 1960s, then received a boost in attention as a consequence of the energy crisis of the early 1970s. In years since, developing theories of global warming and ozone layer depletion have increased the general public's concern over environmental hazards, helping generate support for government action to protect the environment. Major domestic legislation in this period has had a momentum of its own, as the Clean Air Act,[5] Clean Water Act,[6] National Environmental Policy Act,[7] and reams of other environmental laws[8] have emerged. No major public or private construction project can be performed today without considering its environmental consequences. A project's pollution control aspects are often a major portion of the design and construction efforts, particularly in high technology applications.

Computer technology. Computers are revolutionizing just about every aspect of human life. Three of the most significant current trends in the computer field are continued miniaturization, a corresponding increase in memory and capacity, and ever-expanding applications and uses. These developments are bringing greater affordability and vastly expanded usage of computer products. High technology industrial and utility plants lend themselves readily to being controlled, monitored, and regulated by computer systems. This has occurred to some degree with so-called "smart buildings." In the future, greater numbers of contractors in virtually all trades and subtrades will encounter computer systems linked to or interacting with their scope of work in one way or another.

High technology product developments. Advancing technology brings new products on the market that give rise to their own design and installation specialty trades. One such example is halon. First introduced around 1970, halon had great appeal due to its potential for nearly instantaneous fire suppression with little or no harm to equipment, furnishings, and people. In the last 20 years, seven major players have emerged in the U.S. halon industry.[9] The tendency within such subindustries to protect trade secrets, coupled with ever-developing technology, can restrict the number of parties who design and install such systems, which consequently increases the likelihood of design-builders' operating successfully within such specialty areas. Recently, environmental regulators became concerned that halon releases chloroflourocarbons, which can deplete the earth's ozone layer. Undoubtedly, this is pressuring the halon industry to develop a new product that does not have this environmental cost.

---

[5] 42 U.S.C. §§ 7401–7642 (1988).

[6] Properly called the Federal Water Pollution Control Act, 33 U.S.C. §§ 1251–1387 (1988).

[7] 42 U.S.C. §§ 4321–4370a (1988).

[8] *See, e.g.,* Selected Environmental Law Statutes (West 1988).

[9] From a telephone interview with James A. Ready, Jr., Product Manager-Halon for Chemetron Fire Systems, Inc., July 20, 1990.

Most historical trends eventually reach a peak and go into decline. But for now, the graph depicting the use of design-build method in high technology contexts is decidedly an upward curve. It seems safe to predict that the body of law dealing with issues arising from the use of design-build on high technology projects will also expand. However, because litigation occurs in reaction to other events, emerging legal principles should also be expected to lag somewhat behind the construction industry's technological developments. The coming years will likely see the legal issues related to this field evolving through court, board, and arbitrator decisions, until eventually mature and stable legal precepts are established.

PRE-CONTRACT ISSUES

§ 2.4 Contract Award and Bid Protest Issues

Whether the design-build delivery system or some other competing alternative is being used, the earliest stage at which legal disputes between the parties can occur is at the time of contract award or pre-award eligibility determinations. Typically, such issues have been addressed in federal and state government bid protest cases. Bid protests on public projects have been made possible by development of the doctrine that disappointed bidders who might have been eligible for or awarded government contracts have standing to challenge the eligibility and award determinations of contracting agencies. There is no real private sector equivalent of this doctrine, because private parties are free to contract with whomever they want on whatever basis they want, provided they have not somehow obligated themselves to follow a procedure which they then violate.[10] The most common bid protest situations arise when either the lowest or second lowest bidder challenges an eligibility determination in a pre-award context, a responsiveness determination at the time of bid review, or an award decision based upon evaluation factors.

In traditional procurements, in which the contract award will be made to the lowest responsible bidder based upon price alone, the legal issues are fairly finite. However, the movement toward contract awards based upon competitive negotiation, involving the evaluation of factors instead of or in addition to price, has generated a host of additional legal issues and principles. Eligibility determinations, particularly those involving alleged organizational conflicts of interest, are likely to involve legal issues that are of

[10] Tort theories, such as intentional interference with prospective contractual relations, may be the closest thing to a private sector analogue of the bid protest action, but they are beyond the scope of this discussion.

interest in the design-build context, because they call into question the appropriateness of the government's utilizing that method in the context of certain types of work. These are only some examples of the legal issues relating to who gets a contract that can have particular ramifications for design-builders, especially in high technology fields.

The Competition in Contracting Act (CICA) was enacted as part of the Deficit Reduction Act of 1984.[11] The Act was intended to modernize and further standardize federal procurement law and promote open and fair competition in procurement situations in which competitive bidding—meaning award to the low bidder—is desirable. In so doing, CICA preserved the alternative procedure of negotiated procurement, also called competitive negotiation. The legislative history of CICA acknowledged the merits of this alternative:

> Unlike the rigid sealed bid procedures for formal advertising, negotiation allows for considerable flexibility. In a negotiated procurement, contracting officers are permitted to discuss the terms and conditions of the contract with all contractors in a competitive range. 10 U.S.C. § 2304(g); FPR 1-3.804 and 1-3.805-1. Consistent with the flexible nature of negotiation, the evaluation and award procedures for negotiated contracts allow for more discretion. Contracting officers are not required to award to the low offeror, as in formal advertising, but may 'trade off' costs to the government against factors such as technical performance or management capability in selecting the source.[12]

The CICA had a fairly long and detailed legislative history as Congress gathered substantial information from the construction industry and academia, as well as federal agencies themselves. Following extensive hearings in 1982, the Senate Committee on Governmental Affairs identified several problems in the existing procurement system including, inter alia:

> The current procurement statutes are inadequate. The emphasis on formal advertising overshadows negotiation as a legitimate competitive procurement procedure.
>
> Overly-detailed specifications unnecessarily restrict the procuring agency from considering acceptable alternatives, and often result in only one contractor capable of meeting the agency's needs.[13]

Although not readily apparent, both of these sets of remarks suggest the benefits of utilizing design-build capabilities for certain procurements. A negotiated procurement in which technical performance or merit is an evaluation factor necessarily requires a process whereby the contractors'

---

[11] Pub. L. No. 98-369, Div. B, title VII § 2701, 98 Stat. 1175 (1984).

[12] S. Rep. No. 50, 98th Cong., 2d Sess. 1 (1984), *reprinted in* 1984 U.S.C.C.A.N. 2175.

[13] *Id.* at 2181–82.

proposals and subsequent performance involve some degree of design responsibility. Similarly, the caution against overly detailed specifications suggests the benefits of a performance specification approach, another way of placing design-build responsibility on the contractor. And, although there is no focus specifically upon high technology projects in these comments, in actual practice contracting officers are likely to see the opportunity to assess technical merit and to allow the contractor some design flexibility as being particularly beneficial in a high technology context.

Some agencies have taken a greater liking to competitive negotiation than others. Those who have been cited for using it with some regularity include the Defense Department, the Bureau of Reclamation, the Soil Conservation Service, and the Post Office Department.[14] Recently, the Federal Highway Administration has shown an interest in what it calls "innovative contracting," which resembles competitive negotiation because it requires an assessment of factors other than mere price.[15] This would represent a distinct departure from the agency's past practices. The debate is ongoing among agencies and the industry alike over whether competitive negotiation or variations on that approach has merit in the highway context, as a means of improving quality, or whether it fails to result in cost-effective procurements.[16] For the foreseeable future, a substantial volume of federal government contracting, much of it involving high technology applications, will be let by way of the competitive negotiation method.

The subjectivity and broad discretion allowed to a selecting officer under the competitive negotiation alternative creates fertile ground for bid protest cases. The exercise of the selecting officer's discretion, like all federal government agency action, is limited by a requirement that it not be arbitrary and capricious.[17] Additionally, in any competitive negotiation, although the agency is free to set its own criteria or process by which proposals will be evaluated and the award decision made, the agency must follow its own rules. Whatever procedure it establishes must satisfy the overall requirement that all proposals be "fairly and honestly" considered.[18] In *Paxson Electric Co. v. United States,*[19] the central issue was whether the selecting officer's decision to award a contract to a lower scored contractor, after

---

[14] Merwin, *Negotiated Contracts Stir a Furor,* Highway & Heavy Construction 13 (July 1990).

[15] *Id.*

[16] *Compare* Associated General Contractors of America, *Report on Construction Quality: Competitive Negotiation v. Sealed Bids, in* Federal Construction Procurement (1989), *with* Brown, *What? Change the Low-Bid System?,* Highway & Heavy Construction 9 (July 1990).

[17] 5 U.S.C. § 706(2)(A) (1988).

[18] Keco Indus. v. United States, 428 F.2d 1233 (Ct. Cl. 1970).

[19] 14 Cl. Ct. 634 (1988).

evaluation scoring was completed, on the basis of low price—even though price was one of the factors already included in the evaluation itself—failed to meet the applicable fairness standard and amounted to arbitrary and capricious agency action.

The procurement in question called for the design and building of a computerized control system known as a Supervisory Control and Data Acquisition (SCADA) System. The SCADA system's function is monitoring and control of electrical power distribution, street traffic lights, and a sewer system at the naval submarine base in Kings Bay, Georgia, the east-coast home of the TRIDENT submarine fleet.[20] Such systems are technologically advanced. A solicitation calling for a design-build procurement permitted substantial flexibility and variation in the technical capabilities of the system proposed. In this case the protestor, Paxson, a traditional electrical contractor, had acquired expertise in furnishing such advanced systems through prior experience working with a variety of vendors and designers of the pertinent equipment who were regarded as leaders within their own industry.

Section M of the request for proposals (RFP), entitled "Evaluation and Award," indicated that proposals were to be evaluated based upon three factors. It stated:

> The relative order of importance of each element of a proposal will be as follows:
>
> Technical
> Price
> Management.[21]

This section, coupled with bidders' knowledge of agency procurement practice, implied that an initial rating system would be established by the selecting officer and his evaluation board, in which weight factors would be placed on these three elements. As indicated, technical rating would count for more than price and price for more than management. The solicitation did not promise that the proposer with the highest overall score would be awarded the contract.

For this procurement, the navy actually used an evaluation system that assigned the following relative weights to the pertinent factors: Technical—45 percent; price—45 percent; management—10 percent. Thus, the actual scoring that was applied deviated from the solicitation. Technical and price ratings were given equal weight, although the solicitation indicated the technical element would have greater weight.

---

[20] *Id.* at 635.

[21] *Id.* at 636.

Two proposers ended up in the competitive range, Paxson and the ultimately successful bidder, Engineering Design Group, Inc. (EDG). Paxson's technical rating was substantially greater than EDG's, whereas EDG had a substantial advantage on the price evaluation. The overall scores, based on a combined 10,000-point scoring system, favored Paxson by a margin of 8,690 to 8,115. The selecting officer, however, concluded that the two proposals were "virtually equal overall" and made the award decision by using price "as a basis of breaking the tie or tipping the scale."[22] On that basis, the selecting officer awarded the contract to EDG.

Paxson contended there were several abuses in the selection process, which had resulted in an improper award. First, the technical elements had not been weighted more than price; had it been so weighted, Paxson contended, Paxson's scoring advantage over EDG would have been even greater. Second, it was arbitrary and irrational for the selecting officer to use price as a tie breaker, because price had already been taken into account in a scoring system that had resulted in a superior rating for Paxson. To use price as a tie breaker, Paxson felt, would improperly count price double, making price a vastly more important factor than the technical element. Additionally, Paxson took exception to the selecting officer's review of specific elements of the technical evaluation. On some items of the technical evaluation, EDG had received a raw score of zero, but the selection official had concluded that the scorers had misunderstood the scoring criteria. It was Paxson's view that these zero scores should not have been second-guessed by the selecting officer and should have resulted in a determination that EDG's proposal was not adequate technically. Finally, although the evaluation board had given Paxson certain superior ratings on aspects of the technical merit of its proposal, the selecting officer had determined that the technical capabilities of Paxson's proposal were, in some instances, excessive.[23]

In the Claims Court, the United States moved for summary judgment after the factual record had been sufficiently compiled. The court concluded that Paxson was correct in its view that the RFP erroneously listed the order of importance of the evaluation elements, which was inconsistent with the requirements of F.A.R. § 15.401-5(c).[24] However, the court also concluded that Paxson had "failed to establish that it was materially misled or otherwise prejudiced by the violation found here."[25] The court concluded the selecting officer's decision did not amount to an improper double counting of the price element, that it was not arbitrary and capricious, that his review and consideration of the evaluations, including interviews

---

[22] *Id.* at 637.

[23] *Id.*

[24] All F.A.R. cites can be found in title 48 of C.F.R., same section number.

[25] Paxson Elec. Co. v. United States, 14 Cl. Ct. at 641.

with his technical advisors, had been a reasonable process, and thus the protestor was not entitled to relief.[26]

The *Paxson* decision illustrates that the discretion of the selecting official in competitive negotiations of this type is quite broad. Although technical advisors, who have particularized expertise that the selecting officer lacks, may be in place for evaluation purposes, the selecting officer has considerable leeway to analyze and interpret his advisor's findings, and even to disagree with them.

Several lessons can be taken from this experience. In making future proposals in which the technical element is to be afforded the highest or substantial weight, design-build contractors who choose to maximize technical capability at the expense of price had better be able to do an adequate job of selling or risk having the selecting officer conclude that the technical superiority is not worth the price, regardless of the relative importance that was intended to be given to those two elements. Also, on the heels of an economic recession and in an era of government budget crises, design-builders should watch for indications that price will be given more attention than solicitations may indicate. In addition, the continued use of negotiated procurements by the government promises a steady stream of bid protests, which will lead to further development of legal standards for such cases.

§ 2.5 Contract Eligibility Issues

In some instances, a federal agency may be required to render a determination regarding the eligibility of a prospective contractor to compete for or be awarded a certain procurement contract. When an "organizational conflict of interest" exists, a contracting officer must take responsible action. The Federal Acquisition Regulation (F.A.R.) defines an organizational conflict of interest as existing when

> the nature of the work to be performed under a proposed Government contract may, without some restrictions on future activities (a) result in an unfair competitive advantage to the contractor or (b) impair the contractor's objectivity in performing the contract work.[27]

The contracting officer must identify and evaluate such potential conflicts and take actions to "avoid, neutralize, or mitigate significant potential conflicts before contract award."[28] Upon consultation with legal counsel and

[26] *Id.* at 639–43.

[27] F.A.R. § 9.501.

[28] *Id.* § 9.504(a).

technical specialists, the contracting officer's available methods of avoiding such potential conflicts may include advising a prospective bidder or proposer that it is ineligible to receive the contract award. In instances in which the contracting officer sees a significant potential conflict, he must analyze the situation and recommend a course of action to the chief of the contracting officer.[29]

There is a substantial potential for design-build contractors involved in technical lines of work to come across issues that must be resolved under the regulations dealing with organizational conflicts of interest. For example, three major areas of concern that give rise to such a conflict, which may require some restriction on future activities by a contractor, include providing system engineering and technical direction,[30] preparing specifications or work statements,[31] and providing technical evaluation or advisory and assistance services.[32] Examination of these regulatory sections reveals the possibility for definitional problems.

Such concerns are arising in the context of hazardous waste cleanup, to use one illustration. Many federal government facilities, like private industry, have stockpiles of hazardous or toxic materials that eventually must be disposed of, by incineration or other means. Contractors engaged in cleaning up such sites may propose different means and methods of doing so, thus entailing a design-build responsibility. When an agency initially investigates the prospects for entering into such a cleanup contract, it may hire an expert from the industry to perform a study. The study may also involve some sampling or testing of the hazardous materials. The contracting officer who ponders whether the study or testing service performed by the first-stage contractor could give rise to an organizational conflict of interest is faced with the lengthy and complicated descriptions within the regulations of the terms "systems engineering," "technical direction," and other related terms.

However, even upon becoming convinced that a contractor's work satisfies the literal meaning of one of these terms, such as providing technical evaluation, there is no bright line that can be drawn to tell the contracting officer what restrictions, if any, must be placed upon the contractor's eligibility for future work. To begin with, satisfying one of these definitions is a matter of degree, which in turn can have an effect on the extent to which a contractor may have a competitive advantage in future work situations. The degree to which that particular contractor has an advantage clearly must be taken into account when a contracting officer or his chief determines whether the advantage is significant enough to be unfair. The complexity of

---

[29] *Id.* § 9.507.

[30] *Id.* § 9.505-1.

[31] *Id.* § 9.505-1.

[32] *Id.* § 9.505-3.

these determinations and the difficulty of creating absolute standards for resolving potential conflict situations inevitably leaves the agency substantial discretion to exercise subjective judgment.

As with contract award decisions themselves, pre-award eligibility determinations can be protested by potential government contractors. The legal principles for deciding those cases are closely akin to those involved in contract award protests. Construction attorneys experienced with bid protest matters often acknowledge that the contracting officer's freedom to exercise subjective judgment in some areas, coupled with the arbitrary and capricious standard of review, usually make protests against agency award and pre-award decisions an uphill battle.

PERFORMANCE ISSUES

§ 2.6 Testing and Evaluation of Performance

Advanced technology construction projects, by their very nature, are substantially more likely than other types of projects to face difficult questions of whether contract requirements of performance were satisfied once construction is completed. This is particularly so with high technology projects that involve equipment or systems that are operational, as contrasted with bridges, roads, and structures, which are static. Because a design-build project's scope and requirements are defined by performance criteria, there is greater difficulty in determining whether the completed project is what it is supposed to be. The difficulties in determining whether performance criteria are being satisfied by a completed system or project can arise for very mundane or very complex reasons.

An example of the mundane end of the spectrum is the dispute that arose over certain security system equipment installed in the mid-1980s at a maximum security prison in a western state. The prison was located in a remote mountain valley surrounded by undeveloped areas that supported substantial wildlife. The prison site itself was surrounded by a perimeter "T-line" system, a sensory system that consisted of numerous horizontal wires spread from fence post to fence post around the entire prison site, forming an enclosure. Electromagnetic fields are created between the wires themselves which, when linked with sensory monitoring equipment to a central control panel, allow the operator to detect very small movements in the wires and identify the locations of such movements.

The T-line system, when operating properly, cannot be breached by an escaping prisoner without detection. Unfortunately, animals, birds, and even grass coming in contact with the wires could trigger an alarm situation, depending on the sensitivity setting of the system. Guards and prison officials complained that the system was malfunctioning when such alarms occurred. They maintained that the great number of false alarms made the system fail to achieve its performance requirements. In contrast, the manufacturer, assemblers, responsible subcontractor, and general contractor who supplied it all agreed that the T-line system worked exactly as intended but that the users simply had failed to appreciate the system's limitations. Perhaps such a system was not appropriate for the environment in which it was being used, they conceded, but the T-line system completely satisfied the owner's performance criteria, as contained in the contract documents. In essence, the problem in this case was that the prison operators had failed to understand exactly what they were buying. Had they understood such systems better, the prison might have specified something substantially different instead.

An example of the difficulty in determining achievement of performance criteria at the more complex end of the scale involves a flue-gas desulfurization system (FGDS) supplied recently by a design-builder to a southern power authority. The equipment in question was highly complicated to begin with, embodying what was believed to be the latest technology in its field. Monitoring and measuring performance of the system was further complicated because of the many criteria of performance required by the contract. Among other things, the system was required to achieve certain levels of sulfur dioxide (SO_2) removal efficiency, power consumption, limestone consumption, and system pressure drop. The process was also intended to produce a gypsum byproduct meeting certain quality standards. Each of these criteria necessitated extensive performance testing. The testing itself was designed to measure performance over the course of several weeks and was extremely expensive to conduct.

The FGDS was tested shortly after its completion. The design-build contractor who installed it and an independent testing consultant, both of whom were considered leaders in this industry, made observations and recorded data during the course of the test. Although only one such test was run, the reports of these two parties differed drastically in their findings. There were numerous disputed issues, including whether the tests had been run properly, whether either party or both had measured and reported test results correctly, whether certain mathematical extrapolations from data had scientific validity, and other similar disagreements. The technical issues required such detailed scientific understanding of the system that nontechnical management personnel had to rely heavily on their technical cohorts in attempting to evaluate their legal rights. However, the technical staff was not trained to appreciate the contract interpretation issues, such as risk allocation, ambiguity, vagueness, and burden of proof, all of which, combined with the technical facts, played a part in determining the ultimate issue of whether the equipment in place truly failed to meet the contract requirements and whether such a breach could be demonstrated with sufficient legal certainty.

Both of the disputes mentioned above have been resolved, at least tentatively, through settlement. They represent numerous types of cases that can arise in this field which, if resolved short of complete litigation, do not produce legal opinions that assist in advancing our understanding of the legal principles involved. These examples highlight some of the most commonly occurring legal issues relating to performance testing that may arise in advanced technology projects:

1. What testing procedures does the contract establish in order to determine if performance levels are being achieved? At the initial stage, this is a contract drafting issue. When problems arise after contract documents have been prepared, however, this becomes a matter of contract interpretation.
2. Will such tests, if properly conducted, validly indicate whether the performance requirements of the contract are being met? This issue is dependent upon technical determinations, very possibly requiring analysis performed by expert witnesses and questions of evidentiary sufficiency that blend legal and technical issues.
3. Which party to the contract has the burden of proof of showing that a system or equipment works or does not work as intended? This is itself a legal question, although it will never be addressed in a vacuum, because all of the other issues pertaining to the nature and validity of tests will inevitably arise at the same time. Determining allocation of the burden of proof in a particular relationship can sometimes be a matter of contract interpretation and at other times may be determined as a matter of law.

Performance testing also raises a host of other factual and legal questions that deal with the remedies available in the event of total or partial failure to meet performance requirements. That subject is sufficiently detailed that it is addressed in **§§ 2.7** through **2.9**. The three areas of questions outlined above all play a part in arriving at the initial determination of whether there was a breach or not.

The first category of issues, testing procedures or requirements, is the most easily addressed. Either the contract dictates testing procedures, as it should, or the parties will have to utilize some method to arrive at suitable procedures. The second and third categories of issues most likely involve the greater legal challenges.

The law that develops as to test validation in the construction performance testing context will likely follow a history similar to that experienced in other areas that involve scientific or forensic evidence questions. Courts have gone through similar processes in examining, questioning, and accepting or rejecting the validity of devices such as polygraphs, police radar, and DNA testing for paternity.[33] Any process claiming to constitute a valid test of whether a person is lying or a vehicle is speeding or a man is the father of a child will be scrutinized by the courts and must demonstrate that it is founded on correct application of scientific principles, has a substantial level of accuracy, and that this accuracy level satisfies burden of proof requirements for that particular type of case. Test procedures for determining whether equipment as complicated as a flue-gas desulfurization system is operating properly should be put to the same kind of legal scrutiny.

One obstacle to establishing legally acceptable test processes for certain high technology areas is the limited number of similar cases. In contrast to polygraph and police radar cases, which the courts have probably examined hundreds of times, it is unlikely there will be anywhere near that many judicial pronouncements on any particular advanced technology system or product. As a consequence, parties to disputes over whether a high technology system meets its performance criteria can rarely expect that there will already be judicially accepted test procedures for measuring the performance of the type of equipment involved in the case. Such cases are therefore likely to require some degree of pioneering of the legal validity of test procedures and equipment.

§ 2.7 Burden of Proof Allocation

In many of these performance criteria cases, the determination of which party bears the burden of proof regarding the achievement of performance requirements is likely to be pivotal. The law of federal government contracting often provides more guidance than that of any other jurisdiction on particular areas of construction law. Federal procurement regulations and cases have dealt considerably with testing responsibility issues and are somewhat instructive. In government contracting, *inspection* means the examination of supplies and services to determine whether they conform to the contract requirements and may include examination and testing of raw materials, component parts, and intermediate assemblies. *Testing* is the element of inspection that determines the properties or elements of the supplies or components by application of established scientific principles and procedures.[34] The responsibility for testing and inspection is determined by the contract between the parties. If the contract requires a demonstration of

---

[33] *See, e.g.*, Imwinkleried, *Recent Developments in Forensic Science: More Good News, in* Successful Trial Practice (I.C.L.E. of Ga. 1990).

[34] F.A.R. § 46.101.

compliance but does not specify the type of test required, the contractor must submit to the type of test that the government determines is necessary to demonstrate the product's compliance.[35] However, the contractor is entitled to additional compensation for costs incurred if the government imposes improper testing procedures that increase the contractor's requirements.[36] Further, a contractor is entitled to additional compensation if it can show the government imposed new or additional testing requirements that exceeded those specified in the contract.[37]

In the government contracting setting, the contractor is obligated to comply strictly with the requirements of the plans and specifications. The owner's remedy for nonconforming work by the general contractor is either in rejection or warranty. The responsibility for acceptance lies with the government.[38] Therefore, the burden of proof that the material supplied or the work performed meets or does not meet the specifications lies with the government. In *Continental Chemical Corp.*,[39] the government was unable to show that the metal poly submitted for testing by the contractor had not met the contract specifications. The board found that the evidence submitted by the government with respect to the test was inadequate to overturn the contractor's prima facie showing that its product met the specifications.

Once the government meets its burden of proof that the goods supplied or work performed failed to meet the contractual requirements, the burden shifts to the contractor to show that the work complies. In *G. Santoro & Sons, Inc.*,[40] the contractor disputed the government's test findings by submitting results compiled by a private laboratory indicating that the items met the specifications. However, as explanation for the conflicting findings the contractor also submitted evidence that the government had improperly conducted its test. Differing test results may raise a question as to the validity of the results obtained, but they do not constitute proof that the government's methods or results were wrong. Conflicting test results therefore create a question which the trier of fact must resolve to determine whether the work performs as required.

Because these general principles are likely to be followed in other jurisdictions, in both public and private contracts, the design-builder or its

---

[35] RFI Shield-Rooms, ASBCA Nos. 19005, 19038, 19163, 77-1 B.C.A. (CCH) ¶ 12,237 (1977).

[36] N. Fiorito Co. v. United States, 416 F.2d 1284 (Ct. Cl.), *aff'g* ASBCA Nos. 10037, 10041, 66-1 B.C.A. (CCH) ¶ 5,381 (1966).

[37] Virginia Elec. Co., ASBCA No. 18778, 77-1 B.C.A. (CCH) ¶ 12,393 (1977).

[38] F.A.R. § 46.502.

[39] GSBCA No. 2735, 69-2 B.C.A. (CCH) ¶ 7,839 (1969).

[40] VACAB No. 754, 68-2 B.C.A. (CCH) ¶ 7,281; VACAB No. 755, 68-2 B.C.A. (CCH) ¶ 7,282 (1968).

attorney could develop a checklist for avoiding the problems inherent in performance testing cases. At a minimum, that checklist should include:

____ Whenever possible, the client (either owner or design-builder) should have input into designating the type and method of performance test within the contract itself. In the absence of contract documents that specifically dictate the type of testing, the owner may be able to impose on the design-builder whatever test procedures it has concluded will prove whether performance requirements are met.

____ Both parties' technical personnel should have some level of comfort that the required test procedures have been validated.

____ In high-risk projects, defined as projects in which either expected performance is difficult to achieve with existing art or satisfactory testing methods have not yet been validated, there may be some legitimate reason for each party to propose contract testing clauses that shift the burden of proof as to performance achievement to the other party. This may seem like an exercise in avoiding legal responsibility for contract obligations. However, there may be no other plausible alternative for the design-builder whose system or equipment appears to achieve the desired result, with the owner therefore definitely wanting the product, but who cannot prove in a legally sufficient way that the performance requirements have been met. From the owner's perspective, there is nothing wrong with allocating the burden of proof to the design-builder, necessitating that it be able to demonstrate validly that its system works as it should, provided the design-builder recognizes and understands that this burden of proof is on its shoulders. The design-builder can then make an intelligent decision, based upon whether it can prove achievement of contract requirements, as to whether it should enter into a contract in this particular situation at all.

§ 2.8 Allocation of Risk of Impossibility of Performance

Most contractors enjoy the challenge of difficult and innovative projects. A successfully completed project is a source of great pride. In the high technology context, the zeal for taking on extremely challenging assignments may lead certain design-builders into contractual performance responsibilities that prove impossible to fulfill.

Remedies for a design-builder's nonperformance in a high technology project resemble traditional breach of contract remedies whenever those can be determined or imposed. However, the complexity of the contractual undertaking and the responsibilities of the parties sometimes make the questions of appropriateness and measure of remedies quite difficult. These legal issues are particularly intriguing when the issue of impossibility of performance is raised, because the allocation of the risk of impossibility, to either the design-builder or the owner, will affect the initial determination of whether the owner is entitled at all to a remedy for nonperformance or performance deficiencies. Design-builders and their attorneys therefore need a familiarity with the principles that determine who bears the risk of impossibility of performance, as well as an appreciation for the nature and extent of remedies that are being imposed in cases of failed performance.

In the design-build construction arena, the allocation of the risk of impossibility is determined by several factors. Contractors may assume the risk of impossibility by attempting to achieve the contract's requirements or by expressly warranting a satisfactory result. The owner may assume the risk of impossibility through contract changes or by simply drafting the specifications. Two primary factors are usually cited as governing the allocation of the risk of impossibility in the absence of an express undertaking: (1) the nature of the contract and specifications, and (2) the relative knowledge and expertise of the parties.[41]

The first factor, nature of the contract and specifications, boils down to deciding which party took the initiative in drawing up the specifications and promoting a particular method or design. Several considerations come into play: the type of specifications (design or performance); the type of contract (lump sum or cost-reimbursable); the party who drafted the specifications; the level of restrictions in the specifications; and the scheduled completion date (relatively long, indicating the contractor is expected to engage in research and development, versus relatively short, indicating the contractor is expected to go straight into production).

Likewise, the second factor, relative expertise of the parties, is assessed as an indication of which party should be expected to have the greater knowledge of whether the desired performance is achievable. When a contract proves impossible to perform and the government has greater expertise than the contractor with regard to the required performance, the contractor will not be deemed to have assumed the risk of impossibility.[42] However, when a contractor has superior expertise and has defined methods of performance, the risk of impossibility lies with the contractor.[43]

In addition, whether the performance requirements are achievable within the existing state of the art may determine which party assumes the risk of

---

[41] Whittaker Corp., Power Sources Div., ASBCA Nos. 14191, 14722, 14740, 15005, 15628, 79-1 B.C.A. (CCH) ¶ 13,805 (1979).

[42] Foster Wheeler Corp. v. United States, 513 F.2d 588 (Ct. Cl. 1975).

[43] J.A. Maurer, Inc. v. United States, 485 F.2d 588 (Ct. Cl. 1973), *aff'g* ASBCA No. 12071, 69-2 B.C.A. (CCH) ¶ 7,884 (1969).

impossibility. Thus, in some cases, this becomes the third factor in determining the risk allocation. Unless contractors expressly assume the risk of a performance that is beyond the state of the art, such contracts may be considered impossible to perform during the performance period.[44] In determining whether such risks have been assumed, first the terms of the contract and then the contractor's expertise are examined.[45] A contractor must show more than that performance is beyond its own capability to establish that the required performance is beyond the state of the art and is thus impossible.[46]

Decisions arising from public and private construction projects illustrate instances in which the contractor assumed the risk of impossibility. In *Bethlehem Corp. v. United States,*[47] a contractor was properly terminated for default even though the specifications were impossible to perform. The contractor had assured government representatives before award that it could achieve the desired result, so it thereby assumed the risk of impossibility.

Similarly, a contractor may assume the risk of impossibility by making an express warranty. In *Colorado-Ute Electric Association v. Envirotech Corp.,*[48] Colorado-Ute, an electric utility, contracted with Envirotech to provide a hot-side electrostatic precipitator at a coal-fired electric power plant. The contract required the equipment to meet certain performance efficiency requirements calculated to satisfy state air quality standards. The contractor warranted that it would bear all costs of corrective measures and field tests until continuous compliance could be achieved. Installation of the precipitator was completed in December 1974. The first performance test was conducted in October 1975. Envirotech continued attempting to achieve compliance until July 1978, when it asserted that Colorado-Ute had failed to provide the design temperature and flue-gas volume specified in the contract. In October 1978, the contractor disclaimed any responsibility for the precipitator's performance deterioration.

The court, applying Colorado Revised Statutes § 4-2-313(1)(a) (1973),[49] held the contractor had made an express warranty that it could provide the utility with a satisfactory precipitator. By making this express warranty,

---

[44] Firestone Tire & Rubber Co. v. United States, 558 F.2d 577 (Ct. Cl. 1977).

[45] PRB Uniforms, Inc., ASBCA Nos. 21504–21506, 21743, 21957, 80-2 B.C.A. (CCH) ¶ 14,602 (1980).

[46] Video Research Corp., ASBCA No. 14412, 72-2 B.C.A. (CCH) ¶ 9,562 (1972) (contractor failed to rebut government testimony that complying equipment was available from industry at time of contract).

[47] 462 F.2d 1400 (Ct. Cl. 1972), *aff'g* ASBCA No. 10595, 66-1 B.C.A. (CCH) ¶ 5,641 (1966).

[48] 524 F. Supp. 1152 (D. Colo. 1981).

[49] The analogue of Uniform Commercial Code § 2-313(1)(a), dealing with express warranties.

the contractor assumed the risk of impossibility. The court's reliance on the Uniform Commercial Code revealed its willingness to treat the contract obligation as a sale of goods, as opposed to a service contract.

In some instances, the government, as an owner, may assume the risk of impossibility by its actions. In *Ball Brothers Research Corp.,*[50] the government changed a portion of a fixed price contract to a cost reimbursable type. By this change, the government assumed the risk inherent in the development of technically sophisticated detectors to be incorporated into spacecraft instrumentation. Similarly, in *Conrad, Inc.,*[51] the board held that the government, as drafter of defective specifications, assumed the risk of impossibility of performance when the evidence demonstrated that it was impossible to manufacture air conditioning units satisfying the government's specifications. The board reasoned that because there was no express assumption of the risk of impossibility by either party, an implied assumption of risk arises from the implied warranty of adequacy of the specifications. The contract set forth performance requirements for the air conditioning units but imposed certain size and weight limitations; those performance requirements had never before been satisfied within the limitations dictated by the specifications. The time for performance was a relatively short production schedule, 180 days overall, which did not include time for research and development.

In *Whittaker Corp., Power Sources Division,*[52] the contractor was to supply torpedo batteries pursuant to mixed design and performance specifications. The short term production contract did not envision extensive research and development or advancement of the state of the art. On the contrary, the government had previously been involved in the development of the batteries for 18 years. Because of the government's prior experience and superior knowledge that the performance called for was commercially impossible, the contractor's default termination was converted to a termination for convenience, and it was granted an equitable adjustment for the costs of extraordinary efforts made to satisfy contract requirements.

An interesting case involving impossibility in the design-build context was decided in Georgia, based upon a state statute. In *J.C. Penney Co. v. Davis & Davis, Inc.,*[53] a subcontractor, Davis & Davis, brought suit against the owner, J.C. Penney, and the design-builder, ABS. Although the opinion does not explicitly state that ABS had a design-build contract with J.C. Penney, it does state that the contract documents contained the "General Conditions of the Design and Build Construction Contract."[54] These

[50] NASA BCA No. 1277-6, 80-2 B.C.A. (CCH) ¶ 14,526 (1980).

[51] ASBCA No. 14239, 71-2 B.C.A. (CCH) ¶ 9,163 (1971).

[52] ASBCA Nos. 14191, 14722, 14740, 15005, 15628, 79-1 B.C.A. (CCH) ¶ 13,805 (1979).

[53] 279 S.E.2d 461 (Ga. Ct. App. 1981).

[54] *Id.* at 463.

general conditions expressly gave the owner the right to inspect the workmanship and materials utilized in construction and to reject workmanship or materials that did not conform to the specifications. ABS subcontracted with Davis & Davis to perform sheet metal assembly and sheet metal coping work. The specifications provided that "sheet metal items shall be true to line, without buckling, creasing, warp or wind in finished surfaces."[55] Davis & Davis admitted that its work did buckle and crease but contended that faulty or defective design specifications made it impossible to produce work that conformed to all the contractual specifications.

The appellate court reversed a judgment in favor of Davis & Davis and against J.C. Penney and ABS. It held that the contract gave the owner the absolute right to reject work that did not conform to the specifications. Further, the plaintiff had asserted that the specifications were impossible to perform. The court, citing Georgia Code Annotated § 20-111[56] held that Davis & Davis could not bring a breach of contract action on a contract that was void due to impossibility. The court stated: "Where the [plaintiff] contract[s] to perform covenants that are impossible, *not because of an act of God or the conduct of the [defendant],* the failure to perform such covenants is as fatal to the plaintiff'[s] right to recover as a breach of contract for any other reason."[57] This particular statute in Georgia would seem to prevent any situation in which a design-builder could claim a right to damages based upon a contention that the owner had assumed the risk of impossibility.

§ 2.9 Remedies for Nonperformance

In addition to losing its right to a remedy by assuming the risk of impossibility, the owner can also be denied legal recourse for nonperformance when it is guilty of an equal or superior breach of its obligations that excuses a contractor's nonperformance. For example, constant owner involvement in the design process has been held to be a breach of a design-build contract. In *Armour & Co. v. Scott,*[58] the owner awarded a contract to design and build a meat packing plant. During the design phase, the owner increased the size of the building, requiring extensive changes to the refrigeration and electrical plans. The owner also changed the details for hundreds of specially constructed, insulated, and electrically operated doors. Further, the owner became so involved in the design process that it "had become a de facto type

---

[55] *Id.*

[56] Now recodified as O.C.G.A. § 13-3-5 (Michie 1982), that section reads: "Impossible, immoral, and illegal conditions are void and are binding upon no one."

[57] J.C. Penney Co. v. Davis & Davis, Inc., 279 S.E.2d at 464.

[58] 360 F. Supp. 319 (W.D. Pa. 1972), *aff'd,* 480 F.2d 611 (3d Cir. 1973).

of joint enterprise or partnership arrangement between the Armour engineers and the [design-builders] and their engineers," rather than the planned "turnkey operation." This blurring of the lines of responsibility led to delays in the approval of the design. Based on all these factors, the court concluded the owner had breached its contract with the design-builder. However, the design-builder also breached the contract by failing to staff the project with competent designers and commingling labor and materials with the construction of a new residence for the principal of the design-builder. The court held that neither party was entitled to damages because both had breached the contract without measurable benefit to one of the parties.

The failure of a prime contractor to furnish technical format drawings to a design-build subcontractor has been held to be a breach of contract. In *Westinghouse Electric Corp. v. Garrett Corp.,*[59] Westinghouse received a prime contract from the air force to furnish electronic countermeasure pods, which are attached to combat aircraft to counter enemy radar tracking devices. Garrett was a subcontractor to Westinghouse and undertook to design and build the cooling system for those pods. Westinghouse was obligated in the subcontract to furnish Garrett with source control drawings to enable it to go forward with the design of the cooling system. Garrett had the right to rely on the contract that these drawings would be supplied. Westinghouse's failure to timely furnish these drawings was therefore a breach of contract.[60] As in *Armour & Co. v. Scott,*[61] the design-builder Garrett had been equally at fault in the events leading to its termination and therefore did not recover damages.[62]

The case of *Colorado-Ute Electric Association v. Envirotech Corp.*[63] is of great interest on the subject of remedies for the design-builder's nonperformance because it illustrates the dilemma of the contractor who promises too much. After finding the contractor to have made an express warranty as to the performance of certain precipitator equipment at an electrical power plant, as discussed in **§ 2.8**, the court then considered the relief to which the utility was entitled. The utility sought an order that the equipment be made to perform as warranted. Alternatively, it asked for damages for past and future costs to bring the precipitator's performance within the required air quality standards. The court recognized that an electrostatic precipitator is a unique item, specifically designed for that particular plant, and is extremely large, complex, technically intricate, and essentially irreplaceable once it has been installed. Further, the precipitator is of no use to the

---

[59] 437 F. Supp. 1301 (D. Md. 1977), *aff'd,* 601 F.2d 155 (4th Cir. 1979).

[60] 437 F. Supp. at 1332–33.

[61] 360 F. Supp. 319 (W.D. Pa. 1972), *aff'd,* 480 F.2d 611 (3d Cir. 1973).

[62] Westinghouse Elec. Corp. v. Garrett Corp., 437 F. Supp. at 1339.

[63] 524 F. Supp. 1152 (D. Colo. 1981).

utility if it does not meet the bargained-for standards. Taking these factors into account, the court ordered the design-builder to bring the precipitator into compliance with the contract guarantees for its remaining estimated useful life, that is, the remedy was specific performance. The court noted that monetary damages would be sufficient only to bring the precipitator's performance up to the contract guarantees using a chemical injection process. Considering the fact that such a chemical injection process might not be allowed in the future, the court concluded that monetary damages would be inadequate to compensate the utility. The utility had contracted for, and expected to receive, a functioning precipitator to comply with air quality standards; that was exactly what the court decided the owner should get. This precedent could well be a source of concern in future disputes in which owners seek specific performance of projects that the design-builders have argued are impossible to perform.

In a more recent case also involving a division of Envirotech, a court sought to fashion an appropriate damages remedy. In that case, the trial court was convinced that the design-builder's promise of a performance it could not deliver had amounted to fraud, allowing for both compensatory and punitive damages.[64] Aiken County, in South Carolina, had employed an engineering company to design a waste water treatment plant and chose a general contractor to construct the $20 million facility. The general contractor then subcontracted with Envirotech to design and supply the thermal sludge conditioning system, including heat treatment and other related items. The project designer left the design of the thermal sludge conditioning system up to the contractor.

The system chosen and bid upon by Envirotech is known as a sludge-to-sludge heat exchanger. This system involves two pipes, one inside the other. In this particular heat exchanger, cold sludge from the plant is passed through the inner pipe to the reactor where it is broken down and sterilized by heat and pressure. The heated sludge then passes through the outer shell, or annular space, to other parts of the plant for further processing. The purpose of this heat exchanger is to make the process more efficient and more economical by transferring heat from the hot sludge to the cold sludge. The inner tube is held in place within the outer tube by spacers. After construction of the plant, operation never attained the design production rates. Heated sludge in the annular space tended to plug on the spacers, requiring frequent cleaning and reducing production rates.

Throughout the design and installation of this system, Envirotech had made representations as to the suitability and success of the system. When the completed system failed to meet the performance as represented, Aiken

[64] Aiken County v. BSP Div. of Envirotech Corp., 657 F. Supp. 1339 (D.S.C. 1986), *aff'd in part and rev'd in part,* 866 F.2d 661 (4th Cir. 1989).

County brought suit against Envirotech, alleging breach of warranty, breach of contract, and fraud.

The sludge-to-sludge process chosen by Envirotech was a new process that had never been successfully used. In fact, Envirotech's only competitor used a sludge-to-water process. In this process, water instead of sludge passes through the annular space and therefore there is no problem of plugging on the spacers. The sludge-to-water system is a more expensive process than the sludge-to-sludge system.[65]

During design and construction, Envirotech and its engineers continuously assured Aiken County and its designer that the sludge-to-sludge system had been tested. In fact, the court found this system had never been tested, nor had it ever been successfully applied to a waste water treatment plant.[66] This misrepresentation by Envirotech formed the basis of the fraud claim. The breach of contract claim brought by Aiken County was based on the warranty clause of the contract, which promised that the work would be free from faults and defects and would function as intended. Another provision required the system to operate continuously on a 24-hour basis with not more than 15 percent of total time required for maintenance and repairs. For the first three months following start-up, the total time spent on maintenance and repairs was 42 percent, 36 percent, and 42 percent, respectively. The district court and the appellate court deemed this a breach of contract by Envirotech.[67]

The district court assessed damages of $2,650,000, equal to the amount originally bid by Envirotech's competitor for a competing system. To that, the court added $200,000 for the costs of checking design submittals and inspecting the installation of replacement equipment. The court further assessed $1 million as punitive damages for Envirotech's fraud.[68] The court of appeals affirmed the findings of liability as to breach of contract and fraud but differed on the computation of damages. The $2,650,000 figure that represented Envirotech's competitor's bid included, according to Envirotech, far more than the heat treatment system that was now at issue. The court of appeals had other concerns regarding the measure of damages and remanded with instructions. It also reversed the award of punitive damages, based on a South Carolina law under which a remand for reconsideration of compensatory damages requires reconsideration of punitive damages as well.[69]

Certain general conclusions can be gleaned from this overview of cases on liability for nonperformance. In essence, the courts first inquire into which

---

[65] 657 F. Supp. at 1349.

[66] 866 F.2d at 673–76.

[67] 657 F. Supp. at 1356–57.

[68] *Id.* at 1368.

[69] 866 F.2d at 676.

party should be held primarily accountable for the decision to attempt a performance that was ultimately unachievable. If fault lies with the contractor, the second inquiry addresses the legal adequacy of a traditional damages remedy, in the absence of which specific performance might be required. In the design-build context, there is likely to be a greater chance that the contractor ends up being the responsible party because its single-source undertaking often results in there being no other design professional performing for the owner who could assume responsibility for the failure. Because there are myriad ways for an owner's initial design consultant and its design-build contractor to divide the total responsibility for the project, however, each case will be examined on an individual basis to see if the design-builder's total responsibilities were broad enough so the owner should be entitled to some remedy for nonperformance. In the most egregious cases, generous measures of compensatory damages, punitive damages, or a directive to specifically perform something that may be impossible, may all be awarded against the design-builder who promises something it cannot deliver.

OTHER RECURRING PROBLEM AREAS

§ 2.10 Patent Infringement

Advances in technology are patented by their creators whenever possible. Consequently, the more one deals with the high technology field, the more one is likely to be involved with patent law. The subject of patent infringement in a design-build context is treated in more detail in **Chapter 8**. There are, however, several specific legal issues relating to patent rights that affect the design-build contractor performing a high technology project.

The core of a patent law practice involves dealing with the creation of patent rights through the application process and the protection and defense of those rights through infringement litigation. Design-build contractors who operate in high technology areas will likely become involved with these patent law core issues from time to time. The innovative design-builder whose work is on the forefront of its particular specialty area could develop an invention or process that meets the criteria for patentability and could gain a substantial competitive advantage in its field through a successful patent application. As a patent holder, that same contractor may well require legal assistance in protecting its invention from infringement and enforcing remedies against those who do infringe.

Beyond these basic issues of patent law lie the complications that may affect the performance of high technology projects by design-build contractors. The risk that problems will arise as a consequence of a third party's allegation of an infringement exists principally because of the nature of the design-build undertaking. The owner sets forth its requirements schematically, conceptually, or in the form of performance criteria. The design-builder then attempts to meet those requirements through means and methods that are technologically and, it is hoped, legally available. In so doing, the design-builder might intentionally or unwittingly embark on a course of action that results in a third party's asserting that the design-builder, the owner, or both are committing an infringement.

The ancillary legal issues for the design-builder and owner that may arise from a third party's allegation of patent infringement can be illustrated with a hypothetical scenario. The owner (called O) of a planned fossil fuel power plant contracts with a design-build contractor (called DBC) to design and build certain pollution control equipment. The combustion of coal to produce energy results in flue gasses that produce a variety of air pollutants. Equipment must be in place to remove pollutants from the flue gas to a sufficient degree to satisfy prevailing air quality laws. For the sake of simplicity, this scenario focuses on the device which removes sulfur dioxide (SO_2) from the flue gas.

DBC has completed all of its design work and is 50 percent complete with construction, under a $20 million contract, when it is advised that Acme Designs, Inc. (ADI) believes that DBC's flue-gas scrubber violates the patent held by ADI. ADI threatens to seek an injunction requiring DBC to cease and desist from infringing ADI's patent and to request damages consisting of any profits obtained by DBC through its partial contract performance, lost profits to ADI as a consequence of the alleged infringement, interest, costs, and attorneys' fees.

The elements of this simplified scenario undoubtedly exist in the real world with some degree of frequency. There is a wide variety of possible outcomes in such situations, and the parties should be prepared for any of the probable variations:

Infringement action unsuccessful, O bears responsibility. The alternative of an unsuccessful action is considered first because its possible outcomes are the simplest. If ADI is unsuccessful, presumably DBC and O both decide to proceed with performance of the subject contract. Either or both may possibly be awarded attorneys' fees against ADI for being prevailing parties in the action,[70] but whether or not that occurs, other expenses will exist. If the infringement action has substantially delayed project performance, the delay expenses to both parties could easily dwarf the attorneys' fees incurred fighting ADI. Some or all of these expenses could be O's ultimate responsibility. They should be, if the facts warrant a finding that the owner, contractually, was allocated the risk of defending against patent

[70] *See* 35 U.S.C. § 285.

infringement actions, or if the owner somehow caused the bringing of the unsuccessful infringement action.

Infringement action unsuccessful, DBC bears expenses. This outcome could arise if the contract allocates the risk of an infringement action to DBC, or if proximate cause for the bringing of the action can be traced to DBC.

Infringement action successful, ADI grants license, DBC bears expenses. If an actual infringement of ADI's patent rights is determined or conceded to have occurred, O and DBC may seek from ADI a licensing agreement that permits them to go forward with the contemplated project in the contemplated manner. Before opting for this alternative, O and DBC will have to analyze the cost of the licensing agreement versus the alternative cost of performing the contract in a noninfringing manner, if that is possible.

Infringement action successful, licensing agreement granted, O bears expenses. Although this outcome appears less likely to occur than the preceding outcome, it is a possible alternative result, particularly if the owner is held to have induced the contractor to commit the infringement.

Infringement action successful, ADI grants no license, DBC is legally responsible, contract can be performed in alternative manner without infringing patent. ADI's failure or refusal to grant a license in the event an infringement is found to have occurred creates a more complicated search for remedies. Assuming DBC is responsible and an alternative means of meeting the contract's requirements without infringing upon an existing patent is available, the probable outcome is that DBC bears the expenses of the infringement action's defense and is required to perform the contract under the alternative method. Case law suggests, by analogy, that a design-builder refusing to perform in this situation may be ordered to specifically perform.[71] If DBC cannot or will not perform, and O does not seek nor obtain specific performance, the measure of damages should be the cost to "cover" the contract performance.

Infringement action successful, no license is granted, DBC is responsible, contract cannot be performed without infringement of patent, O's damages are ascertainable. This factual situation could easily occur, for example, if DBC were aware of an existing patent that had achieved a performance level that was unmatched in the industry, and DBC believed it had conceived of a way to avoid infringement and produce the same or similar results. When ADI's successful infringement action proves otherwise, DBC

---

[71] See § **2.8**.

finds itself incapable of meeting the contract's requirements without infringing upon the competitor's invention. The contractor cannot perform, so O's remedy must be damages. Those damages could be ascertainable in one of two ways: actual damages are determinable with reasonable certainty, or the contract provided for a valid method of assessing liquidated damages. In this instance, DBC would then bear the costs associated with ADI's successful infringement action as well as the damages owed to O.

Infringement action successful, no license is granted, DBC is responsible, contract cannot be performed without infringement, O's damages are speculative. In the absence of a valid liquidated damages provision, this factual scenario could render a court unable to award the owner damages, or most of its claimed damages, because of the legal requirement that the damages be nonspeculative. In the facts of our hypothetical case, DBC's inability to perform could result in O's power plant's failing to meet its target for removing quantities of SO_2 from its flue gas. Despite this clear failure to meet a contract requirement, however, damages may be indeterminable for a number of reasons. First, although we all benefit from cleaner air, there is probably no intrinsic economic value to O of releasing flue gas into the atmosphere with the reduced SO_2 level that the contract required. Rather, the economic value judgment may be a function of whether O's facility can operate within the guidelines of prevailing pollution control laws. Certain SO_2 emission levels might result in government economic sanctions against O's power plant, or even a shutdown while ameliorative action is taken. However, O may also be able to satisfy government emission guidelines, despite DBC's nonperformance, by switching from the use of a high sulfur coal to a lower sulfur coal. Depending upon market conditions, this might increase the cost of O's operations. The determination of possible damages for the necessity of using a lower sulfur coal would be a function of the useful life of the plant that has been constructed; market conditions over those future years dictating whether low sulfur coal or high sulfur coal should be used; possible changes in air quality laws by the federal government; the laws of supply and demand affecting the price of the respective fuels; and technological advances over the years that might produce an alternative method of satisfying the contract requirements without infringement of the existing patent. Unless certain conditions exist that make the owner's damages nonspeculative, they could be denied altogether as a matter of law, DBC would be answerable to ADI for damages and costs of the infringement action defense, but O could well have no damages remedy.

Infringement action successful, no license granted, O is responsible. This could result in O's bearing the costs of the patent infringement action, paying any damages owed to ADI, and further paying any damages owed to DBC as a consequence. Owner responsibility for this problem could conceivably occur if O, through the use of consultants or through its own expertise, were somehow in a position of having superior knowledge regarding existing patents for the type of work called for in the design-build contract. Although the design-builder will most often be the party most knowledgeable about the type of work involved in the contract, that certainly need not always be the case. Under this alternative outcome, O's scope of responsibility appears to be the same whether or not DBC can perform the contract by some alternative method that does not infringe the existing patent. Even if the contract can be so performed, DBC is likely to still have some damages associated with defense of the infringement action, delay to performance, or both. If the contract cannot be performed without infringement, DBC may also be entitled to its expectations interest in the contract (lost profits, if ascertainable and nonspeculative).

It is also possible that variations on this factual scenario could result in DBC and O each bearing some responsibility for the patent infringement and the resultant inability to perform the contract as intended. When additional facts are added to the above hypothetical case, the number of possible outcomes increases exponentially. However, the outcomes discussed above cover the most probable results and serve to alert design-builders to the major possibilities and problems in this sort of situation.

This hypothetical exercise suggests certain guidelines for those in the high technology design-build arena. When representing the owner, the construction attorney should assure that the client is alerted to the possibility of patent infringement problems any time the design-builder (or traditional contractor) is offering a performance that is on the cutting edge of available technology. The owner may want to have the contract contain substantive remedy clauses, not just procedural dispute resolution clauses, which define the scope of the owner's remedy in the event the design-builder cannot deliver the desired result without infringing the patent rights of the third party. If actual damages are likely to be speculative, the owner should consider reasonable liquidated damages.

The design-builder is cautioned to keep abreast of the patent rights of others in its own field, in order to avoid promising what it cannot deliver. Extreme caution should be exercised when entering into contracts in which there is a high risk that the technology used may be deemed to infringe the patent of another or simply may not work. Ventures with those sorts of risks probably should not be undertaken at all unless the design-builder is confident that the potential costs are built into its pricing or that the contract documents successfully allocate the risk of patent infringement problems to the owner.

Owners, design-builders, and their construction attorneys, confronted with the risk of patent infringement problems, should follow the same precautions. From either side of the contractual relation, the keys to avoiding a crisis are awareness and investigation of the risks of infringing the patent rights of others, drafting contract clauses that allocate the risk fairly but as far away from one's own client as the bounds of fairness allow, and remaining alert to the possibility of requiring licensing agreements from patent holders when it is prudent to do so. Obtaining such licenses may cut profits in some instances and may render some potential projects totally unprofitable. But it is a preferable alternative to paying a patent holder treble damages and being enjoined from performing altogether.

§ 2.11 Environmental Issues

The relationship between environmental issues and the design-build method of project delivery is the subject of **Chapter 9**. This section briefly addresses some particulars of the relationship between environmental issues and advanced technology applications of the design-build method.

A growing world population and the wasteful, polluting habits of mankind which, so far, have not been curtailed, will inevitably force environmental quality standards to become more stringent. Legislatures enacting environmental laws are being called upon to make value judgments concerning acceptable levels of pollution of our natural resources. Many environmental quality standards are already scheduled to require stricter levels in the future. As the population grows and polluting activities continue, standards will have to get tougher simply to maintain the current quality of the environment, without even approaching possible environmental improvement.

As environmental standards rise to new levels, advanced technology must improve. Our society will demand machines, equipment, and processes that are quicker, more fuel efficient, cleaner, less expensive, and better in every tangible sense than their predecessors. This will clearly contribute to the future growth in the use of the design-build method in advanced technology contexts for pollution control and clean-up projects. Design-builders should be mindful that future environmental quality standards will likely push environmental technology to the edge of the universe of its potential advancement. Society will demand advancements that leave the air, water, and land increasingly cleaner until the point is reached where cleaner results become impossible. As this process evolves, the legal issues relating to performance testing, remedies, and legal impossibility will be raised repeatedly.

Advanced technology issues will be involved in the future promulgation and enforcement of all types of environmental legislation. Current environmental laws, in very rough terms, can be divided into two categories, dealing either with clean-up and containment of existing pollution and waste, or control of ongoing emission and pollution activities. In the first category, federal laws such as CERCLA[72] and SARA[73] are addressed to cleaning up toxic and hazardous waste and other substances. With the astronomical costs of such efforts, there is constant pressure on design-builders to advance their technology so that clean-up and containment activities can be more environmentally effective and cost effective.

The regulation of air and water quality, which touches upon the vast majority of ongoing polluting activities in modern society, will demand improved technology to satisfy three major concerns:

1. Society will demand technological advances to manufacture products, produce power, and perform other processes in ways that are cleaner in and of themselves such that the pollution output of those activities, before treatment, is reduced.
2. Technological advances will also be sought to improve pollution control and treatment equipment, processes, and methods themselves. Design-builders will aggressively engage in a quest to clean the air and water to levels of virtually 100 percent purity, or as close to that standard as it is humanly possible to achieve.
3. At the same time, there will be incentives for technological advances that will allow the use of environmentally preferable products or fuels so that society can change its habits of consumption and avoid some of its polluting practices of the past. Many potential environmental trade-offs of this nature are already known and will certainly be studied further. For example, because natural gas and certain other alternative fuels burn cleaner than gasoline, technological improvements are desired that will allow the cleaner alternative fuels to be used in applications in which, under present technology, they are not practical. Other examples would include improvements in the use and application of certain natural products that would diminish or replace the demand for synthetic products that have high environmental costs. One simple example of this is the use of popcorn (unbuttered and unsalted) as an alternative packaging material.

Environmental control and regulation is a growing field, and its growth has paralleled many developments of the advanced technology age. This concurrent growth and development will undoubtedly continue. Advanced

---

[72] The primary provisions of the Comprehensive Environmental Response Compensation and Liability Act that are of interest to environmental and construction attorneys are codified at 42 U.S.C. §§ 9601–9626, 9631–9633, 9641, 9651–9661, 9671–9675 (1988).

[73] The primary provisions of the Superfund Amendments and Reauthorization Act that are of interest to environmental and construction attorneys are codified at 42 U.S.C. §§ 6921 note, 6926, 6928, 6991, 7401 note, 9601–9609, 9611–9614, 9616–9625, 9631–9633, 9641, 9651, 9653, 9656, 9658–9659, 9660–9662, 9671–9675, 11001–11005, 11021–11023, 11041–11050 (1988).

technology holds the key to better pollution control in the future and, everyone hopes, perhaps even a cleaner world.

§ 2.12 Issues for Contracting Parties to Consider

Trial courts, boards of contract appeals, and arbitration panels are the testing laboratories of the American legal system. These tribunals will be performing the "research and development" that will continue the evolution of legal principles relating to the design-build method, particularly as used in advanced technology projects. Judges and arbitrators will see more and more cases of this kind in the future, which will require them to stay abreast of new variations on the traditional roles of parties to a construction contract. They will continue to fashion principles that equitably allocate legal responsibilities and risks in ways consistent with the roles adopted by the contracting parties. The special challenges presented by the advanced technology age will encourage the continued use of the design-build method, or variations upon it. Use of creative types of project delivery systems in high technology ventures will assure that they continue to be a source of significant case law developments. And, as more and more aspects of daily life become affected by the technology boom, these legal developments will have increasing importance and broadened applicability.

For the present, users and practitioners of the design-build method on advanced technology construction projects can cope with their specific legal challenges by keeping a few basic concepts in mind.

1. Attorneys and their clients must be aware of the types of problems that arise at the time of contract formation, when measuring or testing performance, and when applying remedies for breach of contractual promises. Attorneys who foresee and alert clients to potential areas of difficulty can work with their clients toward effective problem avoidance.
2. Construction attorneys given an opportunity to participate in contract drafting should pay particular attention to risk allocation provisions. Important risk allocation features of a contract will always be present in warranty and guaranty provisions, testing clauses and terms pertaining to remedies. However, the attorney must be additionally mindful of less obvious contract features that have risk allocating results. For example, the method of payment provisions of a cost-plus contract place the owner at risk of bearing the extra expenses of unanticipated efforts to achieve required performance, yet those terms do not alert the casual reader to that effect. Risks relating to patent rights and environmental compliance also should be addressed in all good design-build contract documents.

3. Owners should have a natural skepticism of the design-builder who promises a performance that has never before been achieved. Therefore, owners should investigate performance claims thoroughly. References from prior projects should be available to allow the prospective owner to become familiar with the design-builder's past achievements. This does not mean parties should never embark on a contract to achieve things never achieved before, but they must recognize the acute risks of such ventures. Owners' attorneys also need to make certain that contractual remedies are adequate to cover any foreseeable ways that the design-builder could fail to achieve the intended result.
4. The design-builder and its legal counsel ought to be just as cautious in approaching a potential contract that calls for performances exceeding the current state of the art. The contractor must fully understand any risk being assumed, and must have a contract that clearly spells out any risk the owner is expected to assume. As the seller and user of high technology processes and products, the design-builder must be mindful of the ways that patent law issues can intrude upon a project's objectives and turn a profitable contract into a legal battlefield.
5. The key to avoiding failure of performance and defeated expectations, for both parties, is taking preventative steps in the contract formation stage. This is the time when the design-builder's promises are defined and the risks inherent in the contract are allocated. After all, regardless of what is to be built and the method to be used to obtain it, assuring that there is a meeting of the minds, that the project is feasible and achievable, that procedures to be followed during performance are clearly described, and that outcomes are predictable, is the essence of good construction contracting.

CHAPTER 3

THE EFFECT OF LICENSING LAWS ON DESIGN-BUILD PROJECTS

John J. Park, Jr.
E. Mabry Rogers
Walter J. Sears III*

John J. Park, Jr., is an associate with Bradley, Arant, Rose & White in Birmingham, Alabama, where he concentrates his practice in the construction, government contracts, and litigation areas. He graduated from the University of Virginia with a B.A. in history and from Yale Law School with a J.D. After serving in the United States Army JAG Corps, he joined Bradley, Arant, Rose & White in 1985. He is licensed to practice in Alabama and Virginia, and is a member of the bars of various state and federal courts.

E. Mabry Rogers is a partner with the Birmingham, Alabama, office of Bradley, Arant, Rose & White law firm, where his primary areas of practice are litigation and construction contracts. A cum laude graduate of Yale University, he received his law degree, cum laude, from Harvard Law School in 1974. He is licensed to practice in all Alabama courts and various other courts around the country, including the United States Supreme Court. Mr. Rogers has represented owners, contractors, subcontractors, suppliers, designers, and sureties. In addition to lecturing at various construction seminars, he is the author of several books and chapters of books and has had several construction-related articles published. He has served as an arbitrator for the American Arbitration Association and as a special master for the courts.

* The authors wish to thank Nicole Caucci and Jim Davis, law students at the University of Chicago and the University of Virginia, respectively, for their assistance in the preparation of this chapter.

Walter J. Sears III is a partner with Bradley, Arant, Rose & White in Birmingham, Alabama, where he concentrates his practice in construction and litigation. He has substantial experience representing contractors, owners, subcontractors, and suppliers in various courts throughout the country. He graduated cum laude from Princeton University and received his J.D. from the University of Virginia Law School.

§ 3.1 Introduction

The question of whether licensing laws facilitate or prohibit design-build contracting is misleading. All licensing laws discourage practice of the licensed activity by establishing barriers to entry, so the notion that a licensing law could facilitate an activity like design-build contracting must be considered relative. Even so, some state licensing laws facilitate design-build activity to a greater extent than other licensing laws. Still, other licensing laws effectively prohibit or have been construed to prohibit design-build activity. In addition, the public procurement laws of the United States and the states affect design-build activity.

This chapter will discuss the effect of state licensing laws on the design-build market. It will also discuss federal procurement laws because, in general, they limit the ability of public bodies to contract on a design-build basis to a greater degree than do licensing laws. In contrast, private contracts are affected more by licensing laws than by procurement laws. The chapter begins with an overview, then proceeds to a survey of the relevant federal and state laws and regulations.

§ 3.2 Background of Design-Build

"Currently, design-build contracts account for less than 5% of all construction in the United States, but owner demand is driving its use upward."[1] *Engineering News Record* has noted that domestic design-build contracts among its top 400 contractors more than doubled between 1987 and 1990, increasing from $18 billion to $37 billion. The authors foresee increasing resort to design-build in the future, both within the United States and internationally.[2]

This increase occurs against a background of risks that are not always fully sorted out or thought through by the parties involved. For example, design-build alters the liability relationships between and among owner, builder, and the design professional (A/E), and that change has insurance implications. In addition, as discussed in this chapter, A/E and contractor licensing laws add an element of risk to design-build contracts in many states, even in those states in which there is express authority allowing the use of the design-build approach. Thus, licensing laws are an additional hurdle, and a potential hindrance, to the hopeful design-builder.

In each of the states, the professions of architect, engineer, and contractor are regulated for the benefit of the public. In nearly every state, architects, engineers, and contractors are obligated to register, become licensed, or obtain a certificate before engaging in that business. By statute or case law in nearly every state, contracts by unlicensed persons to perform services requiring a license are not enforceable. Sometimes, the courts will look at who performs the services, at other times at who enters into the contract. The risk, however, is clear: a person may perform some or all of a contract but be denied recovery for those services if the person has not complied with an enforcing state's licensing law.

The design-builder may be vulnerable to such a result because it provides a combination of services through a single entity. A design-build entity fronted by a contractor has the license needed to perform construction services but may lack the license needed to perform design services. Conversely, the design-build entity fronted by an A/E may have an adequate design license but not a contractor's license.[3] The design-build joint venture

---

[1] *One-Stop Shopping Has Designers Nervous,* Engineering News Record, Aug. 12, 1991, at 9.

[2] *See id.*

[3] Nearly all states authorize licensed engineers to perform architectural services incidental to the practice of engineering and include a parallel exemption for architects. Because the definition of practicing architecture is usually broader than the definition of practicing engineering, engineers appear more vulnerable to a finding that they have overstepped their bounds by performing more than incidental services. *See, e.g.,* Dahlem Constr. Co. v. State Bd. of Examiners & Registration of Architects, 459 S.W.2d 169 (Ky. 1970).

may be composed of parties who together have the design and construction licenses, but the joint venture may not itself have either license. Legally, then, the design-build entity may be found to lack an element critical to the right to recover on its contracts. The issue may be raised by the owner, to avoid payment, or by professionals jealously guarding their market and professional niches. It has recently been reported, for instance, that the New Jersey board of architects has, over the past 18 months, issued some 300 orders primarily barring contractors from using the term "design-build" in advertisements.[4]

Historically, lawsuits involving design-build licensing problems have arisen most often with contracts that are abandoned during or at the end of the design stage. The licensed contractor, who has provided to the owner a design prepared by a licensed A/E, finds itself confronted by an owner which does not want to use the design and does not want to pay for something it will not use. For example, in *Food Management, Inc. v. Blue Ribbon Beef, Inc.,*[5] the turnkey contractor provided design services for a meat packing plant that was not constructed. The owner did not want to go forward and refused to pay because the construction estimate exceeded the owner's budget. The contractor filed suit for $32,000, representing the balance owed for the design services. The owner counterclaimed for the amounts already paid on the ground that the contractor had defaulted and was not a licensed designer. The court denied the contractor recovery of the amounts not paid, but it also denied the owner's recoupment claim. As this case shows, when an owner has been furnished something it does not intend to use, it has an incentive to avoid paying for it, and licensing issues are a prime defense.

When the defense is raised, the design-build entity is at risk of being found to lack an essential license. This risk will not occur in every state, because some states like Florida, North Carolina, Rhode Island, Washington, and, to an extent, Vermont, have statutorily exempted design-build from the licensing statutes. Several others, including New York[6] and Texas, have done so judicially. Other states, like Iowa and New Jersey, have judicial decisions that interpret the state licensing statutes adversely to the design-build entity. Still more states are unsettled; they may have traditional A/E licensing statutes, court decisions barring recovery in contract to unlicensed persons performing professional services, both, or no precedent one way or the other. In the last group of states, the uncertainty and

---

[4] *Contractor-Design Professional Feud Heats Up,* 15 The Construction Contractor ¶ 286 (Sept. 16, 199[illegible]).

[5] 413 F.2d 716 (8th Cir. 1969).

[6] Practitioners should be aware that recent administrative developments, discussed in **§ 3.5**, may make reliance on this judicial precedent, Charlebois v. J.M. Weller Assocs., Inc., 531 N.E.2d 1288 (N.Y. 1988), uncertain in New York.

the magnitude of the risks involved may be sufficient to discourage design-build activity.

This chapter will discuss both federal and state laws and will provide a survey of the laws of the states. It is presumed that the design-build entity is fronted by a licensed contractor, providing the owner with a design prepared by a licensed A/E, who is acting as a subcontractor to or joint venture partner with the contractor. This presumption appears to be an accurate reflection of the market and further reflects the A/E community's historic distrust of the design-build format. The American Institute of Architects did not fully deem participation in design-build activities to be ethical until 1980.[7] In addition, contractors tend to dominate design-build teams because of their greater bonding capacity and willingness to accept risks.[8] Accordingly, this chapter will presume that a contractor is entering into the contract with the owner and will furnish design services performed by a licensed A/E. The legal issue from the licensing perspective then becomes whether the contractor (or a joint venture that does not have an architect's or engineer's license) needs an A/E license to furnish that design.

§ 3.3 Design-Build in the Federal Sector

With certain specified statutory exceptions discussed below, federal law does not facilitate design-build contracting. In fact, it indirectly prohibits design-build contracts by specifying the ways in which the government will procure A/E and contractor services. When design-build is permitted, the number of projects and freedom to contract are limited. The federal government avoids licensing issues by requiring that A/Es be licensed in some jurisdiction.[9]

The primary limitation on design-build contracting in the federal sector arises from the procurement laws. Procurement of A/E services is governed by the Brooks Act, 40 U.S.C. § 541 in which Congress established federal policy "to negotiate contracts for architectural and engineering services on the basis of demonstrated competence and qualification for the type of

---

[7] R.H. Buesing, *Design/Build Management: The Law Struggles To Keep Pace With The Design/Build Trend,* 10 Construction Law. 14 (Jan. 1990).

[8] In the authors' experience, the design-build licensing issue has often arisen in the context of an A/E's working with an owner in a field of new technology. The A/E convinces the owner to go forward, and the owner agrees so long as the A/E provides a turnkey project. At that point, the A/E begins a "scramble" to find a contractor as a joint venture partner or as prime contractor to solve attendant licensing and bonding problems.

[9] Even this requirement is subject to the limitation that the licensing clause may be omitted when the design is to be performed (a) outside the United States, its possessions, or Puerto Rico, or (b) in a state or possession that does not have a registration requirement for the field involved. *See* 48 C.F.R. § 36.609-4.

professional services required and at a fair and reasonable price."[10] In contrast, the Competition in Contracting Act establishes a general preference for the use of competitive sealed bid procedures in procuring such services, with exceptions to the use of such procedures to be justified.[11] The Federal Acquisition Regulations (F.A.R.) provide, in pertinent part:

> (a) Contracting officers shall acquire construction using sealed bid procedures . . . , except that sealed bidding need not be used for construction contracts outside the United States, its possessions, or Puerto Rico.
>
> (b) Contracting officers shall acquire architect-engineering services by negotiation, and select sources in accordance with applicable law, subpart 36.6 [of the F.A.R.], and agency regulations.[12]

This procurement scheme establishes a preference for separate contracts by the United States with its A/E and with its contractor.

Organizational conflict of interest regulations reinforce the separation of design work from follow-on construction. In pertinent part, the F.A.R. provides:

> If a contractor prepares and furnishes complete specifications covering nondevelopmental items, to be used in a competitive acquisition, that contractor shall not be allowed to furnish these items, either as a prime contractor or as a subcontractor, for a reasonable period of time, including, at least, the duration of the initial production contract.[13]

A similar prohibition applies to the drafting of specifications for and furnishing equipment.[14]

These rules have been applied to the drafting of specifications for construction activities. For example, the comptroller general upheld the air force's disqualification of an operations and maintenance contractor, who participated in drafting the specifications, from participating in the procurement of construction of repairs and alterations at the same base.[15] In another case, a contractor who assisted an A/E in preparing the statement of work for repair of a hangar door was disqualified.[16]

The organizational conflict of interest rules rest on the perception that a party which participates in the design may gain an unfair competitive

---

[10] 40 U.S.C. § 542 (1988).

[11] 10 U.S.C. §§ 2303, 2304.

[12] 48 C.F.R. § 36.103 (1990).

[13] *Id.* § 9.505-2(a)(1).

[14] *Id.* § 9.505-2(A)(2).

[15] *See* Danish Arctic Contractors, B-212957, 84-1 CPD ¶ 131 (Jan. 30, 1984).

[16] Nelson Erection Co., B-217556, 85-1 CPD ¶ 482 (Apr. 29, 1985).

advantage or may not be fully objective in performing the work. The F.A.R. advises:

> An organizational conflict of interest exists when the nature of the work to be performed under a proposed Government contract may, without some restriction on future activities, (a) result in an unfair competitive advantage to a contractor or (b) impair the contractor's objectivity in performing the contract work.[17]

Precluding a design contractor from performing the follow-on contract may help "to avoid a situation in which the contractor could draft specifications favoring its own products or capabilities."[18] In *Nelson,* for example, Nelson's bid price was identical to the government's cost estimate, illustrating a remarkable degree of understanding of the scope of work.

In a backhanded way, the organizational conflict of interest regulations speak to design-build considerations. Design-build projects may represent an "organizational conflict of interest," but the result of the process is intended to be a lower-priced final product. In a conventional procurement, a contractor like Nelson, who participated in developing the scope of work, would have an advantage over other bidders because it had time to evaluate the work, whereas most bidders may not have had the time for a detailed review of the plans. The contractor with advance knowledge should also have a greater understanding of the risk factors. In contrast, design-build entities responding to a negotiated procurement are all equal because each can evaluate the risks and benefits (in terms of constructability) of its proposal and all are allotted the same time period to do so. The owner chooses from among the proposals, selecting the best combination of price and value. In other words, because factors other than price are relevant to design-build, design-build appears highly suited to negotiated procurements.

Notwithstanding the general statutory and regulatory bias in favor of the traditional owner-A/E-contractor relationship, the federal government permits design-build or turnkey contracting to a limited extent.

The General Services Administration (GSA) is reported to be "looking quite hard at the design-build concept."[19] *Engineering News Record* reports that the speedy, timely completion of an office building in Chicago, constructed on a design-build basis, has attracted positive attention at the policy-making level at GSA.[20] Although GSA has statutory authority to

---

[17] 48 C.F.R. § 9.501.

[18] *Id.* § 9.505-2(a)(2).

[19] *GSA, At Least, Still Has Big Plans,* Engineering News Record, Mar. 11, 1991, at 31, 32.

[20] *Id.*

procure A/E and construction services, and also has authority to negotiate 20-year or 30-year leases, the authors are not aware of any specific statutory or regulatory authority for GSA's use of design-build. GSA relies, instead, on the general authority in the Public Buildings Act of 1959[21] for its power to enter design-build contracts.

Congress authorized the secretary of defense to enter into up to three contracts per fiscal year for military construction on a turnkey basis through October 1, 1991.[22] The statute defines *one-step turn-key procedures* as those

> used for the selection of a contractor on a basis of price and other evaluation criteria to perform, in accordance with the provisions of a firm fixed-price contract, both the design and construction of a facility using performance specifications supplied by the Secretary concerned.[23]

Whether this authority will continue to exist appears to depend on the fiscal year 1992 budget, which was not yet enacted when this text was written.

The regulations applicable to the Farmers Home Administration (FmHA) community facilities construction activities establish a preference in favor of traditional contract structures but allow for design-build in some circumstances. In general, an A/E who has prepared plans and specifications or who will be responsible for monitoring the construction will not be permitted to bid on or negotiate for the construction contract.[24] Design and construction services are "normally" to be procured from "unrelated sources," but "[p]rocurement methods which combine or rearrange design, inspection or construction services (such as design-build or construction management) may be used with FmHA written approval."[25] The regulations set forth the kinds of information that should be transmitted to FmHA.

---

[21] 40 U.S.C. §§ 601–607; *but cf.* General Services Administration Acquisition Regulation; Provisions and Clauses (Design-Build Service Contracts), 52 Fed. Reg. 29,207 (proposed June 26, 1991) (soliciting comments on proposed rule authorizing Public Building Service to contract using design-build concept).

[22] 10 U.S.C. § 2862. One commentator opines that, prior to the enactment of this provision, the Corps of Engineers took the position that it was authorized to choose such contracting methods as were in the government's best interest without regard to whether the method involved acquisition of design-build services. In contrast to this view, the legislative history indicates Congress believed it was granting the Department of Defense authority it did not previously have. In either event, the legislation caps the number of such projects at three per fiscal year. *See generally* Jennings, *Government Experience with Design/Build: A View From the Corps of Engineers, in* Design/Build: Issues for the 90's and Beyond, A.B.A. Forum on Construction Industry (1990).

[23] 10 U.S.C. § 2862(a)(2).

[24] 7 C.F.R. § 1942.18(j)(7).

[25] *Id.* § 1942.18(k)(5)(1).

The Environmental Protection Agency has authority to permit grantees to construct certain kinds of waste water facilities, the total estimated cost of which is $8 million or less, on a design-build basis. The proposed construction must be "[c]onsistent with State law."[26]

Department of Energy (DOE) regulations applicable to operations and maintenance contracts note that the Brooks Act "does not directly govern the award of A-E subcontracts by DOE management and operating contractor."[27] The head of the contracting agency, defined to include designated DOE officials delegated the authority to award contracts and appoint contracting officers, is instructed to:

> assure that the purchasing systems and methods of management and operating contractors reflect the essence of the Federal policy [including the Brooks Act] by providing for selection of A-E subcontractors based primarily upon proposer's qualifications; however, this does not preclude the consideration of other factors, including cost or price, in the selection of A-E subcontractors.[28]

In other words, management and operating contractors are not bound but are to be strongly guided by the Brooks Act, just as they are obligated to observe the spirit of federal procurement policy. The regulations discourage combinations of subcontracts for A/E and construction services which may "result in self-inspection of construction work, tend to prevent a subcontractor from rendering an unbiased decision, or create difficulties in segregating costs between subcontracts."[29] Even so, design-build or turnkey subcontracts for the construction of a "discrete facility" are not precluded "so long as the subcontractor assumes all liability for defects in design and construction and consequential damages."[30]

In the federal arena, the principal design-build issue is one of the authority to use this contracting method. State licensing laws have no bearing,[31] unless the federal procuring agency itself requires a prospective contractor to hold a state license in the particular area of work.

---

[26] 33 U.S.C. § 1283(f).

[27] 48 C.F.R. § 970.7104-28(c).

[28] *Id. See also* 48 C.F.R. (DEAR) § 901.101 (defining *HCA*).

[29] 48 C.F.R. § 970.7104-28(f)(1).

[30] *Id.* § 970.7104.28(f)(1)(iii).

[31] Leslie Miller, Inc. v. Arkansas, 352 U.S. 187 (1956) (state cannot require a license of a private contractor engaged solely in the performance of work for the federal government); *see also* Gartrell Constr., Inc. v. Aubry, 940 F.2d 437 (9th Cir. 1991).

§ 3.4 Licensing Problems for Design-Build in the States

To overgeneralize, the states require individuals desiring to practice architecture to satisfy specified educational and other requirements and to obtain a document. The document may be called a certificate or license in the statute. Alternatively, the architect is required to register with the regulatory board. In this chapter, the terms "license," "certificate," and "register" are used interchangeably to mean compliance with the statute, however the compliance may be defined.

In § 3.5, the authors undertake a survey of the A/E licensing in the states. The authors have attempted to identify the statutory provisions and case law defining the practice of architecture, engineering, or both; establishing the penalties for practicing without a license; establishing the criteria for corporate practice; and addressing design-build. If a state has embraced design-build by statute or case law, our discussion is of no lesser importance because the design-build entity must still protect itself against violations of licensing laws. For example, California expressly authorizes design-build for the California State University system.[32] That authorization to the public officials does not solve potential licensing problems for the design-builder, however. Because of the general nature of any survey, practitioners are urged to undertake an independent, in-depth review before advising clients about the law in any particular state.

Typically, the states define architecture and the practice of architecture, engineering and the practice of engineering, and contracting, and they require a license to carry on the particular defined activity. The definitions of architecture or practicing architecture fall into several general categories:

1. Definitions in terms of service or creative work
2. Definitions in terms of "performing" services
3. Definitions in terms of "rendering" services
4. Other definitions.

The form of the definition is important because the states generally prohibit the unlicensed practice of architecture and engineering, but not all activities equate to practicing architecture or engineering or to performing such services. As one commentator has observed, the dictionary definitions of *rendering* include both "perform" and "furnish."[33] If the statute proscribes "rendering" services, does the unlicensed contractor's furnishing of plans prepared by a licensed A/E to the owner constitute rendering?

[32] Cal. Pub. Cont. Code §§ 10503, 10708.

[33] *See* Quatman, *Validity of Design/Build Under State and Federal Law, in* Design/Build: Issues for the 90's and Beyond, A.B.A. Forum on Construction Industry (1990).

Alternatively, so long as the unlicensed contractor is only a conduit for those plans, is the contractor "performing" services? These considerations give rise to uncertainty with respect to the validity of design-build in a number of states.

In addition, the statutes often include other relevant provisions. They exempt a number of activities from the statutory definitions; those exemptions may include preparation of shop drawings, supervision of construction, and design-build. Finally, some states expressly declare contracts by unlicensed persons to be unenforceable.

§ 3.5 State-by-State Survey of Licensing Requirements

Alabama

Alabama prohibits the unlicensed practice of architecture, which is defined in terms of "rendering" or "performing" services. Ala. Code §§ 34-2-30(2), 34-2-31 (1975). The legislative declaration of policy states, inter alia, that only qualified architects should be permitted to practice. *Id.* § 34-2-31. Engineers are permitted to perform incidental architectural services. *Id.* § 34-2-32(d).

General contractors are likewise subject to regulation. A general contractor is one who "undertakes to construct or superintend the construction of any building, highway, sewer, grading or any improvement or structure where the cost of the undertaking is $20,000.00 or more." *Id.* § 34-8-1.

Contracts entered into by unlicensed architects, engineers, and general contractors are void. *See, e.g., J&M Industries v. Huguley Oil Co.,* 546 So. 2d 369 (Ala. 1989) (general contractor); *Southern Metal Treating Co. v. Goodner,* 271 Ala. 510, 125 So. 2d 268 (1960) (dictum; engineer). Even when the owner participated in structuring a contract to avoid the $20,000 limitation on general contractor services, the owner may still raise the lack of a license as a defense in a later dispute with the contractor. *Cochran v. Ozark Country Club, Inc.,* 339 So. 2d 1023 (Ala. 1976). The owner's receipt of a benefit does not defeat the right to claim the defense. *Cooper v. Johnston,* 283 Ala. 565, 219 So. 2d 392 (1969). The lack of a license need not be raised as an affirmative defense. *Brown v. Mountain Lakes Resort, Inc.,* 521 So. 2d 24 (Ala. 1988).

The application of the Alabama licensing laws appears to favor traditional forms of the owner-A/E-contractor relationship. In *Cooper v. Johnston,* for example, the Alabama Supreme Court rejected the attempt of an unlicensed person to "rent" the license of another. The licensed person allowed Johnston to use its license for one-half of 1 percent of the contract price. The court noted that the license holder was in no way responsible for the construction and was not a party "directly or indirectly" to the construction contract. 219 So. 2d at 396. The court found no statutory provision that authorized the use of the license in this manner.

In the authors' experience, joint ventures have been used for Alabama design-build projects. In addition, there are examples of the design-builder's being a large entity licensed both as a contractor and as a designer.

Alaska

Alaska law defines the practices of architecture and engineering in terms of "service or creative work." Alaska Stat. § 08.48.341(7), (8) (Supp. 1990). It also appears to provide for the validity of design-build in private contracts. Although contracts by unlicensed architects are unenforceable, the law recognizes an exemption from licensing for "the execution as a contractor of work designed by a professional architect or engineer." *Id.* §§ 08.48.281, .331(1). In addition, the law includes an exemption applicable to licensed specialty subcontractors; the statute provides that the architect licensing provisions do not apply to:

> a specialty contractor licensed under appropriate Alaska Statutes, while engaged in the business of contracting, designing systems or facilities as otherwise permitted by law for work within the specialty for which the specialty contractor's license was issued to be performed or supervised by the contractor, or any licensed contractor preparing shop or field drawings for work which the specialty contractor has contracted to perform.

Id. § 08.48.33(10). The contract of architects not licensed in Alaska to perform architectural services related to a building to be constructed in Alaska has been held unenforceable even though the architects did most of their work in Washington State. *Hedla v. McCool,* 476 F.2d 1223 (9th Cir. 1973) (applying Alaska law).

Contractors are obligated to allege and prove that they were licensed at the time of contracting for the performance of the work in order to maintain an action on the contract. Alaska Stat. § 08.18.151. The bar to recovery by unlicensed contractors in contract extends to claims under Alaska's Little Miller Act. *Smith v. Tyonek Timber, Inc.,* 680 P.2d 1148 (Alaska 1984).

Arizona

Arizona law defines the practices of architecture and engineering in terms of the professional services involved and provides that holding oneself out as able to "perform" architectural or engineering services may be deemed to be practice. Ariz. Rev. Stat. Ann. § 32-101.3 (1986). Persons desiring to practice architecture or engineering must first procure a certificate. *Id.* § 32-121. Firms and corporations may not practice architecture or engineering "unless the work is under the full authority and responsible charge of a registrant [i.e., one who has a certificate], who is also a principal of the firm or officer of the corporation." *Id.* § 32-141A.

In *Thomas v. Lundgren,* 9 Ariz. App. 4, 449 P.2d 628 (1969), the court held that an unlicensed architect's delivery of existing plans and specifications did not involve the performance of architectural services. The architect was licensed outside Arizona and undertook to provide plans for a hotel but not construction services. The court explained:

> The contract did not involve any "service or creative work", or the "application of the mathematical and physical sciences and the principles of architecture", nor did it involve "consultation, evaluation, planning, design and supervision of construction." Plaintiffs instead agreed only to deliver plans which had been already drawn for another.

Id., 449 P.2d at 630. The court went on to state that it was not endorsing a subterfuge created to avoid the licensing laws. The last comment suggests that Arizona courts may look unfavorably on design-build contracts, especially if the court perceives the contract as an attempt to avoid licensing laws.

Arizona requires contractors seeking to enforce their contracts to allege and prove they were licensed when the contract was entered into and when the cause of action arose. Ariz. Rev. Stat. Ann. § 32-1153. A contractor whose license had expired at the time its cause of action arose was barred from enforcing its contract. *Northern v. Elledge,* 72 Ariz. 166, 232 P.2d 111 (1951); *see also In re Spanish Trails Lanes,* 16 B.R. 304 (Bankr. Ariz. 1981) (contract by unlicensed contractor unenforceable or voidable but not void ab initio). An owner sought to apply that rule to an unlicensed golf course architect, but the court held that the services involved were not architectural services. *Jackling v. Snyder,* 3 Ariz. App. 63, 411 P.2d 822 (1966).

Arkansas

Arkansas law prohibits any person from "practic[ing] architecture in this state, or engag[ing] in preparing plans, specifications, or preliminary data for the erection or alteration of any building located within the boundaries of this state" without being licensed. Ark. Code Ann. § 17-14-301 (Michie 1987). The prohibition is reinforced by a provision making it unlawful for unregistered persons (other than employees collecting a fee as the representative of a registered architect) to collect a fee for architectural services. *Id.* § 17-14-311(c). The contract of an unlicensed person furnishing architectural services has been held void. *Sarkco, Inc. v. Edwards,* 482 S.W.2d 623 (Ark. 1972). The incidental practice of architecture by duly licensed professional engineers is exempt from the prohibition. Ark. Code Ann. § 17-14-302(a)(1).

In *Arkansas State Board of Architects v. Bank Building & Equipment Corp.,* 286 S.W.2d 323 (Ark. 1956), the Arkansas Supreme Court upheld an injunction against the practice of architecture by an out-of-state corporation. The corporation contracted with an owner to furnish plans and specifications and to supervise construction. The court found that the corporation was practicing architecture and that the corporation's unlicensed practice was not validated by the fact that it employed an architect licensed in Arkansas. The corporation's actions violated the Arkansas statute, which then required that "the principal of such corporation whose name appears in the corporation's name [be] a registered architect and . . . each principal [be] so registered." *See* 1941 Ark. Acts No. 270 § 2; *compare* Ark. Code Ann. § 17-14-303 (establishing criteria for corporate practice of architecture).

Although *Bank Building* was a case involving interstate corporate practice rather than design-build, the court's strict interpretation of the statute is troublesome for design-build contracts. The corporate practice statute has been modified since *Bank Building,* so that corporations may practice if two-thirds of the partners or directors are licensed in any state and the person in charge is registered in Arkansas. Ark. Code Ann. § 17-14-303. Under this standard, the activities of Bank Building may have been acceptable, as long as the local architect was "in charge" of the design. The case still represents authority for the proposition that an unlicensed entity cannot satisfy the statute by contracting with a licensed entity.

Unlicensed contractors are not entitled to enforce their contracts. *Id.* § 17-22-103(d) (Supp. 1989). This rule extends to preclude recovery in quantum meruit by virtue of a 1989 amendment to the statute. *See Woodhaven Homes, Inc. v. Kennedy Sheet Metal Co.,* 304 Ark. 415, 803 S.W.2d 508 (1991).

California

California law defines the practice of architecture to include "the offering or performing, and being responsible for, professional services which require the skills of an architect in the planning of sites, and the design, in whole or in part, of buildings, or groups of buildings or structures." Cal. Bus. & Prof. Code § 5500.1(a) (West 1990). Practicing architecture without a license is a misdemeanor, *id.* § 5536(a), but there does not appear to be an express statutory prohibition against recovery on a contract by an unlicensed architect. In contrast, the California law pertaining to contractors provides:

> No person engaged in the business or acting in the capacity of a contractor, may bring or maintain any action, or recover in law or equity, in any court of this state for the collection of compensation for the performance of any act

> or contract for which a license is required by this chapter without alleging and proving that he or she was a duly licensed contractor at all times during the performance of that act or contract regardless of the merits of the cause of action brought by the person, except that this prohibition shall not apply to contractors who are each individually licensed under this chapter but who fail to comply with Section 7029 [joint venture licensure].

Id. § 7031(a); *see also Hydrotech Systems, Ltd. v. Oasis Waterpark,* 803 P.2d 370, 277 Cal. Rptr. 517 (1991) (applying § 7031 in the face of fraud allegations by the unlicensed contractor). According to the California courts, this provision reflects a legislative determination that the misdemeanor penalties for performing without a license (which are like the misdemeanor penalties for unlicensed A/E practice) constituted an insufficient deterrent. *Brown v. Solano County Business Development, Inc.,* 92 Cal. App. 3d 192, 154 Cal. Rptr. 700 (1979).

The California law pertaining to the licensing of architects at one time provided an exemption for unlicensed practice if the unlicensed architect fully informed the other party in writing of the lack of a license. In reliance on this former law, the court in *Walter M. Ballard Corp. v. Dougherty,* 106 Cal. App. 2d 35, 234 P.2d 745 (Cal. App. 1951), held that a corporation which performed hotel consulting, designing, and decorating services but was not licensed as an architect could furnish the services of a licensed architect who subcontracted with the corporation. However, the statutory basis for the court's decision has been amended out of the California Code, so this case may no longer be reliable authority. Cal. Bus. & Prof. Code, former § 5337.

The California Code permits partnerships between architects and nonarchitects but requires the architect's name to appear on all instruments of service, such as blueprints, drawings, and the like, and bars the designation of any nonarchitect as an architect. *Id.* § 5539. The California Supreme Court has held that a partnership composed of licensed architects and a licensed contractor who offered architectural and building contracting services was entitled to recover the reasonable value of architectural services performed. *Joseph v. Drew,* 225 P.2d 504 (Cal. 1950).

Joint ventures may face an additional hurdle. A joint venture composed of two or more licensed contractors must obtain a joint venture license in order to be awarded a contract or act as a contractor. Cal. Bus. & Prof. Code § 7029.1 (Supp. 1991).

Colorado

Colorado defines the practice of architecture in terms of the "performance" of design services and observation and administration of construction without the performance of construction. Colo. Rev. Stat. § 12-4-102(5)

(Supp. 1990); *see also* § 12-25-102(10) (practice of engineering defined in terms of performance of service or creative work for others). Corporations are not licensed, but a business entity may use the word "architects" in its business name if a majority of the officers and directors are licensed architects. *Id.* § 12-4-110(1). Persons lacking a license are prohibited from, inter alia, "[e]ngag[ing] in the practice of architecture." *Id.* § 12-4-113(1)(c)(II). Contracts by unlicensed persons to perform services requiring a license are generally not enforceable. *See Carter v. Thompkins,* 294 P.2d 265 (Colo. 1956) (plumber); *Benham v. Heyde,* 122 Colo. 233, 221 P.2d 1078 (1950). In *Carter,* the court severed the portions of work not requiring a plumber's license (furnishing and installing a furnace) from the tainted portions of the contract (those involving plumbing) and allowed recovery for the former services. In *Mobile Housing Environments v. Barton & Barton,* 432 F. Supp. 1343 (D. Colo. 1977), a design-build contractor who hired the architect as a subcontractor was held liable to the owner for design deficiencies. The case does not raise the licensing issue.

Connecticut

Connecticut also prohibits the practice of architecture without a license. Conn. Gen. Stat. Ann. § 20-290 (West Supp. 1991). The practice of architecture is defined in terms of "rendering or offering to render" architectural services. *Id.* § 20-288(3); § 20-299 (1990) (defining professional engineer in terms of "rendering"). These provisions have been held to bar an unlicensed person's recovery for architectural services performed. *See, e.g., Design Development, Inc. v. Brignole,* 570 A.2d 221 (Conn. App. Ct. 1990). The *Brignole* court also rejected the unlicensed architect's equity-based argument that the bar should not apply because the owner knew Design Development was not a licensed architect or engineer and would be unjustly enriched if it did not have to pay. The court stated:

> We hesitate to agree with the trial court that the parties were, in fact, in pari delicto. The defendants are members of the class that the legislature sought to protect with the enactment of General Statutes § 20-290, and they did nothing that was in and of itself wrong or illegal.

Id. at 223 n. 4.

Delaware

Delaware law defines the practice of architecture as the "rendering or offering to render" architectural services. Del. Code Ann. tit. 24, § 302(5) (1987); *compare* tit. 24, § 2803(7) (practice of engineering defined in terms of services performed for general public). It further prohibits any person from holding himself out as an architect or conveying the impression that he is an architect unless he is licensed. *Id.* tit. 24, § 303(a); *see also* tit. 24, § 2802 (engineering). The licensing statute is not to be construed to prevent the incidental practice of architecture by a registered engineer or by a corporation "if the practice is done under the direct responsibility and supervision of an architect," and also allows incidental practice of engineering by architects. *Id.* tit. 24, §§ 303(b), 2825.

District of Columbia

District of Columbia law defines the practice of architecture in terms of rendering or offering to render professional architectural services. D.C. Code Ann. § 2-214(b) (1988). The statute prohibits practicing architecture without a license. *Id.* § 2-214(a). Corporations are not registered as architects, but a number of architects may constitute a firm. *Id.* § 2-216.

In *Dunn v. Finlayson,* 104 A.2d 830 (D.C. 1954), the court held that architectural services performed by an unlicensed architect before the statutory registration scheme became effective were not invalid. Likewise, performing construction superintendence services after the statute became effective did not invalidate the contract. The court stated, however, "[W]e have no doubt that one who engages in the practice of architecture in violation of the act would have no right to recover for such services." *Id.* at 832 (citing *Rubin v. Douglas,* 59 A.2d 690 (D.C. 1948) (setting forth the general rule)).

Florida

Florida law defines architecture in terms of the "rendering or offering to render" services. Fla. Stat. Ann. § 481.203(6) (West 1987). Persons who are not registered architects are prohibited from practicing architecture. *Id.* § 481.223(a)(1). Licensed architects may practice through a corporation or partnership provided one or more of the principal officers or partners are licensed and all personnel who act as architects in Florida are Florida licensees. *Id.* § 481.219(1).

In 1989, Florida enacted legislation expressly authorizing design-build contracts:

> Notwithstanding the provisions of this part, a general contractor who is certified or registered pursuant to the provisions of Chapter 489 is not required to be licensed as an architect when negotiating or performing services under a design-build contract as long as the architectural services offered or rendered

> in connection with the contract are offered and rendered by an architect licensed in accordance with this chapter.

Fla. Stat. Ann. § 481.229(3); *see also id.* § 471.003(2)(j).

A recent decision by the Florida District Court of Appeals illustrates a key concern for private design-build agreements entered into prior to the 1989 statute. In *Miller Construction Co. v. First Industrial Technology Corp.,* 576 So. 2d 748 (Fla. Dist. Ct. App. 1991), the court held that a contractor who was not licensed as an architect was not entitled to claim a lien for architectural design services provided pursuant to a design-build agreement entered into in 1988. (Because this agreement was entered into prior to the 1989 statute, we presume that is why the court did not mention the 1989 statute in its opinion.) The design-builder entered into a contract which identified the source of the architectural services. *Id.* at 749 n.2. After completing the preliminary design, the contractor performed additional design services and claimed both architect's and contractor's liens when it was not paid. The court rejected the claim for an architect's lien because Miller Construction was not an architect "and therefore cannot perform services as an architect." *Id.* at 750 (citing *O'Kon & Co. v. Riedel,* 540 So. 2d 836, 840 (Fla. Dist. Ct. App. 1988)). The claim for a mechanic's lien was rejected because the furnishing of drawings for the purpose of obtaining financing did not constitute an improvement to real property.

Georgia

Georgia law defines practicing architecture in terms of the "rendering or offering to render" services. Ga. Code Ann. § 43-4-1(3) (Michie 1988). The statute further provides:

> [A]ny person who is engaged in the planning or design for the erection, enlargement, or alteration of any building or group of buildings for others or furnishing architectural administration of construction contracts thereof shall be deemed to be practicing architecture and be required to register under this chapter and to secure all renewals of such registration as a condition precedent to his doing so.

Id. § 43-4-14. The statute includes an exemption allowing architects to perform incidental engineering services. In *Georgia Association of American Institute of Architects v. Gwinett County,* 233 S.E.2d 142 (Ga. 1977), the Georgia Supreme Court held that an engineer's design and supervision of the construction of a fire station did not constitute the unauthorized practice of architecture, because design of a fire station fell within the definition of each practice area.

Although Georgia law does not specifically address the enforceability of a design-build contract, one case reflects a strong administrative and judicial skepticism of such contractual arrangements. In *Wise v. State Board for Qualification & Registration of Architects,* 247 Ga. 206, 274 S.E.2d 544 (1981), an out-of-state architect sought a Georgia license on the basis of reciprocity. His practice experience had been exclusively with a design-build contractor in another state. The Georgia licensing board required him to obtain experience working for an independent architect as a condition to obtaining a Georgia license. The Georgia Supreme Court held that this requirement was not unreasonable, relying on one of the standard critiques of design-build, the alleged conflict of professional loyalty on the part of the architect, as justification for the requirement. The court asserted:

> The job of an architect is to ensure that the plans are followed precisely, irrespective of the additional cost to the contractor. In many respects, the architect is seen as an antagonist to the contractor, as the contractor is seeking the maximum profit, while the architect is seeking the best final product possible. Individuals working in the setting of a "design-build" firm experience a constant conflict of interest not normally present in the setting of an independent architect. Thus, the experience in question is rationally related to the legitimate state interest of ensuring that all licensed architects are properly qualified and will competently practice in the interest of the public health, safety, and welfare.

274 S.E.2d at 546.

Hawaii

Hawaii law defines architect and professional engineer as one holding himself out as able to perform or performing architectural or engineering services. Haw. Rev. Stat. § 464-1 (Supp. 1990). The statute requires a license to practice professional architecture or engineering. *Id.* § 464-2. In *Wilson v. Kealakekua Ranch, Ltd.,* 551 P.2d 525 (Haw. 1976), the Hawaii Supreme Court held that an architect who did not pay a $15 license renewal fee was not barred from recovering for services performed. The court distinguished nonrenewal of a license from initial registration, indicating that an unlicensed architect might not receive the same solicitude. In *Gauschino v. Eucalyptus, Inc.,* 658 P.2d 888 (Haw. Ct. App. 1983), the court found insufficient evidence to show the unlicensed performance of architectural and contractor services; the unsuccessful movant had argued that such unlicensed performance rendered the contract void and unenforceable.

The Hawaii contractor licensing statute requires contractors to be licensed prior to contracting in order to enforce their contracts or to recover in quantum meruit. Haw. Rev. Stat. § 444-22. The Hawaii Supreme Court has held that the statute does not contain an exception for cases in which the owner knows that the contractor is not licensed but enters into the contract anyway. *Butler v. Obayashi,* 785 P.2d 1324 (Haw. 1990).

Idaho

Idaho law defines the practice of architecture in terms of "rendering or offering to render" professional architectural services. Idaho Code § 54-309(1)(c) (Supp. 1991). Practicing architecture without a license constitutes a misdemeanor. *Id.* § 54-310. The statute excludes preparation of shop drawings from the scope of regulated services. *Id.* § 54-309(2)(e). Foreign corporations are permitted to practice in Idaho provided all partners or shareholders are licensed in architecture or in allied professional services in some state, one-third of the partners or shareholders are licensed architects in some state, and the person in charge in Idaho holds no less than a pro rata ownership interest and is licensed in Idaho. *Id.* § 54-316.

In *Johnson v. Delane,* 290 P.2d 213 (Idaho 1955), a Washington engineer entered into a contract to prepare plans and specifications for a building to be constructed in Idaho. The Idaho Supreme Court held that the making of the contract was not sufficient to constitute practicing engineering in Idaho, when the services were performed in Washington. Had the A/E's work constituted the practice of engineering in Idaho, the court's opinion indicates that the court would have followed the general rule denying enforceability of contracts for professional services by unlicensed persons. *Id.* at 215-16.

Illinois

Illinois law defines the practice of architecture to include "the offering or furnishing of professional services." Ill. Ann. Stat. ch. 111, para. 1305. Practicing or attempting to practice architecture without obtaining a license constitutes a misdemeanor. *Id.* ch. 111, para. 1336. A contract employing an unlicensed person to "architecturally prepare the necessary plans, drawings and specifications" has been declared unenforceable. *Keenan v. Tuma,* 240 Ill. App. 448 (1926).

In *Gastaldi v. Reutermann,* 104 N.E.2d 115 (Ill. App. Ct. 1952), however, the Illinois Appellate Court reached a different result in a case resembling design-build. After bids to construct an automobile salesroom and garage according to the plans prepared by a licensed architect (under contract with the owner) exceeded the owner's budget, the contractor proposed a redesign to the architect. The architect was paid by the contractor to prepare revised plans, and the architect contemplated supervising the actual construction. Ultimately, the project did not go forward, but the contractor sought recovery of the stipulated compensation for the services, including the design. The owner denied liability on the ground that the services that had been provided were architectural and the contractor was barred from recovery because it was not licensed.

The court rejected the defense, noting that the contractor never held itself out as an architect and that the licensed architect who prepared the plans intended also to supervise the construction. The court explained, "[T]he contract [does not] call for the rendering of architectural service by the plaintiff, either literally or by necessary implication." *Id.* at 117. The court distinguished *Keenan* on the grounds that *Keenan* involved an unlicensed person's providing services expressly identified as architectural, with no licensed A/E to provide construction supervision services. Finally, the court explained that a case like this, in which the owner was affirmatively aware of the circumstances and a licensed A/E provided the design, was not contrary to the public protection purposes of the licensing statute.

In *U.S.F.&G. v. Continental Casualty Co.,* 505 N.E.2d 1072 (Ill. App. Ct. 1987), the Illinois Appellate Court held that an A/E's services fell within the scope of the "professional services" insurance coverage provided by Continental Casualty. The court rejected Continental's suggestion that design-build services were outside the scope of traditional professional services coverage: "Continental's distinction between a 'traditional architect' and a 'design-build' architect is not reflected in its policy coverage." *Id.* at 1075–1076. Although this case does not involve a licensing issue, it reflects a judicial environment favorable to considering design-build services as architectural or engineering-type services.

Indiana

Indiana law defines the practices of architecture and engineering in terms of the "performance" of professional services. Ind. Code Ann. §§ 25-4-1-17 (Burns 1991); § 25-31-1-2(f) (1991 Supp.). The incidental practice of engineering by architects is exempt from the engineering licensing statutes and vice versa. *Id.* § 25-4-1-11; *see also* § 25-31-1-30 (engineers may engage in incidental architectural practices). Corporations or partnerships may not engage in the practice of architecture "unless the work is under the full authority and responsible charge of a registrant who is also a principal." *Id.* §§ 25-4-1-27, 25-31-1-18.

In *Kolan v. Culveyhouse,* 114 Ind. App. 249, 245 N.E.2d 683 (1969), a general contractor who prepared plans for a home in the hope of obtaining the follow-on construction contract sought to claim a lien when the owner decided to use another contractor to build according to the same plans. The court held that the contractor's actions were within the scope of practicing architecture and that the applicable statute (Ind. Code. Ann. § 25-4-1-13) barred recovery for architectural services rendered by unlicensed persons.

In a case which does not speak to licensing provisions but which demonstrates how difficult design-build may be under public bidding laws, the Indiana Court of Appeals held that the Indiana public procurement laws prevented use of design-build contracts by public bodies in Indiana. *Negley v. Lebanon Community School Corp.,* 362 N.E.2d 178 (Ind. Ct. App. 1977). In a reading of the public procurement laws, however, the court further held that school building corporations that build schools and lease them to school corporations were not covered by public procurement laws, including Indiana's competitive bid laws. Therefore, a design-build contract by a school building corporation was legal.

Iowa

Iowa law defines the practices of architecture and engineering in terms of the "performing or offering to perform" professional services. Iowa Code Ann. §§ 118.16.8, 114.2 (West 1984). The unlicensed practice of architecture is unlawful and constitutes a serious misdemeanor. *Id.* § 118.15. The unlicensed practice of engineering is likewise prohibited. *Id.* § 114.1. In addition to the *Food Management* decision, discussed below, a 1936 Iowa Attorney General's opinion concludes that one who practices a profession without complying with the law may not recover for services performed. 1936 Op. Iowa Att'y Gen. 451.

Corporations may practice architecture in Iowa provided:

1. The entire practice in Iowa is done by or under the responsible supervision of an Iowa architect
2. All directors and the president and vice-presidents of any corporation must be registered in Iowa or some other state.

Iowa Code Ann. § 118.21. The engineering provision is more restrictive, stating:

> Corporations engaged in designing buildings or works for public or private interests not their own shall be deemed to practice professional engineering within the meaning of this Chapter. With respect to such corporations all principal designing or constructing engineers shall hold certificates of registration hereunder. This chapter shall not apply to corporations engaged solely in constructing buildings and works.

Id. § 114.26.

In *Food Management, Inc. v. Blue Ribbon Beef Pack, Inc.,* 413 F.2d 716 (8th Cir. 1969), the court, applying Iowa law, invalidated the design portions of a contract for the turnkey production of a meat packing plant. The contractor subcontracted portions of the design engineering and layout to a licensed Iowa A/E. Before construction began, the owner terminated the contract and sought restitution; the contractor sought to recover for the services provided prior to the termination. The trial court held that the contractor's actions constituted the practice of architecture and engineering and that the contract was not enforceable. On appeal, the court rejected the contractor's contention that, by subcontracting with a licensed Iowa

A/E, the contractor did not engage in the unauthorized practice of architecture or engineering:

> A literal interpretation of the terms of the general contract and subcontract . . . compels the conclusion that [the subcontractor A/E] was not to perform the entire architectural and engineering services, that it was not "in responsible charge" of the work, and that Food Management was not merely executing [the subcontractor A/E]'s plans.

Id. at 723. The court ruled that those portions of the contract relating to architectural and engineering services were illegal and not enforceable, because the contractor acted in contravention of the Iowa licensing statutes. The court stated it was following the "general rule of unenforceability." The court tempered its holding by affirming the denial of Blue Ribbon's counterclaim for restitution, explaining that "[t]o allow both retainment of services and recovery back of money paid is not necessary to effectuate the public policy of the licensing statutes." *Id.* at 727.

Food Management constitutes a barrier to design-build in Iowa. Future turnkey contractors cannot count on receiving partial payment, unless steps, such as joint venturing with a design firm, are taken to address *Food Management*'s holding.

Kansas

Kansas law defines the practice of architecture in terms of the "rendering of service." Kan. Stat. Ann. § 74-7003(e) (1985); *compare* § 74-7003(i) (engineering defined in terms of service or creative work). Kansas law bars the practice or offering to practice a licensed technical profession, including both architecture and engineering, in Kansas without being duly licensed. *Id.* § 74-7001(a).

Kentucky

Kentucky law defines the practice of architecture in terms of the "rendering or offering to render" services. Ky. Rev. Stat. Ann. § 323.010(3) (Michie 1990); *compare* § 322.010(3) (engineering defined in terms of service or creative work). Subject to certain limited exceptions, no person may practice architecture in Kentucky without first obtaining a license. *Id.* §§ 322.00, 323.020. The Kentucky Court of Appeals has held, "[O]ne assuming to act as an architect, who has not procured a license, cannot, under the rule universally recognized, maintain an action to enforce a contract for services rendered by him as an architect." *Board of Education v. Elliott*, 125 S.W.2d 733, 736 (Ky. 1939). Kentucky recognizes an exception to this "general rule" for contracts between persons in the same business field who contracted with knowledge of each other's qualifications. *Kennoy v. Graves,* 300 S.W.2d 568 (Ky. 1957).

In a case involving the procurement of design and construction services from a single entity, the Kentucky Court of Appeals affirmed an injunction against the practice of architecture by a construction company and its principal owners, who were licensed engineers. *Dahlem Construction Co. v. State Board of Examiners & Registration of Architects,* 459 S.W.2d 169 (Ky. 1970). Dahlem undertook to design and construct a nursing home according to plans prepared and stamped by one of Dahlem's principals. Dahlem argued that its activities were legally permitted under the engineering licensing statutes, but the court disagreed. The court read the Kentucky statutes to include the design of "any asylum, hospital, nursing or convalescent home, or home for the aged, regardless of capacity" within the scope of architecture. The court rejected Dahlem's argument that the architectural services it performed were incidental to the practice of engineering and permitted under the engineering licensing statute, stating:

> We suppose it may not be seriously debated that the design and its aesthetic phases were architectural only. There was nothing "incident" to the practice of engineering encompassed in formulating the aesthetic design of the nursing home or in adapting it to the topography so as to attain the maximum artistic effect. Those functions were peculiarly within the expertise of the trained architect.

Id. at 171. This is a case of "close but not enough." Implicit in the case is the assumption that, had Dahlem had another principal who was a licensed architect, the turnkey project may have passed the challenge from Kentucky's architects.

Louisiana

Louisiana law reserves the right to practice architecture and engineering to licensed persons. La. Rev. Stat. Ann. §§ 37:141A, 681 (West 1988, Supp. 1991). The practice of architecture is defined in terms of the "solicitation, offering, contracting to perform, or the performance" of professional services. *Id.* § 37:141B(3). An architect licensed in Texas but not in Louisiana was denied recovery on a quantum meruit basis for services rendered in Louisiana. *Jary v. Emmett,* 234 So. 2d 530 (La. Ct. App. 1970). The decision in *West Baton Rouge Parish School Board v. Ray, Inc.,* 367 So. 2d 332 (La. 1979), holding a contract for architectural services by an architectural corporation void because the firm did not have (and could not then obtain) a license, has been reversed by statute. Louisiana statutes now recognize the legitimacy of professional architectural corporations and allow them to "enter into contracts to provide architectural services and such other contracts as may be consistent with the practice of architecture." La. Rev. Stat. Ann. § 12:1097A.

Maine

Maine law defines the practice of architecture in terms of the "rendering or offering to render" services and prohibits the practice of architecture by unlicensed persons. Maine Rev. Stat. Ann. tit. 32, § 220-A (West 1988). Corporations or partnerships may practice architecture, but one-third of the directors or partners must be licensed under the laws of any state, and the person in charge must be a director or partner and be licensed in Maine. *Id.* tit. 32, § 220.1.13(2). Corporations or partnerships may practice engineering in Maine but only "provided that the practice is carried on only by professional engineers registered in this State." *Id.* tit. 32, § 1253.

Maryland

Maryland defines practicing architecture in terms of the nature of the service or creative work involved. Md. Bus. Occ. & Prof. Code Ann. § 3-101(g) (1989). The statute requires persons to be licensed before practicing architecture. *Id.* §§ 3-302(1), 3-603. Contracts by unlicensed persons to perform architectural services have been held unenforceable. *Snodgrass v. Immler,* 194 A.2d 103 (Md. 1963); *see also Harry Berenter, Inc. v. Berman,* 265 A.2d 759 (Md. 1970) (denying unlicensed contractor right to enforce mechanic's lien and right to recover in quantum meruit).

Maryland law permits licensed architects to practice architecture for others through corporations or partnerships and permits a corporation or partnership to provide professional services through a licensed architect. Md. Bus. Occ. & Prof. Code Ann. § 3-402(a). Corporations and partnerships must also meet compositional requirements, which include the requirement that at least two-thirds of the directors or partners be licensed in Maryland or another state. *Id.* § 3-404(a). In addition, a licensed Maryland architect must be in responsible charge of the architectural practice. *Id.* § 3-404(b).

Massachusetts

Massachusetts law defines the practice of architecture in terms of "performing or agreeing to perform or holding one's self out as able to perform" professional architectural services. Mass. Gen. Laws Ann. ch. 112, § 60A (West 1983). Unlicensed persons are prohibited from engaging in the practice of architecture in Massachusetts. *Id.* ch. 112, § 60K. The licensing statutes do not prohibit, inter alia, "[t]he preparation of any detailed or shop plans required to be furnished by a contractor, or the administration of construction contracts by persons customarily engaged in contracting work." *Id.* ch. 112, § 60L. Likewise, the practice of engineering does not include preparation of shop drawings, plans, or specifications by trades (for example, electrical or plumbing) for work installed or to be installed by the entity preparing those materials. *Id.* ch. 112, § 81R.

Michigan

Michigan law defines the practice of architecture in terms of the kinds of services involved without using the verbs "perform," "render," or "furnish," used in many state statutes:

> "Practice of architecture" includes professional service such as consultation, investigation, evaluation, planning, design or review of materials and completed phases of work in construction, alteration, or repair in connection with any public or private structures, buildings, equipment, works or projects when the professional service requires the application of the principles of architecture or architectural design.

Mich. Comp. Laws Ann. § 339.2001(f) (West Supp. 1991–1992); *see also id.* § 339.2001(h) (engineering practice defined). This definition appears broader than the definitions utilizing the above verbs, but there may not in fact be a substantial difference in application. The statute provides for penalties for using the terms "architect" and "professional engineer" or submitting plans without a license. *Id.* § 339-2014. Firms may practice architecture or professional engineering provided two-thirds of the principals are licensed. *Id.* § 339.2010.

In *Wedgewood v. Jordan,* 157 N.W. 360 (Mich. 1916), the Michigan Supreme Court noted the general rule denying enforcement of contracts for architectural services by unlicensed persons. In that case, a contractor not licensed as an architect obtained plans from another unlicensed person. The court concluded that the contractor was an architect within the meaning of the statute because the contractor planned to supervise the construction if the construction contract were awarded to someone else. The court reasoned:

> Whether plaintiff be regarded as an unlicensed architect, or whether he be regarded as a mere contractor and builder, who knowingly employed an unlicensed architect to do the work, he is barred under the rule from recovering the contract.

Id. at 361.

Minnesota

Minnesota law defines practicing architecture and professional engineering in terms of holding oneself out as able to perform or performing professional architectural or engineering services. Minn. Stat. Ann. §§ 326.02(2), (4) (West 1981). In order to practice architecture or engineering, qualification by registration is required. *Id.* §§ 326.02(1), 326.03(1). It is unlawful to practice architecture or engineering "or to solicit or to contract to furnish work" unless the person is qualified by registration. *Id.* Corporations and partnerships are authorized to practice architecture or engineering provided the person or persons in responsible charge are licensed. *Id.* § 326.14.

In *Scott-Daniels Properties, Inc. v. Dresser,* 281 Minn. 179, 160 N.W.2d 675 (1968), the Minnesota Supreme Court relied on "the general rule" to state that a contract by an unlicensed person was invalid. However, the court upheld the trial court's conclusion that a design contract made by a corporation fronted by an unlicensed person was valid because there was evidence the corporation employed a qualified registered architect. The court cited Minn. Stat. Ann. § 326.14, which authorizes corporations to engage in architectural work if the person in responsible charge was licensed in Minnesota. In *Scott-Daniels,* the evidence permitted the conclusion that the principal, Dresser, who operated James R. Dresser & Associates, Inc., was not licensed but acted only as the corporate agent and that the corporation employed a qualified registered architect. This case, plus the liberal wording of § 326.14, appears to allow a contractor to perform design-build work, so long as an employee of the contractor is registered under the appropriate architectural, engineering, land surveying, or landscape architectural statute.

Mississippi

Mississippi defines the practice of architecture in terms of holding oneself out as able to perform professional architectural services. Miss. Code Ann. § 73-1-3(c) (1972). The practice of architecture without a license is prohibited, *id.* § 73-1-1, and constitutes a misdemeanor. *Id.* § 73-1-25(a). The practice of engineering is defined in terms of service or creative work. *Id.* § 73-13-3 (Supp. 1991). Partnerships and professional corporations may practice architecture or engineering (or both), so long as at least one active member or shareholder holds a Mississippi license and so long as every active member or stockholder holds a valid license in his or her state of residence. No stock company other than a professional corporation is authorized to practice in Mississippi. *Id.* § 73-1-19. A design-build program would therefore likely require a joint venture between a design firm and a contracting firm.

Missouri

Missouri defines the practices of architecture and engineering in terms of "render[ing] or offer[ing] to render" professional services. Mo. Ann. Stat. §§ 327.091, 327-181 (Vernon 1989). By statute, Missouri declares contracts with unlicensed persons for architectural or engineering services invalid and unenforceable by the unlicensed person. *Id.* § 327.461; *cf. Mueller v. Birchfield,* 218 S.W.2d 180 (Mo. Ct. App. 1949) (unlicensed seller of eggs not permitted to enforce its contract). In addition, the unlicensed practice of architecture or engineering constitutes a misdemeanor. Mo. Ann. Stat. §§ 327-111, 327.201.

In *Honig Construction Co. v. Szombathy,* 345 S.W.2d 111 (Mo. 1961), the Missouri Supreme Court rejected the contention that a construction contract was void because the contractor furnished plans but was not licensed. After contracting with the owner to construct a building suitable for lease as a post office, the contractor employed a licensed A/E to prepare plans but not to supervise the construction. The court reasoned that there was no evidence that the contractor agreed to prepare the plans or render architectural services. Rather, the contractor furnished plans prepared by a registered architect to the owner on a cost-plus basis.

Although *Honig* appears to validate design-build contracts by contractors employing a licensed A/E to prepare the design, more recent cases cast doubt on this favorable reading and take a strict and limiting view of the licensing statutes. In *Haith & Co. v. Ellers, Oakley, Chester & Rike, Inc.,* 778 S.W.2d 417 (Mo. Ct. App. 1989), a Tennessee engineering corporation entered into a contract with Haith to provide professional engineering services in connection with the construction of an air cargo facility. The Tennessee corporation was not licensed in Missouri, but two of its principals were Missouri licensees and contended that they were entitled to practice through a corporation and to enforce their contract. The court disagreed, noting that § 327.40(2) required the corporation independently to obtain a certificate of authority and that the corporation was identified as "engineer" in the contract. The corporation's lack of a license rendered the contract unenforceable notwithstanding that the principals in responsible charge were Missouri licensees.

In *Hospital Development Corp. v. Park Lane Land Co.,* 813 S.W.2d 904 (Mo. Ct. App. 1991) (motion for rehearing or transfer to Missouri Supreme Court denied August 27, 1991), the court held that the contract of an unlicensed Missouri corporation, which provided design services to a client through a Missouri-licensed sister subsidiary, was not entitled to recover for design services. The court also rejected HDC's attempts to recover for nonarchitectural services, holding that all the services rendered were architectural in nature. Recovery in quantum meruit was likewise barred because there was no benefit furnished: "Park Lane never used the services, plans, specifications or drawings of HDC; nor was a medical office building ever built using the plans." *Id.* at 910.

Similarly, in *Kansas City Community Center v. Heritage Industries,* 773 F. Supp. 181 (W.D. Mo. 1991), the court held that the contract of a manufacturer of prefabricated modular housing units was invalid for failure to obtain a design license. The court rejected attempts to divide the contract into architectural and nonarchitectural portions (with recovery sought for the nonarchitectural services) and to recover in quantum meruit. Finally, the court required the manufacturer to make restitution for the initial payment, which was deemed to have been made in exchange for the unlicensed design services.

Montana

Montana defines the practices of architecture and engineering in terms of services or creative work requiring professional architectural or engineering knowledge. Mont. Code Ann. §§ 37-65-102(5), 37-67-101(6) (1989). Montana prohibits persons from practicing architecture without having qualified. *Id.* § 37-65-301. Only individuals may be licensed, but "a number of architects constituting a firm may use the collective title 'architects' or 'licensed architects.'" *Id.* § 37-65-302.

Nebraska

In pertinent part, Nebraska law provides, similar to Michigan:

> Any one or combination of the following practices shall constitute the practice of architecture: Consultation, investigation, evaluation, except real estate appraisals, planning, designing or supervision of construction . . . .

Neb. Rev. Stat. § 81-840(2) (1987). The practice of professional engineering is similarly defined. *Id.* § 81-840(1). It is unlawful for unregistered persons to practice architecture or engineering. *Id.* § 81-839.

Nevada

Nevada law defines the practice of architecture in terms of rendering professional architectural services. Nev. Rev. Stat. Ann. § 623.015(4) (Michie 1986). Engineering is similarly defined. *Id.* § 625.050.1.

The Nevada contractor licensing statute, much like the statutes of California and Alaska, for example, requires the contractor seeking to enforce its contract to allege and prove that it was licensed when it submitted its bid and at all times during performance of the work. Nev. Rev. Stat. Ann.

§ 624.320. The Nevada courts, however, have allowed unlicensed contractors to plead fraud causes of action and seek recovery to prevent unjust enrichment. *See, e.g., Day v. West Coast Holdings, Inc.,* 699 P.2d 1067 (Nev. 1985); *Magill v. Lewis,* 333 P.2d 717 (Nev. 1958).

New Hampshire

New Hampshire law defines architecture but not practicing architecture. "'Architecture' means any professional service or creative work" requiring the application of professional architectural skills. N.H. Rev. Stat. Ann. § 310-A:28 (1984). Notwithstanding the lack of a definition, practicing architecture without a license is prohibited. *Id.* § 310-A:37; *cf. William Coltin & Co. v. Manchester Savings Bank,* 197 A.2d 208 (N.H. 1964) (unlicensed foreign corporation barred from recovering for brokerage services in connection with sale of real estate).

New Jersey

New Jersey law defines practicing architecture in terms of "rendering" professional architectural services. N.J. Stat. Ann. § 45:4B-3h (West Supp. 1991). The law permits sole proprietors or business associations that may render engineering services to contract to provide architectural and engineering services if (1) the proprietor or association contracts with the owner in writing for the coordinated rendering of architectural and engineering services, and (2) the architectural services are provided pursuant to a separate written subcontract. *Id.* § 45:4B-8(b). The subcontract must provide: "The licensed architect shall exercise independent professional judgment consistent with accepted standards of the practice of architecture with regard to the project as its circumstances may dictate." *Id.* § 45:4B-8(c)(2).

The reference to preserving the subcontractor architect's independent professional judgment sounds much like one of the standard critiques of design-build. The context, however, is one step removed from design-build because the subcontract at issue is with an engineer, not a design-build contractor.

In *Dalton, Dalton, Little Inc. v. Mirandi,* 412 F. Supp. 1001 (D.N.J. 1976), the court applied New Jersey law and held that a Maryland architect's corporation, not licensed in New Jersey, could not recover fees for architectural services in preparing and certifying plans for a building to be constructed in New Jersey. The court noted that there were two ways for out-of-state architects to render services on New Jersey projects. The first, as subcontractors to a licensed New Jersey architect, was legal. The second, employing an architect licensed in New Jersey to seal the plans, was "inherently illegal," although "[i]n the absence of a dispute which goes to litigation, many such transactions have been made, executed, paid and satisfied." *Id.* at 1004. The court dismissed the fact that the New Jersey architect sealed and certified the plans, noting the New Jersey architect was not a party to the contract with the owner. Significantly, the court dismissed the owner's counterclaim for expenses to correct alleged defects, reasoning that, because the contract was illegal, all parties should be left without a remedy. The court explained:

> New Jersey landowners or developers or builders, as well as unlicensed professionals and foreign corporations, are both to take the consequences of entering into an illegal contract, and their derivative claims can rise no higher than their source.

Id. at 1007.

The statute's focus on independent judgment and the *Mirandi* court's focus on the parties to the contract do not appear to favor contracts by design-build single entities. A joint venture approach, or a design-build contract with the designer as lead, appears to be feasible.

New Mexico

New Mexico law defines the practice of architecture in terms of "rendering or offering to render" professional architectural services. N.M. Stat. Ann. § 61-15-2F (Michie 1978). Practicing architecture without having registered constitutes a misdemeanor. *Id.* § 61-15-10.

New York

New York defines architecture as follows:

> The practice of the profession of architecture is defined as rendering or offering to render services which require the application of the art, science, and aesthetics of design and construction of buildings, groups of buildings, including their components and appurtenances and the spaces around them wherein the safeguarding of life, health, property, and public welfare is concerned. Such services include, but are not limited to consultation, evaluation, planning, the provision of preliminary studies, design, construction documents, construction management, and the administration of construction contracts.

N.Y. Educ. Law § 7301 (McKinney 1985). Similar provisions apply to engineers. *Id.* §§ 7205, 7206, 6508, 6509.

In *Charlebois v. J.M. Weller Associates, Inc.,* 531 N.E.2d 1288 (N.Y. 1988), the Court of Appeals of New York held that a design-build contract was not void as against the public policy of the professional licensing laws. The contract called for the contractor to furnish the services of a licensed professional engineer as part of the overall package of architectural, engineering, and construction services. The court reasoned,

> Pursuant to that arrangement [by which James M. Weller, P.E. performed the design services], James M. Weller, P.E., was not acting in the capacity of an employee of the business corporation, but acted as a professional licensed engineer obligated by contract to exercise his professional judgment in the interest of the public health and welfare, and independent in that sense of unlicensed oversight.

Id. at 1292.

In *Charlebois,* the court distinguished the decision in *American Store Equipment & Construction Corp. v. Jack Dempsey's Punch Bowl,* 21 N.Y.S.2d 117, *aff'd without opinion,* 16 N.Y.S.2d 702 (1939), *aff'd without opinion,* 28 N.E.2d 23 (N.Y. 1940), in which a contractor, not licensed as a designer, contracted for itself to prepare plans and to perform remodeling work according to those plans. The *Charlebois* court affirmed that the *American Store* facts "warranted withholding recovery [for *all* the contractor's work] from the offending contractor." 531 N.E.2d at 1291.

The *Charlebois* arrangement, in which the designer of record is separate from the contractor and is called out and given specific design responsibilities in the design-build contractor's contract with the owner, is one that may work in New York and may withstand scrutiny in other states. However, practitioners should be aware that recent administrative developments may make reliance on *Charlebois* as precedent in New York uncertain. *Engineering News Record* reports that an August 20, 1991 memorandum by Henry A. Fernandez, deputy commissioner for professions in the New York State Education Department, warns against delegation of design responsibility to unauthorized firms. Some contend the memorandum can be read "to prohibit design-build contracts and the performance of design by contractors supplying structural steel, precast concrete, cladding systems or shoring." "New York Lays Down Design Law," *Engineering News Record,* Sept. 30, 1991 at 8; *see also* "New York Designers Pledge Fight," *ENR,* Oct. 14, 1991 at 10. Although the focus of the dispute appears to be delegation of design responsibility to specialty subcontractors, design-build also appears to be involved. These administrative developments make reliance on *Charlebois* uncertain.

North Carolina

North Carolina law expressly exempts design-build from the scope of the architectural licensing provisions:

> Nothing in this Chapter shall be construed to prevent a duly licensed general contractor, professional engineer or architect, acting individually or in combination thereof from participating in a "Design-Build" undertaking including the preparation of plans and/or specifications and entering individual or collective agreements with the owner in order to meet the owner's requirements for pre-determined costs and unified control in the design and construction of a project, and for the method of compensation for the design and construction services rendered; provided, however, that nothing herein shall be construed so as to allow the performance of any such services or any division thereof by one who is not duly licensed . . . ; provided further, that full disclosure is made in writing to the owner as to the duties and responsibilities of each of the participating parties in such agreements; and, provided further, nothing in this Chapter shall prevent the administration by any of the said licensees of construction contracts and related services or combination of services in connection with the construction of buildings.

N.C. Gen. Stat. § 83A-13(b) (1985). The statute also allows corporate practice of architecture by foreign corporations provided a North Carolina licensee is in responsible charge of all architectural work offered or performed in North Carolina. *Id.* § 83-A-8(b).

North Dakota

North Dakota law prohibits the unlicensed practice of architecture but does not define practicing architecture. N.D. Cent. Code § 43-03-09 (1978). The practice of engineering is, however, defined by reference to the kinds of services involved and in terms of "performing" such services. *Id.* § 43-19.1-03.4. North Dakota law also requires a license to act in the capacity of a contractor when the contract sum is greater than $500. *Id.* § 43-07-02.

The corporate of partnership practice of engineering is permitted, "provided all of the partners of such partnership or each officer and shareholder, in case of a professional corporation" are licensed or exempt. *Id.* § 43-19.1-27.2. In addition, the person in responsible charge must be licensed. *Id.* § 43-19.1-27.3.a.

Ohio

Ohio law requires persons practicing architecture to first obtain a license. Ohio Rev. Code Ann. §§ 4703.06, 4703.18(A) (Anderson, Supp. 1990). Although the statute does not define practicing architecture, the Ohio Court of Appeals has stated, "It is generally held that designing a building for another, or furnishing the plans and specifications for such a building for another, constitutes architectural services." *Elephant Lumber Co. v. Johnson,* 202 N.E.2d 189, 191 (Ohio Ct. App. 1964) (dictum). The Ohio Court of Appeals had previously concluded that "a builder who is not a registered architect may contract to furnish plans and specifications for the construction of a building for an owner provided the plans and specifications are prepared by a registered architect." *McGill v. Carlos,* 81 N.E.2d 726, 728 (Ohio Ct. App. 1947). In *McGill,* the court went on to state that the builder who was not a licensed architect could not "prepare complete plans and specifications . . . when expert knowledge and skill are required in such preparation." *Id.*

Contracts by unlicensed persons to perform architectural services are not enforceable. *McGill v. Carlos,* 81 N.E.2d 726; *see also* 1949 Op. [Ohio] Att'y Gen. 273 (recovery in contract, quasi-contract, implied contract, or otherwise barred). Although the statute permits engineers to engage in the incidental practice of architecture, *see* Ohio Rev. Code Ann. § 4703.18(c), an engineer was not allowed to enforce a contract that called primarily for the performance of architectural services in *Fanning v. College of Steubenville,* 197 N.E.2d 422 (Ohio Ct. C.P. 1961), *appeal dismissed,* 174 Ohio St. 343, 189 N.E.2d 72 (1963).

The dictum in *McGill* indicates that a design-build contractor, employing a licensed A/E as design subcontractor, may be able to enforce its contracts.

Oklahoma

Oklahoma law defines the practice of architecture in terms of "rendering" professional architectural services. Okla. Stat. Ann. tit. 59, § 46.3(1) (West 1989). Practicing architecture without a license is prohibited and is a misdemeanor. *Id.* tit. 59, §§ 46.17, 46.22. In addition, Oklahoma law indirectly discourages architects from participating in design-build activities by providing: "It shall be unlawful for an architect, at any time, to bid for a contract for the reparation, alteration or erection of a building for which he has prepared the plans and specifications." *Id.* tit. 59, § 46.27. It is possible that this expression of public policy may not apply to an architect acting as a designer/inspector under a subcontract with a contractor who will build the architect's design.

Oregon

Oregon defines the practice of architecture by reference to the kinds of services provided. Or. Rev. Stat. § 671.010(5) (1989). Oregon statutes prohibit the practice of architecture without a license and bar the enforcement of a contract relating to architectural services unless the claimant alleges and proves that the claimant was licensed when the services were rendered. *Id.* § 671.220(3); *see also Wheeler v. Bucksteel Co.,* 73 Or. App. 495, 698 P.2d 995 (1985) (failure to comply with engineering licensing statute renders unenforceable a contract to perform industrial engineering services even in absence of express statute).

The Oregon Court of Appeals has construed these provisions to prohibit the performance of a contract while unlicensed but not the making of a contract: "The statutes involving licensing of architects . . . do not define the practice of architecture to include the making of a contract for architectural services." *Friedman v. Mt. Village, Inc.*, 640 P.2d 1037, 1041 (Or. Ct. App. 1982); *compare Merrill v. Board of Architect Examiners,* 706 P.2d 556 (Or. 1985) (activities of unlicensed classroom school designer not reviewed by licensed professional constituted unlicensed practice of architecture). In *Friedman,* the court held that the fact that plans for a residential development were partially completed before the designer was qualified in Oregon did not bar recovery because the contract contained a "sufficient guarantee that the final plans" would be the product of a licensed architect. In *Merrill,* the unlicensed person's activities were not protected by a professional engineer's reviewing his work.

Corporations and partnerships are authorized to practice architecture, provided a majority of the stockholders or partners are registered in Oregon. In addition, a majority of the board of directors or of the members must be architects. Or. Rev. Stat. § 671.041(1)(a).

Pennsylvania

Pennsylvania defines practicing architecture in terms of "rendering or offering to render" professional architectural services. Pa. Stat. Ann. tit. 63, § 34.3 (Purdon Supp. 1991–92). Practicing architecture without a license is prohibited. *Id.* tit. 63, § 34.18(a). The statute includes exemptions for persons performing design, construction administration, or construction management services under the personal supervision of an architect, incidental practice of architecture by engineers, and preparation of shop drawings. *Id.* tit. 63, §§ 34.15(1), (2), (3). Partnerships or corporations may practice architecture provided two-thirds of the partners or directors are licensed in some state and one-third are licensed architects. *Id.* tit. 63, § 34.13. Projects for work in Pennsylvania must be under the personal supervision of a Pennsylvania licensee. *Id.* Failure to comply with the licensing statutes renders the contract void, even in the absence of express statutory language to that effect, and there may be no recovery in quantum meruit for the services. *F.F. Bollinger Co. v. Widmann Brewing Corp.,* 14 A.2d 81 (Pa. 1940).

The Pennsylvania statute provides, in part:

> Nothing in this section shall be construed to prevent the practice of architecture by an individual as an employee of a person, partnership or corporation which is not an architectural firm, provided such individual holds a

> certificate to practice architecture in the commonwealth in conformity with the provisions of this act and the architect's seal is affixed to all documents prepared by him or under his supervision for use in this commonwealth.

Id. tit. 63, § 43.14(j). The Pennsylvania Supreme Court construed this provision to allow the architect to work for his employer but not to allow the employer to offer A/E services to the public through the employee-architect. *Consulting Engineers Counsel of Pennsylvania v. State Architects Licensure Board*, 560 A.2d 1375 (Pa. 1989).

Puerto Rico

In Puerto Rico, the practice of architecture or engineering:

> comprises the rendering of any professional work, or the execution of any work of a creative nature, for which the knowledge, training and experience as an engineer or architect are needed. It includes the application of special knowledge, physical science, mathematics, and engineering or architecture in performing such professional services, or in executing such works of a creative nature, as are required in any consulting, studies, investigation, appraisals, drawing up of blueprints, measurements, projects, inspections and supervision of works under construction, in order to ensure that the specifications are complied with, and the adequate execution of what is projected with regard to any public or private works, installation of industrial machinery, methods and procedures, equipment, technical work and systems in engineering or in architecture.

1988 P.R. Laws 173, § 4(a). Licenses are available only to residents, unless a designer forms an association with a designer licensed and domiciled in Puerto Rico, *id.* § 23(b), or is a designer of "renown or international prestige," *id.* § 24. Failure to comply with the licensing provision is a misdemeanor, *id.* § 28, but the statute is silent as to rights to enforce contracts. Given the breadth of the definition in § 4(2), it appears a joint venture is necessary for design-build contracts in Puerto Rico.

Rhode Island

Rhode Island defines the practice of architecture in terms of "rendering or offering to render" professional architectural services. R.I. Gen. Laws § 5-1-2(d) (1987). The law prohibits the unlicensed practice of architecture. *Id.* § 5-1-7(a). Corporate practice is permitted, provided two-thirds of the partners are registered in any state to practice architecture or engineering or one-third are registered architects and the person in responsible charge is a Rhode Island architect. *Id.* § 5-1-7(b).

The statute further provides:

> This section shall not be construed to prevent any person, partnership, corporation or association in the business of building construction and/or construction management from offering to render design and construction services in connection with building construction or construction management executed by that firm provided that services which constitute the practice of architecture, as defined in § 5-1-2(d), shall be performed by one or more registered architects.

Id. § 5-1-7(b). Design-build is thus expressly accommodated by the licensing statute in Rhode Island.

South Carolina

South Carolina defines architectural practice in terms of performing professional architectural activities. S.C. Code Ann. § 40-3-10(2) (Law. Co-op. 1976). A certificate of registration from the State Board of Architectural Examiners is a prerequisite to practice. *Id.* § 40-3-20. The practice of architecture without a certificate is a misdemeanor. *Id.* § 40-3-130.

Individual registered architects may practice through a corporation, provided: (1) one or more of the corporate officers or partners, as applicable, are designated as being responsible for professional architectural services and is registered; (2) all personnel who act as architects are registered; and (3) the corporation has been issued a certificate. *Id.* § 40-3-100.

Unlicensed residential contractors are barred from enforcing their contracts. *Id.* § 40-59-130; *Columbia Pools, Inc. v. Moon,* 325 S.E.2d 540 (S.C. 1985). In *Wagner v. Graham,* 370 S.E.2d 95 (S.C. Ct. App. 1988), the court held that an owner who knew that a contractor was not licensed was not estopped from raising the lack of a license as a defense. The court noted, "If one might avoid the impact of the [licensing] statute by applying the law of estoppel, one could, by similar reasoning, avoid the act by agreement between the Contractor and the Homeowner." *Id.* at 96.

Late registration has been held not to cure the lack of a license at the time the contract was entered into. *Duncan v. Cameron,* 244 S.E.2d 217 (S.C. 1978).

No parallel statutory prohibition appears in the S.C. Code for architects. *See* S.C. Code Ann. § 40-3-140. However, the Supreme Court of South Carolina has held that an unlicensed person should have been held in civil contempt for violating an injunction against unlicensed practice when the person hired licensed architects to work for him in a business styled "George L. Howell & Associates/Architectural Designers." *State ex rel. Love v. Howell,* 328 S.E.2d 77 (S.C. 1985). The evidence indicated that the unlicensed Howell had the licensed architects sign or seal documents as needed, while he continued in responsible charge of the projects. The court stated:

> Howell continued to sign various documents in blanks provided for the architect and continued to perform duties appropriate for architects. He consistently issued orders for the contractors to proceed, authorized change orders and payment orders, tabulated bids, etc.

Id. at 79.

South Dakota

South Dakota law defines architectural and engineering practice in terms of "rendering" professional services. S.D. Codified Laws Ann. § 36-18-4.1(10), (11) (Supp. 1991). No person may practice professional architecture or engineering without having registered. *Id.* § 36-18-5. Persons who violate this prohibition are guilty of a misdemeanor. *Id.* § 36-18-37(1). Corporate registration is permitted, provided: (1) all officers, employees, and agents in responsible charge or who will perform services in South Dakota are registered in South Dakota; (2) the corporation receives a certificate; and (3) the partnership or corporation is responsible for the services of its members. *Id.* § 36-18-31.1.

In *South Dakota Building Authority v. Geiger-Berger Associates, P.C.*, 414 N.W.2d 15 (S.D. 1987), the South Dakota Supreme Court affirmed a judgment in favor of the owner against the architect for damages attributable to the collapse of an air-supported roof. The architect had procured the design from an engineer and sought to hold the engineer responsible in indemnity, on the ground that all the architect did was the mechanical act of stamping the engineer's design. The court rejected the claim and explained that the legislature intended the stamping process to "acknowledg[e] an affirmative obligation to review and insure that the plans were appropriate and architecturally sound." *Id.* at 24. Pursuant to the licensing statutes, the architect could not be a mere conduit.

Thus, South Dakota would likely frown upon any effort to dampen the independence of the design professional, such as might be involved when the designer is a subcontractor to the design-builder. A joint venture approach may avoid this concern, but again, it appears the joint venture itself may be required to obtain the professional license.

Tennessee

Tennessee law declares the unlicensed practice of architecture or engineering to be unlawful. Tenn. Code Ann. § 62-2-101. Practicing architecture or engineering without having registered constitutes a misdemeanor. *Id.* § 62-2-105(b). The practice of architecture or engineering is defined in terms of the use of titles to represent or imply professional qualification. *Id.* § 62-2-105(c). Corporations offering professional architectural or engineering service must have at least one principal or officer in responsible charge and registered in Tennessee. *Id.* § 62-2-601.

The status of contracts performed by unlicensed persons is unclear. The Tennessee statute applicable to contractors provides, in part: "Any unlicensed contractor covered by the provisions of this chapter shall be permitted in a court of equity to recover actual documented expenses only upon a showing of clear and convincing proof." *Id.* § 62-6-103(c). This provision has been held to bar recovery on the contract, but to allow recovery in quantum meruit on a showing of clear and convincing proof. *Chedester v. Phillips,* 708 S.W.2d 407 (Tenn. Ct. App. 1985). There is no parallel statute for A/Es, but an unlicensed person has been held barred from recovering for services rendered as a surgeon and physician. *Haworth v. Montgomery,* 91 Tenn. 16, 18 S.W. 399 (1891). Thus, there is precedent for adherence to the general rule that the contracts of unlicensed professionals are not enforceable.

Texas

Texas law defines practicing architecture or engineering in terms of performing professional services. Tex. Rev. Civ. Stat. Ann. art. 249a, § 10(a)(1); art. 3271a, § 2(5).

In *Seaview Hospital, Inc. v. Medicenters of America, Inc.,* 570 S.W.2d 35 (Tex. Ct. App. 1978), the court held that a turnkey contract with a licensed general contractor for design and construction services was valid. The owner claimed that the contract called for an unlicensed entity to perform architectural or engineering services, but the turnkey builder responded that it had simply arranged, provided, furnished, or procured those services from its subcontractor-designers, who were in compliance with Texas licensing laws for designers. The court found that all of the architectural or engineering work performed was done by persons licensed by Texas or persons working under the supervision of Texas licensees. The court held that a general contractor is not precluded from entering into a turnkey contract calling for it to "provide" or "procure" architectural or engineering services through a subcontract arrangement. *Id.* at 40. It concluded:

> The stated objective of both statutes [relating to licensing of architects or engineers] is to protect public health, safety and the general welfare by insuring that architectural and engineering work be *performed* only by qualified persons who are duly licensed.

Id. The case illustrates the critical nature of the statutory description of what constitutes the practice of architecture or of engineering. Texas clearly favors a concept of public policy that assumes professional designers will discharge their obligation to the public, regardless of what entity (the owner or the design-builder) signs its pay checks.

Utah

Utah defines the practices of architecture and engineering in terms of performing professional services. Utah Code Ann. §§ 58-3-2(7), 58-22-2(7)(a) (1990). Practicing architecture without a license is a misdemeanor. *Id.* § 58-3-7; *see also id.* § 58-22-9. A more general statute provides that unlicensed practice of a licensed profession is unlawful. *Id.* § 58-1-10(1)(a). The engineers' licensing statute expressly provides that unlicensed persons "may not bring or maintain any action in the courts of this state for enforcement of any contract or the recovery of any sums due in connection with the practice of engineering and land surveying in the state." *Id.* § 58-22-11.

In *Dow v. Holley,* 154 F.2d 707 (10th Cir. 1946), an unlicensed excavation subcontractor sought recovery from a licensed contractor. The court, applying Utah law, noted the "general rule" that contracts entered into by unlicensed persons are not enforceable. *Id.* at 710. The court, however, declined to apply the general rule to bar recovery by a subcontractor who had fully performed from a contractor who had been paid in full. The court also indicated a reluctance to bar enforcement of contracts between unlicensed persons and licensed persons to perform professional services. Ten years later, however, the United States District Court for the District of Utah held that unlicensed surveyors, whose work was checked by a licensed surveyor and whose map was also certified by a professional engineer, could not recover on their contract. *Oakason v. Lebanon Valley Uranium Co.,* 154 F. Supp. 692 (D. Utah 1957). The court reasoned that the contract was unenforceable, so the assistance of licensed persons was not significant:

> A more conclusive circumstance is that the practice of surveying in which plaintiffs engaged did not consist so much in the submission of the certified maps as it did in holding out the plaintiffs to the public and to the defendant's predecessors as engineers or surveyors qualified to do the surveying of the mining claims and to enter into the contract for such surveying, and in contracting for and carrying on of such surveying in the field without the statutory qualifications. It did not aid plaintiffs to have the final product of their illegal contract and practice certified by qualified engineers when under no construction was the contract entered into or the work done by or under the supervision of a qualified engineer, whether as partner or otherwise.

Id. at 694. The focus on the licensing status of the contracting parties in *Oakason* represents a barrier to design-build activity by a single entity. The A/E may lack a contractor's license, and the contractor may lack an A/E license. In either event, a licensing hurdle will have to be overcome.

Vermont

Vermont law defines the practice of architecture and engineering in terms of providing professional services. Vt. Stat. Ann. tit. 26, §§ 121(5), 1161(4) (1989). The practice of architecture without a license is prohibited and constitutes a misdemeanor. *Id.* tit. 26, § 122. In *Markus & Nocka v. Julian Goodrich Architects, Inc.,* 250 A.2d 739 (Vt. 1969), the Vermont Supreme Court held that a contract for architectural services by an unlicensed person was unenforceable. *See also Rodgers v. Kelley,* 259 A.2d 784 (Vt. 1969).

Corporations and partnerships may furnish architectural services, provided one member or employee is a licensed architect, the licensed architect is in responsible charge, and the licensed architect signs and stamps the plans and specifications. Vt. Stat. Ann. tit. 26, § 203(b). Vermont law further provides: "A corporation, partnership, association or individual proprietorship with which the architect may practice shall be jointly and severally liable with the architect for the work performed." *Id.* tit. 26, § 203(c).

It appears that design-build is feasible in Vermont, through a contractor, so long as an employee is a licensed Vermont architect.

Virginia

Virginia law defines architecture and engineering by reference to the kinds of services involved. Va. Code Ann. § 54.1-400 (1991). The statutory scheme requires persons to obtain licenses before engaging in the practice of architecture or engineering. *Id.* § 54.1-406A. Preparation of shop drawings by a contractor is exempt from the statute when the licensed A/E for the project will review them. *Id.* § 54.1-402.9. Corporations may engage in the practice of architecture provided the practice "is rendered through its officers, principals or employees who are correspondingly licensed or certified." *Id.* § 54.1-411A. A licensed professional must be responsible and have control of the services rendered. § 54.1-411C.

In *Clark v. Moore,* 196 Va. 878, 86 S.E.2d 37 (1955), the court held that an unlicensed person could not recover for engineering services rendered pursuant to an oral contract. The court found that the services performed, including inspection of the site, study of the plans and specifications, and cost and scheduling work, fell within the scope of civil engineering services.

The court relied on the general rule of unenforceability, set out in *Massie v. Dudley,* 173 Va. 42, 3 S.E.2d 176 (1939) (unlicensed real estate brokerage services).

One commentator has noted that the Virginia Department of Commerce had not acted on complaints that general business corporations were engaging in design-build activities, apparently concluding there was no violation. "Design-Build Contracts in Virginia," 14 U. Rich. L. Rev. 791, 804 and nn. 68-70 (1980). The commentator indicated that the Department of Commerce's action represented only an interim policy "based on anticipated changes in both statutes and regulations rather than upon interpretation of current state law." *Id.* at 807. Absent a change in the law, the commentator characterized the status of design-build contracts in 1980 as "debatable." It does not appear that the statute has been amended so as to allow expressly for design-build, but design-build appears feasible by a general business corporation which has licensed Virginia designers as employees in charge of the design.

Washington

Washington law defines the practice of architecture in terms of the "rendering" of professional services and the practice of engineering in terms of "performing" services. Wash. Rev. Code Ann. §§ 18.08.320, 18.43.020 (West 1989). Subject to certain exceptions, including those set forth below, the practice of architecture or engineering without a license is prohibited. *Id.* §§ 18.08.235, 18.43.020. Contracts by unlicensed persons are unenforceable. *Sherwood v. Wise,* 232 P.2d 309, 309 n.2 (1925); *see also St. John Farms, Inc. v. D.J. Irvin Co.,* 609 P.2d 970 (Wash. Ct. App. 1980) (unlicensed dealer in agricultural products denied recovery).

Corporations are authorized to practice architecture, provided the corporation designates registered individuals to be responsible and to have final decision-making authority on architectural decisions. Wash. Rev. Code Ann. § 18.08.420(b). The corporate bylaws must include a provision "that all architectural decisions pertaining to any project or any architectural activities in this state shall be made by the specified architects responsible for the project or architectural activities, or other responsible architects under the direction or supervision of the architects responsible for the project or architectural activities." *Id.* § 18.08.420(c)(2)(a). Similar provisions apply to corporations practicing engineering. *Id.* § 18.43.130(8).

Washington's architect licensing statutes exempt "Design-build construction by registered general contractors if the structural design services are performed by a registered engineer," from the scope of the regulations. *Id.* § 18.08.410 (1989). In addition, the statute exempts from the scope of the licensing provisions "Any person from designing buildings or doing other design work for structures larger than those exempted . . . if the plans, which may include such design work, are stamped by a registered engineer or architect."

Design-build is thus recognized and accommodated in the Washington licensing format.

West Virginia

West Virginia law defines the practice of architecture in terms of the "rendering" of services. W. Va. Code § 30-12-3 (Supp. 1991). Practicing architecture without a license is prohibited. *Id.* § 30-12-11. Subject to certain exceptions, West Virginia law requires owners of real property who allow construction to be performed on that property to obtain construction administration services from a registered architect or engineer. *Id.* § 30-12-11a(a). The exceptions include "preparation of any detailed or shop drawings required to be furnished by a contractor, or the administration of construction contracts by persons customarily engaged in contracting work." *Id.* § 30-12-12(b). Corporations may practice architecture provided the practice is carried on under the direct supervision of architects registered in West Virginia. *Id.* § 30-12-14(e); *see also id.* § 30-13-9 (engineers).

Again, a contractor apparently can enter a design-build contract, so long as an employee is a licensed designer under West Virginia law.

Wisconsin

Wisconsin law defines the practices of architecture and engineering by reference to the kinds of services involved. Wis. Stat. Ann. § 443.01(5), (6) (West 1988). Wisconsin law prohibits the practice of architecture or engineering without a license. *Id.* § 443.02(2). The licensing statute includes the following exemption:

> Notwithstanding any other provisions of this chapter, contractors, subcontractors or construction or material equipment suppliers are not required to register under this chapter to perform or undertake those activities which historically and customarily have been performed by them in their respective trades and specialties, including, but not limited to, the preparation and use of drawings, specifications or layouts within a construction firm or in construction operations, superintending of construction, installation and alteration of equipment, cost estimating, consultation with architects, professional engineers or owners concerning materials, equipment, methods and techniques, and investigations or consultation with respect to construction sites, provided all such activities are performed solely with respect to the performance of their work on buildings or with respect to supplies or materials furnished by them for buildings or structures or their appurtenances which are, or which are to be, erected, enlarged, or materially altered

> in accordance with plans and specifications prepared by architects or professional engineers.

Id. § 443.14(6). That exemption appears to allow for design-build activities because it requires that the plans and specifications be prepared by architects or engineers but does not state whether the owner or the contractor must contract with the designer. In *Lytle v. Godfirnon,* 6 N.W.2d 652 (Wis. 1942), the Wisconsin Supreme Court reversed a summary judgment denying recovery of amounts due under the contract to an unlicensed person who "furnished" to an owner plans prepared by a registered architect. The court held that if the unlicensed person performed the professional services, there would be no recovery. On the other hand, if the contract with the owner called for the furnishing of services and if the unlicensed person handled the business side of the transaction whereas a registered architect employed by the unlicensed person prepared the plans, there would be a basis for recovery. *Id.* at 653; *see Hickey v. Sutton,* 210 N.W. 704 (Wis. 1926); *see also Adams v. Feiges,* 239 N.W. 446 (Wis. 1931).

Wyoming

Wyoming law defines the practice of architecture in terms of "rendering" or "offering to render" professional services. Wyo. Stat. § 33-4-101(a)(ii) (Supp. 1991). Wyoming requires architects to be registered and prohibits the unlicensed practice of architecture. *Id.* §§ 33-4-112, -114(a)(ii)(B). The statute is silent as to the effect on recovery for a contract entered into without a license.

§ 3.6 Applying Licensing Requirements to Proposed Design-Build Projects

From the foregoing survey, it is clear that licensing often presents a hurdle, if not a complete barrier, to design-build. As a practical matter, of course, the issue may never arise, because a design-build entity that does not squarely meet all the niceties of a particular licensing statute may very well design and build a structure and be paid for its services, leaving a happy owner and a well-protected public. As a legal matter, this practical solution may, in fact, be improper or inappropriate in many states and, before it is pursued, it warrants a thorough examination of the particular state's licensing statutes.

There are two primary issues affecting design-build. The first, with respect to public contracts, is whether design-build is feasible at all, given the constraints of public competitive bidding policies. That issue was addressed, principally in the federal arena, in § **3.3**, and the authors conclude that design-build is not possible, absent special legislative recognition or creative interpretation and administration of legislation, such as the GSA has done. The second issue is presented by state licensing statutes, which hamper the ability of the design-build contractor to provide the design side of its services. From the research underlying this chapter, as well as from the authors' experience in the industry, it is obvious that the licensing laws, particularly with respect to designers, serve an important public purpose. Those licensing laws probably should not be weakened. Instead, the appropriate solution may well be legislative recognition of the legitimacy of design-build contracts, with appropriate licensing safeguards built into that recognition.

If that method is not available in a given state, then the solution presented in the *Charlebois*[34] decision in New York, appears to provide a satisfactory compromise between the protection of the licensing of professionals and the efficiencies many owners associate with design-build approaches. The *Charlebois* structure does preclude, to a small extent, some of the flexibility a design-build contractor may want because *Charlebois* requires that the designer be called out in the contract with the owner. Of course, careful drafting will enable the contractor to change that designer, after appropriate notice to the owner, replacing the initial designer with another designer acceptable to the owner.

Likewise, one may be able to overcome the hurdles of a particular state by a very careful reading of that state's statute. The discussion of the Texas scheme illustrates this approach, because the statute prohibits the performing of services but not the furnishing of those services through another entity which in fact "performed" the design.

Finally, joint ventures may be able to perform design-build contracts in many jurisdictions, particularly in those not requiring the entity furnishing the design to obtain a license. When the joint venture itself must have a design license, the statutes must be researched to determine if there are any compositional requirements (for instance, whether all directors must be licensed architects) that would prevent it from getting such a license. It must also be determined whether the joint venture can obtain a contractor's license, if the statutory requirement applies to the joint venture itself.

The roadblocks presented by the licensing statutes serve the legitimate purpose of protecting the public and assuring, to a degree, the independence of designers. Nevertheless, the authors believe the public interest would also be served if design-build were expressly recognized in the licensing statutes so that contractors may, by subcontract or joint venture

---

[34] 531 N.E.2d 1288 (N.Y. 1988); but see § **3.5** (administrative developments make reliance on *Charlebois* in New York uncertain).

with an appropriately licensed designer, enter into design-build contracts with owners. This statutory development in the law has taken place in several states already, and the authors believe it is an appropriate solution. It certainly recognizes, legislatively, that which is already recognized by the market: the designer does not lose its professional status or integrity simply because it is being paid by a contractor as opposed to an owner.

CHAPTER 4

CHOICE OF FORM OF ORGANIZATION

Frank J. Baltz
Michael E. Lavine
Samuel M. Spiritos

Frank J. Baltz is a partner in the Washington, D.C., and McLean, Virginia, firm of Shaw, Pittman, Potts & Trowbridge, concentrating in design, construction, and real estate development contracts, claims, litigation, and related issues. Mr. Baltz has spoken and published several articles on important subjects affecting the construction industry, including issues involving insurance for design professionals and contractors, negotiating design and construction agreements, and issues involving subcontractor claims against owners and lenders.

Michael E. Lavine is an associate with the Washington, D.C., and McLean, Virginia, firm of Shaw, Pittman, Potts & Trowbridge practicing in the firm's tax group. He is a graduate of the Georgetown University Law Center and the Wharton School of the University of Pennsylvania.

Samuel M. Spiritos, an attorney with the Washington, D.C., and McLean, Virginia, firm of Shaw, Pittman, Potts & Trowbridge, is experienced in all aspects of commercial real estate law, including sales, acquisitions, development agreements, construction contracts, architect agreements, financings, and leases. Mr. Spiritos has represented owners, developers, lenders and tenants in all phases of real estate development and construction projects. Mr. Spiritos received a B.S. from the Wharton School of the University of Pennsylvania, an M.B.A., and J.D. from the State University of New York at Buffalo.

---

§ 4.1 Introduction

An understanding of the economic and legal implications of the various forms of design-build organizations requires comparing the design/build system to the relationship of an owner, an architect and a contractor in a "traditional" construction project. In a traditional project, the owner enters into two contracts, one with an architect or engineer[1] and one with a contractor. In this triangular relationship, the architect's role is to design the project and to provide independent observation of the contractor's work on behalf of the owner. The contractor's role is limited to constructing the project in accordance with the contract documents that the architect has prepared. Generally, the architect completes its plans and specifications before the contractor is hired by the owner,[2] resulting in a "design then build" system.[3] There is also little interaction between the architect and the contractor in a traditional project, except for the architect's observing the contractor during construction.

Design-build projects do not have the separation of roles and responsibilities that characterize traditional construction projects. In a design-build project, the owner enters into one contract with the design-build organization, resulting in a single point of responsibility for the owner.[4] The design-builder is responsible for providing and coordinating all of the work (that is,

---

[1] This chapter uses the term "architect" to refer to both architects and engineers.

[2] J. Sweet, Legal Aspects of Architecture, Engineering and the Construction Process 375 (4th ed. 1989) [hereinafter Sweet, Legal Aspects].

[3] Conner, *Contracting for Construction Management Services,* 46 Law & Contemp. Probs. 5, 5 (1983).

[4] The presence of single point responsibility is one of the primary reasons why owners are using design-build as a method of project delivery. *See, e.g.,* Comment, *Design-Build Contracts in Virginia,* 14 U. Rich. L. Rev. 791, 799 (1980); T. Twomey, Understanding the Legal Aspects of Design/Build 3 (1989) [hereinafter Twomey]; The American Institute of Architects, Design-Build-Bid Task Force Report 8 (1975) [hereinafter AIA Task Force Report].

architecture, engineering, and construction), even though the design-builder may hire subcontractors to perform certain aspects of the project.[5]

The owner benefits because the design-builder can begin various phases of the project simultaneously (including commencing construction before the design is complete), potentially resulting in a reduction in the total project cost and duration of the project.[6] The design-builder benefits because its profit margins may increase, due to the combining of the design and construction responsibilities in the project.[7] These benefits, however, are not without corresponding trade-offs, including the reduction in control by the owner over the performance of the work (due to the absence of tension between the architect and the contractor)[8] and the potential increase in liability undertaken by the design-builder.

This chapter explores the legal, economic, and practical implications of design-build, including an analysis of the various alternative formats for organizing the design-build entity. The correct format for a design-build project will depend upon the facts and circumstances surrounding an individual project. It is impossible to recommend a particular format for all situations. Therefore, this chapter identifies and discusses a variety of issues to be considered when selecting a format for providing design-build services.

§ 4.2 Design-Build Organizations

Although there is an infinite number of possibilities for organizing a design-build entity,[9] these organizations can generally be categorized into one of four basic formats. These formats are easily distinguishable from one another through the identification of the prime contractor (that is, the party who contracts directly with the owner for design-build services) and of the subcontractors (the parties who provide design-build services directly to the prime contractor).[10] The four basic formats are:

---

[5] Sweet, Legal Aspects at 375–76.

[6] Tieder & Cox, *Construction Management and the Specialty Trade (Prime) Contractors,* 46 Law & Contemp. Probs. 39, 44 (1983).

[7] Grant, *A New Look at Design/Build,* 7 Construction Law. 3, 3 (Apr. 1987).

[8] *Id.* In many respects, the architect is an antagonist to the contractor in a typical project; the contractor is seeking to maximize profit, whereas the architect is striving for a well-built project. Wise v. State Bd. for Examination, Qualification & Registration of Architects, 274 S.E.2d 544, 546 (Ga. 1981).

[9] Twomey at 8–12.

[10] No matter which of the four basic formats is used, the design-build project team must ultimately include all necessary expertise and personnel required to complete the project on schedule, within budget, and with the best possible controls on design and construction quality. AIA Task Force Report at 12.

1. The architect as the prime contractor and the contractor as a subcontractor (Prime Architect)
2. The contractor as the prime contractor and the architect as a subcontractor (Prime Contractor)
3. The architect and the contractor form a limited partnership or a joint venture (a general partnership) and the combined entity is the prime contractor (Partnership)
4. The architect and the contractor form a design-build corporation (either an S-corporation or a C-corporation) and the resulting corporation is the prime contractor (Corporation).[11]

The first two types of design-build firms, Prime Architect and Prime Contractor, are commonly referred to as traditional design-build formats because they are easily created through contractual relationships between the parties. Notwithstanding the ease of creation, these formats raise a number of contract, liability, and licensing issues which are briefly discussed in §§ **4.3** through **4.10**.[12] The other two formats are referred to as nontraditional because they may require the creation and maintenance of a separate entity to perform design-build services. As a result, the nontraditional entity requires an understanding of more than mere contract, liability, and licensing issues, but it also necessitates a discussion of the formation, management, and tax issues associated with a separate entity. These issues are discussed in §§ **4.11** through **4.35**, and a summary of tax and business considerations of the partnership and corporate formats is included in § **4.36**.

§ 4.3 Architect as Prime Contractor

The Prime Architect design-build organization[13] is created when an owner enters into a contract with an architect, requiring the architect to provide all of the design and construction services needed to complete the project.

---

[11] *See generally* Twomey.

[12] The contract, liability, and licensing issues are only summarized in this chapter. Other chapters of this work provide more in-depth analysis of these issues. See **Chs. 1, 3, 6, 10, 11, 12**, and **13**.

[13] This design-build arrangement is used less frequently than other design-build formats due, in part, to the typically large disparity in size between design and construction firms. In general, a small design firm has fewer resources than a large construction firm and, as a result, may have greater difficulty competing for design/build projects. Twomey at 15. Nevertheless, a Prime Architect organizational structure may be used by small design firms or individual architects, in association with other design firm or architects, as a way to participate in projects beyond their normal scope of capability. AIA Task Force Report at 19.

The architect then engages a contractor, using a separate subcontract requiring the contractor to provide construction services directly to the architect, not the owner. As is the case in traditional construction projects, the architect is responsible for providing the required design services and for overseeing the timely completion of the contractor's work. However, in addition to the architect's typical responsibilities, the architect, as design-builder, is now directly responsible to the owner for the means and methods of the construction work required for the project, including ensuring that the project is constructed in accordance with the contract documents that the architect prepares.[14]

The contractor in a Prime Architect format has no direct contractual relationship with the owner and is insulated from contract claims made by the owner for defects in the contractor's construction work. The contractor is only contractually obligated to the architect for these defects.[15] The contractor's insulation from contractual liability is the most salient difference between a Prime Architect design-build format and the traditional project delivery system.

Because the Prime Architect form of design-build organization alters the typical allocation of risk in construction projects, resulting in an increase in potential liability to the architect, the architect may attempt to shift some of this additional liability to the contractor. This transfer can be accomplished by the architect's using negotiated provisions in its subcontract with the contractor. The Prime Architect format may also cause the architect to run afoul of state professional licensing statutes. See **Chapter 3**. As a result, the relevant contract, liability, and licensing issues should be thoroughly analyzed before an owner, architect, or contractor determines which form of design-build organization to use.

§ 4.4 —Contract Issues

The Prime Architect design-build format alters the typical allocation of risk and responsibilities between the contractor and the architect, resulting in an increase in economic benefits and potential liabilities to the architect. The architect, however, may not want to retain all of these added liabilities, especially when they relate to work being performed by subcontractors. As a result, the architect will attempt to transfer many of these potential liabilities to the subcontractors through the inclusion of contract provisions in the design-build contracts between owner and architect and between architect and subcontractors. Regardless of which type of format is used, there

---

[14] *See generally* Twomey; AIA Task Force Report.

[15] The contractor will, nevertheless, be liable to the owner and to third parties for its negligent construction work which causes injury to person or property. See **§ 4.5**.

must be a clear understanding among the parties as to who has responsibility for various liabilities and how problems relating to gaps and overlaps in liability insurance coverage will be resolved.[16] The following discussion highlights a number of the most important contract issues.

Independent Review and Conflict of Interest

The architect in a typical construction project is responsible for the design and for providing advice to the owner as to the contractor's work. As a result, the architect usually performs periodic observations of the contractor's work for conformance with the contract documents; interprets the contract documents; certifies payments to the contractor and subcontractors; certifies stages of completion and quality of work; serves as liaison between owner and contractor; serves as arbiter of any disputes that may arise during the course of construction of the project; and ultimately signs off on the final completion of the project to the owner and the owner's lender.[17] These are valuable services provided to the owner, allowing the owner to monitor and manage the progress of the contractor.[18]

In a design-build project, however, the architect's success or failure in the project is closely tied to the contractor's performance, which may create a potential conflict of interest[19] that could hamper the architect's ability to provide independent oversight for the owner. Without supervisory assistance, the owner may be unable to determine if the contractor is delivering substandard work, if the contractor is requesting excessive payments, or if the contractor is failing to pay its subcontractors. Owners, therefore, should consider obtaining alternative, independent representatives when using a design-build project delivery system.

---

[16] When using either a Prime Architect or Prime Contractor design-build format, it is important for the parties to negotiate and fully resolve all of the contract issues in the various design-build contracts executed between the parties. These contracts, as much as is practicably possible, should reflect actual responsibility for the various stages of the project and should anticipate potential problem areas, including compliance with codes, regulations, and professional standards; errors and omissions, both design and construction; management responsibility; third-party liability; the owner's assumption of risk for nonperformance or inadequate performance; and the insurability of the various risks created by the contractual relationship.

[17] Comment, *Design-Build Contracts in Virginia,* 14 U. Rich. L. Rev. 791 (1980); Foster, *Construction Management and Design-Build/Fast Track Construction: A Solution Which Uncovers a Problem For the Surety,* 46 Law. & Contemp. Probs. 95, 100–101 (1983).

[18] Coulson, *Dispute Management under Modern Construction Systems,* 46 Law & Contemp. Probs. 127, 130 (1983).

[19] The architect's interests are so intertwined with the contractor's that the architect is bound to lose its independence. AIA Task Force Report at 10; Sweet, Legal Aspects at 388.

Accordingly, an owner may decide to either use in-house personnel or hire an outside consultant to supervise the design-builder and to provide an independent oversight function similar to what the architect usually provides.[20] Whichever option is chosen, the owner should ensure that its contract with the design-builder specifically provides for this independent review, including a description of who will perform the inspections, how often, and in what detail.

Indemnification Clauses

One of the methods of risk shifting used in construction projects is the use of indemnification clauses requiring the architect and the contractor, as applicable, to indemnify the owner against potential liability as a result of a contracting party's negligent acts.[21] In a design-build project, however, the use of indemnification clauses is complicated because the prime contractor (whether it is the architect or the contractor) will be obligated to indemnify the owner for all liability for both design and construction, arising out of the project, even if the prime contractor was not the cause of such liability. As a result, the prime contractor becomes an insurer of the subcontractor's work.[22] In a traditional construction project, the owner-architect agreement rarely contains an indemnity provision, yet when the architect acts as the design-builder, the owner should require an indemnity provision covering claims arising from design and construction. Therefore, the architect must negotiate this clause carefully and coordinate this clause with its insurance coverage and its subcontract with the contractor.

Because the design-build format alters the typical allocation of risk and responsibility between contractors and architects, the prime contractor should reallocate these risks through its contract with the subcontractor, in order to more accurately reflect actual responsibility.[23] For example, the architect in a Prime Architect format is contractually responsible to the owner for any and all construction problems. However, it is the contractor who is actually responsible for the means and methods of the construction

---

[20] AIA Task Force Report at 10. The owner may also ignore the conflict; however, the author does not recommend this option.

[21] Note, *Allocation of Risk in the Construction Industry: The Nonprofessional Owner and His Construction Manager,* 46 Law & Contemp. Probs. 162 (1983).

[22] The owner must make sure that the prime contractor has sufficient assets to satisfy any such claims, and the owner should request that it be named as an additional insured on the subcontractor's insurance policy, which is usually obtained for the benefit of the prime contractor.

[23] The parties, however, should be cautious to draft the indemnification clauses so that they do not affect the enforceability and insurability of the contract. For example, many states prohibit the contractor from indemnifying the architect for the architect's own design errors. *See* Twomey at 126.

work. The architect, therefore, should require the contractor to indemnify it against all liability arising out of the contractor's performance of its work, whether such claim is made for negligence or under a contractual obligation the architect has with the owner. An indemnification clause makes the contractor ultimately responsible for the damages it causes during the prosecution of the construction work, including late delivery of the project, construction costs exceeding the construction budget, jobsite safety, or defects in the work.[24] The architect, therefore, reduces its liability exposure to the owner as a result of the subcontractor's indemnification.[25]

Cost and Time Parameters

Under the architect's contract with the owner, the architect is contractually obligated to complete the project within the approved project budget and the approved project schedule. However, certain time delays or cost overruns may be caused, in whole or in part, by the actions or inactions of a subcontractor, including the contractor.[26] The architect, therefore, should shift the responsibility for these delays and overruns back to the contractor, through its contract with the contractor.[27]

Dispute Resolution

Typically, the architect is the arbiter of disputes between the owner and the contractor. However, under a Prime Architect format, the architect is not independent enough to officiate project disputes. As a result, the parties should provide a mechanism for resolving any disputes that might arise during the course of the project. Generally, the parties resolve this problem by agreeing to submit all contract disputes to arbitration, using the rules established by the American Arbitration Association or rules agreed to between them, by appointing a third party to mediate disputes as disputes arise,[28] or by agreeing that disputes will be settled in court. Therefore, the design-build contract should contain provisions requiring either

---

[24] AIA Task Force Report at 11.

[25] The parties should be careful to analyze the economic worth of any such indemnification, including reviewing the assets of the party who is giving the indemnity.

[26] This anomaly occurs more frequently in a Prime Architect design-build organization because the contractor performs the construction work and, therefore, is in the best position (if not the only position) to control the construction costs and project delivery date. AIA Task Force Report at 12.

[27] Bynum, *Construction Management and Design-Build/Fast Track Construction from the Perspective of a General Contractor,* 46 Law & Contemp. Probs. 25, 29 (1983).

[28] Coulson, *Dispute Management under Modern Construction Systems,* 46 Law & Contemp. Probs. 127, 127–28 (1983).

arbitration, mediation, or litigation in the event of disputes between the parties. The parties should also consider whether arbitration or mediation will be binding.[29]

§ 4.5 —Liability Issues

In a traditional construction project, one of the owner's major problems is to determine whether the architect or the contractor is responsible when the project fails. Usually, both the contractor and the architect claim that the project's failure was caused by the other party. In the design-build project, however, the owner is protected from this situation because the design-builder is liable to the owner for any default in contract performance caused by either the contractor or the architect, including any failure in design or construction quality.

In addition, an architect in a traditional construction project is insulated from responsibility for construction means, methods, techniques, sequences, and procedures; construction safety precautions; and errors and omissions of the contractor, because the contractor is performing these services.[30] The architect in a Prime Architect format, however, is exposed to these liabilities because the architect is responsible for all aspects of the project, including all construction work. The architect becomes responsible for any failure to construct the project in a good and workmanlike manner and in accordance with industry standards and building codes.[31] The architect is now in a unique position of knowing and supervising all aspects of the project.[32] As a result, the architect is unable to argue that it was only minimally involved in certain portions of the project, because the architect now controls both the design and construction functions.

Correspondingly, the contractor is insulated from contractual liability to the owner for its own construction work. Nevertheless, the contractor in a Prime Architect format is responsible to third parties for the contractor's own negligence, regardless of which design-build format is used. This is because a party will be held responsible for its own negligence that causes injury to person or property, regardless of any contractual limitation.[33] The

---

[29] Twomey at 126.

[30] Block, *Architects' Expanded Liability under Design-Build/Construction Contracting*, 33 Def. L. J. 325, 333–334 (1984).

[31] Twomey at 18.

[32] Block, *Architects' Expanded Liability under Design-Build/Construction Contracting*, 33 Def. L. J. 325, 340 (1984).

[33] *See generally* Twomey.

following areas of liability pose the greatest risk to architects in the Prime Architect design-build format:

Site Control and Safety Precautions

Typically, the responsibility for safety at the jobsite is placed squarely on the shoulders of the contractor. However, in a Prime Architect project, the architect is contractually responsible to the owner for jobsite safety and the project's compliance with state and federal safety regulations, including the requirements of the Occupational Safety and Health Act (OSHA).[34] Architects must comply with OSHA when the architect's role of coordinating the construction work is intertwined with the actual performance of the construction work, that is, when the architect "controls" or "directs" the construction work, either by contract or by its actions.[35] The architect may also be responsible to the general public for construction safety problems, depending upon the jurisdiction of the project.[36]

Insurance

To address the increased risk of liability facing the architect as design-builder, the architect should analyze the various types of insurance available. The most common form of insurance for an architect is the professional liability policy, which protects the architect against liability for its errors and omissions in its design work and for its failure to meet the standards of the profession. However, the professional liability insurance policy typically excludes coverage for design-build projects.[37] Generally, this type of insurance protects the architect only for claims arising out of the performance of its professional services, that is, the practice of architecture. As a result, any contractual obligation or actual activity of the architect beyond the practice of architecture, such as construction work and construction management, will be excluded from coverage.[38] Therefore, the architect is uninsured for the construction portion of the design-build project.

---

[34] Lunch, *New Construction Methods and New Roles For Engineers,* 46 Law & Contemp. Probs. 83, 92 (1983).

[35] *Id.*

[36] Twomey at 18.

[37] *See, e.g.,* Block, *Architects' Expanded Liability under Design-Build/Construction Contracting,* 33 Def. L. J. 325, 353–55 (1984).

[38] *Id.;* Lunch, *New Construction Methods and New Roles for Engineers,* 46 Law & Contemp. Probs. 83, 93 (1983); Bynum, *Construction Management and Design-Build/Fast Track Construction from the Perspective of a General Contractor,* 46 Law & Contemp. Probs. 25, 35 (1983).

The architect, however, can protect itself through the use of indemnification clauses[39] or through the purchase of a commercial general liability (CGL) insurance policy. The CGL policy can protect the architect from a broad range of potential liabilities, including claims for defective manufacture, defective construction work, and the architect's contractual actions that may result in property damage or injury to third parties. The CGL policy, however, excludes claims made against the architect arising out of the performance of its design services. Nevertheless, the architect can protect itself against a number of design-build liabilities through the purchase of both professional and commercial liability insurance.

The architect also should investigate other types of insurance. For example, force majeure insurance may be available to protect the architect in the event of delayed completion. The architect should consult a knowledgeable insurance advisor to properly structure the insurance for a design-build project.

§ 4.6 —Licensing Issues

Design-build projects raise a number of licensing issues[40] that must be considered before an architect or a contractor enters into a design-build project. A design-build project, as is the case in a traditional project, requires both the architect and the contractor to each be licensed by applicable state and federal law to perform their respective services; the architect is licensed for design work, and the contractor is licensed for construction work. However, because the architect in a Prime Architect format is responsible for performing construction functions for which it is not traditionally licensed, some states require the architect to obtain additional licensing or registration when it performs construction services under a design-build contract.[41]

In addition, when an architect performs design services as a professional corporation, the architect's responsibility for the construction process may

---

[39] See § **4.4**.

[40] In addition to running afoul of state and federal licensing laws, design-build projects may also be prohibited by state and local procurement laws. In traditional construction procurement projects (state and local government construction projects), construction services are awarded on a "hard bid" basis, whereas design services are negotiated. Because of the different procurement treatment afforded these two disciplines, design-build formats have been found to conflict with state and local procurement law. See **Ch. 3**. As a result, before entering into a design-build project for a state or local governmental entity, the parties should investigate applicable state and local procurement law to determine if the design-build delivery system is permitted or prohibited. Buesing, *The Law Struggles to Keep Pace with the Trend of State and Local Government Experience with Design/Build,* 11 Construction Law. 4, 22–24 (Oct. 1991).

[41] Twomey at 4.

violate state laws relating to professional corporations, because some states limit the types of activities that professional corporations are permitted to perform. For example, some state statutes prohibit a professional corporation from engaging in activities beyond the scope of its particular professional discipline. An architect who is incorporated as a professional corporation, therefore, should check applicable state law before agreeing to perform a design-build project as the prime contractor.

§ 4.7 Contractor as Prime Contractor

In a Prime Contractor design-build format,[42] the owner contracts directly with the contractor for all design and construction services required to complete the project. The contractor then enters into a separate subcontract directly with an architect who will be responsible for providing the contractor, as design-builder, with its design services. The contractor then constructs the project in accordance with the architect's contract documents.

When the contractor is the prime contractor in a design-build organization, the contractor is exposed to similar risk, reward, and liability issues that affect the architect in a Prime Architect organization. The contractor is liable to the owner for all problems associated with the project, including the architect's design work. The architect is shielded from direct contractual responsibility to the owner for design defects because the architect does not have a contract with the owner. Nevertheless, the architect must perform its services in accordance with the applicable standard of care.[43] In addition, the owner loses the architect as an independent advisor because the architect's interests are so intertwined with the contractor's interests that the architect is bound to lose its independence.[44]

Because the contractor, not the architect, is now responsible to the owner for errors and omissions in the design, the contractor should attempt to address liability concerns by negotiating contract provisions to be inserted in its subcontract with the architect. The contractor would want the architect to be ultimately responsible if the design of the project fails to conform to applicable codes or standards of professional practice. The most important contract, liability and licensing issues affecting a Prime Contractor format are discussed in §§ **4.8** through **4.10**.

---

[42] This format is one of the most frequently used of the design-build formats due to the relative size of contracting firms compared to design firms and because this form of organization can be easily created. Twomey at 19.

[43] *See, e.g.*, Playskool, Inc. v. Elsa Benson, Inc., 147 Ill. App. 3d 292, 497 N.E.2d 1199 (1986); Twomey. The architect will also be liable to the owner and to third parties for its negligence. See § **4.9**.

[44] See § **4.8**.

§ 4.8 —Contract Issues

In a Prime Contractor design-build format, the contractor becomes contractually obligated to the owner for all aspects of a construction project, including all design work. This alters the traditional allocation of risk and responsibilities, resulting in an increase in both economic benefits and potential liabilities to the contractor. The contractor, however, may seek to avoid these added liabilities by transferring many of them to the architect by means of various contract provisions. To accomplish this transfer, the parties must have a clear understanding of the allocation of potential liabilities and how gaps and overlaps in liability coverage will be resolved. The following discussion highlights a number of the most important contract issues.

Independent review and conflict of interest. As in the Prime Architect format,[45] the owner loses the architect as an independent observer of the contractor's work during the prosecution of the Prime Contractor project.[46] The architect is an employee of the contractor and has no contractual obligations to the owner. Owners, therefore, should consider obtaining alternative, independent representation, either in-house personnel or an outside consultant, for the project. If the owner requires this independent review, the owner should include a provision in its contract with the contractor specifically providing for this independent representation.

Indemnification clauses. The contractor in a Prime Contractor format is contractually responsible to the owner for any and all project design problems. Because the architect is the party who actually prepares the design documents, the contractor should shift the liability associated with design responsibility to the architect by using indemnification clauses in its subcontract agreement. These clauses require the architect to indemnify the contractor for any losses resulting from the architect's defective design, including the architect's failure to design the project in accordance with applicable codes and its failure to meet professional standards of conduct.[47]

Cost and time parameters. In the Prime Contractor format, the contractor has the responsibility to complete the project on time and within the approved budget. However, the contractor should ensure that the architect, as one of the contractor's subcontractors, is responsible for any delay in construction (such as through the late delivery of drawings) or an increase

---

[45] See § **4.4**.

[46] The architect's interests are so intertwined with the contractor's that the architect is bound to lose its independence. AIA Task Force Report at 10; Sweet at 388.

[47] S. Stein, Construction Law, § 13.06[9] (1990).

in the budget (for example, through improper design requiring reconstruction) caused by the architect's performance. The contractor, therefore, should include provisions in its contract with the architect to address these issues.

Dispute resolution. As a subcontractor to the contractor in a Prime Contractor format, the architect is unable to be the arbiter of disputes between the owner and the contractor. The owner, therefore, may require that all disputes be decided by an independent third party and not by the architect. If the owner so desires, the owner should ensure that the various design-build agreements provide for an alternate dispute resolution mechanism. The agreements should specify whether disputes will be resolved by arbitration, mediation, or litigation.

§ 4.9 —Liability Issues

Because the design-builder is a single point of responsibility, the contractor in a Prime Contractor format has increased potential liability, as compared to typical projects.[48] The contractor is exposed to liability for design errors caused by the architect. The architect, however, is not contractually liable to the owner for design errors. However, the architect may still be liable to third parties for its negligence which causes injury to person or property.[49] The architect's liability to third parties exists despite the architect's insulation from contractual liability to the owner.

The increased design liability incurred by the contractor is the greatest drawback to the contractor in the Prime Contractor format. The contractor now controls and oversees the design portion of the project and is liable if the design fails to conform to professional standards or to the applicable codes, rules, and regulations. The contractor also loses the protection of certain defenses usually available to a contractor in a traditional construction project, such as the defense that the architect's drawings were inadequate or incomplete. The contractor is obligated to provide the owner with a design that complies with all codes, including building code requirements. The contractor cannot insulate itself from these liabilities because it is also responsible for the project design.

The contractor may attempt to protect itself from this liability for design errors by purchasing a professional liability insurance policy. However, this type of insurance is only available to contractors who use their own design personnel (that is, in-house architects) and is unavailable to contractors

---

[48] Comment, *Design-Build Contracts in Virginia,* 14 U. Rich. L. Rev. 791, 799 (1980).

[49] *See* Playskool, Inc. v. Elsa Benson, Inc., 147 Ill. App. 3d 292, 497 N.E.2d 1199 (1986); *see generally* Twomey.

who hire outside architectural firms.[50] Because the contractor's normal insurance (builder's risk and commercial general liability) does not provide coverage for design errors,[51] the contractor should require the architect to indemnify it for any resulting design liability[52] or convince the owner to purchase design professional liability insurance for the project.

§ 4.10 —Licensing Issues

A contractor in a Prime Contractor format is contractually obligated to the owner to provide not only construction services but also the design services for the project, including the drafting and "sealing" of the contract documents. However, all 50 states, as well as the District of Columbia, require that the practice of architecture only be performed by professionally licensed architects.[53] In addition, if the architect is a corporation, many states require the architect to obtain corporate authorization from the state to perform design services.

Because contractors are not licensed or authorized to render architectural services, they are potentially liable under state licensing laws for performing architectural services without a professional license.[54] In some states, it is also unlawful for an architect to contract with a contractor to provide design services, because this would involve the architect in illegal fee splitting.[55] As a result, the contract between the owner and the design-builder may be void or unenforceable because it requires the performance of architectural services without a license.[56] This may result in great liability to the design-builder, who is contractually responsible to the owner for rendering architectural services.[57]

---

[50] S. Stein, Construction Law, ¶ 13.06[9] (1990). If the contractor is performing the design work in-house, the contractor may be able to obtain, in some states, professional liability insurance protecting it from its own design errors. This type of insurance is not available to contractors who use outside architectural firms. *Id.*

[51] Bynum, *Construction Management and Design-Build/Fast Track Construction from the Perspective of a General Contractor,* 46 Law & Contemp. Probs. 25, 35 (1983).

[52] See § **4.8**.

[53] Halsey & Quatman, *Design/Build Contracts: Valid or Invalid,* 9 Construction Law. 29 (Aug. 1989). See also **Ch. 3**.

[54] Design-build projects may also not be permitted under state and local procurement laws. *See* Buesing, *The Law Struggles to Keep Pace with the Trend of State and Local Government Experience with Design/Build,* 11 Construction Law. 4 (Oct. 1991).

[55] Buesing, *Design/Build Contract Management: The Law Struggles to Keep Pace with the Design/Build Trend,* 10 Construction Law. 14 (Jan. 1990).

[56] Halsey & Quatman, *Design/Build Contracts: Valid or Invalid,* 9 Construction Law. 29 (Aug. 1989).

[57] See § **4.7**.

These potential risks and problems, however, may be evaporating because many states now allow design-build firms to enter into contracts to provide architectural services, provided a validly-licensed architect is providing such services and "sealing" construction drawings.[58] Similarly, many states are now amending their laws to authorize architects to enter into design-build projects.[59] Contractors, therefore, should not enter into a Prime Contractor design-build project unless there is established legal precedent giving the contractor such authority.

Before offering or soliciting design-build work, the design-builder should either (1) ensure that its subcontract with an architect is authorized by state laws and by the state licensing board, or (2) apply to the state licensing board directly for a certificate of authority to practice architecture.[60]

§ 4.11 Partnership Format

Several issues are important if the architect and the contractor form either a general or a limited partnership to conduct design-build operations.[61] Because the partnership format offers the architect and contractor considerable flexibility in structuring a business arrangement and may receive favorable tax treatment, in many cases it is well-suited for design-build projects.

A general partnership is defined as "an association of two or more persons to carry on as co-owners a business for profit."[62] General partners have joint and several liability for partnership obligations and are presumed to share equally in the management and profits of the partnership. As parties to a voluntary contractual association, however, the partners have considerable flexibility in defining their relationship.[63] Thus, capital contributions need not be pro rata, and one partner may bear a disproportionate share of the risks of the business, control day-to-day operations, and be responsible for making major decisions for the association, all in a manner that the partners consider appropriate. No formal filing is usually required

[58] Halsey & Quatman, *Design/Build Contracts: Valid or Invalid,* 9 Construction *Law.* 29, 29–33 (Aug. 1989); Block, *Architects' Expanded Liability under Design-Build/Construction Contracting,* 33 Def. L. J. 325, 367 (1984).

[59] Buesing, *Design/Build Contract Management: The Law Struggles to Keep Pace with the Design/Build Trend,* 10 Construction Law. 14 (Jan. 1990).

[60] Sweet, Legal Aspects at 388.

[61] Detailed discussions of the factors influencing the choice of entity are set forth in E. Manning & S. Koppelman, Choosing the Business Entity, Tax Transactions Library (CCH) (1989) and Solomon, Lurie, & Boutwell, 456 Tax. Mgmt. (BNA) *Choice of Entity* (1987).

[62] Unif. Partnership Act § 6, 6 U.L.A. 22 (1914).

[63] *See* J. Crane & A. Bromberg, Law of Partnership 38–44 (1968).

under state law to form a partnership, and a partnership may operate simply on the basis of an informal oral understanding.[64]

A limited partnership is a hybrid entity that has many features of a general partnership but also offers limited partners the protection of limited liability. A limited partnership is defined as "a partnership formed by 2 or more persons . . . having one or more general partners and one or more limited partners."[65] Limited partners usually do not participate in the day-to-day management of a limited partnership. The remaining terms of the partnership agreement are, however, open to negotiation. Thus, as in the case of a general partnership, the partners have considerable flexibility with respect to capital contributions and the sharing of profits and losses. As in the case of a corporation, a limited partnership is formed by filing a certificate with the appropriate state authority.[66]

§ 4.12 —Liability Issues

A principal advantage to the owner in the design-build situation is the single point of responsibility. There is, of course, a corresponding shift of liability to the architect, contractor, or design-build entity that assumes responsibility for the project. In a Prime Architect design-build project, the architect is exposed to risks previously borne by the contractor, and in a Prime Contractor design-build project, the contractor is exposed to risks previously borne by the architect. The following discussion highlights the transfer of risk that occurs when the architect and contractor form a general partnership to act as the prime contractor of a design-build project.

Architect's Liability

General partners are liable for the contractual obligations and torts of the partnership.[67] Further, each partner is an agent of the partnership for the purpose of partnership business and, if acting within the scope of the partnership business, may bind the partnership.[68] Thus, when an architect and contractor do business as general partners, each is liable for the acts of the other.

---

[64] It is advisable, however, to set forth in writing the partners' rights and obligations with respect to financing, control, liability, transferability of interests, and sharing of profits and losses. J. Crane & A. Bromberg, Law of Partnership 43 (1968).

[65] Rev. Unif. Limited Partnership Act § 101(7), 6 U.L.A. 271 (1985). *See also* Unif. Limited Partnership Act § 1, 6 U.L.A. 562 (1916).

[66] Rev. Unif. Limited Partnership Act § 201 (1976).

[67] Unif. Partnership Act § 15 (1914).

[68] *Id.* §§ 9, 15.

In a traditional construction project, the architect is not responsible for safety at the jobsite, construction means or methods, or the defective workmanship of the contractor. If the architect and contractor are general partners, however, the architect will be exposed to liability for these items in its capacity as a partner. The architect also becomes responsible for cost overruns and late delivery of the project.

The case of *Kishwaukee Community Health Service Center v. Hospital Building & Equipment Corp.*[69] illustrates the architect's increased exposure to liability when design-build operations are conducted jointly. In *Kishwaukee,* the owner executed an agreement with the contractor for services in designing and constructing a hospital. The agreement indicated that the architects were employed by the contractors and that the contract sum included the architects' charges. The owner sought to recover damages from the architect and contractor for negligent design and construction and breach of express and implied warranties. The court noted that the defendants were hired as one cohesive group, with each liable (presumably for both design and construction errors) under the contract.[70]

An architect's professional liability insurance policy covers malpractice claims arising from the performance of professional services. Breach of warranty claims and claims arising from participation in a partnership in which the architect holds an equity interest usually are excluded. Therefore, the architect must obtain business or general liability coverage to protect against claims arising from design-build operations.[71]

It is important in arranging insurance coverage to ensure that there are no gaps between the professional liability and general liability policies. The issue of such a gap was raised in *United States Fidelity & Guaranty Co. v. Continental Casualty Co.*[72] The architect had separate professional liability and multi-peril liability insurance policies. Both insurers attempted to deny coverage. The professional liability insurer argued that design-build services were beyond the scope of its policy, and the multi-peril liability insurer argued that such services were excluded from coverage under its policy.

Apart from insurance, an architect may take a variety of steps to shift or reduce its risk of liability for acts of the contractor. For example, an

---

[69] 638 F. Supp. 1492 (N.D. Ill. 1986).

[70] *Id.* at 1503. In a subsequent motion for summary judgment on plaintiff's warranty claims, the court did not distinguish between the architect and contractor, noting that both were subsidiaries of Hospital Building and Equipment Corp. In this regard, the court stated that any such distinction "deserves glossing over." Kishwaukee Community Health Serv. Ctr. v. Hospital Bldg. & Equip., No. 80-C-1850, 1988 WESTLAW 31434, at 10 n.1 (N.D. Ill. March 28, 1988).

[71] *See* Block, *Architects' Expanded Liability under Design-Build/Construction Contracting,* 33 Def. L. J. 325, 355–56 (1984).

[72] 505 N.E.2d 1072 (Ill. App. Ct. 1987).

architect who pays damages as a result of the contractor's acts or omissions may be entitled to seek indemnification from the partnership, with the contractor sharing its portion of this liability through contribution.[73] It also may be possible for an architect to form a wholly owned corporation that would enter into a partnership as a general partner, along with the contractor. The architect then could perform its professional services pursuant to a contract with the partnership. If this structure were utilized, the architect's exposure through the partnership would be limited to its investment in the corporation. The architect's exposure under the contract to perform services then would be similar to that encountered in a traditional construction project.

Contractor's Liability

In a traditional construction project, the contractor is not responsible for the design errors and omissions of the architect. The contractor is exposed to liability for such errors and omissions, however, if business is conducted through a general partnership. Professional liability insurance ordinarily is not available to a contractor to reduce exposure for this risk.[74] In addition, a contractor cannot be named as an additional insured on the architect's professional liability policy.[75]

A contractor who suffers a loss as a result of the design errors of the architect may be entitled to seek indemnification from the partnership, with the architect sharing its portion of this liability through contribution.[76] Alternatively, the contractor could form a wholly owned corporation that could enter into a partnership with the architect. The contractor then could perform its services pursuant to a contract with the partnership. If this structure were utilized, the contractor's exposure through the corporation would be limited to its investment in the corporation, and its risk of liability under the contract would be similar to the risks undertaken in a traditional construction project.

---

[73] An architect who pays a judgment attributable to the contractor's acts or omissions apparently may shift the loss to the partnership but not wholly to the contractor. Conversely, if the architect is sued for its own malpractice, it may not recover in contribution from a nonnegligent contractor. *See, e.g.,* Marcus v. Green, 13 Ill. App. 3d 699, 300 N.E.2d 512 (1973); *See also* A. Bromberg & L. Ribstein, Partnership § 4.07(h) (1988).

[74] *See* Twomey at 139.

[75] *Id.*

[76] *See, e.g.,* Marcus v. Green, 13 Ill. App. 3d 699, 300 N.E.2d 512 (1973); *see also* A. Bromberg & L. Ribstein, Partnership § 4.07(h) (1988). It may be possible for the contractor to assure performance of this obligation by purchasing (or funding the purchase of) additional professional liability insurance for the architect.

Limited Partnerships

Limited partnerships provide a method to limit the liability of the architect and/or contractor while preserving many of the other desirable attributes of a general partnership. General partners and limited partners play different roles in a limited partnership. General partners manage the operations of the limited partnership and are liable for the obligations of the partnership in much the same manner as partners in a general partnership.[77] Limited partners, in contrast, usually do not participate in the management of the partnership and generally are not personally liable to creditors of the partnership.[78]

Limited partners may lose the protection of limited liability if they participate in the management of the partnership.[79] An architect or contractor who is willing to accept this passive role ordinarily can avoid liability in contract to the owner or subcontractors. However, the architect or contractor still would be exposed to tort liabilities, such as possible liability for defective plans or inadequate site supervision.

The architect and contractor usually would want to participate in the management of a design-build partnership but would desire to limit their exposure for the liabilities of the entity. It may be possible to satisfy these competing interests by their forming a corporation to serve as general partner of the partnership. The architect and contractor then could participate in the management of the partnership through their interest as shareholders of the corporation. This arrangement would limit the partners' exposure to contractual liability to their investment in the corporation, but it would not limit possible exposure to tort liabilities, such as for design defects. Owners and subcontractors may insist that the partnership entity or corporate general partner have adequate capitalization or that some form of guarantee be provided.

In summary, the limited partnership form offers some protection from liability and is in many cases well-suited for design-build operations. An architect or contractor owning a limited partnership interest in a partnership conducting design-build operations would be an equity participant in the project, sharing the profits and losses of the enterprise. The limited partner would not, however, be exposed to the potential liabilities of the partnership or to the risks typically borne by its counterpart.

---

[77] *See* Rev. Unif. Limited Partnership Act §§ 401–405 (1985).

[78] *See id.* § 303.

[79] *Id.* Limited partners also may be responsible for the debts of the partnership if their name appears in the name of the partnership or if they hold themselves out as general partners. *Id.* § 303(d). In addition, limited partners may be liable for promised but unpaid capital contributions or, in certain circumstances, for capital withdrawn from the partnership.

§ 4.13 —Management and Licensing Issues

An architect and contractor who form a design-build general partnership would be free to allocate management authority in any manner they consider appropriate.[80] There may be less flexibility in a limited partnership, because a limited partner who participates in management decisions may lose the protection of limited liability. In states that have adopted a statute that corresponds with the Revised Uniform Limited Partnership Act, an architect or contractor limited partner could act as an agent or employee of the partnership, or approve specified major partnership decisions, without endangering his status as a limited partner.[81]

One issue that arises in connection with the operations of a design-build partnership relates to licensing under state law.[82] The laws of each state require a license or authorization to perform architectural services. Consequently, licensing requirements must be reviewed to ensure compliance whenever architectural services are performed by a design-build partnership. Some states require that each partner of a partnership performing architectural services be a licensed architect. This creates an obvious problem when an unlicensed contractor is a member of a design-build partnership. Other states require only one licensed architect. In certain states, licensing requirements are satisfied if the design-build entity agrees with the owner to provide (through a licensed architect) rather than perform architectural services.[83]

The consequences of violating state licensing requirements also vary from jurisdiction to jurisdiction. For example, in Food Management Inc. v. Blue Ribbon Beef Pack, Inc.,[84] the court declared the portion of a contract relating to architectural services void and unenforceable because the corporation performing such services was not licensed as an architect.[85] A contrary result was reached in *Pacific Chromalox Division v. Irey,*[86] which involved the

---

[80] Unif. Partnership Act § 18 (1914).

[81] *See* Rev. Unif. Limited Partnership Act § 303(b)(1) (1985).

[82] See **Ch. 3**. Licensing issues are discussed in detail in Halsey & Quatman, *Design/Build Contracts: Valid or Invalid,* 9 Construction Law. 29 (Aug. 1989). *See also* Comment, *Design-Build Contracts in Virginia,* 14 U. Rich. L. Rev. 791 (1980).

[83] *See, e.g.,* Seaview Hosp. v. Medicenters of Am., 570 S.W.2d 35, 39–40 (Tex. Ct. App. 1978) (holding that contract to provide architectural and engineering services was not a contract to perform such services but to arrange for those services, and finding it valid even though neither contractor nor any of its employees were licensed to practice architecture or engineering).

[84] 413 F.2d 716 (8th Cir. 1969).

[85] *Id.* at 724–25; *see also* West Baton Rouge Parish School Bd. v. T.R. Ray, Inc., 367 So. 2d 332 (La. 1979) (holding contract for architectural services invalid because firm was not licensed).

[86] 787 P.2d 1319 (Utah Ct. App.), *cert. denied,* 800 P.2d 1105 (Utah 1990).

violation of engineering licensing laws in connection with the design and construction of a heating coil production machine. The court in *Pacific Chromalox* enforced the contract to avoid an unreasonable forfeiture.

§ 4.14 —Partnership Tax Considerations

Tax considerations may favor conducting design-build operations through a partnership. Partnerships are flow-through entities for federal income tax purposes and thus avoid the potential second level of tax that is characteristic of corporate taxation.[87] Instead, each partner reports on its income tax return, and takes into account in determining its own income tax, its allocable share of the partnership's income, gain, loss, and deduction.[88]

§ 4.15 —Tax Status as a Partnership

The characterization of an entity for state law purposes as a partnership, corporation, or trust is not determinative of its federal income tax treatment.[89] Instead, the status of an entity for federal income tax purposes is determined by the Internal Revenue Code and regulations.[90] An entity that has associates and an objective to carry on business for a joint profit will be treated as a partnership, and not as an association taxable as a corporation, if it has less than three of the following four corporate characteristics:

1. Continuity of life
2. Limited liability
3. Centralization of management
4. Free transferability of interests.[91]

An entity formed to conduct design-build operations will have associates and an objective to carry on business for joint profit. Consequently, the status of the design-build entity for federal income tax purposes will depend upon the presence of the enumerated corporate characteristics. As the discussion below illustrates, it usually is quite easy for design-build partnerships or limited partnerships to qualify as partnerships for federal income tax purposes.

---

[87] I.R.C. § 701 (1991).

[88] *Id.* § 702. For a comprehensive treatment of partnership taxation, *see* W. McKee, W. Nelson, & R. Whitmire, Federal Taxation of Partnerships and Partners (1990).

[89] Treas. Reg. § 301.7701-1(c) (as amended in 1977).

[90] *Id.*

[91] Treas. Reg. § 301.7701-2(a)(2) (as amended in 1983); Rev. Rule 88-76, 1988-2 C.B.360.

Continuity of Life

Continuity of life does not exist if the death, insanity, bankruptcy, retirement, resignation, or expulsion of any member causes a dissolution of the organization.[92] Under the Uniform Partnership Act, a general partnership dissolves upon the death or bankruptcy of any partner.[93] Therefore, design-build general partnerships formed in accordance with a statute corresponding with the Uniform Partnership Act will lack the corporate characteristic of continuity of life.

In the case of a limited partnership, continuity of life does not exist if the retirement, death, bankruptcy, or insanity of a general partner causes a dissolution of the partnership, unless the remaining general partners agree to continue the partnership or unless all remaining partners agree to continue the partnership.[94] Under the Uniform Limited Partnership Act, the bankruptcy, death, or incompetence of a general partner generally will cause a dissolution of the partnership unless the remaining general partners or, if there are no general partners remaining, all the limited partners agree to continue the partnership's business and to appoint at least one general partner.[95] Therefore, a design-build limited partnership formed in accordance with the Uniform Limited Partnership Act also will lack continuity of life.

Limited Liability

An organization has the corporate characteristic of limited liability if under local law there is no member who is personally liable for its debts.[96] Limited liability is lacking in the case of a design-build general partnership, because the architect and contractor each would be liable for claims against the partnership.

The issue is slightly more complicated in the case of a design-build limited partnership. A limited partnership lacks the corporate characteristic of limited liability if there is at least one partner who is personally liable for the debts of or claims against the partnership. The general partner of a limited partnership is personally liable if it has "substantial assets" other

---

[92] Treas. Reg. § 301.7701-2(b)(1) (as amended in 1983). A *dissolution* means an alteration of the identity of an organization by reason of a change in the relationship between members as determined under local law. *Id.* § 301.7701-2(b)(2). Thus, a dissolution may occur upon the withdrawal of a member even if the remaining members continue the business of the partnership.

[93] Unif. Partnership Act § 31(4), (5) (1914).

[94] Treas. Reg. § 301.7701-2(b)(1) (as amended in 1983).

[95] Rev. Unif. Limited Partnership Act § 801(4) (1985); Unif. Limited Partnership Act § 20 (1916).

[96] Treas. Reg. § 301.7701-2(d)(1) (as amended in 1983).

than its interest in the partnership, but the level of net worth a general partner must have to satisfy this requirement is unclear.[97] It may be necessary, therefore, to have an individual architect or contractor with substantial assets or a well-capitalized corporation serve as the general partner.

Alternatively, a general partner will be considered personally liable under the regulations if it is not a dummy acting as the agent of the limited partners. If either the architect or the general contractor acts as the general partner and does not own an interest as a limited partner, the general partner should not be viewed as an agent of the limited partners, and the partnership should lack limited liability.

Centralized Management

Centralized management exists if any person has continuing exclusive authority to make the management decisions necessary to conduct the partnership business. Because an act of either the architect or the contractor within the scope of the partnership business binds a design-build general partnership, such a partnership does not have centralized management. In the case of a limited partnership, centralized management ordinarily exists if substantially all of the interests in the partnership are owned by the limited partners. Therefore, a design-build limited partnership will have centralized management unless the general partner has a substantial interest in the partnership.[98]

Free Transferability of Interests

For free transferability of interests to exist, each of the partners of a partnership, or those owning substantially all of the interests in the partnership, must have the power, without the consent of other members of the partnership, to substitute in their place a person who is not a member of the partnership. This power of substitution does not exist if a member can, without the consent of other members, assign only its right to share in profits and not its right to participate in management. For obvious reasons, the partners in a design-build partnership would want to limit the transferability of

---

[97] *See* Rev. Proc. 89-12, 1989-1 C.B. 798. If the net worth of corporate general partners is at least 10 percent of the total contributions to the limited partnership, then, for advance ruling purposes, the partnerships will generally be deemed to lack limited liability. *Id.*

[98] The IRS will not issue a private ruling that a limited partnership lacks centralized management if the limited partners own in excess of 80 percent of the partnership. *See* Rev. Proc. 89-12, 1989-1 C.B. 798. For a discussion of the IRS' ruling standards under Rev. Proc. 89-12, see Howard, *Partnership Rulings Eased by New Limited Liability, Net Worth Tests,* 70 J. Tax'n 334–39 (1989).

partnership interests and the transferor's right of substitution. Therefore, avoiding the corporate characteristic of free transferability of interests will not harm the party's underlying economic agreement.

In sum, a general partnership that is formed to conduct design-build operations typically will lack the corporate characteristics of continuity of life, limited liability, centralized management, and free transferability of interests. A limited partnership formed for this purpose typically will lack continuity of life and free transferability of interests, and also may lack limited liability and/or centralized management. The favorable tax treatment according to partnerships will, therefore, usually be available to design-build partnerships and limited partnerships.

§ 4.16 —Taxation of Partnership Formation

Ordinarily, a design-build partnership would not own tangible assets. The partnership instead enters into a contract with the owner and arranges subcontracts for the actual construction work. The architect and contractor may form such a partnership by contributing cash in exchange for their partnership interests. Alternatively, the design-build partnership may perform some or all of the construction work, and the contractor may contribute the necessary equipment to the partnership in exchange for its partnership interest. In either case, the formation of the partnership ordinarily is not taxable to the architect, the contractor, or the partnership.

The contribution of money or property to a partnership generally is viewed as a mere change in the form in which business operations are conducted and is not taxable to the contributing partner.[99] Instead, the contributing partner takes a basis in its partnership interest equal to the basis of the contributed property.[100] If the contributed property is either a capital asset or depreciable property used in a trade or business, the partner's holding period for its partnership interest will include the period during which it held the contributed asset.[101]

Consistent with the view that the formation of a partnership is merely a change in form, the receipt of cash or property by the partnership also would not be taxable.[102] Instead, the partnership takes a basis in the contributed property equal to the property's basis in the hands of the contributing partner.[103] The partnership's holding period for contributed property

---

[99] I.R.C. § 721 (1991).

[100] *Id.* § 722.

[101] *Id.* § 1223(1).

[102] *Id.* § 721.

[103] *Id.* § 723.

will include the period during which such property was held by the contributing partner.[104]

In the vast majority of cases, the formation of a design-build partnership will not be taxable to the partners or the partnership. However, this general rule does not apply in two situations that are potentially relevant to design-build operations. The first exception would apply if, for example, the contractor contributed encumbered property to the partnership. Upon such a contribution, the contractor would receive a constructive distribution of cash equal to the amount of debt encumbering the property.[105] This constructive distribution would be taxable to the extent it exceeded the contractor's basis in its partnership interest.[106]

A second exception may apply if a partnership interest were issued in connection with the performance of services.[107] This exception would be relevant if, for example, the contractor contributed property to the partnership in exchange for a 50 percent interest in partnership capital and profits, and the architect agreed to perform any necessary professional services in exchange for a 50 percent interest in partnership capital and profits. The transfer of an interest in partnership profits and capital in exchange for services performed for the partnership is taxable, so the architect would be taxed upon receipt of the partnership interest.[108] The tax treatment of the transfer of an interest in partnership profits in exchange for services is not settled, but it is typical of the recipient of a profits interest to claim no immediate taxation because of the speculative value of the interest received.[109]

---

[104] *Id.* § 1223(2).

[105] I.R.C. § 752(b).

[106] *Id.* § 731(a).

[107] Any such transfer is not governed by the nonrecognition rule of I.R.C. § 721 because it is not a contribution of property.

[108] *See* United States v. Frazell, 335 F.2d 487, 489 (5th Cir. 1964), *cert. denied,* 380 U.S. 961 (1965); 1 W. McKee, W. Nelson, & R. Whitmire, Federal Taxation of Partnerships and Partners 915.01, at 5-2 (1990). The leading case on this issue, Diamond v. Commissioner, 56 T.C. 530 (1971), *aff'd,* 492 F.2d 286 (7th Cir. 1974), which held that a service partner's profit interests are taxable, has generated considerable controversy and commentary. *See, e.g.,* Robinson, *Diamond's Legacy—A New Perspective on the Sol Diamond Decision,* 61 Taxes 259 (1983).

[109] In Campbell v. Commissioner, 59 Tax Ct. Mem. Dec. (CCH) 236 (1990), *rev'd in part,* No. 9-2730, 943 F.2d 815 (8th Cir. 1991), the IRS persuaded the Tax Court that a service partner should be taxed on the receipt of partnership profits interests. The 8th Cir. Court of Appeals reversed the Tax Court's decision, holding that the profits Campbell received were without fair market value and, therefore, should not have been included in income. No. 9-2730, 943 F.2d 815 (8th Cir. 1991). The *Campbell* decision also has generated considerable commentary. *See, e.g.,* Townsend, *The Controversy Over Campbell: Slicing the Bologna too Thin,* 52 Tax Notes 83, 90 (1991).

The rules governing the formation of a partnership are similar to the rules governing the formation of a corporation, and the formation of a design-build corporation typically is not a taxable event. The rules governing the formation of a partnership are more flexible than the rules governing the formation of a corporation, and in certain circumstances these differences could be relevant. For example, the contribution of property to a corporation will result in current taxation if the debt encumbering the property exceeds the shareholder's basis in the property.[110] In contrast, a contributing partner would not be taxed currently on the contribution of encumbered property to a partnership if its basis in its partnership interest (which includes the basis of other contributed property and a share of certain partnership liabilities) exceeds the amount of debt assumed by the partnership. In addition, because stock ordinarily represents a claim against the corporation's capital as well as its future profits, the issuance of stock in connection with the performance of services could be taxable currently, whereas the issuance of an interest in partnership profits might not be.

§ 4.17 —Taxation of Operations

A corporation is treated as an entity separate from its shareholders for tax purposes and is taxed currently on its net income.[111] A partnership, in contrast, is simply a reporting entity that computes its taxable income, and each partner takes its allocable share of such income into account in determining its own income tax. A partnership's taxable income generally is computed in the same manner as that of an individual.[112] In computing its income, a partnership, like a corporation, may deal with the partners in their individual capacities.[113] Thus, a design-build partnership could pay fees to the architect or contractor for services they perform, and these fees

---

[110] I.R.C. § 357(c) (1991).

[111] The taxation of S-corporations is discussed in § **4.34**. The shareholders of a C-corporation are not to be taxed on the corporation's earnings, but they are taxed as distributions are made to them to the extent such distributions represent (1) corporate earnings and profits or (2) the return of capital in excess of basis.

[112] Because this income is reported on the partners' tax returns, however, items of income that could be subject to limitation on a partner's return (such as capital gains and losses, § 1231 gains and losses, and investment interest) must be separately stated and retain their separate character in the partner's hands. *See* I.R.C. § 702(a), (b). For example, an individual partner's share of investment interest incurred by the partnership would retain its character as investment interest in the partner's hands and would be deductible only to the extent that the partner's aggregate investment interest did not exceed its net investment income. In addition, a partnership is not allowed a deduction for such items as charitable contributions or personal exemptions. *See id.* § 703(a)(2)(C).

[113] *See* I.R.C. § 707(a), (c).

would be income to the recipient and, to the extent capitalization is not required, deductible to the partnership.

Once the design-build partnership's income or loss has been computed, it must be allocated among the partners.[114] This allocation ordinarily is governed by the partnership agreement.[115] The allocation of tax items set forth in the partnership agreement will be respected if it has "substantial economic effect" or is in accordance with the partners' interests in the partnership. If it does not, the Internal Revenue Service (IRS) may reallocate tax items in accordance with its determination of the partners' interests in the partnership.[116]

The IRS has issued a series of complex regulations for determining whether an allocation has substantial economic effect. These regulations apply a two-part test; first, the allocations must have "economic effect,"[117] and second, the allocations must be "substantial."[118] A meaningful discussion of these complex rules is beyond the scope of this work. It should be noted, however, that they accommodate a wide variety of transactions that are more difficult to arrange if design-build activities are conducted through the corporate form. For example, losses attributable to cost overruns on a fixed-price contract could be specifically allocated to the contractor, thereby reducing its capital account and the amount of cash the contractor would receive on liquidation of the partnership. This special allocation would, in effect, cause the contractor to suffer the economic (and tax) consequences associated with the cost overrun.

---

[114] It also is possible to "specially allocate" particular items of partnership income.

[115] I.R.C. § 704(a).

[116] *See id.* § 704(b); Treas. Reg. § 1.704-1(b)(1) (as amended in 1988).

[117] Treas. Reg. § 1.704-1(b)(2)(ii). An allocation will have economic effect if (1) throughout the full term of the partnership the partners properly maintain capital accounts; (2) upon liquidation of the partnership (or any partner's interest in the partnership), liquidation proceeds in all cases are distributed in accordance with the partners' capital account balances; and (3) following the liquidation of any partner's interest in the partnership, such partner is unconditionally liable to restore any deficit in its capital account. *Id.* If the partnership agreement contains a "qualified income offset," the absence of the duty to restore a deficit will not invalidate an allocation to a partner to the extent the allocation does not create or increase a deficit in the partner's capital account. *Id.* § 1.704-1(b)(2)(ii)(d). A partnership agreement contains a *qualified income offset* if it provides that a partner who unexpectedly receives an allocation or distribution that creates or increases a deficit in such partner's capital account will be allocated items of income and gain in an amount and manner sufficient to eliminate any deficit balance in such partner's capital account as quickly as possible. *Id.*

[118] Treas. Reg. § 1.704-1(b)(2)(iii). The economic effect of an allocation will be substantial if there is a reasonable possibility that the allocation will affect substantially the dollar amounts to be received by the partners from the partnership, independent of tax consequences. *Id.*

The rules governing partnership distributions also give the architect and contractor considerable flexibility that is difficult to match in a corporate setting. Partnership distributions need not be pro rata, and the architect and contractor are free to use preferential distributions that reflect the underlying economic transaction. For example, to reward the contractor for saving money on a fixed-price contract, the partnership agreement could make a preferential distribution of 75 percent of the cost savings to the contractor, with the remaining partnership cash flow being distributed on a pro rata basis.

Partnership operating distributions may be taxed more favorably than distributions from a corporation. Unless a corporation pays out all of its earnings as deductible interest, salaries, or bonuses, distributions that it makes to its shareholders are taxed as dividends to the extent of the corporation's current or accumulated earnings and profits.[119] Thus, unless the corporation zeros out its income, tax will be paid at the corporate level and at the shareholder level. In contrast, because partnership income flows through and is taxed to the partners, only one level of tax is paid. Partnership cash distributions are not taxable unless they exceed the recipient's basis in its partnership interest.[120] Distributions in excess of basis generally are eligible for favorable capital gains treatment.[121]

A design-build partnership usually does not own tangible property and, therefore, ordinarily will not make operating distributions of property. In the unusual situation in which the partnership performs some of the actual construction work and tangible property is distributed back to the contractor, the tax treatment compares favorably with the treatment accorded a design-build corporation, because operating distributions to a partner of partnership property generally are not taxable to the partnership or the recipient.[122]

§ 4.18 —Limitation of Flow-Through of Losses

Partnership income and loss flows through the partnership and is taxed to the partners. The tax consequences of flow-through treatment are particularly favorable if a design-build partnership expects to incur losses during its initial operating periods, because such losses may be available to the partners to offset their current income from other sources.[123] There are,

---

[119] I.R.C. § 316 (1991).

[120] *Id.* § 731(a).

[121] A portion of a distribution may be taxed as ordinary income if the partnership has "unrealized receivables" or "substantially appreciated inventory." *Id.* § 751.

[122] *See id.* § 731(b).

[123] In contrast, losses of a corporation may be carried to other years but are available only to offset the corporation's income.

however, several limitations that restrict the extent to which the architect or contractor may deduct properly allocated partnership losses.

First, regardless of whether the partnership is a cash or accrual basis taxpayer, long-term contracts generally must be accounted for using a modified percentage of completion method.[124] This accounting method in effect matches contract revenues with costs over the life of the contract. A partnership that is required to use this method may be less likely to incur a taxable loss that would flow through to the partners.

Second, the basis and at-risk rules may limit the extent to which the architect or contractor can deduct partnership losses.[125] These rules could apply if the partnership borrows money or if allocations and distributions are not made ratably in accordance with contributions.

Third, the *passive loss rules* may limit a partner's ability to utilize tax losses generated by a design-build partnership.[126] Under the passive loss rules, losses from passive activities, which generally are businesses in which the taxpayer does not "materially participate," are deductible only to the extent of income from those types of activities. Any disallowed passive losses are losses carried forward indefinitely to offset future income from those activities, including gain from the eventual disposition of the activity.

§ 4.19 —Taxation upon Liquidation

The liquidation of a design-build partnership typically involves collection of any amounts owed by the owner, payment of any amounts owed to the

---

[124] *See* I.R.C. § 460. For a discussion of the long-term contract rules, *see generally* Seago, *Final Look-Back Regs. Provide Practical and Simplified Procedures,* 73 J. Tax'n 384 (1990); Pollack, *IRC Section 460: Long-Term Construction Contract Issues,* 68 Taxes 30 (1990).

[125] A partner's adjusted basis in its interest initially equals the amount of cash and the basis of any property contributed to the partnership and is increased by the partner's share of items of partnership income and gain. I.R.C. § 705 (1991). In addition, under a complex set of rules, a partner may include in its basis a portion of certain partnership debts. *See id.* § 752; Treas. Reg. § 1.752-1T to 4T (as amended in 1989). A partner's basis is decreased by distributions of cash and property and by the partner's share of partnership losses and deductions. If a partner's share of partnership losses exceeds such partner's basis at the end of any taxable year, such excess loss may be carried over indefinitely and deducted to the extent that, at the end of any succeeding year, the partner's adjusted basis exceeds zero. *See* I.R.C. § 704(d). A taxpayer generally is considered to be at risk to the extent of (1) the amount of money and the adjusted basis of other property contributed to an activity, and (2) under limited circumstances, amounts borrowed for use in the activity. I.R.C. § 465(b). A taxpayer's amount at risk is reduced by its share of losses and cash distributions. *See id.* § 465(a). Losses in excess of the taxpayer's amount at risk are suspended and are carried over indefinitely and deducted to the extent that at the end of any succeeding year its amount at risk exceeds zero. *Id.*

[126] *See* I.R.C. § 469.

subcontractors, and distribution to the partners of any remaining cash. The distribution of cash would not be taxable to a partner, however, unless such distribution exceeds a partner's basis in its partnership interest.[127] In the case of a liquidating distribution of property, the architect or contractor would not recognize gain and would take a basis in the distributed property equal to the basis in its partnership interest, as reduced by any cash distributed in the same transaction.[128]

§ 4.20 —Taxation of Retirement Plans

Partnerships, like corporations, may maintain retirement plans. Such plans are accorded favorable tax treatment if certain qualification requirements are satisfied. Most notably, a partner generally may deduct the amount of contributions made by the partnership on such partner's behalf to a retirement plan.[129] In addition, earnings on the contributions may accumulate on a tax-free basis, so taxation of the contributions and earnings is deferred until distributions are made from the plan.

Partnership retirement plans generally are subject to more restrictive qualification rules than corporate retirement plans. In this regard, special rules apply to a partner who owns more than 10 percent of a partnership (a 10 percent partner), and it is likely that these rules would be relevant to partners in a design-build partnership.

If a 10 percent partner "controls" (or a group of 10 percent partners collectively "control") more than one business, the partnership retirement plan that covers the 10 percent partner(s) is aggregated with the retirement plans of all controlled businesses to determine whether the qualification requirements are satisfied.[130] "Control" means the ownership, by a 10 percent partner individually or by a group of 10 percent partners collectively, of (1) 100 percent of the interest in a sole proprietorship, or (2) more than 50 percent of the interest in a partnership.[131] If the control requirement is met, no plan may be established for any 10 percent partner unless a plan has been established for the employees of each other controlled business.[132] In addition, the plan for the employees of each other controlled business must provide contributions and benefits that are at least as favorable as those provided to any 10 percent partner.

---

[127] I.R.C. § 731(a).

[128] *Id.* § 732(b).

[129] I.R.C. § 62(a)(6); Treas. Reg. § 1.62-1T(c)(7) (as amended in 1990).

[130] I.R.C. § 401(d)(1)(A).

[131] *Id.* § 401(d)(1)(B).

[132] *Id.* § 401(d)(2).

Unlike a corporation, a 10 percent partner is prohibited from obtaining a loan from the retirement plan maintained by the partnership.[133] Such a loan is subject to a penalty tax, and the use of the 10 percent partner's plan benefits to secure such a loan is an impermissible assignment of plan benefits that disqualifies the retirement plan.[134]

§ 4.21 —Taxation of Fringe Benefits

A partnership may also provide partners with several types of fringe benefits. Fringe benefits that are excludable from a partner's income include: (1) death benefits of up to $5,000 if paid under a qualified plan, (2) "working condition fringe" benefits, such as company-provided automobiles for business use, under certain circumstances, periodicals, and memberships in professional organizations,[135] and (3) "de minimus fringe" benefits, such as occasional personal use of company secretarial service or equipment and occasional company parties or picnics.[136] However, the costs of the following types of fringe benefits are taxable to a recipient partner:

1. Premiums paid for accident and health insurance[137]
2. Death benefits not provided through a qualified pension or profit sharing plan
3. Certain group term life insurance[138]
4. Meals and lodging provided by the partnership for the convenience of the partnership.[139]

---

[133] *Id.* § 4975(d).

[134] *Id.* §§ 401(a)(13); 4975(a), (b).

[135] Treas. Reg. § 1.132-5(a)(1) (1989).

[136] *Id.* § 1.132-6(a).

[137] If the total amount of the expenses paid for medical care of the partner, his spouse, and dependents during a taxable year exceeds 7.5 percent of a partner's adjusted gross income, such partner may deduct the excess amount. I.R.C. § 213. A special rule also allows a partner to deduct 25 percent of the premiums paid for accident and health insurance, but this special rule is scheduled to expire after June 30, 1992. I.R.C. § 162(l). A partnership, however, may deduct all of the premiums paid for accident and health insurance on behalf of partners. *See* Rev. Rul. 91-26, 1991-15 I.R.B. 23.

[138] I.R.C. § 79(a); Treas. Reg. § 1.79-0 (as amended in 1983).

[139] The majority view is that the exclusion under I.R.C. § 119 of the value of meals and lodging furnished for the employer's convenience only applies to common law employees and not to partners. *See* Wilson v. United States, 376 F.2d 280, 296 (Ct. Cl. 1967). One court has held, however, that a partner could exclude from his income the value of meals and lodging provided by the partnership for the convenience of the partnership if he performed services for the partnership in the capacity of an employee rather than a partner. Armstrong v. Phinney, 394 F.2d 661 (5th Cir. 1968).

Moreover, unlike a corporation, a partnership is precluded from maintaining a cafeteria plan that permits participants to choose between cash and one or more types of tax-free fringe benefits.

§ 4.22 Corporation Format

When the architect and contractor form a corporation to conduct design-build operations, a variety of issues arises. The principal advantage to conducting design-build operations through a corporation is insulation from liability. This advantage may be offset, however, by the unfavorable tax consequences of doing business through the corporate form.

A corporation is an entity created under state law and generally is treated as a separate legal being from its shareholder owners. Thus, shareholders generally are not responsible for the debts or liabilities of the corporation. Further, the corporate existence is unaffected by the death of a shareholder or the transfer by a shareholder of corporate stock. Most corporations (so-called C-corporations) also are treated as separate legal entities for tax purposes and are taxable on their net income, and a second level of tax is imposed when earnings are distributed to shareholders. Certain qualifying corporations (S-corporations) may, however, elect flow-through tax treatment similar to that accorded to partnerships.

§ 4.23 —Formation and Maintenance

A corporation is formed by filing a certificate of incorporation with the appropriate state officials.[140] This filing typically is accompanied by a filing fee, which is based on the corporation's capital structure.[141] The incorporation process also involves an organizational meeting at which the directors of the corporation are elected.[142] Once the corporation is organized, its affairs are governed by the laws of the state of incorporation and by its certificate of incorporation and its by-laws.[143] Corporations usually pay annual franchise taxes to the state of incorporation and are required to

---

[140] *See, e.g.*, Delaware General Corporation Law, Del. Code Ann. tit. 8, § 101 (1983 & Supp. 1990).

[141] *See, e.g.*, *id.* § 391.

[142] In some states, the initial directors may be named in the certificate of incorporation. *See id.* §§ 102(a)(6), 107, 108. *See also* E. Folk, R. Ward, & E. Welch, Folk on the Delaware General Corporation Law 14 (1988).

[143] *See* E. Folk, R. Ward, & E. Welch, Folk on the Delaware General Corporation Law 40–54 (1988).

qualify in each state (other than the state of incorporation) in which they do business.[144]

§ 4.24 —Limited Liability

A major advantage of conducting design-build operations through the corporate form is limited liability.[145] In general, shareholders of a corporation are not responsible for the corporation's debts or liabilities.[146] Thus, a shareholder ordinarily is at risk only to the extent of its stock or debt investment in the corporation.

The attribute of limited liability may not be available in all cases, however. For example, an owner or surety may require the architect or contractor to guarantee the performance of the corporation, and lenders frequently require the shareholders of a closely held corporation to guarantee the corporation's debts. In addition, in certain circumstances courts may "pierce the corporate veil" and hold shareholders responsible for liabilities of the corporation.[147] Further, even if design-build operations were incorporated, the architect and contractor remain exposed to potential tort liability for services provided to the corporation.

Performing design-build operations through a corporation complicates the task of obtaining adequate insurance coverage. Professional liability insurance is unavailable to contractors and may be unavailable to a corporation performing design-build operations.[148] In addition, the architect's professional liability policy ordinarily would exclude projects in which the architect holds an equity interest.[149] Thus, unless a policy is specifically tailored to the project, both the corporation and the architect may be uninsured with respect to design defects.

§ 4.25 —Management and Licensing Issues

A corporation's affairs are governed by the laws of the state of incorporation and by the corporation's charter and by-laws. The corporation's

---

[144] *See, e.g.,* Delaware General Corporation Law, Del. Code Ann. tit. 8, § 371 (1983 & Supp. 1990).

[145] *See* W. Cary, Corporations 22–25 (1969).

[146] *See* Delaware General Corporation Law, Del. Code Ann. tit. 8, § 325 (1983 & Supp. 1990); E. Folk, R. Ward, & E. Welch, Folk on the Delaware General Corporation Law 344–47 (1988); Amsted Indus. v. Pollak Indus., 382 N.E.2d 393 (Ill. App. Ct. 1978).

[147] *See* H. Henn & J. Alexander, Laws of Corporations 344–52 (1983 & Supp. 1986).

[148] *See* Twomey at 139.

[149] *Id.*

shareholders do not directly participate in the management of the corporation, although certain corporate actions, such as amendment of the corporate charter, require shareholder approval.[150] Instead, they elect directors who as a group are responsible for the management of the corporation.[151] The directors, in turn, appoint officers, who are agents of the corporation and carry on the business of the corporation.[152] It is not unusual in a closely held corporation for a shareholder to serve as an officer and director.

Each share of stock is generally entitled to one vote in the election of directors.[153] In the design-build context, this arrangement may not be satisfactory if, for example, one party owns a minority interest but wants to participate equally in the management of the corporation. To accommodate this situation, the corporation could issue two or more classes of stock with different voting rights, or the architect and contractor could enter into a voting trust or shareholders' agreement.[154] These arrangements will likely be satisfactory to achieve the desired sharing in management but generally are more cumbersome to structure than a similar arrangement in a partnership. Whether design-build operations are conducted through a corporation or a partnership, the architect and contractor should have a buy/sell agreement or some other exit mechanism in place in the event that irreconcilable differences arise.

Licensing problems also arise when design-build operations are conducted through the corporate form. If a design-build corporation is not properly licensed, it may be unable to recover for all or a portion of the services rendered to the owner.[155] In certain states, general business corporations may not perform architectural services.[156] It may be possible to avoid this problem in some states if the corporation merely agrees to "furnish" such services through a licensed architect rather than agreeing to "perform" them.[157]

---

[150] *See, e.g.*, Delaware General Corporation Law, Del. Code Ann. tit. 8, §§ 109, 242, 271, 273 (1983 & Supp. 1990).

[151] *See, e.g., id.* § 141.

[152] *See, e.g., id.* § 142.

[153] *See, e.g., id.* § 212.

[154] *See, e.g., id.* § 218(c).

[155] *See* Food Management, Inc. v. Blue Ribbon Beef Pack, Inc., 413 F.2d 716 (8th Cir. 1969) (denying recovery for portion of contract attributable to engineering services performed in violation of licensing requirements).

[156] *See* West Baton Rouge Parish School Bd. v. T.R. Ray, Inc., 367 So. 2d 332 (La. 1979) (citing Louisiana statute which requires two-thirds of shareholders of corporation to be licensed as architects if corporation is to perform professional services).

[157] *See* Seaview Hosp. v. Medicenters of Am., 570 S.W.2d 35, 39–40 (Tex. Ct. App. 1978) (holding contract valid when services were furnished by corporation through licensed architect rather than performed by corporation).

§ 4.26 —Free Transferability

One attribute of a corporation that frequently is viewed as desirable is that corporate stock usually is freely transferable. The architect and contractor likely would consider this attribute to be a disadvantage, however, because each has an obvious interest in selecting its business partner. Accordingly, the architect and contractor should consider restricting stock transfers in the charter, by-laws, or in a shareholders' agreement.[158]

§ 4.27 —Corporate Tax Considerations

Corporations are separate legal entities for federal income tax purposes and are taxed on their net income.[159] In addition, the shareholders pay a second level of tax when corporate earnings are distributed. Further, in certain circumstances, the rules governing events such as formation and liquidation are less favorable than in the partnership setting. Consequently, conducting design-build operations through a corporation may result in less favorable tax results than if such operations are conducted through a partnership. An overview of the principal rules of corporate taxation is set forth below.

§ 4.28 —Taxation at Formation of Corporation

Shareholders generally will not be taxed when they contribute cash or property to a corporation solely in exchange for stock of such corporation.[160] In order to qualify for nonrecognition treatment, the contributing shareholders taken as a group must control the corporation after the transfer.[161] The control requirement ordinarily is not a concern on the initial formation of a corporation. Thus, the formation of a design-build corporation typically will not be taxable.

There are, of course, exceptions to the nonrecognition treatment. For example, gain is recognized if, for any particular shareholder, the corporation

---

[158] *See* Delaware General Corporation Law, Del. Code Ann. tit. 8, § 202 (1983 & Supp. 1990) (authorizing certain restrictions on the transfer of shares).

[159] H. Henn & J. Alexander, Laws of Corporations 132–38 (1983 & Supp. 1986). For a comprehensive review of the taxation of corporations, see B. Bittker & J. Eustice, Federal Income Taxation of Corporations and Shareholders (1987).

[160] I.R.C. § 351 (1991).

[161] *Control* is defined for this purpose as ownership of at least 80 percent of the total combined voting power of all voting stock and at least 80 percent of all other classes of stock of the corporation. I.R.C. § 368(c).

assumes debt or takes property subject to debt that exceeds the aggregate basis of property contributed.[162] In addition, in contrast to the issuance of an interest in partnership profits, about which the law is unsettled, the issuance of stock in exchange for services may be taxable.[163]

If property is contributed in a nonrecognition transaction to a corporation, the shareholder's basis in the stock received equals the basis of the contributed property minus the value of any other property and money transferred to the shareholder, plus any income recognized by the shareholder.[164] If the shareholder contributes a capital asset or a trade or business asset, the holding period of the stock received includes the holding period of the contributed asset.[165] The basis to the corporation of contributed property equals the basis of such property in the hands of the shareholder, plus any gain recognized by the shareholder.[166] In addition, the corporation's holding period for contributed property includes the period such property was held by the contributing shareholder.[167]

The foregoing rules are similar to the rules governing the formation of a partnership; the most notable difference is that partners need not be in control of a partnership in order for the nonrecognition provisions to apply. This ordinarily would not be a concern in the formation of a design-build corporation, because both the architect and the contractor would be contributing money or property, and together they would control the corporation. A problem could arise, however, if the corporate form is selected and the architect and contractor later decide to admit another shareholder. That shareholder usually would not control the corporation and, therefore, would not be able to contribute property on a tax-free basis.

§ 4.29 —Taxation of Operations

A corporation is a separate legal entity for federal income tax purposes. As such, it is taxed on its net income at graduated rates of up to 34 percent.[168] In contrast to the treatment of partnerships, losses incurred by a design-build corporation would not be available to the architect or contractor to offset income from other sources.[169] Instead, such losses may be carried

---

[162] I.R.C. § 357(c).

[163] *Id.* § 351(d).

[164] *Id.* § 358(a).

[165] *Id.* § 1223(1).

[166] *Id.* § 362(b).

[167] *Id.* § 1223(2).

[168] I.R.C. § 11(b) (1991).

[169] The taxation of electing S-corporations is discussed in § **4.34**.

back to offset income earned by the corporation in the preceding three years or carried forward to offset income earned in the succeeding 15 years.[170]

Distributions by a design-build corporation may be taxable to the architect and contractor.[171] Distributions are taxed as dividends if such distributions are attributable to current or accumulated earnings and profits.[172] Distributions in excess of current and accumulated earnings and profits are considered first to be a return of the shareholder's basis in its stock.[173] Any distributions in excess of the shareholder's basis are treated as gain from the constructive sale of stock.[174]

A simplified example illustrates the consequences of the second level of corporate taxation. Assume a design-build entity earns $100, pays its tax liability, and distributes the remainder to its individual owners, the architect and contractor. If the entity is a partnership, there is no entity level taxation. Accordingly, architect and contractor each receive $50 cash, and each has $50 of taxable income that could result in tax liability of $15.50. This leaves the partner with $34.50 of after-tax cash flow.

On the other hand, if the entity is a corporation, it could owe $34 of tax, leaving only $66 to distribute. Architect and contractor each would receive $33 of cash, which would result in $10.23 of tax. This leave architect and contractor with only $22.77 of after-tax cash flow. The consequences of paying tax at both the corporate and shareholder level may be reduced or eliminated if the corporation is able to pay out substantially all of its income as deductible interest, salaries, and bonuses.

A second level of tax also would be imposed if a design-build corporation distributed appreciated property.[175] This situation could arise if the contractor contributed property to a design-build corporation in order to enable the corporation to perform some of the actual construction. If the fair market value of the property exceeds its tax basis when it is returned to the contractor, the corporation would recognize gain on the distribution. Further, any such gain would generate current earnings and profits, possibly causing the distribution to be treated as a dividend to the contractor.[176] In contrast, a distribution of appreciated property by a partnership ordinarily is not taxable.

---

[170] I.R.C. § 172.

[171] *Id.* § 301. A dividends received deduction may be available to corporate recipients of dividends. *See id.* § 243.

[172] *Id.* §§ 301(c), 316.

[173] *Id.* § 301(c)(2).

[174] *Id.* § 301(c)(3).

[175] *Id.* § 311(b).

[176] I.R.C. § 312(b).

§ 4.30 —Taxation upon Liquidation

As a result of the Tax Reform Act of 1986, a corporation recognizes gain or loss on a liquidating distribution of its assets.[177] Thus, a corporation generally is taxed in the same manner whether it sells its assets and distributes the cash or distributes the assets in kind to the shareholders. Amounts received by the shareholders of a corporation in a distribution in complete liquidation are treated as received in exchange for their corporate stock.[178] Thus, the shareholders generally recognize capital gain or loss on the liquidation of the corporation.

One exception to these rules applies in the case of a complete liquidation of a subsidiary. This exception only is available, however, if the parent corporation owns at least 80 percent of the voting power and 80 percent of the value of the stock of the subsidiary.[179] Consequently, this preferential nonrecognition treatment may not be available to a corporation formed to conduct design-build operations either because no shareholder owns the requisite percentage of stock or because the shareholders are not corporations.

§ 4.31 —Reducing the Second Level of Taxation

A number of steps are available to the architect and contractor to reduce or eliminate the second level of taxation that is characteristic of the treatment of corporations. One simple strategy involves making deductible payments of salaries, bonuses, or fees to the shareholders, thereby reducing or eliminating the corporation's taxable income. In order to be deductible, however, such payments must be reasonable in amount.[180] A similar strategy would involve capitalizing the corporation with debt rather than equity so that profits may be paid out as interest or leasing property to the corporation rather than contributing it in exchange for stock.

Alternatively, dividends received by the architect or contractor may be eligible for the "dividends received" deduction.[181] If the recipient and the distributing corporation are members of the same affiliated group of corporations, the dividend is entirely eliminated by the deduction. The amount of the dividend that is offset by the deduction falls to 80 percent if the recipient owns 20 percent or more of (by vote and value) the distributing corporation,

---

[177] I.R.C. § 336. Gain or loss is not recognized if the liquidating distribution is made to a corporation that owns 80 percent or more of the stock of the distributing corporation. *See id.* § 337.

[178] *Id.* § 331(a).

[179] *Id.* § 337.

[180] I.R.C. § 162(a) (1991).

[181] *Id.* § 243.

and it falls to 70 percent if the recipient owns less than 20 percent of the distributing corporation.

The unfavorable aspects of the second level of taxation are nearly eliminated if the design-build corporation files a consolidated return with a corporate shareholder. Such a return could be filed if a corporate shareholder owns 80 percent of the voting power and 80 percent of the value of the stock of the corporation.[182] In such a case, the design-build corporation would not be taxed separately, and its income would be included in computing the income of the consolidated group.[183] Further, any losses incurred by the design-build corporation would be available to offset income earned by other members of the group.

§ 4.32 —Taxation of Retirement Plans

As with a partnership retirement plan, a retirement plan maintained by a corporation is accorded favorable tax treatment if certain qualification requirements are satisfied.

Contributions to the plan by a corporation generally may be deducted by the corporation.[184] Further, earnings on the contributions may accumulate on a tax-free basis, so taxation of the contributions and earnings generally is deferred until distributions are made from the plan.

Corporate retirement plans are subject to less restrictive qualification rules than partnership retirement plans. Retirement plans of a "controlled group" of corporations are aggregated and treated as a single plan for determining whether the qualifications requirements are satisfied. A *controlled group* generally means parent-subsidiary corporations or brother-sister corporations connected through 80 percent common stock ownership.[185] In contrast, a broader aggregation rule applies to partnership plans that cover a 10 percent partner.

Unlike a partner, a shareholder-employee covered by a corporate retirement plan, except for a shareholder who owns 50 percent or more of a corporation, may obtain a loan from the plan using his or her account balance as security for the loan, subject to the plan loan rules.[186]

Certain stock-based plans, by their nature, can only be maintained by a corporation and not by a partnership. These include employee stock ownership plans, stock bonus plans, cash or deferred arrangements that are part

---

[182] *Id.* §§ 1501, 1504.

[183] *See id.* § 1502 and the treasury regulations promulgated thereunder.

[184] I.R.C. § 404 (1991).

[185] *Id.* § 414(b).

[186] *Id.* § 4975(d).

of stock bonus plans, incentive stock options, nonqualified stock options, and stock appreciation rights.

§ 4.33 —Taxation of Fringe Benefits

In the fringe benefits area, a corporation enjoys significantly more tax advantages than a partnership. In addition to those benefits available to a partnership, a corporation generally may deduct, and its shareholder employees may exclude from income, the costs of all of the following fringe benefits:

1. Premiums paid for accident and health insurance[187]
2. Cost of up to $50,000 of group term life insurance[188]
3. Death benefits not in excess of $5,000
4. Meals and lodging provided by the employer for the convenience of the employer[189]
5. Fringe benefits provided under a cafeteria plan.[190]

§ 4.34 —Subchapter S Corporations

An S-corporation is simply a qualifying small business corporation that has elected to be taxed under Subchapter S of the Internal Revenue Code.[191] Thus, except for the tax considerations described below, the issues that are relevant to the formation and operation of a design-build C-corporation apply equally to a design-build S-corporation.

With certain limited exceptions, Subchapter S provides for flow-through treatment of the corporation's items of income and deduction, thereby eliminating the second level of tax that is characteristic of corporate taxation.[192] There are, however, restrictions on eligibility to elect S-corporation status. These restrictions, generally designed to limit favorable tax treatment under Subchapter S of the Internal Revenue Code to closely-held corporations, in many cases makes the S-corporation unsuitable for design-build projects.

---

[187] I.R.C. §§ 106, 162 (1991).

[188] *Id.* §§ 79, 162.

[189] *Id.* §§ 119, 162.

[190] *Id.* §§ 125, 162.

[191] I.R.C. § 1361(a) (1991).

[192] *Id.* §§ 1363, 1366. For a comprehensive review of the taxation of S-corporations, see J. Eustice & J. Kuntz, Federal Income Taxation of S Corporations (1985).

Eligibility for Subchapter S Treatment

Congress enacted Subchapter S to permit the operation of small businesses in the corporate form without the incidence of taxation at both the corporate and the shareholder levels.[193] Consistent with this policy, an S-corporation may not have more than 35 shareholders.[194] In addition, only individuals (other than nonresident aliens) and certain estates and trusts may hold stock of an S-corporation. Further, an S-corporation may not be a member of an affiliated group of corporations and, therefore, it may not own 80 percent or more of the stock of another corporation. Finally, an S-corporation may not have more than one class of stock, and the shareholders of the corporation must bear corporate income and loss in accordance with their proportionate stock ownership.[195]

Two of these limitations may eliminate the S-corporation from consideration as a design-build entity. First, because only individuals and certain estates and trusts may hold stock of an S-corporation, this form of ownership would not be available if either the contractor or the architect is a corporation or a partnership. Second, in many cases the contractor and architect would want to use varying allocations of income and loss and preferred returns of cash flow. Such arrangements could violate the one class of stock requirement and, therefore, could terminate or invalidate the corporation's S election.

Formation

The rules that govern the formation of a C-corporation also govern the formation of an S-corporation. Thus, in contrast to a partnership, the architect and contractor must be in control of the corporation after the contribution to receive nonrecognition treatment. The control requirement ordinarily is not a problem on initial formation but could be troublesome if an additional shareholder is admitted subsequently. In addition, an S-corporation shareholder will recognize gain upon the contribution of encumbered property subject to liabilities in excess of basis, whereas a partner may not be taxed upon such a contribution to a partnership.[196]

---

[193] S. Rep. No. 640, 97th Cong., 2d Sess. (1982).

[194] I.R.C. § 1361(b).

[195] For a discussion of recently proposed regulations dealing with the one class of stock requirement, see Bolling, *Treasury's Attempted Repeal of Subchapter S: An Analysis of the "One Class of Stock" Proposed Regulation,* 69 Taxes 236 (1991).

[196] I.R.C. §§ 357(c), 721.

Operations

Although both partnerships and S-corporations offer flow-through treatment, partnerships nevertheless are taxed under a more favorable regime. For example, income and loss of an S-corporation flow through to the shareholders pro rata based upon their stock ownership.[197] Partnerships, on the other hand, offer considerable flexibility in allocating income and loss. Further, losses of an S-corporation are deductible to the extent of the shareholder's basis in the stock and debt of the corporation, but such basis does not include any portion of the corporation's debts to third parties.[198] In contrast, a partner's basis in its partnership interest may include a share of the partnership's debts.[199]

Cash distributions by an S-corporation are not taxable unless such distributions exceed the shareholder's basis in the stock.[200] Because a partner may include certain partnership debts in the basis of its interest while an S-corporation shareholder may not, cash distributions are less likely to be taxed currently to a partner than to an S-corporation shareholder. Further, distributions of appreciated property by a partnership generally are not taxable, whereas distributions of such property by an S-corporation result in gain which passes through to the shareholders.

Liquidation

The rules that govern the liquidation of C-corporations also control the liquidation of S-corporations. Thus, an S-corporation will be taxed on a liquidating distribution of its assets as if such assets had been sold at their fair market value, and any resulting gain will flow through and be taxed to the shareholders.[201] In contrast, partnerships generally are not subject to tax on liquidating distributions of property.

Retirement Plans

Although the law is unclear, the majority view is that retirement plans of an S-corporation generally are subject to the qualification rules applicable to retirement plans of a C-corporation rather than those applicable to a

---

[197] *Id.* §§ 1366(a)(1), 1377.

[198] *Id.* § 1366.

[199] *Id.* § 752(a).

[200] *Id.* § 1368(b).

[201] *Id.* § 336(a).

partnership.[202] Therefore, the discussion in § **4.32** on the qualification rules that govern corporate retirement plans also applies to retirement plans maintained by an S-corporation, except that plan loans to an S-corporation shareholder generally are prohibited.[203]

Unlike a corporation, an S-corporation is precluded from maintaining an employee stock ownership plan which purchases its stock because such a plan cannot be an S-corporation shareholder. In addition, an S-corporation's maintenance of a stock bonus plan or issuance of incentive and nonqualified stock options could cause the number of its shareholders to exceed 35, resulting in the termination of its S status.

Fringe Benefits

In the case of fringe benefits other than retirement plan benefits, S-corporation shareholders generally are treated like partners.[204] Therefore, the discussion in § **4.33** on the tax treatment of fringe benefits (other than retirement plan benefits) provided to a partner generally also apply to an S-corporation shareholder.

§ 4.35 Special Retirement Rules for Multiple Business Entities

If the design-build entity is organized by two or more business entities (the *organizing entities*), the organizing entities and the design-build entity may be subject to the special rules that apply to "leased employees," "affiliated service group," "controlled group of corporations," or "commonly controlled trades or businesses" for purposes of testing certain qualification requirements imposed on retirement plans. These rules are designed to prevent employers from evading the qualification requirements by establishing multiple business entities.

Leased Employees

The organizing entities may lease their employees to the design-build entity. Because such employees perform services on behalf of the organizing

---

[202] *See, e.g.*, Wile, *Limitations on Fringe Benefits Provided by S Corporations and Partnerships,* 43 Tax Notes 479 (1989).

[203] I.R.C. § 4975(d). This prohibition does not apply to a shareholder who owns 5 percent or less of an S-corporation.

[204] *Id.* § 1372(a)(1). However, shareholders who own less than 2 percent of an S-corporation are treated like shareholders of a C-corporation. *Id.* § 1372(a)(2).

entities for the design-build entity, they remain employees of the organizing entities and may continue to accrue benefits under the retirement plans of the organizing entities. On the other hand, if the employees terminate their employment with the organizing entities and become employees of the design-build entity, their accrued benefits under the retirement plans of the organizing entities may be reduced or eliminated due to the break in service with the organizing entities.

If the employees of the organizing entities perform services for the design-build entity under the leasing arrangement on a substantially full-time basis for at least one year ("leased employees"), the design-build entity generally may be required to treat the leased employees as its own employees for most retirement plan purposes,[205] regardless of whether any one of the organizing entities or the design-build entity is a partnership, a corporation, or a sole proprietorship.[206] In such case, the benefits provided under the organizing entities' retirement plans that are attributable to services performed for the design-build entity are treated as provided by the design-build entity.[207]

Affiliated Service Group

If one or more of the organizing entities and the design-build entity constitute an *affiliated service group,* employees of all of the entities will be treated as employed by a single employer for most retirement plan purposes,[208] regardless of whether any one of the organizing entities or the design-build entity is a partnership, a corporation, or a sole proprietorship.[209]

In general, an organizing entity and the design-build entity constitute an affiliated service group if the design-build entity is a "service organization" and:

1. The organizing entity is a *service organization* that regularly performs services for the design-build entity or is regularly associated with the design-build entity in performing services for third parties
2. A significant portion of the organizing entity's business is the performance of services for the design/build entity, those services are

[205] I.R.C. §§ 414(n)(1)(A), (n)(2) (1991); Prop. Treas. Reg. § 1.414(n)-1(a), -2(a) 52 Fed. Reg. 32502 (1988).

[206] Prop. Treas. Reg. §§ 1.414(n)-1(b)(1), (2), (6).

[207] I.R.C. § 414(n)(1)(B); Prop. Treas. Reg. § 1.414(n)-2(b).

[208] I.R.C. § 414(m)(1); Prop. Treas. Reg. § 1.414(m)-1.

[209] Prop. Treas. Reg. §§ 1.414(m)-2(e), -5(a)(2).

historically performed by employees in the service field of the design/build entity, and 10 percent or more of the interests in the organizing entity is held by highly compensated employees of the design/build entity

3. The principal business of the organizing entity is performing management functions for the design-build entity on a regular and continuing basis.[210]

For purposes of the affiliated service group rule, a service organization includes an organization that provides architectural, engineering, or consulting services and an organization for which capital is not a material income-producing factor.[211] A design-build entity most likely would be considered a service organization.

Controlled Group of Corporations

The employees of an organizing entity and the design-build entity will also be treated as employed by a single employer for most retirement plan purposes if the organizing entity and the design/build entity constitute a *controlled group of corporations.*[212] A controlled group of corporations is found when the organizing entity and the design-build entity are corporations connected through 80 percent stock ownership interests.

Commonly Controlled Trades or Businesses

In addition, the employees of an organizing entity and the design-build entity will be treated as employed by a single employer for most retirement plan purposes if the organizing entity and the design-build entity constitute *commonly controlled trades or businesses.*[213] The organizing entity and the design-build entity generally constitute commonly controlled trades or businesses if they are connected through 80 percent ownership interests and (1) the organizing entity and the design-build entity are both partnerships, (2) one entity is a partnership and the other entity is a corporation, or (3) the organizing entity is a sole proprietorship and the design-build entity is a partnership or a corporation.

---

[210] I.R.C. §§ 414(m)(2), (m)(5); Prop. Treas. Reg. §§ 1.414(m)-2, -5.

[211] Prop. Treas. Reg. § 1.414(m)-2(f).

[212] I.R.C. § 414(b); Treas. Reg. § 1.414(b)-1 (1988).

[213] I.R.C. § 414(c); Treas. Reg. §§ 1.414(c)-1, -2, -3, -4, -5 (1988).

§ 4.36 Summary of Tax and Business Considerations

An architect or a contractor may choose among a variety of formats when constructing a project using the design-build method. The architect or the contractor may contract directly with the owner and enter into a subcontract with the other. Otherwise, the architect and the contractor may create a partnership (general or limited), or one or both of them may create a corporation to perform design-build services.

The choice of format will depend upon a variety of factors. Important considerations are:

1. What form of entity are the architect and the contractor
2. Will the architect or the contractor be in control of the project
3. Will this be the only design-build project or the first of many
4. What are the licensing considerations for the architect and the contractor
5. What are the insurance implications of the choice of format
6. Which format offers the best protection from liability
7. What format will be the least expensive and most convenient to create and administer
8. Which format offers the most advantageous tax consequences.

It is impossible to choose the best format without analyzing the circumstances surrounding a particular project. The issues discussed in this chapter should be helpful, however, in determining which format is best.

The information in **Table 4–1** sums up the tax and business factors that should be considered by the parties when deciding the form of organization to pursue.

Table 4–1

Summary of Tax and Business Considerations

	Limited Partnership	General Partnership	S-Corporation	C-Corporation
Tax Treatment:	Flow-through entity; only one level of income tax.		Generally a flow-through entity, with one level of income tax, except for certain distributions of property and financing proceeds.	Separate taxable entity; two levels of tax except to the extent profits are paid to shareholders as salaries or bonuses.
Liability:	General Partner is personally liable for obligations of partnership. Minimally capitalized corporation may be general partner, but could jeopardize tax characterization as partnership.	All partners personally liable for obligations of partnership.	Shareholders not liable for obligations of corporation, but shareholders may often be required to sign personally for corporation debts.	
Management and Control:	Day-do-day management is by general partner, but general partner can be an entity jointly controlled by several owners.	Management can be divided among owners by terms of partnership agreement.	Shareholders elect directors, who appoint officers, who are in charge of day-to-day management.	
Retirement Plans & Fringe Benefits:	Subject to more stringent rules for qualified retirement plans and tax-free fringe benefits. For example, a 10% or more partner cannot receive a loan from retirement plan.		In general, an S-corporation is under C-corporation rules for retirement plans, but under partnership rules for fringe benefit provisions.	C-corporations generally can provide more tax-free fringe benefits and have less stringent rules for qualifying a retirement plan. For example, using a C-corporation allows full deductibility of health insurance costs.

CHAPTER 5

BONDING DESIGN-BUILD CONTRACTS

Kenneth N. Ryan

Kenneth N. Ryan is the executive vice president and manager of Willis Corroon's Construction Industry Division in Los Angeles, California. He provides consulting and brokering services in bonding, project financing, owner controlled, and privatized projects. Mr. Ryan received a B.A. from St. Martins College and a J.D. from Gonzaga Law School. Mr. Ryan has lectured and written extensively throughout the U.S. and Europe on his specialities for numerous construction and related industry associations and firms.

§ 5.1 Surety Fundamentals

This chapter may be shortest in this book because surety companies are not interested in bonding design-build contracts. The primary reason is simple: they are not willing to accept the design performance exposure. The real reason, however, is much more complicated and will be explained in this chapter.

Before attempting to explore the sureties' rationale, it is very important that the reader have a clear understanding of suretyship. Surety (bonding) is rooted in the principles of finance and credit, not in the fundamentals of insurance or the laws of probability. The rules of finance and credit require that a principal possess the ability and commitment to perform the obligation to be bonded by the surety. Additionally, the principal must have the financial capability to indemnify the surety if the surety is required to pay or perform as a result of a default by the principal. Therefore, the surety must thoroughly examine the principal's business to evaluate its ability to provide indemnification.

Over the years, suretyship has produced some confusion or, perhaps, mystery, in part because insurance companies are sureties rather than banks (a fluke of history). That confusion is further compounded by the fact that no money is actually loaned; only unsecured credit is extended.

Historically, surety underwriters have used the 3 Cs—capital, capacity, and character—of credit to prequalify a principal. The surety, like a bank extending a loan, must be convinced that the borrower or principal has the financial strength to repay the loan or perform the transaction. The surety does this by analyzing whether the principal has an organization sufficiently staffed and focused to perform the contract that is to be bonded. It also analyzes whether the principal will honor all of the commitments made under the contract. The significant point is that the surety must be comfortable that the principal can financially, organizationally, and managerially perform the contract for the obligee, who is traditionally the owner of the project.

It is essential for the reader to understand these fundamentals. If there is a lack of appreciation of these basics, then the ability of the contractor (principal) or its organization to comply and maintain a meaningful surety relationship will be impossible. It may be easier to understand if the reader could imagine why a bank would lend a borrower money if the banker knew in advance that the borrower had no intent or ability to pay back the loan. The surety, in the same way, must be convinced the contractor can perform the contract.

In the case of design-build, many of the sureties are very skeptical that a traditional construction firm possesses the necessary design skills in-house to complete the project. This would even be true if there were a joint venture between an architect/engineer (A/E) firm and a contractor. The surety is just not sure of the design exposure or even how to measure it. We will explore later in this chapter some suggestions to ease this skepticism.

§ 5.2 The Bond

Let's take a minute to look at the bond issued by the surety to the obligee (owner) and examine what exactly it does. The bond simply stated, promises to the owner that if the contractor fails to perform per the terms and conditions of the contract, the surety will. The bond adheres to the construction contract with all its provisions. If the contractor (principal) performs and the owner pays according to the terms of the contract, then the surety's obligation is terminated.

There are a great many legal cases that could be cited to point out some of the legal ramifications surrounding this triparty agreement. Without going into a legal dissertation, the most fundamental of the legal elements surrounding bonding are:

A surety will be responsible to an owner (obligee) if the contractor (principal) breaches its agreement or is terminated on the contract.

A surety is responsible to the owner (obligee) even if the contractor (principal) fails to pay the premium. The reason is that the consideration for the bond is the obligee's change in position by entering into the contract with the principal.

Misrepresentation by the principal does not invalidate or void the surety bond. The obligee may enforce the bond against the surety unless the obligee was a party to the fraud or misstatement.

A surety has the right to subrogate against the principal if it pays the obligee. This right can be enforced in the name of the obligee or the surety.

Not all defenses against the obligee that are available to the principal are also available to the surety.

Historically, most of the public works in the U.S. have been awarded to the low bidder. The *low bidder* is the firm that submits the lowest price for the work to be done according to the terms and conditions of the contract. This system has been perpetuated because it maintains a competitive objectivity and generally works to the benefit of the owner. In reality however, there have been some real horror stories, such as cost overruns, excessive change orders, poor quality materials and workmanship, as well as bid rigging and kickbacks. Part of the reason for these failures is that the competition among the bidders can be fierce. A review of the process shows that a bidding contractor must take a set of plans and specifications, properly cost them, and provide for contingency and profits. If successful, the contractor must then mobilize its firm as well as the subs to perform. The principal's objective is to complete the contract on time, within the budget, and make a profit.

§ 5.3 Historical Perspective of Design-Build

Some of the more successful contractors and A/Es (principals) of the 80s are now poised to continue their success into the 90s. During the last decade, several changes that affected construction can be identified. The first is the computer. It has had some very significant benefits, particularly in estimating. The more successful principals have enhanced their computer applications to speed up calculations and eliminate errors in estimating. The computer also has provided the principal with the ability to obtain, retain, and analyze historical job data much more easily.

At the same time, the principal's financial people have become able to use the data in a timely manner and provide meaningful financial information to the credit people much sooner than in the past. Both the estimating and financial departments of the principal have greatly enhanced the data available to the surety and have given the surety the ability to track the current work on hand more closely.

During this same period, many of the primary sureties were developing their own computerized informational systems. Their new systems give them an overall perspective of their entire book as well as individual accounts. Both the primary surety and its reinsurers have become better able to review and analyze their exposures in order to determine capital utilization and effective rates of return. The systems also allow principals to be tracked from one surety to the other.

The other change which emerged in the 1980s and certainly will continue into the 90s is in management. The more successful principals have adopted advanced management principles and practices. This upgrading of skills has occurred not just at the university or academic level but inside the contracting organizations. This was important because the construction environment has become very regulatory and "hyperlegal." Most new construction managers and executives are well versed in areas other than just brick and mortar. Financial analysis and strategic planning have become very important and are being used by construction managers. Also, successful management developed the ability to communicate this vital information to the sureties.

These influences have forced the construction industry to change how they construct, as demonstrated by the design-build, earlier referred to as fast-track construction. Traditionally, the principal obtains plans and specifications prepared by an A/E on behalf of the owner. The A/E was generally the approver of change orders, progress payments, scheduling, and overall interpretation of the contract. This practice has created a certain amount of adversity between the contracting parties, which tended to slow the construction process or at times delay it dramatically. As a result, all the parties suffered financially. However, under the design-build concept, the tardiness and hostility has changed. Under the design-build contract, the principal is responsible for the design and construction of the project. The primary motivation is self evident. The contractor and architect feel that time and money can be saved if both disciplines are joined. The owner, of course, echoes their sentiment of "build faster because time is money." Litigation is also reduced when the parties work together. With all of these benefits, what could the surety possibly find wrong with this concept?

The surety questions whether the benefits are substantive and whether they really aid the surety. The answer is a mixed yes and no. The design-build concept does allow the project to progress much quicker from conception to completion. The designer and the contractor do share a common goal and are both responsible for the successful completion. Under the traditional system, both parties had the goal of a successful job but there was no contractual or financial mutuality of interest. Under design-build there is. The parties are bound together rather than being separately accountable to the owner.

In addition, time has shown that there have been real time and cost savings and a clear reduction of litigation surrounding the project. Therefore, from a surety's viewpoint, it should be a win-win situation. The surety still has some doubts, however.

In order to understand the surety's position, it is necessary to explore how the surety prequalifies the principal before deciding to bond it. The surety analyzes the 3 Cs: capital, capacity, and character.

§ 5.4 Capital Analysis of the Principal

A successful principal must have sufficient capital to prosecute its work program without causing a problem to a surety. Adequacy of capital is determined by reviewing three years' financial statements. In most cases, these financials should be audited by CPAs because anyone contemplating lending serious capital should have the assurance that the financials are accurate.

The adequacy of the financials is in some part dependent upon what the surety is asked to bond or what work program the principal intends to undertake. In broad, general terms, the *primary* or *critical ratios,* those that determine whether a principal is stretched or has the liquidity and equity base to support a given work program, should show at least a 5 percent working capital to aggregate work program ratio and a 10 percent net worth to aggregate work program ratio. These ratios are broad and are only the starting point for a further detailed financial analysis. The surety must determine whether the principal has sufficient capital, including available cash flow, to handle current and future work.

Financials are more than just the numbers. Their presentation should be impressive and according to industry standards. The contractor has an excellent opportunity to demonstrate that the firm or joint venture is financially sound and has the ability to earn money over time.

The timeliness of the financials is very important. Financials should not just be provided annually, they should be provided quarterly or at least semi-annually. Also, work on hand (WOH) information should be provided monthly. Remember, this is the most important continuing information the principal can provide the surety. If these are good numbers presented in a proper format, the only question the surety would have should be, "How much surety credit do you want?" Nothing excites a surety more than profit and prompt presentation of that information.

In design-build contracts, the surety should be shown how the financials are protected by insurance. The principal must demonstrate that the firm's insurance program, particularly the errors and omissions policy (project or practice), has adequate limits with a financially strong carrier. It must also show how the proper tail (future) coverages are available for the specific project and how the insurance program will respond and keep the surety out of any possible deep pocket scenario.

The surety is also interested in the principal's prior work experience and its profitability. Does the principal estimate and prosecute work in an expeditious manner, enabling the firm to make a profit and retain it? Historically, A/E firms generally have small retained earnings on their balance sheets; most of their income has been dividended or distributed to the partners. Sureties are very reluctant to bond companies having insufficient capital. This is one of the problems the surety has in bonding a design-build contract. Even in a joint venture the A/E firm generally brings no substantial retained earnings to the venture.

§ 5.5 Capacity Analysis of the Principal

The principal's entire organization will be reviewed by the surety. This review will consist of an historical examination principally directed at the type, location, and size of the work performed. This will allow the surety to become knowledgeable about the principal's successes or failures. By examining the past work, the surety has the opportunity to get indirect information regarding the principal's overall organization and identify individuals who have completed the successful jobs or pinpoint those who have lost money by poor performance.

It cannot be overemphasized that the manner in which this information is provided can go a long way in determining whether the surety will be interested in continuing the relationship with the principal. The principal should spend some time and thought on how and in what format this information should be provided. It should show that the firm is organized properly and that management has functioned effectively to produce a profit from work performance.

It is also critical that the principal not prepare the information just to impress the surety during the initial meeting. The information should flow easily from the organization and be made available to the surety on a regular basis. Remember, don't promise information that the organization can't provide regularly. So many times, contractors develop and provide useful information to the surety for their annual meeting, only to have that same information unavailable on a regular basis during the year. This leaves the surety completely confused for several reasons. First, if the promise to provide the information was made by the owner or CEO, the same person who then fails to provide the continuing information, the surety wonders who is really running the company. Secondly, when the follow-up information does not continue, the surety wonders whether it was really important or whether it was prepared merely to impress the surety but not really used by the company. The principal should not leave the surety with any confusion about its account.

The basic capacity information supplied to the surety should include:

____ **1.** Key personnel, showing experience
____ **2.** Organization chart and/or information flow chart
____ **3.** Experienced personnel to cover future work
____ **4.** Company policies on safety, accounting procedures, and contract administration
____ **5.** Job history, showing past completed jobs with detailed descriptions
____ **6.** Complete exhibit of current work on hand (WOH).

This information should be continually updated as it changes. It is important to remember that even though the principal is very familiar with this information, the surety is not, so it is incumbent on the principal to make sure the right story is told. The surety will review and analyze this information very thoroughly.

The principal should provide a complete exhibit of current work on hand (WOH). Most sureties have their own WOH format, which should be used if possible. This WOH schedule will show the principal's ability to perform work timely, profitably, within the estimate, and without litigation (if everything goes as planned). It will also show where there are problems and their scope. This is why the surety insists on these schedules. The principal must make sure they are accurate. If there are problems on a job, the principal must be prepared to give reasons for them but more importantly be prepared to show how the problem will be solved and for how much. Here is the real test for a principal. Realistic accuracy must be portrayed to the surety. The principal is cautioned to not guess at solutions nor tell the surety "not to worry." Even a problem can work to the principal's benefit if the problem is solved in a manner and for the amount committed to the surety. This capacity analysis is a real look by the surety into the principal's organization and its ability to manage crisis.

This is equally true in the case of a design-build contract. All the information regarding the design capability should be demonstrated. Past work, key employees, and similar work should all be pointed out very clearly to the surety.

§ 5.6 Character Analysis of the Principal

The third element examined by the surety is character, or the management skills of the principal. The character of a corporation is not just that of the founder or key stockholder. It is the ability, skill, and ethic of the management team. Reputation for sound and ethical business practices is the essential ingredient a surety is looking for in a client.

How can a principal ensure that the surety properly evaluates its reputation or character? Basically, the principal must identify its management team or people and show their backgrounds and how and why they were selected for management positions. It is important that the individuals are good, solid people who have and would conduct themselves ethically in the future.

The principal should point out to the surety how personnel have functioned in the past, using prior jobs as the exhibit, and show the day-to-day synergy between members of the team and how this translates to future successes. It would also be important to show the surety how the group has developed a written business plan; when and how it was implemented; how the long and short goals have been or are being attained. The company's written crisis management plan with specific actions should also be submitted to the surety. If possible, a job that had problems should be discussed in order to enforce the point that not only does management have a plan but that in a crisis it was followed.

The surety is always concerned with change and how the changes will be handled by management. Of paramount concern to the surety is whether management has a contingency plan to handle a significant downturn in business. The principal should make sure there is a plan and that management has the power and desire to follow it.

The surety is also keenly interested in management's plan for continuity of the business. This must be addressed by management, because without such a plan the surety will not willingly give long-term credit. In addition, does the company or stockholders have a buy-sell agreement? Equally important is how the buy-sell is funded. If it is funded with insurance, is the amount provided adequate?

In the case of design-build contracts, the principal must show how management has analyzed its risk exposure, with the design exposure and the construction exposure dealt with separately. It is important to explain and demonstrate the analysis management went through and why the decision was made to go forward. The principal must clearly demonstrate how the risk could be handled financially and operationally, showing how it has contractually eliminated any long-term performance requirements or how they have been insured adequately, or both.

§ 5.7 The Future of Bonding Design-Build Projects

Change is inevitable. In the construction process, the change of design-build is here to stay. Some forerunners in the construction industry have successfully proven that design-build can be accomplished, and as successfully as contemplated. Sufficient time and successful projects have clearly shown that design-build is acceptable. Sureties seeing the clear evidence of this success will be willing to provide credit for such projects. However, as with all surety credit, the principal must clearly and convincingly prove to the surety two things: that the performance required by the contract can be completed successfully and that there is no risk of loss to the surety.

CHAPTER 6

INSURANCE ASPECTS OF DESIGN-BUILD CONSTRUCTION

Betty L. Hum*

Betty L. Hum is a partner in the Phoenix, Arizona, law firm of Lewis and Roca. Ms. Hum received a B.A. degree from the University of Minnesota in 1971 and a J.D. degree from the University of Minnesota Law School in 1975. She is admitted to practice in Arizona and Minnesota. She has been actively engaged in representing owners, developers, and contractors in all aspects of construction law, specializing in alternative dispute resolution methods and litigation. She has written and spoken on various topics including construction claims, alternative dispute resolution procedures, and construction documents. She is a member of the forum committee on the construction industry of the American Bar Association (ABA) Design Build Committee and the panel of arbitrators for the American Arbitration Association. She is a fellow of the American College of Construction Lawyers and serves as the Phoenix affiliate member of the Arizona Building Chapter Board of Directors.

*Much of the material contained in this chapter has been adapted from an article co-authored by Betty L. Hum and Timothy M. O'Brien for the Fall 1990 ABA Forum on the Construction Industry. Copyright © 1990 by the American Bar Association. Reprinted by permission of the American Bar Association.

§ 6.1 Introduction

Owners have turned to design/build construction with the expectation of obtaining a completed project on which the budgetary, performance, and time constraints will be established and observed. Integral to such an assumption is the corresponding expectation that the risks associated with such an undertaking will be allocated on a clear, and even rational, basis. The juxtaposition of the roles of the design professional and the contractor, inherent in the design-build process, results in the fusion of their efforts and has, to some extent, changed the traditional risk allocation characteristics of a project. The project owner properly views the design-build process as an amalgamation of effort and responsibility that should significantly limit exposure or loss in the resolution of the dichotomy between design and construction, whereas the design professional and the contractor and their insurers are being called to venture upon, or as the cynic might say, "walk" upon uncharted waters.

The world of design and construction risk is complex and multi-faceted. Under the traditional construction process with its parallel but discrete design and construction elements, considerable legal authority and comment abound to address the respective liabilities of the design professional (and inferentially its professional liability insurance carrier) and the contractor (and its surety in the event of the contractor's insolvency). A comparable situation has not yet developed with respect to participants in the design-build process. A relatively sparse body of insurance law has developed about the consequence of merging the design and construction process.

§ 6.2 Professional Liability Insurance

Professional liability insurance was developed to cover claims against design professionals arising from professional negligence or malpractice.[1] Other types of insurance written to cover losses or claims during the construction process, such as builder's risk or commercial general liability, typically exclude claims arising from design services.

During the period from the late 1970s to the late 1980s, the professional liability insurance market for design professionals became soft as premiums

---

[1] Professional liability policies are commonly referred to as errors and omissions, or E&O, or malpractice policies. The terms will be used interchangeably in this chapter.

and deductibles rose dramatically with the increase in litigation against design professionals. Since that time, the market for professional liability insurance has improved, and architects and engineers have been able to more readily obtain professional liability insurance.[2]

The professional liability insurance that is currently available is written on a claims-made basis, which covers claims that are made during the policy period. The loss experience under claims-made policies enables insurers to predict with reasonable certainty losses and to set premiums and calculate revenues. Based on historical data, insurers have determined that roughly 85 percent of design claims are reported within five years of completion of construction, and the remaining 15 percent are reported after five years of completion. Consequently, most insurers write professional liability insurance on an annual aggregate limit basis but offer the option of extended discovery or reporting period endorsements for a negotiated period of time.[3]

Prior to the mid-1980s, insurers also wrote professional liability insurance on an occurrence basis. Under this type of policy, claims would be covered if made during the policy period or after the expiration of the policy as long as the occurrence arose during the policy period. Unlike a claims-made policy, insurers found that they could not reasonably predict how many claims would be made against an occurrence policy at the expiration of the policy.[4]

The most common type of available coverage is a standard policy that is written on an annual basis. Such a policy covers claims that are made during the policy year and during any period for which prior acts coverage has been added to the policy.[5]

The insured on professional liability policies is typically the design professional firm and its principals. Generally, the insurer will not include the owner or the contractor as an additional or named insured.[6] However, the professional liability insurance will protect the design professional from claims arising from the errors and omissions of its consultants, unless that risk is specifically excluded.

Professional liability insurance generally covers the design professional from claims relating to errors, omissions, or negligent acts arising out of the performance of professional services. A *claim* has been defined as a

---

[2] Howard, *A&E Market Resurfacing Experts Say,* National Underwriter Property & Casualty 3 (Employee Benefit ed. May 29, 1989) [hereinafter Howard].

[3] *Id.*

[4] S. Stein, Construction Law § 13.06(2) (1990).

[5] Howard at 3.

[6] The design professional should identify all names used by the design firm for inclusion in the policy and key persons. Failure to do so may jeopardize coverage. Berger, *Understanding Liability Insurance; Architects Liability,* 67 Progressive Architecture 53 (1986).

"demand for money or services, or the filing of a suit or institution of arbitration proceedings naming the insured and alleging an error, omission, or negligent act."[7]

The scope of coverage under professional liability insurance is better understood by examining the exclusions which more explicitly define the range of activities that professional liability insurance does not cover. Typical exclusions include, but are not limited to:

1. Services or activities that are not ordinary or customary to the design professional
2. Warranties and guarantees of design
3. Faulty workmanship
4. Subsurface surveys of ground conditions, tunnels, or bridges (unless there is a specific endorsement)
5. Infringement of copyright, trademark, or patent advice
6. Failure to advise about insurance
7. Delays in completing the original contract drawings and specifications
8. Express warranties
9. Estimates of probable costs of construction
10. Dishonest, fraudulent, criminal, or malicious errors or omissions
11. Personal injury or death of an employee during employment by the insured
12. Performance in whole or in part by the design professional of any erection, construction, fabrication, installation, assembly, manufacture, or supplying of equipment or materials
13. Ownership, maintenance, or use of an aircraft, boat, automobile, or trailer
14. Punitive damages
15. Payment of professional fees.

For a claim to be made under a professional liability policy, the design professional is required to give written notice of a claim to the insurer during the policy period. Generally, under a basic policy without an extended reporting period, most policies require that notice be given no later than 60 days after the policy expires. Some policies require the design professional to report any potential incident that may give rise to a claim during the policy period. This type of requirement actually benefits the design professional if the actual claim is reported after the policy expires.[8]

---

[7] S. Stein, Construction Law § 13.06(2)(a) (1990).

[8] *See* Architect and Engineer Liability: Claims Against Design Professionals § 3.4 (R. Cushman et al. eds., John Wiley & Sons 1987).

The claims-made policy covers claims for errors and omissions that are made on or after the policy's retroactive date specified in the declaration page of the policy or in an endorsement to the policy. Without a retroactive endorsement or specified retroactive date, it is possible that an insurer may become liable for negligent acts that occurred years before the policy became effective but for which claims are made during the policy period.[9] The retroactive endorsement may exclude claims arising from prior acts before a specified time period. Such retroactive periods are negotiable. If the design professional is aware of or knows of any possible claim that might be asserted, the insurer must be notified of such items, otherwise the insurer has a defense to the claim when it is made.

As with other types of insurance, the larger the deductible, the greater the risk the design professional self-insures in the amount of the deductible. Conversely, the lower the deductible, the higher the premium. As with other types of insurance, the design professional must exercise business judgment to determine the amount of the deductible and risk to be assumed.

Virtually all professional liability policies include coverage for the costs of investigating, defending, and settling claims. The difference in the policies is whether the defense costs are in addition to the policy limits or are included within the limits of liability.

For example, if defense and claims settlement costs are not included in the policy limit, and the insurance company has expended \$1 million to defend a given claim, and no claim has been paid, the entire policy limit is intact and remains available for other claims. However, if the defense costs are included within the limit of the policy, the \$1 million in defense costs would reduce the limits of the coverage; in other words, the coverage is depleted or wasted, to the extent of defense costs.

All major professional liability carriers give the design professional the right to approve settlement offers to the claimant. The insurer is not permitted to settle a claim without first receiving the insured's consent. However, the provision also stipulates that if the insurer suggests a certain settlement amount and the insured refuses to consent, the figure becomes a maximum the insurer will pay in settlement regardless of the eventual resolution of a claim. Assume a design professional has a policy with a \$1 million annual aggregate coverage limit and is sued for losses arising out of a negligently designed structure. If the insurer offers \$750,000 to settle with the owner, this amount becomes the maximum amount the insurer would be obligated to pay if the insured refuses to consent to settle for \$750,000.

The limits of the policy depend on the business and the nature of business of the design professional and the type of project.[10] A limit per claim and an

---

[9] S. Stein, Construction Law § 13.06(2) (1990).

[10] Furr, *Insurance Planning for Construction Projects,* 85-10 Construction Briefings 4 (Oct. 1985).

aggregate limit applies to all claims that arise during the policy period. The aggregate limit is generally written on an annual basis. The per claim limit has resulted in disputes about what constitutes a single error, omission, or negligent act or what related acts, errors, or omissions pertain to a single claim. The characterization of whether acts, omissions, or errors constitute a single claim or multiple claims will affect the number of deductibles that the design professional must pay.

§ 6.3 Project Insurance

Another type of policy that is used more commonly on large projects is project insurance, which is purchased by the owner to wrap up coverage for potential professional liability exposure. Typically, such policies cover the design period and the construction period plus a specified period ranging from two to ten years to allow for discovery of claims. Project policies are written to cover all the design professionals who provide services on a construction project, which may include the architect, engineer, design-builder, and even construction managers.[11]

This type of policy gives the owner the assurance that professional liability insurance is in place for all design professionals and is guaranteed and noncancelable for a specified term of years. With a substantial number of design professionals "going bare," that is, without E&O coverage, the project policy offers the owner protection from design errors that might not otherwise be covered because design professionals on a project may not be able to obtain coverage or cannot get adequate limits. In addition, the owner's interests are further served by the fact that the limits of liability will not be decreased by claims against the design professionals arising from other projects.

One benefit to the design professional is that project insurance permits the design professional to exclude the revenues from the insured project from its gross revenues for purposes of calculating the premium for professional liability coverage it otherwise carries. However, because project insurance is written on a claims-made basis and expires within a specified time period, it is conceivable that potential claims may be identified during the policy period but not actually reported until after the project insurance terminates. Hence, to protect against contingent liability, the design professional must take steps to cover such possible claims arising from a project under its own professional liability insurance. This risk reduces the attractiveness of project insurance from the design professional's viewpoint.

[11] International Risk Management Inst., Construction Risk Management Professional Liability ch. VIII, C.24 (Nov. 1989).

§ 6.4 Design-Build Organizational Options

The types of insurance available to the design-builder depends, in part, on the type of organizational arrangement under which the design-builder conducts business. There are several basic configurations which the design builder can take.

First, there is the design-build constructor who is staffed with in-house architects and/or engineers. A variation of this option is supplementation of the in-house design professional staff with outside design professionals who participate in the design process or who approve the design and provide the requisite seal for a project. If the design-build constructor has in-house capability to provide design services, it has the advantage of being able to control and coordinate the project as a single entity without having to communicate or coordinate with third parties, such as independent architects or joint venture partners. The design-build firm can maintain a single business focus and purpose, unlike the design-build organization comprised of joint venture partners who must share responsibility and the decision-making process.

Second, there is the design-build contractor who subcontracts the design portion of the contract to outside architects and engineers. A strong contractor can apply its experience of coordinating trade subcontractors and material suppliers to maintain complete control of the project. In its role as a subconsultant to the design-build constructor, the design professional technically owes its contractual obligations and responsibilities to the constructor, which should theoretically permit the design-build constructor to construct a design-build project more efficiently and more quickly. The historically adversarial relationship between the contractor and the architect is eliminated, because the contractual obligations run to the contractor rather than to the owner.

Third, the design-build entity can be controlled by the architect who furnishes the design services but subcontracts the construction portion of the work to a contractor. During the early to mid-1980s, many architectural firms decided to expand their revenue bases by undertaking design-build projects. Unlike the contractor-controlled design-build option, the architect-driven option faces greater difficulties because of architects' relative lack of experience in coordinating and resolving jobsite problems. Contrary to the traditional architect relationship to the owner, the design-build architect promises to provide the owner with a project that will function as designed and constructed.[12] This represents a higher standard of performance and stricter contractual responsibility than the architect would normally satisfy under traditional methods of contracting.

---

[12] *See* Loulakis & Love, *Exploring the Design Build Contract,* 86-13 Construction Briefings 14 (Dec. 1986).

Finally, a separate design-build entity can be established in the form of a joint venture, partnership, or corporation. Depending upon the complexity of the project, the design-build entity may subcontract the design portion of a project to an outside firm of design professionals, or to a design professional with an interest in the design-build entity, or to a joint venture responsible for the design. The design-build entity may also subcontract the construction portion of the project. Under this arrangement, a contractor and architect can cooperate to facilitate the design and construction for greater financial rewards. There is no doubt this type of arrangement requires careful preparation of the contractual agreement to define liabilities, responsibility, and management of disputes.[13]

§ 6.5 Owner's Expectations of Design-Build Projects

Regardless of the method of contract delivery, the owner wants a quality project that is constructed on time and on budget. In evaluating the various methods of contracting, the design-build approach offers the owner certain perceived advantages. The most significant is the owner's ability to deal with a single entity for design and construction of a project. This single entity should enable the owner to avoid involvement in protracted disputes that historically often arise between the design professional and the contractor, because the design-builder has the total responsibility for design and construction.

The ability of a single entity to control the design and construction should result in lower costs through value engineering, closer coordination between the design professionals and the contractor, and the ability to complete the project more quickly, whether on a fast-track basis or through economies achieved by means of the closer relationship between the design and construction functions.[14]

Moreover, the owner expects the design-builder to furnish a project that will perform as designed and will be constructed as designed. This expectation can be said to create warranties and guarantees that may be broader than those available under traditional methods of contracting. In contrast, in a conventional project, a design professional does not warrant the design

---

[13] *Id.* at 15.

[14] Design-build is often linked with the process of completing construction on a fast-track basis in which design documents are prepared in phases. Construction proceeds as each phase of the design is completed. Theoretically, a project can be completed in a shorter period of time because construction can proceed before all the construction documents have been completed. *See* Bynum, *Construction Management and Design-Build/Fast Track Construction from the Perspective of a General Contractor,* 46 Law & Contemp. Probs. 25, 34 (1983).

of a project but is required only to exercise a standard of minimum professionally acceptable conduct. This implies that the design professional will follow customary procedures but does not become strictly liable for the consequences of design errors and omissions.[15] In one sense, the owner expects broader warranties and guarantees because it can be said to be buying an end product rather than only construction services. Hence, the design-builder may be held to standard of performance wherein the design can be said to be warranted to meet the owner's specified program and criteria and be constructed within the budget. However, there have been no cases that directly examine the scope of insurance coverage available if the design-build project is characterized as a product rather than a furnishing of services.[16]

Under a design-build approach, the tasks and functions of a normal construction project do not change. Responsibility is, however, shifted entirely to the design-builder for design and construction.

§ 6.6 Available Policies for the Design-Build Project

It is only during the last 10 to 15 years that owners have extensively utilized the design-build approach to construct projects. The design-build approach can apply to construction ranging from specialty trade installations, such as air conditioning or plumbing, to commercial buildings, or to unique and complex projects, such as waste management plants. The design-builder is generally required to furnish proof of professional liability coverage to the owner.

---

[15] Block, *Architects' Expanded Liability Under Design-Build/Construction Contracting,* 33 Def. L. J. 325 (1984).

[16] The Uniform Commercial Code (UCC) generally excludes construction from the definition of goods. UCC §§ 2-102, 2-105. *See also* International Risk Management Inst., Construction Risk Management Professional Liability ch. VIII (Nov. 1989).

In Omaha Pollution Control Corp. v. Carver-Greenfield, 413 F. Supp. 1069 (D. Neb. 1976) liability was analyzed. A sewage treatment plant was designed, built and sold to the city and the city's nonprofit corporation. Numerous defects and operational problems arose. The court decided the deficiencies in the completed plant constituted the sale of a product under the UCC. This case is aberrational. The change in parties to a single entity which provides the design and construction services should not be analogized to a selling of a product. Each design-build project is generally unique. The liability of the design-builder has been analogized to that of a manufacturer. *See, e.g.,* Shipper v. Levitt & Sons, Inc., 44 N.J. 70, 207 A.2d 314 (1965). The court found that Levitt's mass construction and sale of tract homes was similar to the mass production and sale of automobiles. The court concluded that the same public policy arguments that support the imposition of strict liability in tort on auto manufacturers applied to design-build vendors. This type of decision, however, should not be applied to design-builders who generally do not build on a repetitive or mass scale.

The professional liability insurance forms and coverage for design professionals under contract with design-builders or for design-build entities are quite similar to the professional policies that design professionals obtain under traditional methods of contracting. Design-build professional liability coverage is provided under what is referred to as contractor's errors and omissions, contractor's professional liability, or contractor's malpractice policies.

There are two basic variations of contractor's professional liability policies that are available. One provides coverage for negligent errors, omissions, and acts of design professionals but excludes faulty workmanship or construction that is not in accordance with the design of the project or the construction documents, failure to complete construction in a timely manner, and consequential losses arising from such acts.[17]

The other variation of contractor's professional liability insurance includes all the standard coverages but broadens coverage by adding provisions that include direct or contingent liability for faulty workmanship for work performed by or for the design-builder.[18] The scope of the professional liability insurance, including faulty workmanship coverage, can be written in the declarations of the policy or can be added through a professional activities endorsement that is attached to the architect's or engineer's professional liability policy.[19] The faulty workmanship provision covers damages arising from the replacement of the faulty work itself.

---

[17] This type of policy has been available from Heath Syndicate of Lloyd's of London through Illinois R.B. Jones, 250 South Wacker Drive, Chicago, Illinois 60604, (312) 993-0505; Lexington Insurance Company through Professional Managers, Inc., 2 North Riverside Plaza, Suite 1460, Chicago, Illinois 60606-2640; the Homestead Insurance Company through William B. Turner and Associates, Inc., 221 North LaSalle Street, Suite 1137, Chicago, Illinois 60601-1304; CNA Insurance Company through Victor O. Schinnerer and Company, Inc., Two Wisconsin Circle, Chevy Chase, Maryland 20815-7703.

[18] This type of coverage has been available since 1972 but only in limited markets. Prior to early 1990, it was available from H.S. Weaver's Underwriting Agency, but it is no longer being offered by Weaver's. It is currently being offered by Lloyd's of London through Professional Underwriters Agency, Inc., 600 Enterprise Drive, Suite 200, Oak Brook, Illinois 60521. In addition, Federated Insurance Co., 121 E. Park Square, Owatonna, Minnesota 55060-2401, provides contractors' errors and omissions coverage for specialty trade contractors and smaller general building contractors directly through its own agents. The maximum limits of liability on a per claim and annual aggregate basis are $500,000. Federated Insurance provides coverage for specialty contractors that generally have gross revenues of around $10 million.

[19] Coverage under a professional activities policy or endorsement includes but is not limited to: (1) design errors and omissions; (2) professional liability as a consultant or advisor to the owner on all aspects of planning for the mechanical phases of construction; (3) professional liability for reviewing plans and specifications and offering advice or making recommendations about construction feasibility, availability of materials and labor, and possible economies in construction; (4) liability for supervision, inspection, or review performed by the design professional; (5) direct or contingent liability arising

The design portion of a design-build project is insured in several ways. The design-builder having in-house design staff capabilities can procure contractor's E&O coverage to cover the total potential design liability. Design professionals who are employees cannot generally obtain this type of insurance on an individual basis.

In the situation in which the design-builder subcontracts the design work, there are several options for obtaining professional liability coverage. The design-builder can elect to cover the entire design liability by obtaining a professional liability policy and not rely on any insurance from the design professional it has under contract. In the alternative, the design-builder can, as a matter of contract, require the design professional to carry professional liability insurance and impose that requirement on all design consultants working on a project.[20] The design-builder can rely on the design professional and its consultants to provide the primary professional liability coverage. However, the design-builder may not be comfortable with the limits of liability reflected in those policies, especially if the design professionals have been or are engaged in numerous other projects. It is conceivable that claims from other projects may consume the aggregate limits during the policy period. From the design-builder's perspective, total reliance on the design professional's insurance may not protect it from the contingent liability it retains for design. Therefore, the prudent design-builder should purchase contractor's professional liability to protect itself against contingent design liability.

Another alternative is to use project insurance to cover all design professionals who directly work for the design-builder or as consultants for the project. The owner and design-builder can benefit from project insurance for the reasons discussed in **§ 6.3**. One of the advantages project insurance would provide for the design-builder is the greater opportunity to use design consultants who might not otherwise have insurance coverage sufficient to satisfy an owner's requirements. Another benefit of project insurance is that the aggregate limits would not be reduced by claims related to other projects.

---

from awarding contracts to others on behalf of the owner; (6) liability arising from scheduling or coordinating operations; (7) direct or contingent liability for injuries to workers or others; (8) direct or contingent liability for faulty workmanship and work performed by the insured or for the insured; and (9) direct or contingent liability to the public for work performed by or on behalf of the insured.

[20] If the design professional's professional liability coverage is written on a blanket basis, no endorsement is necessary to cover the project. However, some policies are written on a per project basis and would require a specific endorsement to add the project. Certificates of insurance do not necessarily indicate whether the design professional's professional liability coverage is on a blanket or per project basis. Copies of the policy should be reviewed to verify scope of coverage.

If project insurance is purchased for a design-build project, the design-builder should clarify with all design professionals how the deductible will be paid. Allocation of responsibility for design issues can be difficult, so the design-builder needs to address the issue during the contract negotiation stage with the design consultants.

Design-build contracts are generally negotiated and involve unique projects.[21] Professional liability insurance is based upon broad categories of risks that have been identified through past experience, with the traditional roles of the contracting parties, the owner, the contractor, architect, subcontractor, supplier, lender, or surety defined by custom and case law. There is not sufficient loss experience in design-build to give the underwriter rating categories that are as clearly defined. The underwriting process is highly subjective and a function of the underwriter's experience in assessing risks. Consequently, the design-builder must look to conventional types of insurance covering the design and construction process to protect against claims and losses. Currently, no single policy of insurance covers the risk of design and construction. The insurance market has developed a product to respond to the additional risks assumed by the design builder. The design-builder must carefully review the exclusions, because the design-builder assumes overall responsibility for design and construction.

§ 6.7 Underwriting Considerations for Professional Liability Policies

The insurer determines the premium by considering various factors to evaluate the risks associated with the design builder's responsibility for a project. Many of these concerns are expressed in the questions directed to the design-builder in the application form for design-build professional liability insurance. The typical application form requests information about the history of the design-builder and the design firm or professionals who will be furnishing design services. This includes an examination of the firm's most recent financial data and three to five years of income statements. Policies carry high deductibles, and the insurer wants to assure itself that the design-builder will be able to pay the deductible in the event claims occur.

Other information sought by the insurer relates to prior and current insurance coverage, including professional liability, builder's risk, and general liability. This information enables the insurer to determine whether the design-builder has been able to maintain professional liability coverage. Insurers have determined that design firms that maintain

---

[21] Public agencies are starting to turn to the design-build approach for major infrastructure projects. *See* Randich, *Take Two for Design-Building Contracting,* Construction Bus. Rev. (Mar./Apr. 1991).

insurance over longer period of time are more likely to maintain insurance in the future.[22]

The underwriter will require a copy of the firm's most recent general liability policy, to determine how broad the coverage is, and information about the prior three to five years of general liability losses, to establish the kinds of losses the design-builder has experienced. In addition, the underwriter will request a copy of the owner's builder's risk policy for the project to review the scope of coverage. The main concern is whether the builder's risk policy has been extended to cover the cost of damage that is a direct result of design errors, faulty workmanship, and faulty materials. Underwriters are concerned about the frequency of losses under general liability and builder's risk policies rather than the amount of loss, as an indication of the level of professional competence. A single major claim may be an unusual occurrence and not be indicative of the quality of the design work, whereas frequent claims may point toward professional incompetence.

The application also requests information about prior and current projects. This assists the underwriter in assessing the other risks undertaken by the design-builder. The underwriter considers the nature of the particular project. Insurers view design-builders as engaging in hazardous construction, because of the total design responsibility and control over construction, which includes supervisory activity on the jobsite.[23]

Another concern of the insurer is the extent of contract liability assumed by the design-builder. Generally, the insurer requests a copy of the contract to review the type of express warranties, indemnity, and hold harmless agreements included in the contract. If the design-builder prepares its own plans and specifications as the design professional, the design-builder guarantees not only the performance of the work but that the work will conform with the plans. When design and construction functions are merged, it can become difficult to ascertain whether the responsibilities for errors lie in the design or construction. The contract can clarify responsibility by carefully defining the scope of the design work as distinguished from the construction work. Even so, some professional liability insurers may exclude coverage for any administrative activities in the construction phase because of the difficulty in separating design from construction activities. It is also difficult to determine if an error or omission is negligent or non-negligent or results from noncompliance with the contract plans and specifications.

---

[22] Howard at 4.

[23] Based on experience, insurers have ranked design activities from the most hazardous to the least. The following are some of activities, ranked from most to least hazardous: (1) soils design; (2) structural design; (3) combined architectural and engineering efforts; (4) mechanical design; (5) architecture; (6) civil design; (7) electrical design; and (8) land surveying. International Risk Management Inst., Construction Risk Management Professional Liability at B.20 (Nov. 1989).

The information provided on the insurance application becomes the basis for issuing the professional liability policy. Each application form requires the design-builder to certify that the information is true. The design-builder should understand that the insurer may treat the information as being warranted as accurate for purposes of providing coverage.

§ 6.8 Checks and Balances

One perceived disadvantage to design-build is that the traditional checks and balances between the design professional and contractor are discarded. Although this would seem to be of most concern to the owner, it is likely that the owner may be willing to live with such an arrangement in return for the other advantages that flow to it as a consequence of the design-build approach. The owner's acceptance is even more likely to occur if it insists that the design-builder be bonded and that the bond extend to all obligations of the design-builder.

The surety is likewise impacted by the elimination of the design professional as an independent evaluator of the adequacy of the design and the compliance with the plans and specifications by the design-builder in the performance of the construction obligations. Moreover, the surety is further impacted by the fact that it no longer has an independent entity in place to assure that contract funds are paid out on a proper basis.

The surety has two ways to deal with the fact the design professional is no longer closely aligned with the interests of the owner. First, the surety can account for the additional risk by charging even higher premium rates. Second, the surety can engage an inspecting architect to evaluate work in place to ensure conformance with project plans and specifications and to monitor payments to the design-builder.

Close coordination of insurance requirements is required on a design-build project in order to protect common interests. The owner and the design-builder should structure their agreement in such a fashion as to allocate risks on an equitable basis. Certainly, to the extent that construction risk can be guaranteed by a surety and design risk can be insured by a liability carrier, normal expectations will be realized.

The insurance coverages the design-builder obtains should be carefully reviewed to assure that there are no glaring liability expenses that are not covered. This means that the exclusions and endorsements to builder's risk, commercial general liability, and professional liability coverage should be analyzed to assure that both construction performance claims and design errors and omissions are adequately covered. The design-builder assumes a higher degree of risk than under traditional construction projects.

In today's market, the professional liability insurance available to design-builder is not very different from the traditional errors and omissions policy. The insurance market has not reacted by creating new insurance to cover the potentially expanded construction and design risks. The risks and exposures are best covered by maintaining as separately as possible the traditional architecture and constructor responsibilities, in order to preserve the available insurance coverages for both design error and construction defects or deficiencies.

§ 6.9 Commercial General Liability Insurance

Although a single entity, the design-builder, must obtain commercial general liability insurance (CGL), which traditionally provides coverage to contractors against claims for bodily injury or property damage arising from construction work, no insurance policy currently exists to provide coverage for both construction and design claims against a design-builder. The CGL coverage comes in two forms: occurrence and claims-made. Most policies are written on a claims-made basis. CGL policies are written on an aggregate limit basis that is depleted during the policy period by the amounts paid on separate claims. The numerous exclusions to the CGL policy, in one sense, better define what is available for claims.

It is critical for the design-builder to understand that the CGL policy does not provide any professional liability coverage. Therefore, regardless of the organizational form of the design-builder, professional liability coverage needs to be separately purchased to protect against professional liability exposures.

In the case in which the design-builder subcontracts with a design professional, the design-builder should determine what an adequate professional liability limit would be and make sure that all design professionals on the project have professional liability coverage.[24] It is possible to obtain a professional liability endorsement to be attached to the CGL policy. The effect of the endorsement, however, is to specifically exclude "the design portion" of the design builder's obligations from CGL coverage. Under present market conditions, the design-builder would be wise to purchase a separate professional liability policy.

The typical exclusion for design in the CGL policy also excludes any supervisory activities in engineering services.[25] Another exclusion that

---

[24] Under the AIA standard form of agreement between contractor and consultant, there is no provision that specifies that the design professional must carry errors and omissions coverage.

[25] Typically, constructors provide the engineering for false work, scaffolding, and form work as part of their work. It is possible that such activities could be considered to be design. In the design-build context, there could be a gap in coverage for problems related to these types of activities which may be excluded from CGL coverage and not covered by E&O insurance.

restricts design errors and omissions is what is known as the *sistership exclusion,* or damage caused by the removal or replacement of the insured's product. The effect of this exclusion is to preclude coverage in the event that there is defective construction that necessitates removing nondefective work in order to effectuate repairs.

One of the more troublesome exclusions is the *work product exclusion,* which excludes coverage for property that has been damaged under the "care, custody or control" of the insured, as well as property that the insured is currently working on, and damage to the work arising in whole or in part because of the work in progress or arising out of damage from completed operations.

The majority of jurisdictions have held that the CGL policy does not indemnify the constructor for the cost of correcting or replacing its own work, on the policy basis that the losses attributable to defective workmanship should be carried as a business expense or risk by the constructor.[26] The CGL policy, unlike a performance bond, is intended to shift the risk of poor performance away from the owner but not away from the constructor. Therefore, courts have been reluctant to permit the constructor to be paid by the owner and then indemnified by the CGL carrier for the cost of repairing or replacing the deficient work. There have been many disputes between general liability carriers and professional liability carriers about the scope of coverage afforded for activities that may be characterized as design errors and omissions. There are many gray areas as to what activities of the design professional should be defended by the E&O carrier versus the general liability carrier.[27]

---

[26] *See* Knutson Constr. Co. v. St. Paul Fire & Marine Ins. Co., 396 N.W.2d 229 (Minn. 1986). *See generally* Mack, *Construction Claims under the Comprehensive General Liability Policy,* 40 S.C. L. Rev. 1003 (1989). The minority of jurisdictions has found that the CGL policy is ambiguous as to the coverage for breach of warranty claims, so claims for breach of an insured's warranty of good workmanship would be considered to be covered. *See, e.g.,* United States Fidelity & Guar. Corp. v. Advance Roofing & Supply Co., 163 Ariz. 476, 788 P.2d 1227 (App. December 14, 1989), *rev. denied,* (Apr. 17, 1990); Federal Ins. Co. v. P.A.T. Homes, Inc., 113 Ariz. 136, 547 P.2d 1050 (1976).

[27] *See, e.g.,* First Ins. Co. of Haw. v. Continental Casualty Co., 466 F.2d 807 (9th Cir. 1972). The engineers on a project successfully defended themselves from claims asserted by a former superintendent of a contractor that he had been fired as a result of the engineers' false accusations. The E&O policy excluded coverage against claims for acts or omissions "not arising out of the customary and usual performance of professional services for others in the insured's capacity as architect and engineer." The engineers' contract authorized them to review the quality of workmanship and recommend that the contractor discharge any employee they considered to be incompetent. Because the engineers were responsible for quality control, the court held that there was coverage under the E&O policy. *See also* Shaw v. Aetna Casualty & Sur. Co., 407 F.2d 813 (7th Cir. 1969); United States Fidelity & Guar. Co. v. Continental Cas. Co., 153 Ill. App. 3d 185, 505 N.E.2d 1072 (1987); American Employers' Ins. Co. v. Continental Casualty Co., 85 N.M. 346, 512 P.2d 674 (1973). For additional references, see Henderson,

Claims-made policies disallow claims that are made to the insurer after the policy has expired, even if the bodily injury or property damage occurred during the policy period. One way to protect against such an occurrence is to obtain an extended reporting period. The basic reporting period can be extended for up to five years from the end of the policy. The normal reporting period runs for 60 days from the expiration of the policy. A five-year tail would cover claims arising out of incidents that have occurred before the end of the policy but are reported more than 60 days after the end of the policy period as extended. The basic tail of 60 days is a grace period in which the insured has to report claims for damages occurring during the policy period. It is provided by the terms of the claims-made policy.

The reporting period can also be extended through a supplemental tail, which requires an additional premium to be paid. The insured must request it within 60 days after the end of the policy period. The supplemental tail takes effect after the end of the basic five-year tail for claims arising out of an occurrence reported to the insurer within 60 days after the end of the policy period or the 60-day tail for claims resulting from occurrence not previously reported to the insurer. The effect of the supplemental tail is to extend the reporting period for an indefinite duration, in effect turning a claims-made policy into an occurrence policy.

Another major exclusion is the *contractual liability exclusion.* Under this exclusion, claims that arise from the assumption of liability on a contract or agreement are not covered. Coverage is available for "insured contracts," which include such written agreements as license agreements, indemnification of a governmental entity required by ordinance or statute, or a part of a contract or agreement under which the insured assumes the tort liability of another to pay damages arising out of bodily injury or property damage to the third person or entity, if the agreement was made prior to the bodily injury or property damage. Only the indemnification portion of a contract is considered to be an insured contract.

The CGL policy does not cover bodily injury or damages that arise from an architect's, engineer's, or surveyor's preparing, approving, or failing to prepare or approve maps, drawings, opinions, reports, surveys, change orders, designs, or specifications, or giving directions or instructions or failing to give them. The general manner in which such an exclusion occurs is by way of a separate endorsement attached to the policy to preclude direct claims for professional liability.

Insurance Protection for Products Liability and Completed Operations—What Every Lawyer Should Know, 50 Neb. L. Rev. 415 (1971); Note, *Liability Coverage for Damages Because of Property Damages Under the Comprehensive General Liability Policy,* 68 Minn. L. Rev. 795 (1984); Patin & Johnson, *Liability Insurance,* 89-9 Construction Briefings (Aug. 1989); Braude & Patin, *Comprehensive General Liability Insurance,* Construction Briefings (Mar. 1982).

§ 6.10 —Problem Areas in CGL Coverage

If the design-builder's CGL policy includes an exclusion for engineers', architects', or surveyors' professional liability by way of an endorsement or specific exclusion, the CGL policy will not cover the "professional services" that the design-builder provides to the owner for what would otherwise be considered incidental design for such activities as the engineering for false work or scaffolding. This means that the design-builder must make sure that the exposure is covered under a separate professional liability policy for the entire design-build entity. If the design-builder has subcontracted the design, separate E&O coverage must be obtained by the design professional and its consultants to cover such design services. If the CGL policy does not include this exclusion, arguably the incidental design services may be covered.

The CGL policy further restricts coverage for design services by the definition of what constitutes an occurrence. Many policies define *occurrence* as "an accident, including continuous or repeated exposure to substantially the same general, harmful conditions."[28] This definition raises the issue of whether design errors can constitute an accident.

Another area of risk under the CGL policy concerns potential gaps in coverage for work performed by subcontractors. If the design-builder requires that the subcontractors also carry CGL coverage, the design-builder should as a requirement for the insurance provide that the subcontractors' CGL policy run concurrently with the retroactive date and reporting period of the design-builder's own CGL coverage. Otherwise, if a subcontractor's reporting period lapses before that of the design-builder, the subcontractor's CGL coverage will not respond to claims made and reported after the expiration of the reporting period. If the owner has requested the design-builder to provide extended reporting coverage, the design-builder should as part of the contract negotiations with the subcontractors extract the same commitment to purchase extended reporting coverage.[29]

Frequently, the contract between the owner and design-builder requires that the design-builder and owner waive their rights against each other and any of their representatives, subcontractors, subsubconsultants, and design consultants for damages for bodily injury or property damage covered by property insurance. In addition, builder's risk and professional liability coverage often include similar waivers of subrogation. As a single entity, the design-builder should implement a review of the various types of insurance to make sure that there are no gaps in the waivers of subrogation.

---

[28] *CGL Coverage Form* Insurance Services Office, Inc. (1983, 1987).

[29] *See* Buoncristiani, *Special Risks and Problem Areas Under the New CGL Policy,* ABA Forum Comm. on Construction (Jan. 1987).

The purpose of waivers of subrogation is to shift the risk of loss of covered perils to the insurance carrier. If some entity in the construction process is not included within the waiver of subrogation, the insurance carrier may be able to sue the party responsible for causing the insured peril under its rights of subrogation. This is particularly important in the design-build process in order to avoid the insurance carrier's coming back against the design-builder if one of the subconsultants is not included or one of the other insurance policies, such as builder's risk or professional liability, does not include as broad a waiver of subrogation. Coordination of the waivers of subrogation for consistency is necessary to avoid such problems.[30]

In the current insurance market, the design-builder has no alternative except to obtain insurance coverages through separate policies, because no single policy exists to cover both construction and professional liability losses on a project. Risk management is generally not changed by the design-build approach, however, the design-builder may be found to have provided an end product that is warranted not only for construction but for design purposes. This characterization of the design-build project can pose problems for insurance coverage, which does not respond to the expanded warranty of design responsibility under traditional professional liability coverages. If insurance does not respond to such risks, the design-builder should negotiate limitations on such liability in the contract with the owner. The key is to obtain the advice of an experienced insurance counselor to put together a responsive insurance program, and to analyze potential exposures with legal counsel in order to determine what provisions can be negotiated with the owner to offer the best protection for the owner and the design-builder within the current available coverages.

---

[30] *See, e.g.,* LeMaster Steel Erectors, Inc. v. Reliance Ins. Co., 546 N.E.2d 313 (Ind. Ct. App. 1989) (in subrogation action against the subcontractor and contractor, contract language did not specifically include subcontractor and insurer was entitled to seek subrogation against the subcontractor); St. Paul Fire & Marine Ins. Co. v. Freeman-White Assocs., Inc., 322 N.C. 77, 36 S.E.2d 480 (1988) (in subrogation action brought by builder's risk carrier against architect, owner-architect agreement required architect to maintain professional liability insurance to cover errors and omissions during the life of the project, but inclusion of a waiver of subrogation for builder's risk and the requirement of the architect to maintain professional liability insurance rendered the contract ambiguous as to the scope of the waiver); Hartford Ins. Co. v. CMC Builders, Inc., 752 P.2d 590 (Colo. Ct. App. 1988) (modification to owner-contractor indemnification clause indicated that loss of property would be covered by the builder's risk insurance and that the waiver of subrogation would prevent the builder's risk carrier from pursuing the contractor); Dyson & Co. v. Flood Eng'rs, Architects, Planners, Inc., 523 So. 2d 756 (Fla. Dist. Ct. App. 1988) (in an action against A/E firm brought by contractor and builder's risk carrier for damages caused by a fire resulting from allegedly negligent design, court held A/E firm had a "insurable interest to the extent that the firm could become legally responsible for damages as a result of its own negligence," so A/E was covered by builder's risk policy).

CHAPTER 7

CONTRACT AWARD AND ELIGIBILITY ISSUES

James L. Hawkins*

James L. Hawkins is chairman of the Construction Law Practice Group of Greensfelder, Hemker & Gale, P.C., St. Louis, Missouri. His practice is devoted primarily to construction law, representing prime contractors, subcontractors, and design professionals. Mr. Hawkins graduated with honors from St. Louis University School of Law and previously taught courses on credit transactions and suretyship at that institution. He is a member of the American Bar Association, where he serves on the Section of Public Contract Law and the Forum on the Construction Industry.

*The assistance of senior law student, Cheryl A. Lovell, Bachelor of Engineering, Civil Engineering, in gathering research materials for this chapter is gratefully acknowledged.

§ 7.1 Introduction

Design-build contractors who submit proposals to perform construction work expect fair and impartial procedures to govern the award process. The request for proposals normally describes the criteria upon which an award will be based. In public works, applicable statutes, ordinances, and regulations often govern the award process and, in some instances, provide a procedure for protest by an unsuccessful bidder or proposer. There are no comparable protections in private works contracting. This chapter will examine award and eligibility issues relating to design-build contracting.

PROBLEMS WITH DESIGN-BUILD FOR PUBLIC WORKS

§ 7.2 Protests of Private Design-Build Awards

Private construction projects (private works) may be defined as those projects that are funded solely with private money and not directly or indirectly with public tax revenues.

A private works bidder, invited to bid in competition with others on a lump-sum basis, would seem to have just grounds for complaint if its low bid is not accepted and the contract is awarded to another. If pre-approved bidders all quote on the same design documents, and price is the reason for the competition, shouldn't the low bidder be entitled to the award? In fact, however, challenges to the award of such private works contracts and lawsuits against the awardee based upon tort theories are usually unavailing. For example, a bidder on a private work who disregarded the instructions to bidders, conducted private pre-bid negotiations with the owner, and submitted a nonconforming bid that was accepted by the owner, was held by the Missouri Court of Appeals in *Briner Electric Co. v. Sachs Electric Co.*[1] not to be liable to an unsuccessful competitor-bidder for tortious interference with a valid business expectancy. The court cited the justified business

[1] 680 S.W.2d 737 (Mo. Ct. App. 1984).

competition exception of the *Restatement of Torts (Second)* § 768. The court further found that all bidders were notified in advance that the owner reserved the right to waive irregularities in the bids and that such a provision allows the owner to permit nonconforming bids and otherwise "control compliance" with the bidding documents.

In *St. Luke's Hospital v. Midwest Mechanical Contractors, Inc.*,[2] the Missouri Court of Appeals held that a rejected low bidder is not the "contractor," and despite being "pre-qualified" to bid, such bidder may not demand arbitration pursuant to the contract if the owner reserved the right to reject "any and all bids."

Proposals by private works contractors to private owners, including lump-sum bids, generally are considered to be offers which can be accepted or rejected at will. Design-build proposals offer alternative designs, materials, and configurations. Analysis of such proposals for award purposes involves subjective judgment concerning functional and aesthetic features and, therefore, the comparative basis for challenge by an unhappy proposer is more elusive and ephemeral than in the case of lump-sum bidding.

§ 7.3 Protests of Public Design-Build Awards

Public works are designed and constructed with tax dollars. Conventional wisdom concerning the prudent expenditure of taxes calls for open, advertised, competitive public bidding on identified products, services, and real property improvements. Traditionally, the award of the contract is to be made to the lowest responsive, responsible bidder whose price is within appropriated fund limits. This principle is well established by numerous federal, state, and local procurement laws and ordinances. The obvious benefits of such competitive bidding are: (1) price competition; (2) clear identification of the work purchased; and (3) avoidance of corruption, fraud, favoritism, and politics in the expenditure of public money through open, public, objective selection methods.

A new trend toward design-build in public works has been observed in recent years. Procedures for design-build competitive procurements are under development in federal, state, and municipal agencies. Of course, awards of such contracts must not violate existing laws and ordinances and must be governed by fair and impartial procedures if proposers are to have faith in the integrity of the system. The cost of preparing and offering such proposals is often very substantial.

Suppose a public works contract is not awarded in accordance with the criteria published with the bid documents or with relevant procurement laws and regulations? What remedies are available to the frustrated bidder

[2] 681 S.W.2d 482 (Mo. Ct. App. 1984).

or proposer, or to others, such as interested taxpayers? An array of forums has evolved in federal procurement law for protest against improper solicitations and awards. Some remedies are also available under certain federal grant programs. However, comparable state and municipal protest remedies generally are not available under many state and municipal procurement systems.

§ 7.4 Protests in the Federal System

Federal procurements, aggregating hundreds of billions of dollars over the last half-century, have spawned innumerable protests. Early appeals were essentially administrative complaints resolved in the form of decisions issued by the head of the General Accounting Office (GAO), the comptroller general.

In 1956, the U.S. Court of Claims provided a remedy of sorts by recognizing damages for breach of an implied-in-fact contract between the government and its bidders that all bids and proposals will be fully and fairly considered. The relief granted was limited to the offeror's bid and proposal preparation costs, however.[3]

In 1970, the United States Court of Appeals for the D.C. Circuit held that an unsuccessful bidder may be "aggrieved" by government agency action within the meaning of the Administrative Procedure Act and have standing to obtain judicial review in the federal district courts of alleged arbitrary or capricious agency procurement action or abuse of discretion.[4]

In 1985, the General Services Board of Contract Appeals (GSBCA) was authorized by statute[5] to hear protests regarding automated data processing equipment procurements.

The federal experience is an important source of precedent in any consideration relating to the development of state and municipal award evaluation systems.

§ 7.5 —General Accounting Office Role

The comptroller general as head of the GAO is charged by Congress[6] to settle all accounts of U.S. government agencies and, as an incident of that function, issues decisions indicating GAO requirements for proper procurement actions. Early on these decisions were directed to procurement

[3] Heyer Prod. Co. v. United States, 140 F. Supp. 409 (Ct. Cl. 1956).

[4] Scanwell Labs., Inc. v. Shaffer, 424 F.2d 859 (D.C. Cir. 1970).

[5] 40 U.S.C. § 759(f) (1988).

[6] 31 U.S.C. § 3526 (1988).

officials of the government and offered only moral, indirect relief to the disappointed bidder.[7]

In 1985, a section of the Competition in Contracting Act (CICA)[8] provided a new, comprehensive statutory basis for GAO resolution of protests concerning federal government procurement. This statute directs the GAO to decide protests "without regard to any cost or disruption from terminating, recompeting or reawarding the contract." The GAO is to act on protests timely filed by "interested" parties by giving a notice to the federal agency involved "within one working day." The GAO notice has an injunctive effect, as it will suspend award of the contract unless the "head of the procuring agency" makes a written finding that "urgent and compelling circumstances that significantly affect interests of the United States will not permit" the delay involved in the protest procedure.

If the GAO sustains a protest, it shall recommend that the federal agency:

> (A) refrain from exercising any of its options under the contract;
>
> (B) recompete the contract immediately;
>
> (C) issue a new solicitation;
>
> (D) terminate the contract;
>
> (E) award a contract consistent with the requirements of such statute and regulation;
>
> (F) implement any combination of recommendations under clauses (A), (B), (C), (D), and (E); and
>
> (G) implement such other recommendations as the Comptroller General determines to be necessary in order to promote compliance with procurement statutes and regulations.[9]

Also, if the protest is sustained, the GAO may declare an appropriate interested party to be entitled to the costs of "(A) filing and pursuing the protest, including reasonable attorneys' fees; and (B) bid and proposal preparation."[10]

The GAO considered a protest involving a design-build procurement in *Shirley Construction Corp.*[11] The Army Corps of Engineers solicited competitive proposals for a fixed-price contract for the design and construction of a commissary at Fort Eustis, Virginia. Six offerors responded, one was

[7] The early history of the GAO as a forum for protests of federal contract awards was summarized in Wheelabrator Corp. v. Chafee, 455 F.2d 1306 (D.C. Cir. 1971).

[8] 31 U.S.C. §§ 3551–3556 (1988).

[9] *Id.* § 3554(b)(1).

[10] *Id.* § 3554(c)(1).

[11] 70 Comp. Gen. 62 (1990). *See also* Paxson Elec. Co. v. United States, 14 Cl. Ct. 634 (1988) (government "performed a technical/price tradeoff and concluded that the technical superiority of [the losing] proposal simply was not worth the extra $1.7 million in price.").

selected. Shirley protested the $8,984,000 award to Donohoe Construction Company, the third lowest offeror. Shirley's price proposal was $6,645,202. Shirley complained that the agency failed to follow the proper evaluation procedure or make a "reasonable" trade-off between technical factors and price. The GAO decision states Shirley's complaint as follows:

> The protester contends that since its price was 35 percent lower than the awardee's and its technical score was only 17 percent lower than the awardee's, the government could not reasonably determine that the award to Donohoe, the higher priced offeror, was most advantageous to the government.
>
> In a negotiated procurement, the government is not required to make award to the firm offering the lowest price unless the RFP specifies that price will be the determinative factor. University of Dayton Research Inst., B-2271115, Aug. 19, 1987, 87-2 CPD para. 178. Since the RFP did not provide for award on the basis of the lowest priced technically acceptable proposal, but instead stated that the award would be made to the offeror whose offer is most advantageous to the government, considering price and other factors, the contracting officer had the discretion to determine whether the technical advantage associated with Donohoe's proposal was worth its higher price. This discretion exists notwithstanding the fact that price and technical factors were of equal weight. McShade Gov't Contracting Servs., B-232977, Feb. 6, 1989, 89-1 CPD para. 118. Agency officials have broad discretion in determining the manner and extent to which they will make use of the technical and cost evaluation results. Thus, technical/price tradeoffs may be made subject only to the test of rationality and consistency with the established evaluation factors.[12]

Shirley's protest attacked the award with evidence of inconsistent awards by the government in other, similar commissary procurement actions:

> Shirley contends that the agency has failed to maintain the integrity of the competitive bidding system because the evaluation of offers under the RFP at issue was inconsistent with the evaluations under other solicitations with similar evaluation criteria. The protester cites two other commissary procurements where its design subcontractor was selected for award based on the same basic design as proposed in the current procurement and a third procurement where another, lower priced offeror was selected despite the technical advantage offered by the protester's subcontractor. The protester in essence argues that it reasonably assumed that the evaluation in this case would result in an award to the low priced, technically acceptable offeror, and prepared its offer accordingly.
>
> Each procurement action is a separate transaction; thus, the evaluation conducted under one is not relevant to the propriety of the evaluation under another for purposes of a bid protest, especially when there are different evaluation team members, different offerors, and varying proposals. See

[12] 70 Comp. Gen. 62, 66 (1990).

> Ferrite Eng'g Labs, B-222972, July 28, 1986, 86-2 CPD para. 122. Rather, the issue is whether the evaluation is consistent with the evaluation criteria in the RFP. Given our finding that the evaluation was proper, we see no basis to challenge the selection of Donohoe.
>
> The protest and the claim for proposal preparation and protest costs, including attorneys' fees, are denied.[13]

This decision of the comptroller general illustrates the special problems encountered in attempting to protest a design-build award. An apples-to-apples, objective comparison is extremely difficult.

The GAO will dismiss any pending protest if the matter is the subject of litigation before a court of competent jurisdiction, unless the court requests an advisory decision from the GAO.[14] The complete GAO bid protest regulations are found at 4 C.F.R. §§ 21.0 through 21.12 (1991).

In overview, we see that the GAO, a powerful federal office, is the procurement proctor for the federal system, charged with providing consistent, principled guidance for the system, plus a relatively inexpensive, swift recourse for interested parties when a solicitation, proposed award, or award does not comply with federal statutes or regulations.

Should state auditors or procurement boards be authorized to perform similar functions with respect to state and municipal contract solicitations and awards?

In view of the subjective factors in design-build selection, a reasonable, effective degree of oversight and vigilance is advisable. The mere existence of a review process would serve to encourage propriety in the solicitation and award of design-build contracts for public works.

§ 7.6 —The United States Claims Court

After the decision in *Heyer Products Co. v. United States*[15] in 1956, the U.S. Court of Claims was open to disappointed bidders who were able to allege injury for breach of an implied-in-fact contract to fairly and impartially consider bids and proposals. It remains open to this type of action.

The Federal Court Improvement Act (FCIA) of 1982[16] conferred jurisdiction on the U.S. Claims Court (successor to the U.S. Court of Claims) to award injunctive relief in the pre-award stage of the procurement process.[17] Decisions of the court in cases filed pursuant to FCIA jurisdiction have

---

[13] *Id.* at 67.

[14] 4 C.F.R. § 21.9 (1991); *see* Olympia USA, Inc. v. United States, 6 Cl. Ct. 550 (1984).

[15] 140 F. Supp. 409 (Ct. Cl. 1956).

[16] Pub. L. No. 97-164, 96 Stat. 25 (1982) (codified as amended at 28 U.S.C. § 1491(a)(3) (1988).

[17] United States v. John C. Grinberg Co., 702 F.2d 1362 (Fed. Cir. 1983).

made it clear, however, that such relief is difficult to obtain, especially when the discretion of the agency is a factor in the award.[18]

§ 7.7 —The Federal District Courts

Scanwell Laboratories, Inc. v. Shaffer[19] conferred standing on aggrieved rejected bidders or proposers to seek relief under the Administrative Procedure Act.[20] A flood of injunction actions to prevent the alleged improper award of government contracts immediately followed *Scanwell,* moving the *Scanwell* court in 1971 to counsel judicial restraint in the issuance of injunctions and, further, that "courts should not overturn any procurement determination unless the aggrieved bidder demonstrates that there was no rational basis for the agency's decision."[21]

§ 7.8 —Summary of Federal Experience

The federal system for protests against arbitrary denial of a public-works contract is far from perfect,[22] but an aggrieved bidder has certain administrative remedies available as an alternative to litigation. Moreover, contracting officers and their technical staff have available a body of precedent to provide guidance in making "award" decisions. They also know that their final judgment may be subjected to the scrutiny engendered by a bidder's protest. These are salutary protections for the integrity of a procurement system that each year awards contracts for billions of hard-earned taxpayer dollars.

§ 7.9 Protests of State, Municipal, and Other Public Contract Awards

For the most part, existing state and local procurement laws were not enacted with design-build in mind and, absent enabling legislation, represent a virtual mine field which both the design-build owner and contractor must traverse en route to their common objective: a successful project.

---

[18] Essex Electro Eng'rs, Inc. v. United States, 3 Cl. Ct. 277 (1983); Electro-Methods, Inc. v. United States, 3 Cl. Ct. 500 (1983), *aff'd in part, rev'd in part,* 728 F.2d 1471 (Fed. Cir. 1984).

[19] 424 F.2d 859 (D.C. Cir. 1970).

[20] 5 U.S.C. § 702 (1988).

[21] M. Steinthal & Co. v. Seamans, 455 F.2d 1289 (D.C. Cir. 1971).

[22] *See* Pachter, *The Need for a Comprehensive Judicial Remedy for Bid Protests,* 16 Pub. Cont. L. J. 298 (Aug. 1986).

The procurement systems utilized by the states and local public bodies have often been held to be for the protection of the public and not those submitting proposals.[23] Louisiana stands as an exception, recognizing that a low bidder, arbitrarily rejected without a hearing as "not responsible," has liberty and property rights cognizable under the 14th Amendment of the U.S. Constitution. The Louisiana jurisprudence on this subject is set forth in the case of *Haughton Elevator Division v. State.*[24] Generally, however, state and local procurement systems have not provided a protest procedure for use by the person most likely to finance a challenge: a disappointed bidder.

In Georgia, Florida, Minnesota, Illinois, New York, Idaho, and other jurisdictions,[25] bidders arbitrarily denied award of a public works construction contract have been allowed to maintain an action based upon promissory estoppel principles, in order to recover bid preparation and submittal costs. The claimants generally were denied recovery of lost profits and attorneys' fees. In many jurisdictions, however, as discussed in §§ **7.10** and **7.12**, taxpayers are accorded standing to challenge illegal contracts.

§ 7.10 —Sealed Bids and Competitive Proposals

Formally advertised, open, competitive bidding is termed *sealed bidding,*[26] and the phrase "competitive proposals" is now used in lieu of "negotiation" in federal procurement terminology[27] and in the *Model Procurement Code for State and Local Governments* developed as a project of the American Bar Association.[28]

---

[23] Tectonics, Inc. v. Castle Constr. Co., 496 So. 2d 704 (Ala. 1986); Metcalf & Eddy Servs., Inc. v. City of St. Charles, 701 S.W.2d 497 (Mo. Ct. App. 1985).

[24] 367 So. 2d 1161 (La. 1979). Denial of Fourteenth Amendment equal protection rights has been a focal point of protests by disappointed construction bidders in J.A. Croson Co. v. City of Richmond, 822 F.2d 1355 (4th Cir. 1987), *aff'd,* 488 U.S. 469 (1989), and its progeny.

[25] City of Atlanta v. J.A. Jones Constr. Co., 260 Ga. 658, 398 S.E.2d 369 (1990); City of Cape Coral v. Water Servs., of Am., Inc., 567 So. 2d 510 (Fla. Dist. Ct. App. 1990); Telephone Assocs., Inc. v. St. Louis County Bd., 364 N.W.2d 378 (Minn. 1985); State Mechanical Contractors, Inc. v. Village of Pleasant Hill, 132 Ill. App. 3d 1027, 477 N.E.2d 509 (1985); Spencer, White & Prentis, Inc. v. Southwest Sewer Dist., 103 A.D.2d 802, 477 N.Y.S.2d 681 (1984); Neilsen & Co. v. Cassia & Twin Falls County Joint Class A Sch. Dist., 103 Idaho 317, 647 P.2d 773 (Ct. App. 1982). *See* Annotation: *Public Contracts: Low Bidders Monetary Relief Against State or Local Agency for Nonaward of Contract,* 65 A.L.R. 4th 93 (1988).

[26] 10 U.S.C. § 2304(a)(2) (1988).

[27] *Id.* §§ 2304(a)(2)(b), 2304(c).

[28] American Bar Association, The Model Procurement Code for State and Local Governments—Recommended Regulations, §§ 3-202, 3-203 (3d printing Sept. 1990).

Generally, sealed bids are publicly opened. They are subject to inspection by other bidders for responsiveness. The contract is awarded to the lowest responsive, responsible bidder, without discussion or negotiation. An identity of the contract terms advertised and bid upon with the contract awarded characterizes competitively bid contracts.

Design-build procurements also are competitions in the sense that each competitive proposer is addressing the general criteria specified in the request for proposals (RFP) in competition with the other contestants. The solutions proposed to satisfy general performance, space, and other criteria often differ significantly, however. Is the element of competition in such design-build competitions sufficient to satisfy state statutes that require "sealed bids?"

The case of *North Country Development Corp. v. Massena Housing Authority*[29] involved a competitive procurement for a HUD-subsidized housing project to be built on a design-build, turnkey basis. The lowest priced proposal was rejected and the disappointed proposer obtained a statutory show cause order. The court held:

> Any attempt to circumvent the requirement for sealed proposals for bids on construction contracts, no matter how well intended, cannot be looked on with favor by this court. Whether this project involved a straight construction contract or the so-called "turn-key" procedure, the result is the same, and the statutes for the protection of the taxpayers should be strictly followed; and this regardless of whether the project is financed through the Federal Government, State Government or by local taxes.[30]

Failure to comply with existing, applicable statutory requirements for sealed bidding may result in an injunction or may render a contract illegal and void. In the *Massena* case, the court remitted the matter to the housing authority for new bids, "if so advised, complying with legal requirements."

The *Massena* case was distinguished in a later New York case, *Marino v. Town of Ramapo,*[31] on the grounds that the housing authority in *Massena* at all times owned the property on which the construction occurred, whereas *Ramapo* concerned a "pure" turnkey contract providing for the owner to purchase the project land and buildings only upon full completion. The court found authority in Massachusetts[32] and New Jersey[33] to support this exception to the usual competitive bidding requirements, and alternatively supported its decision by the federal supremacy clause of the

---

[29] 65 Misc. 2d 105, 316 N.Y.S.2d 894 (1970).

[30] 316 N.Y.S.2d at 902.

[31] 68 Misc. 2d 44, 326 N.Y.S.2d 162 (1971).

[32] Commissioner of Labor & Indus. v. Lawrence Hous. Auth., 358 Mass. 202, 261 N.E.2d 331 (1970).

[33] Lehigh Constr. Co. v. Housing Auth., 56 N.J. 447, 267 A.2d 41 (1970).

U.S. Constitution, Article VI, Section 2, to the effect that if New York law were applicable, it "must yield to HUD regulations" authorizing such procurement as applied to a pure "turn-key" project.

A Wisconsin court carefully considered the validity of design-build selection procedures respecting eight public buildings in *J.F. Ahern Co. v. Wisconsin State Building Commission.*[34] The Wisconsin State Building Commission, composed of the governor, six legislators, and a citizen appointed by the governor, waived the application of the competitive bidding statute. This waiver was clearly authorized by a related section of the Wisconsin statutes. Two Wisconsin taxpayers, who were held to have "standing to test the constitutionality of statutes which result in public expenditures," charged, however, that despite the waiver action the procurement violated another Wisconsin statute providing that no public body shall enter into construction contracts costing "in excess of $15,000, by any means whatsoever, *without completion of final plans.*"[35] The court held that "the final plans requirement . . . is satisfied when the commission has such plans as are sufficiently definite to allow the letting of contracts consistent with the process chosen for a particular project."[36] Of course, the process chosen was design-build, and the plans upon which the contract was let were considered sufficient for that process by the commission.

In *Ahern,* the statutory establishment of a building commission with authority to waive competitive bidding requirements was found to be permissible under the Wisconsin constitution. The court stated:

> Because there are ascertainable standards for the commission to determine whether waiver is in the best interest of the state, and because judicial review of commission waiver decisions protects against arbitrary, unreasonable or oppressive conduct, sec. 13.48(19), Stats., does not constitute an unlawful delegation of legislative power to the commission.[37]

The *Ahern* case illustrates vividly the need for constitutionally sound, statutory authority for the employment of design-build procurement in state and local procurement systems.

A majority (3–2) of the Supreme Court of Alaska decided[38] that one Betty Breck was guilty of inexcusable delay in bringing a pro se lawsuit to enjoin work on a $5+ million parking and tourist facility in Juneau. The contract was let by the City and Borough of Juneau (CBJ) despite at least nine appearances by Breck before the CBJ legislative assembly to protest against the proposed design-build contract as a violation of CBJ laws

---

[34] 336 N.W.2d 679 (Wis. Ct. App. 1983).

[35] *Id.* at 687 (emphasis added).

[36] *Id.* at 688.

[37] *Id.* at 689.

[38] City & Borough of Juneau v. Breck, 706 P.2d 313 (Alaska 1985).

requiring competitive, sealed bidding. However, Breck's suit was not filed until eight months after the City advertised its RFP. By this time construction was 50 percent complete. The trial court nonetheless issued a preliminary injunction based upon Breck's showing of a high probability of success on the merits.

On review, the Alaska Supreme Court reversed on the basis of long delay by Breck and evidence of greatly increased cost to CBJ if the injunction were made permanent. The dissent notes, however, that Breck timely raised objections to the contracting method and that the trial court found any injury to CBJ would be due to "their own haste in proceeding with the project despite the serious questions raised."[39]

The plaintiff Breck subsequently filed a new action, seeking personal liability judgments against the individuals who were CBJ assembly members when the design-build contract was let, for knowingly authorizing illegal payments in violation of CBJ charter provisions requiring competitive bidding. The Alaska Supreme Court upheld the defense offered by the CBJ legislators based upon the doctrine of qualified legislative immunity. The assembly members had received advice from the assistant city-borough attorney concerning exceptions in the CBJ code "where calling for bids on a competitive basis is unavailing" or when procuring professional services is involved. The court held:

> At the time the contract was being considered by the assembly members, CCBJ § 53.50.090 excepted from the requirement that competitive sealed bidding be used to award contracts, both contracts for professional or specialized services such as architects and engineers, and contracts in circumstances where the call for competitive bidding was "unavailing." Thus, it was within the assembly members' authority to award certain public improvement contracts on a non-competitive basis.[40]

The issues raised in the two Breck litigations undoubtedly were disturbing to the CBJ officials involved and to the contractor as well. The injunction caused a work suspension, which resulted in a claim by the contractor against CBJ for damages. The claim was settled (over Ms. Breck's objection). What if Breck's complaint had been promptly filed? It seems that in such case the citizen challenge could have been successful at both the trial and appellate levels. An early injunctive challenge appears to be a favored remedy.

In *Sutter Brothers Construction Co. v. City of Leavenworth,*[41] the Supreme Court of Kansas held that a disappointed bidder has no right of

---

[39] Breck v. Ulmer, 745 P.2d 66 (Alaska 1987).

[40] *Id.* at 72.

[41] 238 Kan. 85, 708 P.2d 190 (1985).

action for damages but has available the remedy of "injunctive relief preventing the award of the contract to one not legally entitled thereto." The court cited with approval *Funderburg Builders v. Abbeville City Memorial Hospital,*[42] which, after holding that a disappointed low bidder has standing to seek equitable relief, stated:

> Injunction and mandamus are the proper remedies to compel compliance with public contract award procedures. *Carpet City, Inc. v. Stillwater Municipal Hospital Authority,* 536 P.2d 335 (Okla. 1975); *Federal Electric Corp. v. Fasi,* 527 P.2d 1284 (Haw. 1974); *City of Phoenix v. Wittman Contracting Co.,* 20 Ariz. App. 1, 509 P.2d 1038 (1973); *City of Inglewood v. Superior Court,* 7 Cal. 3d 861, 103 Cal. Rptr. 689, 500 P.2d 601 (1972); *Cf. Gulf Oil Corp. v. Clark County,* 575 P.2d 1332 (Nev. 1978). In the present case, it is clear that an injunction and declaratory judgment are the only adequate means of protecting the public interest, the integrity of the competitive bidding process, and the rights of the individual bidder. If the Hospital is allowed to proceed with award to other than the lowest responsible, responsive bidder, Funderburg, the public has no legal remedy for the senseless and unlawful waste of public funds. Moreover, if it is learned that Abbeville County is not required to comply with statutory requirements and its own representations that it will award to the lowest responsible bidder, competition for county [projects] will no longer receive the benefit of the lowest competitive price.
>
> * * *
>
> For a contractor to arbitrarily be deprived of one of the jobs on which it is the lowest responsible bidder, not only deprives it of anticipated profit but also throws an undue overhead burden on the remainder of the contractor's work and may cause the contractor to lose key field personnel that it cannot readily employ. Nevertheless, notwithstanding this severe adverse impact, it has been uniformly held that a disappointed bidder may not recover even its anticipated profits. *Paul Sardella Construction Co. v. Braintree Housing Authority,* 329 N.E.2d 762 (Mass. App. 1975); *Swinerton & Walberg Co. v. City of Inglewood,* 40 Cal. App. 3d 98, 114 Cal. Rptr. 834 (1974). It is this clear lack of an adequate legal remedy that will dissuade contractors from competing where competitive bidding procedures are not equitably enforced.

In summary, absent a specific state statute or local ordinance governing challenge of a solicitation or an imminent improper award of a public works design-build contract, injunction or mandamus should be considered. Generally, the challenge must be pursued by a taxpayer to satisfy standing requirements. Recent cases tend to confer broad standing upon taxpayers to challenge illegal state contracts.[43]

---

[42] 467 F. Supp. 821 (D.S.C. 1979).

[43] *See* Tichenor v. State Lottery Comm'n, 742 S.W.2d 170 (Mo. 1989).

§ 7.11 —Design-Build as a Violation of State Design Procurement Law

Design-build has been attacked as an evasion of state laws enacted to provide an impartial, systematic method of selecting design firms for public works on the basis of their qualifications rather than a low bid. Such laws were enacted to complement traditional sealed bidding procedures applicable to construction contracts. Often such laws are called "little Brooks Acts" after the governing federal statute known as the Brooks Act.[44]

In *City of Lynn Haven v. Bay County Council of Registered Architects, Inc.,*[45] the court enjoined a design-build construction solicitation, accepting the position of the plaintiff-architects that the statutorily prescribed Florida selection procedure for engaging design professionals had not been followed. This principle was supported by an opinion of the Florida attorney general dated November 29, 1988 to the same effect.[46] As a result of these opinions, Florida enacted comprehensive statutory provisions to authorize the design-build method of construction procurement.

The attorney general of Texas addressed this issue at the request of a county attorney and the executive director of the State Board for the Registration of Professional Engineers and concluded:

> [b]ecause the Professional Services Procurement Act, V.T.C.S. article 664-4, prohibits the procurement of architectural or engineering services through competitive bidding, we conclude that a commissioners court does not possess the authority to award a design/build contract for the construction of a public work on the basis of competitive bids where architectural or engineering services comprise a component of the contract.[47]

These challenges to design-build for public works underscore the need for a solid legal foundation in the state or local jurisdiction undertaking such a program.

§ 7.12 —The Serious Risk of Unlawful Public Works Contracts

Traditionally, taxpayers have been accorded standing by the courts to enjoin payments to contractors pursuant to contracts awarded in violation of statutory procurement requirements.

---

[44] 40 U.S.C. § 541 (1988).

[45] 528 So. 2d 1244 (Fla. Dist. Ct. App. 1988).

[46] Op. [Fla.] Att'y Gen., 1988 Fla. AG LEXIS 57 (Nov. 29, 1988).

[47] Op. No. JM-1189, July 24, 1990.

In the early case of *Hillside Securities Co. v. Minter,*[48] the public authority awarded what amounted to a design-build contract for the construction of six bridges without complying with competitive bidding laws. The county engineer had prepared plans and specifications and advertised for bids. One bidder used those specifications, including profiles, as criteria documents to prepare alternate plans and a proposal offering a price 5 percent lower than the other bids received. A contract was awarded to that enterprising bidder based upon the alternate plans.

The plaintiff, a corporate taxpayer, sued various defendants, to enjoin:

1. Certification by the county surveyor of estimates of progress necessary for payment
2. Issuance by the county administrative officials of warrants authorizing payment
3. Payment by the county treasurer of any warrants issued in payment for said bridges
4. Collection by the contractor of such warrants.

In ruling on the issue of the plaintiff's standing to maintain the injunction action, the court held that a taxpayer "has the clear right to challenge the authority of the county [administrative] court to pay out public money under a void contract."[49]

The contractor then argued that the bridges and culverts constructed conformed to the profiles and specifications of the published bid documents, and that the alternate plans were in all respects as good as, if not better than the plans prepared by the highway engineer. The contractor's evidence was uncontradicted. The court found that the alternate plans were different from the published plans and that "no other person or company bid, or was given an opportunity to bid, upon the alternate plans."[50] The Missouri Supreme Court affirmed the injunction against payment, holding that the contract was void and expressing this opinion:

> Counties are permitted to be bound under the terms of contracts of this character only when such contracts are entered into in compliance with the express statutory provisions. Persons contracting with county courts must be held to know the law and to know that contracts not entered into in compliance with such statutory provisions are void.[51]

---

[48] 300 Mo. 380, 254 S.W. 188 (en banc 1923).

[49] 254 S.W. at 193.

[50] *Id.* at 190.

[51] *Id.* at 193.

The contractor alternatively sought a quantum meruit recovery, claiming that the bridges and culverts were fully completed and in use, so it would be inequitable for the county to have the benefit of these improvements without payment. The court responded:

> To permit recovery under such contract for the reasonable value of the work done thereunder by denying [the] injunction sought by a taxpaying citizen would be to permit the county to do indirectly that which it is forbidden to do directly and would furnish a ready means of evading the law. Such course of action may not be sanctioned.

In a more recent Missouri case citing *Hillside,* the court confirmed that an injunction against a void contract is the proper remedy and stated: "[The] taxpayer represents the public interest of all the citizens of city when he alleges and proves the expenditure of public funds in violation of city charter."[52]

Numerous other jurisdictions recognize taxpayer suits as a proper method to prevent implementation of contracts entered into in violation of legal requirements or, put another way, without compliance with legally mandated procurement procedures.[53]

The heavy risk lies with the contractor, whose right to payment might be challenged by a civic-minded taxpayer despite the fact that both the awarding authority and the contractor have acted honestly and in the good-faith belief that the contract entered into is perfectly lawful. The public owner may suffer delay and embarrassment but would seem to have far less to lose should a taxpayer's challenge be successful.

The prospect of a mid-project taxpayer's action, with the possibility of enjoined payments and denial of a recovery in quantum meruit, argues strongly for statutory and constitutional provisions which clearly validate design-build procurement for state and local public works.

---

[52] Riney v. City of Hannibal, 712 S.W.2d 49 (Mo. Ct. App. 1986).

[53] 65 Am. Jur. 2d *Public Works and Contracts* § 234 (1972); City & Borough of Juneau v. Breck, 706 P.2d 313 (Alaska 1985); Marino v. Town of Ramapo, 68 Misc. 2d 44, 326 N.Y.S.2d 162 (1971); J.F. Ahern v. Wisconsin State Bldg. Comm'n, 114 Wis. 2d 69, 336 N.W.2d 679 (Ct. App. 1983). North Broward Hosp. Dist. v. Fornes, 476 So. 2d 154 (Fla. 1985) holds that the taxpayer must allege a special injury distinct from other taxpayers in the taxing district to maintain suit, absent a constitutional challenge; but note the stinging dissent objecting to this burden on the right of a taxpayer to challenge tax waste.

SOLUTIONS

§ 7.13 ABA Model Procurement Code for State and Local Governments

Obviously, design-build contracting as a valid method of public procurement should not be sustained solely on strained interpretations and vague exceptions of existing laws requiring sealed bidding and selection of design professionals based on qualifications, not price. What solutions are available for state and local enactment, and what precedent is available for examination?

In an effort to respond to a perceived need, the American Bar Association authorized a project for the development of a Model Procurement Code for state and local governments. The ABA text summarizes its provisions as follows:

> This American Bar Association Model Procurement Code for State and Local Governments provides (1) the statutory principles and policy guidance for managing and controlling the procurement of supplies, services, and construction for public purposes; (2) administrative and judicial remedies for the resolution of controversies relating to public contracts; and (3) a set of ethical standards governing public and private participants in the procurement process.[54]

The development of the Code was supported by federal, state, and local government funding grants. Public participation was broadly solicited through publication of working papers, symposia, and direct liaison with purchasing organizations. The code is a *model* code, not a *uniform* code, because of differences in state organizational structures and needs. Alternative provisions and organizational structures are suggested in some cases. Code sections are short, leaving implementation of details to regulations, which can be adjusted more readily as required. The final version of the Code was approved by the ABA for publication in February 1979. Recommended regulations supporting the Code have been prepared, approved by the relevant ABA committees, and published by the ABA.[55]

The Code, the regulations, and three supplementary annotation booklets commenting on cases from Code jurisdictions represent thousands of hours of work and millions of dollars in value, dedicated to the improvement of

---

[54] American Bar Association, The Model Procurement Code for State and Local Governments (4th printing Dec. 1987).

[55] American Bar Association, The Model Procurement Code for State and Local Governments—Recommended Regulations (3d printing Sept. 1990).

public procurement procedures, including design-build construction. This important work product should be the starting place for anyone undertaking to establish a valid state statutory scheme for newer, innovative procurement procedures, including design-build and construction management.

By 1990, 13 states and one U.S. territory had enacted procurement codes and statutes based on the ABA Model Procurement Code (MPC).[56] Of those, 12 states include provisions allowing competitive negotiations or competitive sealed proposals in addition to conventional competitive sealed bidding.[57]

When is design-build considered for use under the MPC? MPC § 3-203 prescribes these conditions for use:

> When, under regulations promulgated by the Policy Office, the Chief Procurement Officer, the head of a Purchasing Agency, or a designee of either officer above the level of the Procurement Officers determines in writing that the use of competitive sealed bidding is either not practicable or not advantageous to the [State], a contract may be entered into by competitive sealed proposals.

The section also describes in outline terms how the procurement is to be conducted. The Code's commentary and the recommended model regulations implementing MPC § 3-203 define in rather complete detail what is meant by *not practicable* and *not advantageous.* MPC Regulation R3-203.02.2 offers as background rationale for use by procurement officers who are considering the use of competitive proposals the following:

> The key element in determining advantageousness is the need for flexibility. The competitive sealed proposals method differs from competitive sealed bidding in two important ways:
>
> (a) it permits discussions with competing offerors and changes in their proposals including price; and
>
> (b) it allows comparative judgmental evaluations to be made when selecting among acceptable proposals for award of the contract.

Absent a material mistake, the competitive sealed bidding process excludes negotiations and discussions between the awarding authority and the bidders after bid opening. Accordingly, if it is not practicable for a contract to be "awarded solely on the basis of information submitted by bidders at

[56] American Bar Association, Annotations to the Model Procurement Code for State and Local Governments, at vi–vii (2d Supp. 1990).

[57] American Bar Association, Annotations to the Model Procurement Code for State and Local Governments, Analytical Summary of State Enactments 85–88 (2d Supp. 1990).

the time of [bid] opening, competitive sealed bidding is not practicable or advantageous."[58]

MPC Regulation R3-203.02.3 undertakes to list the factors to be considered in any determination that sealed bidding is not *practicable*:

(a) whether the contract needs to be other than a fixed-price type;

(b) whether oral or written discussions may need to be conducted with offerors concerning technical and price aspects of their proposals;

(c) whether offerors may need to be afforded the opportunity to revise their proposals, including price;

(d) whether award may need to be based upon a comparative evaluation as stated in the Request for Proposals of differing price, quality, and contractual factors in order to determine the most advantageous offering to the [State]. Quality factors include technical and performance capability and the content of the technical proposal; and

(e) whether the primary consideration in determining award may not be price.

Finally, MPC Regulation R-203.02.4 indicates that sealed bidding may be determined to be *not advantageous* when (1) prior procurements have indicated that competitive sealed proposals may result in more beneficial contracts for the state, or municipal subdivision thereof, and (2) the flexibility provided by subsections (b), (c), and (d) of MPC Regulation R-203.02.3 above is desirable in conducting a procurement.

Of course, in order to gain maximum participation, provisions of the MPC and the proposed MPC regulations establish procedures for prominent advertisement and notice of contracts to be let on the basis of competitive sealed proposals. The RFPs "shall state all of the evaluation factors, including price, *and their relative importance.*"[59] "Factors not specified in the Request for Proposals shall not be considered."[60]

After proposals are initially evaluated and unacceptable proposals are rejected, discussions are held between the remaining offerors and the awarding authority to (1) promote understanding of owner's needs and how the proposal will meet such needs, and (2) facilitate arriving at an acceptable contract.[61] Fair and equal treatment is required for all offerors, and "auction techniques (revealing one offeror's price to another) and disclosure of any information derived from competing proposals" is prohibited.[62]

---

[58] MPC Regulation R3-203.02.2.

[59] MPC Regulation R3-203.13.1.

[60] MPC Regulation R3-203.13.2.

[61] MPC Regulation R3-203.14.2.

[62] MPC Regulation R3-203.14.3.

Best and final offers (BAFOs) are requested from all offerors after adequate discussions have been held; such BAFOs are submitted concurrently at a date and time established by the procuring agency.[63] The proposal considered most advantageous to the awarding agency is accepted, and the award is publicized.

In summary, competitive sealed proposals are contemplated for use when competitive sealed bids are not practicable or advantageous. Such proposals seem to be a likely choice: when the scope of work is not sufficiently defined or definable for the purpose of estimating and bidding; when price is not the sole or principal determinate factor; when time is critically short; when program and technical discussions with offerors are necessary or highly desirable; or when the prospective bidders are few and negotiation is likely to result in a better price.

§ 7.14 —Protests under MPC Procedures

What provisions are included in the MPC to deal with protests of improper solicitations or awards? MPC article 9, entitled "Legal and Contractual Remedies," contains § 9-101, which gives any "actual or prospective bidder, offeror or contractor who is aggrieved" the right to protest to the chief procurement officer or head of the purchasing agency.

The protest must be filed within 14 days after the facts giving rise to the protest were known or should have been known. If a resolution of the problem is not achieved, the procurement official receiving the protest must issue a written decision stating reasons for the action taken and advising the aggrieved party of its right to judicial or administrative review of the decision.

Procurement is stayed during the protest unless the chief procurement officer makes a written finding that award of the contract "without delay is necessary to protect the substantial interests of the [state]." If the protest is sustained after the contract has been awarded to another, the protesting party shall be entitled to reasonable costs, other than attorneys' fees, incurred due to the solicitation, including bid or proposal preparation costs.

The MPC also contains an "optional part" in § 9-501, entitled "Creation of the Procurement Appeals Board (PAB)." The PAB would hear direct protests concerning awards as well as appeals from award determinations made by the chief procurement officer. The PAB also would hear and administratively decide contract claims and disputes, with such resolution to be final on the facts unless "arbitrary, capricious, fraudulent or clearly erroneous."

---

[63] MPC Regulation R3-203.14.4.

§ 7.15 The Florida Experience

Public agencies in Florida desiring to use design-build as a construction method were met with organized opposition in the form of a lawsuit styled *City of Lynn Haven v. Bay County Council of Registered Architects, Inc.*,[64] decided in 1988, and an adverse Florida attorney general's opinion issued in 1988.[65]

In 1989, the Florida legislature undertook to validate design-build construction for public agencies by enacting statutes which at once authorized the process and removed existing barriers to its use.

Florida Statute § 287.055 (1990) is known as the Consultants Competitive Negotiation Act. It defines design-build firm, design-build contract, design criteria package, and design criteria professional, and sets forth the procedures for public announcement, qualification of design-build firms, competitive selection, and competitive negotiation of contracts. A *design-build firm* may be a partnership but must be certified under Florida Statute § 489.119 to engage in contracting "through" a certified or registered contractor, and certified under other statutes to practice engineering, architecture, or landscape architecture. It is not clear whether a licensed contractor who engages a licensed design firm as a subcontractor will be held to be a design build firm. This point should be considered by any jurisdiction using Florida as a basis for legislative enactments.

Florida Statute § 337.11 (1990) requires a determination by the "head of the department" that a design-build contract is in the "best interests of the public." It further requires adoption of regulations governing: prequalification of applicants; announcements of design-build projects; criteria for selection of those permitted to submit proposals; criteria for RFPs; evaluation of proposals; awards; and reports to the legislature on results obtained from a test program of up to $50 million in public works.

Florida Statute § 471.003 (1990) was amended to exempt from the requirement to register as an engineer "any general contractor, certified or registered pursuant to the provisions of Chapter 489, when negotiating or performing services under a design-build contract as long as the engineering services offered or rendered in connection with the contract are offered and rendered by an engineer licensed or registered in accordance with this chapter." Florida Statutes §§ 481.229 and 481.329 (1990) exempt "a general contractor" from engineering license requirements as an architect or landscape architect under like conditions to § 471.003.

Florida Statute § 489.103 exempts engineers, architects, and landscape architects from registration as a contractor when engaged in design-build

[64] 528 So. 2d 1244 (Fla. Dist. Ct. App. 1988).

[65] Op. [Fla.] Att'y Gen., 1988 Fla. AG LEXIS 57 (Nov. 29, 1988).

work, so long as "the contractor services to be performed" are offered and rendered by a "certified or registered" (in Florida) general contractor.

Florida has endeavored to fashion a complete solution but has left open the question of whether a public body can accept a design-build proposal from a Florida-licensed contractor who proposes to furnish the design by subcontracting all design work to a Florida-licensed architect or engineer. In arriving at a solution that unequivocally supports the design-build process for public works, it is essential to assure maximum competition that enabling laws clearly permit this approach, so often employed in private design-build projects.

§ 7.16 Legislative Authority for Special Projects

In a number of instances, states have taken an ad hoc approach to legislative authorization of individual design-build projects or categories of projects, or authorization for certain public agencies to contract on a design-build basis.

The California Public Contract Code generally requires state agencies to obtain "at least three competitive bids or proposals for each contract."[66] The Code gives the agency two choices in evaluating proposals. One choice requires a two-envelope system in which an unpriced proposal is tendered in one sealed envelope, and the price and cost information is submitted in a second sealed envelope. All unpriced proposals are analyzed; all "acceptable" proposals are identified, and all others are rejected. The price envelopes for the acceptable proposals are then publicly opened and the contract is awarded to the "lowest responsible bidder meeting the standard."[67] The other choice involves evaluation of competitive proposals by an agency committee to determine acceptability under the published RFP criteria. The Code mandates that "[a]ny evaluation and scoring method shall ensure that substantial weight in relationship to all other criteria utilized shall be given to the contract price proposed by the bidder."[68] The proposal receiving the highest score wins the contract.

The California Code also contains provisions which directly authorize "design and build" and other contracting methods, including CM and cost-plus-fee and the like, for use by the regents of the University of California "as the regents determine to be in the best interest of the university."[69] The trustees of California State University are also authorized to employ "design and build" for their projects, with the contractor selected "by a

---

[66] Cal. Pub. Cont. Code § 10340(a).

[67] *Id.* § 10344(b).

[68] *Id.* § 10344(c).

[69] *Id.* § 10503.

competitive bidding process which employs selection criteria in addition to cost."[70]

In New York, the legislature expressed the following rationale for using design-build for solid waste recovery facilities:

> It is further the intent of the legislature to acknowledge the highly complex and innovative nature of resource recovery technology for processing mixed solid waste, the relative newness of the variety of resource recovery systems now available, the desirability of a single point of responsibility for the development of facilities and the economic and technical utility of contracts for resource recovery projects which include in their scope various combinations of design, construction, operation, management and/or maintenance responsibilities over prolonged periods of time and that in some instances it may be beneficial to the municipality to award a contract on the basis of factors other than cost alone, including but not limited to facility design, system reliability, energy efficiency, compatibility with source separation and other recycling systems and environmental protection.[71]

This language is part of a statute authorizing a negotiated design-build prime contract with a developer for "solid waste management-resource recovery facilities" provided that the "building shall be constructed through construction contracts awarded through public competitive bidding."[72] The law contains certain formal provisions for effective public awards, which, if met, limit the time for bringing a court action to contest the validity of the award to 60 days.[73]

The Oxford-Rochdale Wastewater Treatment Facility in Massachusetts was authorized by special design-build legislation, which elaborated the procedures for issuing RFPs, for solicitation and analysis of proposals, and for making an award.[74]

In Minnesota, a light-rail transit system was deemed by the legislature to be a fit subject for the turnkey implementation method.[75]

Virginia has authorized "competitive negotiation"[76] and design-build[77] for state contracts pursuant to statutes based on the ABA Model Procurement Code. But Virginia also has authorized "[d]esign-build or construction management contracts for public bodies other than the Commonwealth," including the city of Richmond (a visitors' center), various

---

[70] *Id.* § 10708.

[71] N.Y. Gen. Mun. Law § 120-w, 4(e).

[72] *Id.* § 120-w, 7.

[73] *Id.* § 120-w, 6.

[74] 1989 Mass. Adv. Legis. Serv. ch. 707 (Law. Co-op).

[75] Minn. Stat. § 473.3993.

[76] Va. Pub. Procurement Act, Va. Code Ann. § 11-41.C.2.

[77] *Id.* § 11-41.2.

combinations of specifically named counties and cities (regional and municipal jails), and the city of Chesapeake (replacement of a bridge).[78] The enabling act authorizes "payment to no more than three responsive bidders who are not awarded the design-build contract if such governing bodies determine that such payment is necessary to promote competition."

Public agencies are increasingly attracted to design-build construction. It is a new contracting option which seems to offer greater choice and flexibility, faster performance, and single-point legal responsibility.

Well-established laws requiring open, competitive bidding for construction contracts, and qualifications-based selection of licensed designers who are independent of the bidding contractor constitute formidable barriers to quick and easy adoption of design-build contracting for public works.

Solutions structured to give the appearance of formal compliance with such laws, but which in fact circumvent the intent of such laws, are dangerous for contractors. The risk of delay or denial of payment as a result of a taxpayer's action must be considered.

Solutions should be adopted to provide a well-founded legal basis for design-build authority for certain projects or types of projects, or for certain specific public agencies, or for the entire state and municipal public procurement system. Such solutions would consider removal of all existing barrier laws and related state constitutional provisions, the enactment of open, fair procurement procedures, and the creation of a system for protest appeals and sanctions. These steps seem essential to the development of maximum competition for design-build awards and to safeguard the integrity of a proposal and selection process which depends, in part, upon subjective considerations.

---

[78] *Id.* § 11-41.2:1.

CHAPTER 8

ENVIRONMENTAL ISSUES

Steven J. Comen

Steven J. Comen is a partner in the law firm of Hinckley, Allen, Snyder & Comen located in Boston, Massachusetts, and Providence, Rhode Island. He received an A.B. degree from Brown University and his J.D. from the University of Michigan Law School. The firm is active in providing legal services to the construction industry, representing contractors involved in public works projects in the New England region, architect/engineers, owners, material suppliers, and specialty subcontractors for construction projects throughout the United States and internationally. Mr. Comen has represented clients in state and federal courts, arbitration and medication proceedings, boards of contract appeals, and before administrative agencies throughout New England and New York, Washington, Michigan, California, Puerto Rico, and the Virgin Islands. An author and coauthor, he has also lectured extensively to various professional groups of lawyers, contractors, architects, and engineers.

§ 8.1 Introduction

Over the last 20 years, the environmental regulations that potentially affect the typical construction site, along with the liabilities that flow from them, have increased astronomically. The federal, state, and local agencies responsible for implementing and enforcing these regulations have also grown not only in size and complexity but also in effectiveness. With fines that can easily reach six figures or more, design-build contractors must be aware of the risks of violating environmental standards, even if through simple ignorance of the law. With this in mind, the purpose of this chapter is to present the environmental statutes and regulations that usually affect the typical construction site. The focus will be on those matters that are principally construction related, but they are also of concern to the design member of the design-build team.

§ 8.2 Hazardous Wastes

Dusts, fumes, gases, liquids, pastes, and vapors usually are the most common mediums for a variety of chemicals associated with construction sites, such as cleaning and degreasing solvents, lubricating oils, paint removers and strippers, waxes, and wood preservatives. When construction generates waste, that waste is considered hazardous if it is either a *listed waste* or *characteristic waste* under the Resource Conservation and Recovery Act of 1976 (RCRA).[1]

The Environmental Protection Agency (EPA) has officially designated listed wastes as hazardous wastes, and they include discarded commercial chemical products. Under RCRA, chemical products are not considered to be wastes until they are discarded or spent. Characteristic hazardous wastes are ignitable (flashpoint of less than 140 degrees), corrosive (pH less than or equal to 2 or greater than or equal to 12.5), reactive (unstable), or toxic. Acids, bases, ignitable wastes, and solvents are common construction materials that frequently fall into one or more of these categories. Acetic, sulfuric, and hydrochloric acids are consistently used during construction. Typically used solvents in the construction context are acetone, ethylene, methylene chloride, perchloroethylene, toluene, and 1,1,1-trichloroethane.

Ignitable construction waste includes glue, paint and lacquer waste, and spent solvents generated by cleaning, degreasing, painting, and refrigeration/air-conditioning maintenance. In addition, hazardous gases may result as a by-product of high temperature work, such as soldering and welding.

---

[1] 42 U.S.C. §§ 6901–6992k (1988).

Upon completion of construction, equipment is often performance-tested to guarantee the satisfaction of standards and specifications. Chemical products used in testing can become RCRA hazardous wastes once discarded if they are not carefully selected beforehand.[2]

Some hazardous waste may be inadvertently generated by construction contractors. Some hazardous waste may be discovered during the course of construction, such as finding asbestos during a renovation project or a leaking underground storage tank or past hazardous waste dumping site during earth removal operations.

Note that state statutes may define hazardous waste more broadly than RCRA. The definition of hazardous waste under RCRA and the applicable state law should be examined before reaching any determinations about whether a particular substance is a hazardous waste. Note also that some statutes regulate waste oil explicitly,[3] unlike RCRA.

§ 8.3 CERCLA Liability

When contractors encounter hazardous waste on the construction site, they meet more than simply the wastes they discover. The Comprehensive Environmental Response, Compensation, and Liability Act of 1980 (CERCLA),[4] commonly referred to as Superfund, extends strict liability for the necessary cleanup costs to four categories of *potentially responsible parties:*

1. The current owner and operator of the site
2. The owner and operator of the site at the time of disposal of the hazardous substance
3. Any party that transported hazardous material to a disposal or treatment facility
4. Any party that arranged for the disposal or treatment of hazardous material at the site or for the transportation of such material to the site.

The question facing construction contractors today is whether they can be held to be responsible parties under CERCLA.

The Fifth Circuit Court of Appeals answered this question in *Tanglewood East Homeowners v. Charles-Thomas, Inc.*[5] The case involved a

---

[2] Meech & Bazany, *Construction Creates Own Set of Hazardous Wastes,* Hazmat World 74–77 (Aug. 1991).

[3] *See, e.g.,* Mass. Hazardous Waste Act, Mass. Gen. L. ch. 21C (1991).

[4] 42 U.S.C. §§ 9601–6992k.

[5] 849 F.2d 1568 (5th Cir. 1988); *see* Koegel, *Construction Contractors, Meet Superfund,* N.Y. L.J. 1 (Dec. 21, 1989).

division that had been developed on a site previously operated by a wood treatment facility. Creosote pools at the site were filled in and graded and replaced with a residential development. Construction companies, a lending institution, residential developers, and real estate agents and agencies were designated collectively as defendants. The circuit court agreed with the subdivision property owners that the "definition of *disposal* does not limit disposal to a one-time occurrence—there may be other disposals when hazardous material are *moved, dispersed, or released during landfill excavations and fillings.*"[6]

Defining disposal in such a broad manner could prove disastrous for construction contractors because of their common practice of moving soil and water throughout the site during construction. In the course of grading, they may be unaware that they are, in fact, dispersing hazardous wastes. In addition, when, in the course of securing a foundation, a contractor drives a steel piling through one or more buried barrels of toxic wastes, thereby releasing the liquid into the surrounding environment, is this a disposal subject to CERCLA liability?[7]

Another court recently defined disposal in a way more favorable to construction contractors. In *Ecodyne v. Shah,*[8] the key issue was whether the general migration of a hazardous substance, in this case chromium, commonly used as a wood preservative and previously introduced to the site by the plaintiff, constituted a continuous disposal under CERCLA, subjecting all the successive defendant-owners of the site to liability as owners at the time of disposal of a hazardous substance. In finding for the defendants, the court focused upon the meaning of disposal and concluded that the "clearest example," that is, "placing," meant "introducing—putting—formerly controlled or contained hazardous substances into the environment."[9] The court concluded that the plaintiff, not the defendants, introduced the chromium to the site, and thus, the defendants were not liable under CERCLA for its disposal during their consecutive ownerships.

Ecodyne might be good news for construction contractors if it is adopted by other courts because it would free contractors from liability when, during construction, they encounter hazardous wastes introduced to the site by another party. Under *Ecodyne,* construction contractors could move hazardous wastes around without incurring liability, because they did not introduce the wastes to the site.[10]

Although placing CERCLA liability upon construction contractors who innocently encounter hazardous substances during the course of

---

[6] Tanglewood E. Homeowners v. Charles-Thomas, Inc., 849 F.2d 1568 (emphasis added).

[7] *See* Koegel, *Construction Contractors, Meet Superfund,* N.Y. L.J. 1 (Dec. 21, 1989).

[8] 718 F. Supp. 1454 (N.D. Cal. 1989).

[9] *Id.* at 1457.

[10] *See* Koegel, *Construction Contractors, Meet Superfund,* N.Y. L.J. 1 (Dec. 21, 1989).

construction is difficult to justify in an equitable sense, substantial public policy reasons have been cited for doing so. For example, the threat of CERCLA liability could force construction contractors and, indirectly, architects, engineers, and owners to investigate sites more carefully before construction begins. In addition, and in keeping with CERCLA's theory of imposing liability upon those parties most able to assume the cost, construction contractors could provide yet another source of cleanup revenue.[11]

This public policy argument was squarely rejected in *Edward Hines Lumber Co. v. Vulcan Materials Co.*[12] by the Seventh Circuit Court of Appeals. *Hines* is particularly pertinent because it involved a design-build contractor. In *Hines,* the court found that although the contractor "designed and built the plant, furnished the toxic chemical, trained [the plaintiff's] employees, and reserved the right to inspect ongoing operations,"[13] it was not the owner or operator of the plant in the CERCLA sense. Once the contractor had designed and built the plant, the plaintiff became the owner of the finished product. Thereafter, the plaintiff also had day-to-day control over the plant, making it, and not the contractor, the true operator of the facility.

Many states have their own mini-Superfund law. Care should be taken to determine whether these statutes create any liability in addition to the liabilities that exist under CERCLA.

§ 8.4 RCRA Liability

RCRA establishes "cradle-to-grave" hazardous waste management requirements in subtitle C.[14] Regulations promulgated by the EPA implement the statutory requirements of subtitle C, which are:

1. To identify and list hazardous waste
2. To regulate generators and transporters of hazardous waste
3. To regulate facilities that treat, store, or dispose of hazardous waste (TSDFs)
4. To establish permit requirements for TSDFs.[15]

Although RCRA wastes are usually generated, treated, or stored at operating facilities, they can also be generated during a facility's construction phase. Hazardous waste generated during construction must be managed

---

[11] *Id.*

[12] 861 F.2d 155 (7th Cir. 1988).

[13] *Id.* at 157.

[14] 42 U.S.C. §§ 6921–6939b.

[15] 40 C.F.R. §§ 260–272 (1990).

according to the provisions of subtitle C. Construction contractors must also be aware that state and local authorities may require additional management and disposal practices.

RCRA defines *hazardous waste generation* as "the act or process of producing hazardous waste."[16] A *generator* is defined as "any person . . . whose act or process produces hazardous waste . . . or whose act first causes a hazardous waste to become subject to regulations."[17] These definitions have been broadly construed to include any entity or activity type that could generate hazardous waste. These definitions also do not provide any exceptions for infrequent or minimal spills or accidents. The definitions are also very site-specific, and more than one entity at a site can be designated as a generator.

Generator, transporter, or facility status determines who will be ultimately responsible for manifesting, complying with hazardous waste transportation regulations and obtaining permits, recordkeeping, personnel training, and emergency preparedness, in addition to specific design performance and operating requirements. At a construction site, generator status can be allocated through contractual arrangements between the general contractor and subcontractors.

The amount of hazardous wastes generated each month determines the reporting, storage, and management requirements under RCRA. RCRA contains three categories of hazardous waste generator:

1. Conditionally exempt small quantity generators, who produce no more than 100 kilograms or less per month of hazardous waste and no more than 1 kilogram per month of acutely hazardous waste.
2. Small-quantity generators, who produce 100 to 1,000 kilograms monthly.
3. Large-quantity generators, who produce 1,000 or more kilograms per month.

Conditionally exempt small quantity generators are not included in RCRA's subtitle C regulatory program.

During the course of construction, a contractor may find it more cost effective to allow waste to accumulate on-site before sending it to a licensed hazardous waste management facility. Although this is permissible under RCRA, construction contractors should make note of the following conditions in order to avoid liability:

1. Large quantity generators are permitted to store hazardous waste on-site for up to 90 days. The hazardous waste, however, must be placed

---

[16] 42 U.S.C. § 6903.

[17] 40 C.F.R. § 260.10.

in appropriate containers located in areas meeting specified requirements, with the contents of the container and date of storage clearly identified.

2. Small quantity generators are permitted to accumulate hazardous waste on-site for up to 180 days if the accumulation does not exceed 6,000 kilograms and the waste is appropriately contained and labelled.
3. Production of less than 100 kilograms of hazardous waste or less than 1 kilogram of acutely hazardous waste may be stored on-site if amounts do not exceed 1,000 kilograms of hazardous waste or 1 kilogram of acutely hazardous waste.

§ 8.5 Identifying Environmental Hazards at the Construction Site

Construction contractors should be concerned with identifying the kinds of incidents at a construction site that give rise to reporting or emergency response obligations under the forgoing environmental statutes. That obligation often arises from accidental spills, usually transportation-related, or from an unexpected encounter with a hazardous substance either above or below-ground, usually related to remodeling or excavation.

In the construction context, a typical CERCLA incident most likely results when there is a "release" of a "hazardous substance" from a "facility." Under CERCLA, a *release* can be "any spilling, leaking, pumping, pouring, emitting, employing, discharging, injecting, escaping, leaching, dumping or disposing into the environment." A *facility* means:

> any building, structure, installation, equipment, pipe or pipeline (including any pipe into a sewer or publicly owned treatment works), well, pit, pond, lagoon, impoundment, ditch, landfill, storage container, motor vehicle, rolling stock, or aircraft, or any site or area where a hazardous substance has been deposited, stored, disposed of, or placed, or otherwise come to be located.[18]

The identification of a solid waste as hazardous is the triggering event for RCRA regulation. In order to be a hazardous waste, a waste must first meet RCRA's definition of *solid waste,* which is:

> any garbage, refuse, sludge from a waste treatment plant, water supply treatment plant, or air pollution control facility and other discarded material, including solid, liquid, semi-solid, or contained gaseous material resulting from industrial, commercial, mining, and agricultural operations, and from community activities, but does not include solid or dissolved material in domestic

---

[18] 42 U.S.C. § 101(9).

> sewage, or solid or dissolved materials in irrigation return flow or industrial discharge which are point sources subject to permits under [§ 402 of the Federal Water Pollution Control Act], or source, special nuclear or byproduct material as defined by the Atomic Energy Act of 1954, as amended.[19]

RCRA defines *hazardous waste* as:

> a solid waste, or combination of solid wastes, which because of its quantity, concentration, or physical, chemical, or infectious characteristics may - (A) cause, or significantly contribute to an increase in mortality or an increase in serious irreversible, or incapacitating reversible, illness; or (B) pose a substantial present or potential hazard to human health or the environment when improperly treated, stored, transported, or disposed of, or otherwise managed.[20]

As noted in **§ 8.4**, this definition is further refined in RCRA by the hazardous waste characteristics of ignitability, corrosivity, reactivity, and toxicity.

The Federal Water Pollution Control Act (FWPCA)[21] regulates the *discharge* of pollutants into the waters of the United States. Permitting and reporting requirements are in place under the FWPCA for certain discharges; these requirements apply to any company that discharges into a body of water or sewer system, utilizes a stormwater collection system, or commences construction within a wetland. In addition, unlike CERCLA, FWPCA applies to discharges of both oil and hazardous substances. In many instances, therefore, a release under CERCLA can also be a discharge under FWPCA.

Under FWPCA, a permit is required for any discharge of pollutants into waters from a *point source,* which is broadly defined as "any discernible, confined and discrete conveyance, including but not limited to any pipe, ditch, channel, tunnel, conduit, well, discrete fissure, container, rolling stock, concentrated animal feeding operation, or vessel or other floating craft from which pollutants are or may be discharged."[22] The court in *United States v. Tull*[23] concluded not only that "[f]ill material composed of sand and debris would necessarily be considered an offending pollutant" under FWPCA, but it also stated that "[*b*]*ulldozers* and *dump trucks* constituted point sources from which pollutants can discharged within the meaning of [the] Federal Water Pollution Control Act."[24]

---

[19] *Id.* § 1004(27).

[20] *Id.* § 1004(5).

[21] 33 U.S.C. §§ 1251–1387.

[22] *Id.* § 1362(14).

[23] 615 F. Supp. 610 (1983).

[24] *Id.* at 622 (emphasis added).

National Pollutant Discharge Elimination System (NPDES) regulations, which became effective on December 17, 1990, limit point sources to two categories; stormwater discharges from municipal separate storm sewer systems that serve a population of 10,000 or more, and any "stormwater discharge associated with industrial activity." *Stormwater discharge associated with industrial activity* is defined to include "discharges from construction operations, including clearing, grading, and excavation, that result in the disturbance of five acres or more of land."[25] One commentator has said:

> "The threshold of 5 acres is based in part on the thought that construction projects on larger tracts of land are likely to use heavy equipment such as dump trucks, cranes, and bulldozers for removing earth and vegetation, and may entail the installation of hauling roads, drainage systems, and holding ponds that are commonly identified with industrial activities."[26]

§ 8.6 Reporting Requirements and Liabilities

It is essential that construction contractors be aware that each of the major environmental statutes, namely CERCLA, RCRA, and FWPCA, have reporting requirements that must be observed in order to avoid civil or criminal liability, or both.

Under CERCLA, any person in charge of a vessel or facility must immediately report a release of reportable quantities of a hazardous substance to the National Response Center.[27] Reporting must take place as soon as that person has knowledge of the release. In addition, *person* is defined by CERCLA as meaning not only an individual but also a corporation, a partnership, or a commercial entity.[28] For example, in *United States v. Carr,*[29] the court discussed the meaning of *in charge* under CERCLA and found that Congress "intended that the reporting requirements of CERCLA's section 103 to reach a person—even if of relatively low rank—who, because he was in charge of a facility, was in a position to detect, prevent, and abate a release of hazardous substances."[30] Failure to report a release is punishable under CERCLA by a fine of not more than $10,000, or imprisonment of up to one year, or both.[31]

---

[25] 40 C.F.R. § 122.26(a)(14)(x).

[26] Meagher, *New NPDES Stormwater Regulations Affect Construction Sites and Sewer Systems,* Construction Outlook 17 (Jan. 1991).

[27] Reports can be made by calling 1-800-424-8802 or 1-202-426-2675 in Washington, D.C.

[28] 42 U.S.C. § 9601(21).

[29] 880 F.2d 1550 (2d Cir. 1989).

[30] *Id.* at 1554.

[31] 42 U.S.C. § 9603(c).

Under RCRA, hazardous waste generators, transporters, and owners and operators of treatment, storage, and disposal facilities have an obligation to report. *Generators* under RCRA, however, have reporting obligations dependant upon generator class. See **§ 8.5**. For example, conditionally exempt small quantity generators are not required to report spills or comply with the manifest system.

Small-quantity generators, on the other hand, must immediately notify the National Response Center "in the event of a fire, explosion, or other release which could threaten human health outside the facility or when a generator has knowledge that a spill has reached surface water."[32] Such notification must include:

1. The name, address, and EPA identification number of the generator
2. The date, time, and type of fire or spill
3. The quantity and type of material involved
4. The extent of any injuries
5. An estimate of the amount and disposition of any recovered material.

Large-quantity generators, owners and operators of TSDFs, and those who store hazardous waste on-site for up to 90 days must develop emergency plans that "minimize hazards to human health or the environment from fires, explosions, or any unplanned sudden or non-sudden release of hazardous waste or hazardous waste constituents to air, soil, or surface water."[33]

Transporters on land are required by RCRA to take "appropriate action" in the event of a release of hazardous waste during transportation.[34] This includes immediate action to protect human health and the environment, such as contacting the local authorities and diking the spill area.[35]

Under FWPCA, a reportable discharge is any spill of a harmful quantity of a hazardous substance or oil from a vessel or facility into the waters of the United States. Such a spill must be reported and removed, unless the discharge is permitted under the National Pollutant Discharge Elimination System. Therefore, immediately upon discovery of the spill, the "person in charge" of the vessel or facility from which the spill originated must notify federal authorities.[36]

---

[32] 40 C.F.R. § 262.34(C).

[33] *Id.* § 265.51(a).

[34] *Id.* § 262.30(a).

[35] *Id.*

[36] 33 U.S.C. § 311(b)(5).

Negligent failure to notify under FWPCA is punishable by a fine of not less than $2,500 nor more than $25,000 for each day of the violation, or by imprisonment of up to one year, or both.[37] Knowingly failing to notify, however, is punishable by a fine of not less than $5,000 nor more than $50,000 for each day the violation, or by imprisonment for up to three years, or both.[38]

§ 8.7 Emergency Response

Any spill or discovery of hazardous substances at a construction site requires an appropriate response, containment of the spill or securing of the substance, and eventual removal of the contaminated material from the work area. On the construction site, these tasks must be performed in an efficient manner that not only minimizes disruption of work but also protects workers and complies with federal and state regulations.

The scope of the Occupational Safety and Health Act (OSHA)[39] covers, inter alia, emergency response actions and post-emergency response operations for hazardous substance releases.[40] An *emergency response* under OSHA is defined as:

> a coordinated response effort by employees from outside the immediate release area or by outside responders (i.e., mutual aid groups, local fire departments, etc.) to an occurrence which results, or is likely to result, in an uncontrolled release of a hazardous substance.[41]

Responses to releases that can be "absorbed, neutralized, or otherwise controlled at the time of release by employees in the immediate release area," however, are not emergency responses within the scope of OSHA.[42] Neither are responses to releases when the concentration of hazardous substance falls below established permissible exposure limits.[43]

Under OSHA, every employer engaged in either hazardous substance response operations under CERCLA, corrective actions taken in clean-up operations under RCRA, operations involving hazardous waste storage, disposal, and treatment facilities (except small-quantity generators or those

---

[37] *Id.* § 309(c)(1)(B).

[38] *Id.* § 309(c)(2)(A).

[39] 29 U.S.C. §§ 651–678.

[40] 29 C.F.R. § 1910.120.

[41] *Id.* § 1910.120(a)(3).

[42] *Id.*

[43] *Id.*

employers within the 90-day exception), or engaged in emergency response actions for release of hazardous substances or post-emergency release response actions, must establish a *safety and health program,* which is designed "to identify, evaluate, and control safety and health hazards and provide for emergency response for *hazardous waste operations.*"[44] The term *hazardous waste operations* is, in turn, defined as "any operation involving employee exposure to hazardous wastes, hazardous substances, or any combination of hazardous wastes and hazardous substances."[45] OSHA also requires that the safety and health plan, at a minimum, address:

1. Pre-emergency planning
2. The roles of personnel, lines of authority and communications, training
3. Recognition of emergencies and their prevention
4. Safe distances and shelters
5. Site control and site security
6. Evacuation procedures
7. Decontamination procedures
8. Medical treatment
9. Emergency alter/response procedures
10. Response critique
11. Emergency/protective equipment for personnel.

The nature of the substance discovered or spilled as well as the site conditions will be determinative of the type of response required of the construction contractor. For example, the nature of the substance might include not only the size or extent of the discovered or spilled substance but also its toxicity, flammability, and potential for an explosive reaction. Site conditions that may affect the type of response include soil permeability, drainage patterns and runoff potential, weather conditions, and proximity to sensitive receptors, such as residential developments or drinking water supplies. In some cases, proper emergency planning will enable the contractor to segregate the hazardous substance in such a way as to allow work to continue. This action, however, most likely also will require appropriate site security in order to restrict vehicles and personnel from entering the contaminated area. Contractors should also be aware that whenever a hazardous substance is discovered or a hazardous spill occurs, those workers who must participate in the containment process should be instructed in proper decontamination procedures, so that toxicity remains contained at

---

[44] 29 C.F.R. § 1910.120(b)(1) (emphasis added).

[45] *Id.* § 1910.120(a)(3)(iv).

the site and does not spread by way of contaminated clothes or equipment to other areas, other workers, or family members.[46]

Contractors frequently encounter both asbestos, commonly in the form of some type of insulation, and polychlorinated biphenyls (PCBs), commonly contained within discarded transformers, at construction sites. These are two very dangerous substances that must be handled with care when they are initially encountered and eventually transported and disposed of.

In the case of asbestos, the Clean Air Act[47] and the Toxic Substance Control Act (TSCA)[48] contain the standards that govern the two activities construction contractors may perform upon encountering it during the course of construction, namely asbestos transportation and disposal. In appendix D to subpart E of the TSCA regulations, certain guidelines are set forth that apply specifically to the transportation of asbestos waste from where it originated to final disposal.[49] For example, there cannot be visible emissions to the air during the course of transportation of the asbestos waste, the asbestos waste must be "properly wetted and containerized," a chain-of-custody, signed by the generator, should be required by the transporter, and the vehicle used for the transportation must have an enclosed carrying compartment or canvas covering capable of preventing not only damage to the contained asbestos waste but also the release of asbestos fibers into the air.

Asbestos should only be removed by trained, qualified workers operating in strict compliance with all applicable federal, state, and local laws. Asbestos waste should be disposed of in such a way as to prevent any release of fibers into the atmosphere or water. Isolation in a landfill is the most recommended form of asbestos disposal because soil virtually immobilizes the asbestos fibers. Likewise, TSCA reiterates EPA's requirements that, once disposed of, asbestos waste must be covered within 24 hours by at least six inches of nonasbestos material, normally meaning soil. TSCA also states that many state and local agencies have much more stringent requirements for handling asbestos, and these agencies normally publish a list of licensed asbestos disposal sites, which is usually available upon request.

In addition to asbestos guidelines, TSCA also sets forth requirements for handling PCBs.[50] For example, whenever a PCB spill directly affects either surface water, sewers, or drinking water supply, the responsible party must notify the appropriate EPA regional office to receive guidance as soon as possible within a 24 hour period. Areas where a PCB spill of less than one

---

[46] I. Reid & J. Lifschitz, Environmental Problems on the Jobsite, 187–88 (1990).

[47] 42 U.S.C. §§ 7401–7671q.

[48] 15 U.S.C. §§ 2601–2671.

[49] 40 C.F.R. § 763, subpart E, app. D (1990).

[50] 40 C.F.R. § 761.25.

pound has occurred must be double washed and rinsed, and all the soil within the spill area must be evacuated within 48 hours, unless delayed by circumstances beyond the party's control, such as adverse weather conditions or lack of access to the site. If the construction contractor is responsible for the spill, it must document the cleanup "with records and certification of decontamination," which must be kept for at least five years. For PCB spills of one pound or more, the responsible party must notify the EPA regional office and the National Response Center, cordon off and restrict the spill area, record and document the area of visible contamination, and initiate the cleanup. All these actions must be taken within 24 hours of the spill, unless reasonably delayed, as noted above.

TSCA and RCRA contain detailed requirements for the disposal of PCBs; among them is the requirement that PCBs at concentration of 50 parts per million or greater be disposed of in an incinerator approved by an EPA administrator or the director of the exposure evaluation division.[51]

§ 8.8 Environmental Risk Management

It is becoming more important than ever for design-build contractors to understand their potential environmental liabilities. The need to identify, evaluate, and reduce environmental liabilities has greatly increased. This is due, in part, to the incredible amount of money presently required to clean up the typical hazardous waste site and the potential of being held liable for funding either some or all of the cleanup.

Environmental risk management is a field that should be of great concern to design-build contractors, because it is based upon the premise that regulatory compliance is an insufficient indicator of pollution liabilities. Simply stated, liabilities associated with the construction site are likely to arise outside the arena of environmental regulations. Therefore, it behooves design-build contractors to identify environmental risks associated with particular activities scheduled to take place at the construction site.[52]

Environmental risk is assessed by evaluating each construction site separately. The risk associated with each site is assessed by evaluating four individual factors:

1. *Environmental routes,* which is an analysis of all the possible pathways material from the site could move off-site, such as groundwater and surface water, air, and soil

---

[51] *Id.* §§ 761.60, .71.

[52] Miller & Murphy, *Insuring and Assessing Hazardous Waste Contractors, in* Hazardous Waste Disposal and Underground Construction Law 305 (R. Cushman et al. eds., John Wiley & Sons 1987).

2. *Target populations,* which involves identifying populations that could be adversely affected by material moving off-site, such as neighborhoods in close proximity of the construction site
3. *Facility operation,* which is an analysis of the way that materials will be handled both on- and off-site
4. *Material characteristics,* which means identifying and analyzing the properties of materials to be present on-site, such as toxicity and ignitability.[53]

A case example involving PCBs on a project can offer insight into how an environmental risk assessment functions. At this hypothetical project, assume that the environmental routes most accessible to PCB contamination are storm water runoff, foot traffic, accidental spills from trucks, employee clothing (especially footwear), groundwater, surface water, and air. The target population always includes the surrounding neighborhood, both human and nonhuman because of the bioaccumulative effect of PCBs. The potential for release is always connected to the effectiveness of facility operation, including design, overall management and employee training programs, environmental compliance status, and emergency response preparedness. How well the particular characteristics of PCBs are understood by facility personnel is the last ingredient in order to properly assess the facility's environmental risk, such as the stability of PCBs, their effect on reproduction, how easily PCBs are absorbed through the skin, and for what the chemical was used so that its presence can be anticipated.[54]

Construction contractors handling hazardous substances like PCBs are usually not able to effectively transfer their environmental liabilities through insurance. The comprehensive general liability policies of most contractors contain total pollution exclusions.[55]

§ 8.9 Environmental Permitting

In the context of design-build, the owner may try to shift to the design-build contractor the responsibility of identifying and obtaining the federal, state, and local environmental permits, licenses, and approvals required for the construction of the proposed project. Obviously, it is crucial during the first phase of environmental permit identification that both the characteristics of the site for the proposed project, such as the location of wetlands or tidelands, and the environmental impacts of the project itself are adequately

---

[53] *Id.* at 306.

[54] *Id.* at 307–09.

[55] *Id.* at 310.

identified by both the designer and the project owner. For example, it would be necessary to determine whether the site will produce a regulated storm water discharge.

The design-build contractor should also perform a *critical flaw analysis* once it has determined which permits are necessary for construction of the project. This involves a review of the necessary improvements associated with the project in light of permitting, licensing, and approval criteria. The question to be analyzed in a critical flaw analysis in this context is whether there were certain aspects of the project or project site for which permits could not be obtained. For example, the project might require the filling of wetlands for access to an extent prohibited by wetlands regulations.

In certain instances, the applicable requirements may be unclear. For example, it may be unclear whether an area to be filled is considered wetlands. In such situations, serious consideration should be given to submitting the question for resolution by the permitting authority along with a detailed analysis of the facts and law in question.

The design-build situation also raises questions about which operations the design-build contractor is required to obtain permits for and which are the responsibility of the owner. For example, a project that requires various stacks and vents may need an air discharge permit. However, the permit is dependant upon the emissions discharged through various stacks and vents. Other examples would be permits for storm water and waste water discharges, which are also dependant upon operational practices. The permitting responsibilities should be clearly understood and responsibilities allocated between the contractor and the owner/operator.

§ 8.10 Government Environmental Contracting

"Governmental contractors and subcontractors doing business in the environmental cleanup arena face serious potential liability arising out of their performance, far beyond that normally encountered by other federal contractors."[56] The dollar amount capable of being levied upon those found to be responsible is staggering. This is due, in part, to the fact that responsible parties are held strictly liable under CERCLA, that is, liability without fault is imposed for any environmental damage, including cleanup costs. In addition, the courts have further held that liability can be apportioned in such a way as to hold each responsible party jointly and severally liable for the entire cleanup cost. An extreme, but accurate, interpretation of this theory

---

[56] M. Charness & J. Dobbs, Contract Performance Issues, Government Environmental Contracting, 19–20 (1990).

would hold a responsible party who contributed a very small amount of hazardous waste to a site liable for the entire cleanup cost.[57]

§ 8.11 Indemnification

In addition to the liability mentioned in **§ 8.10**, § 119 of CERCLA, as amended by the Superfund Amendments and Reauthorization Act of 1986 (SARA),[58] gives the president discretionary authority to indemnify response action contractors against any liability, including litigation or settlement expenses, for negligence arising out of response action activities at hazardous waste sites, both those sites on the National Priorities List and removal action sites. This indemnification does not, however, cover negligence, gross negligence, or intentional misconduct on the part of the contractor.[59] *Response action contractor* is defined as:

> (A) any (i) person who enters into a response action contract with respect to any release or threatened release of hazardous substances or pollutant or contaminant from a facility and is carrying out such a contract; and (B) any person who is retained or hired by a person described in subparagraph (A) to provide any services relating to a response action.[60]

In order to enter into an indemnification agreement with the government, the contractor must meet the following requirements:

> (A) *The liability covered by the indemnification agreement exceeds or is not covered by insurance available, at a fair and reasonable price,* to the contractor at the time the contractor enters into the contract to provide response action, and adequate insurance is not generally available at the time the response action contract is entered into.
>
> (B) The response action contractor has made *diligent efforts* to obtain insurance coverage from non-Federal sources to cover such liability.
>
> (C) In the case of a response action contract covering more than one facility, the response action contractor agrees to continue to make such diligent efforts each time the contractor begins work under the contract at a new facility.[61]

---

[57] *Id.*

[58] 42 U.S.C. § 9619.

[59] *Id.* § 9619(a)(2).

[60] *Id.* § 9619(e)(2).

[61] *Id.* § 9619(c)(4) (emphasis added).

§ 8.12 Design-Builder's Protection

Before committing to a new project, design-build contractors should consider taking the following precautions:

1. Seek *indemnification* from the owner for all costs associated with cleaning up pre-existing hazardous substances and borne by the construction contractor
2. Insert *contract provisions* allowing the contractor to cease working if hazardous substances are encountered on the jobsite and to allocate damages for the cost of delay
3. Conduct a thorough site *examination* (for example, take soil and water tests and check the records of the appropriate environmental agency for past site activity) before bidding on a project or signing a contract.[62]

---

[62] Robert B. Koegel, *Construction Contractors, Meet Superfund,* N.Y. L.J. 1 (Dec. 21, 1989).

CHAPTER 9

ALLOCATION OF RISKS BETWEEN DESIGNER AND BUILDER

Michael Evan Jaffe
Coralyn Goode

Michael Evan Jaffe is a partner with Arent Fox Kintner Plotkin & Kahn, a law firm headquarterd in Washington, D.C., with offices in New York, New York, and Budapest, Hungary. He is a senior litigation partner specializing in construction law issues with the firm, which has an established construction law transactional and litigation practice. Arent Fox has represented owners, design professionals, and contractors in a wide variety of design-build projects in the United States and abroad.

Coralyn Goode is a partner in the law firm of Arent Fox Kintner Plotkin & Kahn. The firm is headquartered in Washington, D.C., with offices in New York, New York, and Budapest, Hungary. She is a specialist in construction transactional matters. Arent Fox has an established construction law transactional and litigation practice, and represents owners, design professionals, and contractors in a wide variety of design-build projects in the United States and abroad.

§ 9.1 Introduction

In ancient times, the architect served as both the designer and builder. To the ancient Egyptians, it probably seemed sensible to have the person responsible for designing a structure also be responsible for carrying out the design intent. But with the overlay of modern financial and legal concerns, this practice changed so that the functions of designer and builder were separated. Today, in many projects, we are reverting to the combination of tasks. Advantages cited for the design/build model are numerous: it saves time, it can save money, it consolidates the responsibility for project success in one entity. But without adequate attention to the potential risks and liabilities inherent in the design-build model, designers and builders can be subject to some bad surprises.

In any business venture, it is of paramount importance to allocate the risks and benefits of the business venture in advance, so that each party can evaluate its expected gains against its possible losses and make an intelligent decision regarding its participation in the venture. In a design-build project, it is first necessary to allocate risks between the owner and the design-build contractor. But because the design work and the construction work are seldom performed by the same entity, it is also necessary to allocate responsibility for potential project risks between the designer and the builder. Although many of the basic project concerns mirror those in a traditional construction project, such as cost overruns, liability for delay, warranties, and performance guaranties, the design-build model can offer a unique context for organizing these risks.

For example, the centralized coordination of various activities can make it more difficult to trace or categorize efforts as strictly related to design or construction. Both the designer and the builder will be contributing their expertise throughout the project, from bid preparation and scheduling through supervision and performance testing. Although this cooperation promotes efficiency, reduces overall project time, and facilitates harmony of design concepts and buildability, it obscures the chain of responsibility for cost overruns, delays, building systems, or structural failures, to note only a few of the ways that a project can go awry. Moreover, the design-build model not only affects the designer-builder relationship, but it alters as well the architect's relationship with the owner.

The strategies and models for allocating risks between the designer and builder vary greatly and depend on factors such as project type, bargaining strength, owner involvement, owner requirements, amount of risk assumed by the owner, and the parties' sophistication in the use of the design-build model. In all cases, however, it is critical to the success of the venture that the parties (1) identify project risks and the context in which they are likely to arise at the earliest stages of project planning, (2) attempt to maximize the allocation of these risks to the owner or design-build subcontractors through appropriate contract language, and (3) negotiate the allocation of any remaining risks between the designer and builder and memorialize such allocation through contract language.

The focus of this chapter is to identify and discuss risks that must be anticipated in any design-build project and to suggest various methods for allocating such risks between the designer and the builder. Unlike the traditional construction model, which frequently utilizes standard contract forms produced by various organizations, including the AIA and the AGC, no standard form has found general use in the design-build model. This chapter will raise the questions that are often the focus of concern and will suggest some answers.

Not all of the risks discussed in this chapter will be present in each design-build project, nor will the risks listed herein be comprehensive. Moreover, the allocation methods suggested may not be best for the parties involved. Thus, this chapter should be used only as a guideline for designers and builders, who must analyze the risks inherent in their own project and devise their own solutions for allocating risk and responsibility.

ALLOCATING RISKS

§ 9.2 Coordination of the Design and Construction Efforts

One of the principal burdens of the design-build contractor is the coordination of the design and construction efforts and the resolution of any discrepancies or conflicts between the two tasks. Under the traditional construction model, the owner hires an architect to design the project and the owner makes the design choices which will later have an impact on construction. In this model, the owner is generally responsible, vis-à-vis the contractor, for any errors in the design documents, any delays created by the architect's failure to perform its tasks in a timely fashion, or any excess costs incurred if the architect's design exceeds the project requirements. In the design-build scenario, the design-build contractor must ensure that the design meets the technical and performance requirements of the contract and is completed in a timely fashion to permit construction to occur on schedule and within budget.

§ 9.3 Bid Preparation

Clearly, the first requirement for coordination of the design and build components is during the bid or proposal preparation process. It is critical that the designer and builder both agree on the scope and nature of the project to be constructed so that the project effort can be priced accurately. Because the solicitation documents normally only provide for some performance and quality standards, many variations are possible when responding to the solicitation requirements. It would be disastrous to merely request that the designer prepare a proposal covering the cost of its design effort and the builder prepare a proposal covering the cost of its construction effort without ensuring that each entity was building the same project.

For this reason, both the designer and builder must work together to develop the elements of the builder's price. They should agree on items such as material quantities, equipment requirements, and basic scheduling requirements. Only after reaching agreement on the basic project parameters can each entity prepare cost estimates for its portion of the work.

The safest method by which to ensure that the designer and builder have equivalent understandings of the project scope is to have both entities prepare detailed cost and quantity estimates for the project and then to compare their estimates for discrepancies. When discrepancies are discovered, the designer and builder must meet to discuss and resolve them. The contract documents establishing the relationship between the designer and builder should give one of the entities the responsibility for ensuring that the bid proposal coordination effort occurs and the ultimate power to resolve any disputes that arise.

§ 9.4 Scope of Work

One of the primary factors in allocating risk is allocating the scope of work. At first blush, this may appear simple: the designer undertakes all work items relating to design and the builder undertakes all work items relating to construction. This simplistic approach, however, is unacceptable. It ignores categories of work, like project administration, that are not design or construction functions. It also ignores that other items of work, such as scheduling, involve both design and construction and are not easily separated. Further, it does not take into account that certain items of work that apparently fall into one category are traditionally performed by firms in the other. For example, the preparation of shop drawings involves significant design considerations but is routinely a contractor's responsibility. These examples are sufficient to demonstrate why the contract between the designer and builder must clearly specify the division of duties.

Perhaps the best method of apportioning the work is for the designer and the builder to review painstakingly each item of work identified in the design-build contract and assign responsibility for each to one of the entities. If the parties review, paragraph by paragraph, the obligations of the design-build contract and delegate, in writing, the burden of fulfilling that obligation, the possibility of later confusion and misunderstandings is minimized.

Special attention must be given to the bonding and insurance obligations. It can be difficult, and expensive, to obtain bonds and insurance that both cover construction and professional design services and afford coverage for the full amount required for the entire design-build project. For this reason, design-build contractors frequently offer separate policies and bonds for the design work and the construction work. Although this approach is usually acceptable to an owner with respect to insurance, owners often insist on a single performance bond to cover all performance responsibilities.

Performance bonds must be backed by indemnification agreements of the parties covered by the bonds. Neither designers nor the builders desire to be liable to indemnify the bonding company for the liabilities of the other party. And although a special purpose entity may be established to perform the design-build contract to limit the liability of the principals under that contract, a bonding company is not likely to accept the indemnification of a special purpose company to back the bonds.

It would be optimal if the bonding company would accept from the designer and the builder indemnification agreements tied to that party's scope of work and share of the prime contract price. It is highly unlikely, however, that a bonding company would accept this arrangement, because it would be unwilling to become involved in disputes between the designer and builder as to which is responsible for a particular problem. The bonding company merely wishes to ensure that it is reimbursed for all monies that it is required to pay under the bond.

It is possible that the bonding company may accept indemnification agreements from the designer and builder with a specified ceiling amount if (1) the two ceiling amounts, in the aggregate, at least equal the penal amount of the bond, and (2) the credit of each party is sufficient for that party's portion. Although this arrangement still exposes the designer and builder to liability to the bonding company for the mistakes of the other party, at least the liability is more limited. To back this arrangement, the designer and builder would have to enter into additional indemnification agreements with each other to cover payments made to the bonding company due to the fault or negligence of the other party.

The least desirable arrangement is to have one party offer the entire bond, which would be backed by another bond offered by the other party for its portion of the work. Under this arrangement, one party would be responsible for the entire loss, and all or a portion of that loss may be covered by another bond. The disadvantages of this arrangement are that (1) two bond premiums must be paid, (2) the bonding capacity of the partner providing the large bond is used to a greater extent than necessary, and (3) only one of the partners receives limited liability.

§ 9.5 Scheduling

In traditional construction projects, the design is normally completed before the construction contractors submit bids. Thus, only minimal scheduling coordination between the designer and builder is required.[1]

In a design-build scenario, however, scheduling can become very complex. Many design-build projects are scheduled on a fast-track basis in which the design and construction occur simultaneously. The design and construction activities must be coordinated on one integrated schedule, and the designer must comply strictly with the schedule or the project may

[1] The builder provides certain design details even under the traditional construction method, such as shop drawings and connection details. The review of these drawings must be coordinated so as not to interfere with the construction schedule. This coordination, however, normally can be accomplished with a minimum of difficulty.

be delayed. Because designers are not ordinarily held to strict schedules, they must be sensitized by the design-build contractor to those portions of the schedule which are critical and must be given priority. The design-build contractor must monitor the progress of the designer carefully to ensure that delays do not adversely affect the project's critical path. In addition, it is important when selecting a designer to ensure that sufficient manpower is available to accomplish the required tasks in accordance with the schedule to avoid any delays.

§ 9.6 Design Review

In the traditional model, as between the owner and contractor, design responsibility is borne by the owner and the design process is largely completed before the construction contractor is selected. Little risk exists that the design review process will interrupt construction progress. Moreover, if the design proves to be flawed, the owner assumes, vis-à-vis the contractor, all costs associated with those flaws and any delay impact while the problems are being corrected.

The design-build model greatly complicates this process. Most owners exercise their rights to review the design-build contractor's design in a fairly aggressive fashion. Owners often believe that they must review the design with care, to prevent the design-build contractor from cutting corners. For these reasons, the review process can be lengthy and may involve the owner's revision of the drawings.

It is critical to keep careful records of the owner's revisions to the drawings and the effect of these revisions in terms of, among other items, scope, time, cost, structural integrity, and material compatibility. If revisions that are not required by the design-build contract are requested, then the design-build contractor must object to those revisions and make a claim for a change in a timely fashion. Because designers typically work on an hourly basis rather than on a scope of work basis, the designer on a design-build project must be alert to identify revisions not required by the terms of the contract. Obviously, it is best for both the designer and builder if the liability and risk for design changes are the owner's responsibility.

If the owner's revisions are required by the contract scope or otherwise indicate a flaw in the design-build team's design, then responsibility for such revisions may well rest with the design-build contractor, and likely with the designer. Liability of the designer in such instances may be addressed in a general liability clause as follows:

> Designer shall indemnify builder and hold it harmless from and against any loss, liability, claim, cost, or expense (including reasonable attorneys' fees) arising out of or resulting from the designer's performance of the work.

Most designers would insist on a limitation of their indemnification responsibilities to exclude responsibility for losses to the extent the loss, liability, claim, cost, or expense was caused by the acts of the builder.[2]

If the parties would rather address the designer's obligation for drawing revisions more specifically, the following clause may be used:

> Designer shall be responsible for performing all revisions and corrections to its work requested by owner if such revisions or corrections are required due to the failure of the work to meet the requirements of the design-build contract or applicable law or otherwise are the result of any negligent act or omission of the designer. In such event, designer shall indemnify builder and hold it harmless from and against any loss, liability, claim, cost, or expense, including, but not limited to, extended or unabsorbed overhead and other daily expenses, liability to third parties, and attorneys' fees, arising out of or relating to such failure, negligent act, or omission.

This clause should be accompanied by an obligation to identify all revisions that the designer contends are not required by the terms of the contract or applicable law at the time such revisions are requested so that the parties can preserve their right to make a changes claim against the owner.

Although designers are reluctant to provide indemnifications, even the more limited indemnifications as suggested above, the costs that can result from defective design work are real and can be significant. The designer's reluctance notwithstanding, it is not unreasonable to expect the designer to cover this risk.

§ 9.7 Construction and Construction Supervision

In the traditional construction project, the designer usually performs the owner's oversight of the builder's work. Clearly, this role cannot be assumed by the designer in a design-build project. This oversight is usually filled by a consultant retained by the owner.

Yet even in the design-build model, the designer may have a role in ensuring that construction is being performed as designed. Some projects have the designer serving as a quality control check on behalf of the contractor rather than the owner. In such event, which party—the designer or the contractor—bears the ultimate burden of guaranteeing that the project is constructed as it was designed? The contractor will want to place that burden on the designer if the designer is the quality control entity, and the designer will argue that the contractor is "always" responsible for building in accordance with the design.

---

[2] In addition, there should be a mirror indemnification clause by the builder to the designer.

If the builder provides internal quality control as on a traditional project and does not rely on the designer to discover quality control problems, then the builder will be responsible for its failure to build as designed. If the designer is intended to be the quality control check, and especially when the designer is compensated to perform this function, the builder may prevail in making the designer responsible for assuring quality control. In any event, this issue must be discussed and coordinated prior to project commencement.

COMMON RISKS

§ 9.8 Budget Overruns

If the project fails to make anticipated profit, not infrequently that disappointment is due to budgeting errors. These errors can be caused not by external factors, such as the owner's interference or misinformation, but rather by incorrect assumptions underlying the bid. As between the designer and the builder, who should assume responsibility for the errors?

Obviously, in many cases, it will depend on the reasons for the budget overrun. Among the more frequently encountered reasons are quantity variations, quality variations, subcontractor cost overruns, and unforeseen circumstances. To illustrate methods of responsibility allocation, the cost overrun causes just mentioned are discussed separately below.

Quantity variations can be caused both by design errors and by contractor errors. As discussed in **§ 9.3**, the designer and builder should coordinate their efforts during the bidding process so that each is comfortable with the quantities anticipated. But when the anticipated quantities are short, who picks up the tab?

The initial burden will fall on the builder. Regardless of the budget, the builder has an obligation to the owner to build the structure promised in the contract documents. The builder must purchase and install the additional quantities without interrupting construction to determine responsibility for the error.

Ultimate responsibility for the error should be determined by attempting to ascertain the probable cause of the error. If a design error can be pinpointed, the builder would argue that the designer should bear the additional expense. Under the traditional model, the designer does not warrant results, only that its work will be performed in a nonnegligent manner, using the level of skill and judgment expected from comparable professionals. Thus, when architects give cost estimates, they do not usually guarantee cost, only that the estimate was not performed in a negligent fashion. If actual costs prove to be much higher than estimated, the owner may not have any recourse against the designer.

Similarly, if the contract between the builder and designer only specifies that the designer's services will not be negligently performed, the builder may not have recourse against the designer if the quantities prove to be underestimated. One way for the builder to avoid this problem is to have the designer guarantee results, that is, the designer guarantees that the quantities will fall within specific ranges. The designer must complete the design within the specified ranges or bear the cost of failing to do so.[3]

The budget can also be overrun if *quality requirements* are underestimated. Quality problems can occur in two ways: (1) mistakes can be made in interpreting the quality requirements of the design-build contract, or (2) the project can be over-designed, that is, more quality is designed into the project than is required by the design-build contract. The latter problem hopefully can be resolved through enhanced coordination by the designer and builder during the design and bidding process. Because the builder is likely to bear the bulk of the expense of over-designing, the builder's interpretation should be preferred in quality disputes between the two parties. And if the builder proves to be wrong in its determination of the quality requirements, the builder should bear that cost.

The first problem, that of a mistake in interpreting the quality requirements, is more difficult to resolve. This mistake is likely to be a mutual one, not attributable to either the designer or the builder. In such a case, it seems more appropriate that the builder bear this risk, because the builder's share of the design-build contract is ordinarily much larger than that of the designer, and the builder is more capable of establishing a contingency to cover these risks.

Another source of budget overruns is *underestimating subcontractor costs.* Of course, these underestimates can relate to quantity or quality errors, as discussed above. But in other instances, a subcontractor's estimated cost simply may be wrong, perhaps because certain costs escalated rapidly between the bid date and the time the subcontract is placed.

The risk of increased subcontract costs normally should fall on the builder. The builder has the primary responsibility for estimating these costs and the sole ability to minimize the risk of escalation by obtaining binding subcontractor quotes and bid and performance bonds. The designer may be responsible if its design specifies the use of only one subcontractor, and that subcontractor proves to be unusually expensive. But even in this case, if the specification is required due to the terms (express or implied) of the design-build contract, the designer cannot be held responsible.

Finally, and most importantly, the budget may be overrun due to the effect of *unforeseen circumstances.* Design-build contracts vary greatly with respect to the contractor's right to a compensation adjustment for

[3] This provision could be supplemented with a bonus payment to the architect if the quantities prove to be lower than the specified range.

force majeure events. Some contracts permit the contractor time but not money, or they place the entire force majeure risk on the owner. More typical are provisions that allow compensation for certain types of force majeure events but not all, for example, allowing compensation for acts of God and acts of government but denying compensation for strikes.

To the extent the contractor bears any risk for force majeure, that risk must be allocated between the designer and builder. The easiest solution is to allow each party the risk of force majeure to the extent it affects that party's work. This rule would place the principal force majeure burden on the builder. But again, because the bulk of the design-build contract price is for the builder's work, the builder seems best positioned to assume such risk and include contingencies in its price to cover it.

§ 9.9 Delay Costs

Delays can be caused by major events: the owner's actions or orders, failure by the designer, the builder, or both parties to meet schedules, faulty work, or force majeure. It would be impossible to address all the possible variations in the causes for delay and to suggest resolutions for each. However, it would be useful to review some of the major issues that the parties should anticipate and address in their contractual arrangement.

If one party is solely responsible for project delay, it would be fairly easy to require that party to assume the cost of that delay.[4] But in the authors' experience, it is extremely rare for any one entity to be entirely responsible for a delay. And when there are three parties (designer, builder, and owner) working simultaneously, as would occur in a fast-track design-build project, the likelihood that the delay would be attributable to only one party would be rarer still.

The first issue to consider is the effect of *concurrent delay*. As between the owner and the contractor, concurrent delay typically means that the contractor will receive additional performance time but not money. Under a similar theory, if both the designer and the builder cause a delay, then each should bear its own costs of that delay. This rule would force the builder to bear the more significant risk of delay, but it is no different than the result in the traditional model.

The second issue to discuss is that of ownership of the float, which is the time built into the schedule to allow for early completion and/or flexibility in sequencing non-critical path activities. This issue is complicated in the traditional model, because the owners and contractors are always arguing

[4] Most designers are not accustomed to bearing responsibility for delay costs and would resist this provision even when the delay is entirely the fault of the design firm.

about ownership of the float. In the design-build model, the designer will also demand entitlement to use of float time.

Float issues can arise in a couple of contexts. First, float can mean the amount of time available for non-critical path activity until delay for that activity would affect the overall completion date. When early completion is scheduled, float can also mean the time between scheduled completion and contract completion. The second type of float can be referred to as *end-float.*

With respect to non-critical path activities, absent contract language to the contrary, it would seem that the designer and builder have equal rights to use float time. Thus, if the designer were late in completing its design work, but the work was not on the critical path, the builder would not have a claim for delay. For the builder to have the right to use non-critical path float, specific language should be included to recognize that right.[5]

For example, the contract could state:

> All design work must be completed strictly in accordance with the time limits contained herein. If such work is not completed in a timely fashion, then the parties expressly agree that such delay will be presumed to have delayed the project for at least an equal period of time. Without limiting the preceding sentence, designer may not use as a defense to a delay claim by the builder the availability of float time in the construction schedule equal to or exceeding the amount of delay in the design work.

If the delay affects end-float and the designer or builder is denied the opportunity to complete early due to the delay of the other party, there is a stronger argument for imposing delay costs on the designer.[6] The result should not depend on interpretation of contract language that was not intended to deal specifically with this issue. Rather, the designer and builder should address the issue directly. And, in the usual design-build relationship, it may best serve the design-build team's collective interest to have a provision that neither will be liable to the other except when the deadline specified in the design-build contract is passed or acceleration is required to achieve completion by that deadline.

The final delay issue to discuss is that relating to unforeseen circumstances. The same considerations discussed in **§ 9.8** relating to budget

---

[5] This rule would be consistent with court decisions that contractors are not entitled to a time extension from the owner until float is exhausted by the delay. Titan Pac. Constr. v. United States, 17 Cl. Ct. 630 (1989); Indiana & Mich. Elec. Co. v. Terre Haute Indus., Inc., 507 N.E.2d 588 (Ind. 1987).

[6] In the traditional context, owners have been held liable for delays affecting end-float. *See* Weaver-Bailey Contractors v. United States, 19 Cl. Ct. 474 (1990); Metropolitan Paving Co. v. United States, 163 Ct. Cl. 241 (1963); Callanan Indus., Inc. v. Glenn Falls Urban Renewal Agency, 403 N.Y.S.2d 594 (1978); Grow Constr. Co. v. State, 391 N.Y.S.2d 726 (1977).

overruns would apply to delay costs. Again, the easiest solution to this problem would be to allow each party the risk of force majeure to the extent that it affects that party's work.

§ 9.10 Owner's Failure to Pay

The business structure of the design-build contractor can have a significant impact on which party bears the risk of the owner's failure to pay (either due to bankruptcy or other reasons) and who has the responsibility to institute legal action to recover amounts due from the owner. If the design-build contractor is a corporation, then the corporation would have the responsibility of collecting payments from the owner, and the designer and builder would each be at risk to the extent of their subcontracts with the design-build corporation, plus their ownership interest in the design-build corporation. If the design-build contractor is a partnership, then the designer and builder would be at risk in accordance with the terms of the partnership agreement, and each would have to finance any litigation as required thereunder. If the design-build entity has been established as a prime/sub teaming arrangement, then the parties must deal with this issue in their contract, or the prime contractor will likely bear the entire burden of collection.

§ 9.11 Liability to Owner

Which entity bears the risk of paying the damages from a successful breach of contract claim by the owner? Under the traditional model, the owner would often sue both the designer and the builder when causation was unclear, and the court would decide allocation of fault. In a design-build model, however, the design-build contractor is the focus of single point responsibility, because it is the entity contracting to provide a complete product for the owner. To the extent that an owner can convince a court that a breach has occurred, the design-builder must now resolve the distribution of fault internally.

§ 9.12 —Delay Claims

One specific type of owner claim is a claim for delay damages, either in the form of actual damages or liquidated damages. The design-builder is faced with the task of determining which activity caused the delay, if responsibility is to be apportioned between the designer and the builder other than in proportion to their respective ownership interest in the design-build entity. This may be a daunting challenge, considering the level of cooperation and integration required from both disciplines throughout the project, including scheduling. The designer is no longer considered an agent of the owner, so that his delays must now be added to that of the contractor as opposed to cancelling them out as being concurrent. Moreover, the interdependence between the two tasks of design and construction tend to spread the effect of delay throughout all phases of the project, especially when they concur simultaneously, as in a fast-track project. Another aspect of this changed relationship is that the design-builder is now policing itself with respect to delay and loses the benefit of the estoppel and waiver defenses available for the actions or representations of the architect or engineer in the traditional model.

Many of the considerations that govern the allocation of internal delay costs also govern the allocation of the owner's delay costs. The principal difference is that these costs must actually be paid by one or both of the design-build entities or their bonding companies. The solution cannot be as simple as "each party bears the costs incurred by that party."

Also significant is the fact that the parties may have to go through multiple litigations to have this issue resolved. Depending on the dispute resolution mechanisms in the various contracts, the disputes may have to be resolved in different forums. Furthermore, it would be strategically advantageous for the designer and builder to cooperate in the litigation against the owner, which will not be possible if the parties are litigating against each other in the same proceeding. In any event, the issues of liability, responsibility for funding any litigation against the owner, and procedural issues regarding the conduct of the litigation should be addressed in the contract between the designer and builder.

§ 9.13 —Performance and Warranty

The combination of design and construction responsibilities also leads to a synthesis of liability standards as they relate to the performance requirements of the project. Traditionally, the designer is liable to the owner based upon a negligence standard, that is, it had to perform up to the same level of professional competence and skill as other designers in the field. The contractor, on the other hand, is required to perform its services in a workmanlike manner in accordance with the plans and specifications provided by the owner, who generally would be held to have warranted the viability of those plans if they are followed. See **Chapter 1**.

In the design-build model, however, the owner typically only supplies performance requirements for the end product, and it is now up to the contractor to develop the appropriate plans and specifications. Therefore, the design-build contractor may well be held to a higher professional standard than either the individual designer or builder under the traditional approach, because it is now supplying the plans as part of a complete product.[7]

The designer and builder must allocate risk based upon the expanded liability of the design-build contractor rather than each party's assuming the liability under the traditional model. These issues must be discussed by the parties and allocated in their contract.

§ 9.14 Liability to Subcontractors

The allocation of risk must also take into account the possibility that the design-build entity may be exposed to liability from subcontractors. The general contractor has traditionally been responsible for coordinating the various subcontractors and is held liable when its failure to do so results in damages. With the owner removed from the design responsibility in the design-build scenario, the design-builder's duty to coordinate the trades intensifies.

As a member of the construction management team, the designer can no longer insulate itself from damages claimed by subcontractors by claiming the defense of lack of privity. The designer is now directly supplying the plans and specifications, which the owner would have warranted in the traditional model. Furthermore, absent some interference from the owner, the subcontractor can also look to the design-builder for any potential delay damages. The subcontractor therefore need only look to one entity, the design-builder, for damages based on either defective design or construction management. The level of integration between the designer and builder in a successful project makes it difficult to isolate or allocate the causation issues relevant to specific subcontractor claims.

Also, depending upon the contract with the owner, the designer and builder may need to determine how to hold the owner harmless from a subcontractor's claims and how to bear the burden of bonding off any lien that may be invoked. Traditionally a problem for the general contractor, the builder may seek to share this responsibility with the designer.

---

[7] Specifically, the designer is not usually held responsible under any theories of implied warranties or strict liability in tort when performing services under the traditional model. However, implied warranties and strict liability in tort may be found under the design-build model. *See, e.g.,* Kellogg Bridge Co. v. Hamilton, 110 U.S. 108 (1884); Kriegler v. Eichler Homes, Inc., 269 Cal. App. 2d 224, 74 Cal. Rptr. 749 (1969); City of Mounds View v. Walijarvi, 263 N.W.2d 420 (Minn. 1978); Schipper v. Levitt & Sons, Inc., 207 A.2d 314 (N.J. 1965).

§ 9.15 Licensing

Another obstacle that the design-builder must overcome is the acquisition of all appropriate licenses. Depending upon local statutes, the design-builder may need to be licensed as a general contractor as well as an engineer or architect. Obtaining all required licenses may be made more difficult by state restrictions on the type of organizational corporate structure that may be licensed to do this work. See **Chapter 3** for a discussion of licensing issues.

In addition, various building permits or licenses are required for the product itself, whether it be an office building, power plant, or other structure. Responsibility for these efforts must be delegated within the design-build team, because delays in obtaining required occupancy certificates or approval for local building codes can lead to construction delays and cost overruns. Often, problems at this level are simply the product of bureaucratic red tape and cannot be traced to the applicant's neglect.

Both the designer and builder must be prepared to equitably allocate any unforeseen costs arising from this process. The requirements for professional licenses should be addressed in the initial stages of determining which sort of arrangement will be selected for the design-build entity. As for obtaining building permits and certificates, those issues can be specifically addressed in the underlying documents that form the entity. Language such as that found in Article 3.7.1 of AIA Document A201 could serve as a basis for language allocating the responsibility to one of the parties:

> Unless otherwise provided in the Contract documents, the Contractor shall secure and pay for the building permit and other permits and governmental fees, licenses and inspections necessary for proper execution and completion of the Work which are customarily secured after execution of the contract and which are legally required when bids are received or negotiations concluded.

§ 9.16 Other Risks

Among the other risks a design-builder must anticipate is the potential for injuries to employees at the jobsite. Generally, this risk has been predictable and to some extent quantifiable for contractors, because the level of compensation a worker could recover would be limited by workers' compensation insurance. This has not been the case for designers, however. The architect/engineer has often had to defend itself against personal injury actions by construction workers over whose work it had no control. As a member of the design-build team, however, the architect or engineer may now partake in the protection that workers' compensation offers to the employer. In return, the contractor may seek to spread the cost of this insurance with its new partner.

In addition, tortious injuries to third parties, such as the ultimate users of the building, must also be foreseen. In the traditional model, the injured party would have to successfully attack either the architect for design defects or the contractor for construction defects. Now, with a single entity responsible for both, the plaintiff will have an easier task at proving causation. Strict liability may be imposed, because the design-builder is providing a complete package.[8] Specific causation need not be determined at trial, so the designer and builder will need to allocate responsibility internally. As with later repairs for warranty defects, the personal injury lawsuit may not develop until years after the project has been completed. Careful planning must be initiated to develop a strategy for mutually defending against such suits as well as paying successful claims.

The potential for acquiring insurance for the project must also be considered. To the extent that insurance is available, the risk may be shifted for a determinable premium shared by both parties. Care must be taken, however, as general liability or builder's risk insurance policies applied to contractors generally exclude errors and omissions in design. Similarly, a designer's policy covering the design excludes construction errors.[9] Simply procuring both policies may leave the design-builder with a gap in coverage, or one policy may be held to apply to a specific situation.

The allocation of uninsured losses may depend upon the form that the design-build entity takes. A designer placed in the role of subcontractor will be less likely to share in such risks because it may have little or no control over jobsite conditions. A compromise may be reached by increasing the designer's responsibility in relation to supervising the construction site.

§ 9.17 Shifting Risks

In addition to allocating respective risks among themselves, the designer and builder should pursue the parallel strategy of shifting as much risk away from the design-build entity as possible. Obviously, the more successful this is, the less tension will develop in trying to allocate responsibility

---

[8] *See,* Miller, *The Architect in the Design-Build Model: Designing and Building the Case for Strict Liability in Tort,* 118 Case W. Res. L. Rev. 116 (1982). This is already often the case in relation to builder/vendors of mass-produced homes. Although many of the public policy considerations applicable to homes may not apply to the sophisticated owner/developer of a commercial property, the possibility of strict liability for defects must be considered.

[9] Bynum, *Construction Management and Design-Build/Fast-Track Construction: A Solution Which Uncovers a Problem for the Surety,* 46 Law & Contemp. Probs. 95 (Winter 1983).

between two parties who traditionally have been cast in somewhat adversarial roles. The primary method of accomplishing this goal is to employ appropriate contract language with the owner and subcontractors, and this topic is covered in detail in **Chapter 12**.

It is useful, however, to review the subject matter addressed by some of those clauses in the context of risk between the designer and builder as well. In addition to identifying specific risks for which the entity may be liable, the clauses may also serve as an example for adapting the language to the agreement the designer and builder ultimately enter with each other.

CHAPTER 10

PROTECTING OWNER WITH CONTRACT CLAUSES

James F. Butler III*

James F. Butler III is a partner with the Atlanta law firm of Smith, Currie & Hancock, concentrating in construction and environmental law. Mr. Butler writes and speaks on construction contract claims, the quantification of damages, project documentation, claims avoidance, environmental issues, and design-build projects for a variety of professional and trade organizations. In 1990 he was awarded the Rich Allen Meritorious Service Award for his work on design-build projects and contracts with the National Society of Professional Engineers. He is an arbitrator and mediator for the American Arbitration Association and is a graduate of Duke University and the University of Kentucky College of Law.

*This chapter is reprinted from *Alternative Clauses to Standard Construction Contracts,* edited by James E. Stephenson. Copyright © by John Wiley & Sons, Inc. Used with permission.

§ 10.1 Introduction

The design-build method of project delivery theoretically shifts all significant design and construction risks to the single source responsible design-builder. However, unless the contract between the owner and design-builder is consistent with the decisive shift of project risks, the owner has lost the foremost advantage of this method of project delivery. Design-builders are marketing their expertise in design, construction, and construction management, and then are tendering proposed contracts that emasculate their sole source responsibility for design and construction risks. The purpose of this chapter is to suggest approaches to contract formation on design-build projects that allow the owner to better manage and minimize its own risks.

The chapter uses AIA Form A191 (1985)—*Standard Form of Agreement Between Owner and Design-Builder*—as a vehicle for discussing some of the issues that should be addressed by the owner during contract formation for a design-build project. The discussion of suggested modifications to A191 is followed by a general checklist for the owner's use in the review of any proposed design-build contract.

§ 10.2 Overview of AIA Form A191

The AIA's form A191 is a commonly used form for the design-build project. It is a two-part agreement that provides for the evolution of the project concept from design development to working drawings to prosecution and completion of the work. Each part of the agreement provides for an independent scope of services and pricing. A191 provides an integrated skeletal system for the design-build project, but it requires modification for each project.

The single most important fact to consider in modifying A191 is that design-build contracts are scope driven. Your emphasis and concentration should be on defining the project. What scope of work do you as the owner expect? The scope of work should define the general nature and character of the project, establish performance specifications and identify the major components of the work. A191 generically describes the basic services, but an identification of the scope of work is necessary for each specific project.

This chapter addresses legitimate owner concerns and interests with the idea of strengthening the owner's contractual position through modifications to A191. It should be stressed, however, that the best way for an owner to strengthen its position or obtain that killer owner design-build contract is with precision of scope, not with exculpatory language and risk-shifting clauses. Although there is little to limit the possible modifications and amendments to A191, this chapter proposes possible modifications and amendments using the existing organizational structure found in A191.

The modifications and amendments are intended to address those areas of risk which need clarification or alteration in order to shift decisively the risk from the owner to the design-builder. Each of the proposed modifications or amendments is followed by commentary which explains the rationale behind the proposed change. The explanation is intended to assist the owner in obtaining design-builder understanding and acceptance of the proposed change.

Each design-build project is different. Accordingly, uniform application of any modification or amendment is not appropriate. Also, the interrelationship of contract provisions and unique characteristics of each project mandate that owners obtain the advice of an attorney familiar with A191 before finalizing any modifications or incorporating any amendments into the contract documents.

An awareness of the risks of design-build projects is necessary for the owner to minimize its exposure through careful contract formation. Negotiation of a contract with such an awareness facilitates a better mutual understanding of each parties' respective roles and responsibilities.

The suggested modifications and amendments are intended to allow the owner to obtain a less ambiguous contract and one which amplifies the single source responsibility of the design-builder.

PART 1—PRELIMINARY DESIGN AND BUDGETING

§ 10.3 Article 1—General Provisions

A191 provides a very brief and general description of the project and the work. Some owners may wish to amend the stated relationship between the owner and third parties to provide explicitly that the owner is an intended third-party beneficiary of the design-builder's contracts. The following amendment addresses that desire.

1.2.2

Paragraph 1.2.2 is deleted in its entirety and the following is substituted in lieu thereof:

1.2.2 Nothing contained in the Design/Builder Contract Documents shall create a contractual relationship between the Owner and any third party; however, it is understood and agreed that the Owner is an intended third-party beneficiary of all contracts for design or engineering services, all subcontracts, purchase orders and other agreements between the Design/Builder and third parties. The Design/Builder shall incorporate the obligations of this contract into its respective subcontracts, supply agreements and purchase orders.

Commentary: The amendment proposed above strengthens the owner's legal standing and rights vis-a-vis the designers, subcontractors and suppliers of the design-builder. As written, A191's Paragraph 1.2.2 states that nothing contained in the contract documents creates a professional obligation or contractual relationship between the owner and any third parties. Unless amended, the architect and consulting engineers could argue that they have no professional obligation to the owner. Although the owner perceives the design-builder as the single entity responsible for design and construction of the project, additional security is available if the design professionals and their errors and omissions insurance carriers are also liable for any design defects. This also reiterates that the purchase of design and construction services as a package includes design services in accordance with the appropriate professional standard of care.

Also, by establishing that the owner is the intended beneficiary of the design-builder's subcontracts and purchase orders, the owner is in a stronger position to enforce warranties or guarantees and is in a better position to terminate the design-builder and take over completion of the project if such a course of action becomes necessary. Although the defense of privity of contract has eroded, it still remains an obstacle in certain circumstances. This proposed modification attempts to avoid that obstacle by use of third party beneficiary law permitting the owner to proceed directly, if it desires, against the third parties employed by the design-builder.

§ 10.4 Article 2—Design-Builder

Article 2 of A191 sets out that design services will be performed by qualified design professionals selected and paid for by the design-builder and that construction services will be performed by qualified construction contractors and suppliers. Article 2 also attempts to eliminate any professional obligation owed by the design professionals to the owner. As noted above, this situation can be addressed by modifying the article.

2.1.1

Change the last sentence of Paragraph 2.1.1 to read:

Nothing contained in Part 1 shall create a contractual relationship between such persons and the Owner except as noted in Paragraph 1.2.2 above.

Commentary: A191 Paragraph 2.1.1 requires modification in order to establish the professional obligations of the design professional and the third party beneficiary status of the owner. Otherwise, the owner could have difficulties if it attempts to assert any direct claims against third parties involved in the construction of the project.

2.1.2

At the end of Paragraph 2.1.2 add the following:

The Design/Builder shall also be responsible to the Owner for acts and omissions of the subcontractors, suppliers, agents, and employees of those in privity with the Design/Builder.

Commentary: This modification emphasizes the design-builder's role of the single responsible party. The intent is to lessen the possibility that the owner will be responsible for the acts or omissions of any party in the design-builder's chain of privity.

2.3

Paragraph 2.3 is amended by inserting the words "including the cost of said services" after the words "in writing" in the second line.

Commentary: This proposed modification of Paragraph 2.3 requires the design-builder to provide the owner with the costs of any additional services to be provided by the design-builder prior to the owner becoming obligated for payment of additional services.

§ 10.5 Article 3—Owner

A191's Article 3 sets out a very brief and general description of the owner's responsibilities to render decisions and provide services for the project. The owner and its attorney must carefully examine the obligations and services set out in order to tailor desired obligations to the particular project. Article 3 requires an owner to respond with reasonable promptness to questions and to notify the design-builder of any observed defects in the work. Also, Article 3 obligates the owner to provide all geotechnical services.

These responsibilities increase the owner's exposure. Some owners may wish to delete portions of Article 3. The following are proposed changes, but each project will have different owner requirements.

3.2

Delete Paragraph 3.2 in its entirety.

Commentary: Paragraph 3.2 requires an owner to set up separate line item contingencies for changes in design and construction and other costs which are the responsibility of the owner. The owner should employ contingency funds at its election for undefined portions of the work. This paragraph provides no protection to the owner. Rather, it imposes obligations on the owner, while the design-builder benefits from the ambiguity and lack of clarity of the paragraph.

3.3

Delete all that portion of Paragraph 3.3 after the sentence: "The Owner shall designate a representative authorized to act on the Owner's behalf with respect to the Project."

Commentary: The deleted portion of the paragraph imposes an affirmative obligation on the owner to examine documents submitted by the design-builder and to render a decision promptly to avoid delay in the progress of the work. This provides the design-builder with strong contractual ammunition for the recovery of delay damages, e.g., extended jobsite costs and extended home office overhead. Any implied obligations similar to that set out in the deleted language should be limited or avoided by the use of a no damage for delay clause as set out in Part 2, Article 4.

3.4

Delete all that portion of Paragraph 3.4 after the clause: "The Owner shall cooperate with Design-Builder in identifying required permits, licenses and inspections."

Commentary: The concept of design-build is based upon owner reliance on the single point responsible party, the design-builder. To the extent that the owner assumes responsibilities or duties, it loses its ability to turn solely and unambiguously to the design-builder to provide the finished project without hitch, problem or involvement. The first part of Paragraph 3.4 requires the owner's cooperation in the identification of required permits, licenses and inspections. If the design-builder is the expert, it should not be necessary or even desirable for the owner to participate in the identification process. The obligation of cooperation creates the possibility that the owner would be found jointly responsible for the costs or delays associated with an overlooked permit, license or inspection. Deletion of the entire paragraph eliminates any possible ambiguity and should be considered as an alternative to the partial deletion above.

For certain projects, however, the owner's cooperation is necessary to identify the permits, licenses and inspections. Even in those circumstances, no reason exists to include the last clause of Paragraph 3.4 which reads: "and shall take appropriate action with reasonable promptness." This vague and ambiguous clause is an invitation for claims against the owner by introducing two factual variables into interpretation of the contract, that is, what is appropriate action and what is reasonable promptness. This modification is highly recommended.

3.5

Delete Paragraph 3.5 in its entirety; *or* amend to delete the word "complete" and substitute "available" in line 7, and delete the word "full" in line 8.

Commentary: Paragraph 3.5 defines certain owner responsibilities that will be appropriate for some projects and inappropriate for others. This paragraph involves an assignment of risk that should be investigated and allocated to either the owner or the design-builder. If the owner does decide to assume the site risks, the obligation to investigate can be tempered slightly by reducing the investigation to provide "complete" data and "full" information. In the absence of these value laden words, the owner should be held only to a standard of reasonableness.

The major decision for the owner revolves around who will bear the risk of differing site conditions. The owner can shift this risk to the design-builder who will have to protect itself with necessary site studies, tests, borings and investigations. Reasonable site investigation will be necessary in either case and the owner will have to pay a premium to get the design-builder to take the risk of the site unless the design-builder is also providing the site. Each project should be considered individually in the allocation of this risk.

3.6

Delete Paragraph 3.6 in its entirety.

Commentary: As worded, Paragraph 3.6 is a potential problem for the owner and an open checkbook for the design-builder. A better course is to require that the design-builder have the reasonable and necessary geotechnical services performed as part of its design-build package. The requirement that the owner provide these services shifts to the owner the risks of additional costs and delays caused by inaccurate studies, erroneous reading of data, overinspection or untimely testing or performance.

The owner can require that the design-builder provide these necessary services as part of its total contract price or it can be set up as an allowance item. Regardless of how payment is structured, the better practice is to allocate this risk to the design-builder to ensure perpetuation of single point responsibility. If the owner has any role in this area, it should be limited to the right to receive all reports, data and logs of any investigation or test performed.

3.7

Delete Paragraph 3.7 in its entirety; *or* amend to end the paragraph at the word "expense."

Commentary: For the reasons stated in the commentary for Paragraphs 3.5 and 3.6, the better practice is to place the responsibility and associated risk of testing and investigation of site conditions on the design-builder.

The paragraph, as written, explicitly sets the owner up for the design-builder claims. Therefore, if the owner is going to furnish the services, information, surveys and reports at its expense, deletion of the clause "and the Design-Builder shall be entitled to rely upon their accuracy and completeness," changes the owner's burden from an explicit contractual obligation to an implied obligation of completeness and accuracy. This implied obligation can be softened further through the use of a "no damage for delay" clause, as discussed in Part 2, Article 4.

3.8

Delete Paragraph 3.8 in its entirety.

Commentary: The owner has contracted with the design-builder for the design and construction of a project. The owner should not have to act as inspector of quality control and should not have to respond to later allegations that if it knew the work was defective, it should have told the design-builder. This paragraph allows the design-builder to argue that the owner's silence was acceptance of deviating work. No owner interests are served.

3.9

Delete Paragraph 3.9 in its entirety.

Commentary: The owner should avoid affirmative obligations "to avoid delay," such as that contained in this paragraph. Such obligations run counter to the intent of the "no damage for delay" clause set out in Part 2, Article 4, and could be interpreted as either ambiguous or as specific exceptions to the "no damage for delay" clause.

3.10

In the first line, delete the word "only" and add "or with the Design-Builder's knowledge" at the end of 3.10.

Commentary: If the owner can foresee circumstances which are going to require direct communication or coordination with the design-builder's contractors, it is preferable to establish that right, rather than operate in the face of the preclusion established in Paragraph 3.10. However, the practice is to follow the mandate of the paragraph and channel all communications through the design-builder. Every direct contact and communication between the owner and a contractor of the design-builder is a possible source of claims or excuses from performance for the design-builder. Thus, the owner may prefer to leave Paragraph 3.10 intact.

§ 10.6 Article 4—Time

4.1

Delete the phrase "as expeditiously as is" from Paragraph 4.1.

Commentary: The deleted language vitiates the owner's desired intent of the paragraph. The owner wants the services completed with reasonable skill and care and on time. As originally worded, the paragraph has an internal conflict between the concept of timeliness and that of as expeditiously as is possible, given the restraint of reasonable skill and care. The reasonable skill and care is a contract requirement that must be exercised during the specific time of contract performance.

§ 10.7 Article 5—Payments

Article 5 of A191 sets out a payment scheme that may be appropriate and desirable for some projects. Owners should examine this proposed scheme and timetable to determine whether it should be employed on a particular project.

5.1

Delete Paragraph 5.1 in its entirety.

Commentary: There are few contracts that require an upfront payment such as the initial payment required in A191. The owner should select a design-builder with the financial resources and capability to commence performance prior to payment. Although there will be some circumstances which justify the concept of the owner making an initial payment upon execution of the contract, those should be the exception, rather than the automatic rule suggested in Paragraph 5.1.

5.3

Substitute "thirty" for "ten" in the first line of Paragraph 5.3.

Commentary: Ten days for the receipt, verification, processing and funding of an application for payment is unrealistic for many projects. Evaluate the particular project, the complexity of measuring and verifying work-in-place, the administrative procedures that will be employed and any time lags or constraints that will result from the involvement of financial institutions or lenders before agreeing to the ten day timetable suggested. Be realistic in the assessment of the necessary time for payments and alter the contract language accordingly. Otherwise the owner will not meet the payment schedule and will be liable for interest and possibly work stoppages.

5.4

Delete all that portion of Paragraph 5.4 after the clause "specified in Paragraph 9.5."

Commentary: Specify the rate of interest in Paragraph 9.5. Do not allow the possibility that the owner will have to pay an interest rate applicable in the state where the design-builder's office is located. By stating a specific rate of interest, the owner can effectively limit its exposure to interest on late payments.

§ 10.8 Article 6—Arbitration

Article 6 of A191 sets out the standard arbitration clause providing for binding arbitration in accordance with the Construction Industry Arbitration Rules of the American Arbitration Association. A discussion of the merits of arbitration versus litigation is beyond the scope of this work and the inclusion of an arbitration clause is a matter of preference and tactics.

The following proposed arbitration clause contains features intended to give the owner greater flexibility and control over the arbitration of disputes.

Article 6, including Paragraphs 6.1, 6.2, 6.3, 6.4, and 6.5, is deleted in its entirety and the following Article 6 is substituted in lieu thereof:

6.1 All claims, disputes and other matters in question between the Design/Builder and the Owner arising out of, or relating to this Agreement, the Project, the Work, the Contract Documents or the breach thereof may, at the Owner's sole option, and only upon the exercise of that sole option by the Owner, together or separately as the Owner sees fit, be decided by arbitration in accordance with the Construction Industry Arbitration Rules of the American Arbitration Association then obtaining as modified hereby.

Any arbitration arising out of or relating to this Agreement, the Project, the Work, the Contract Documents, or the breach thereof may include by consolidation, joinder or in any other manner, at the Owner's sole option, any other entities or persons whom the Owner believes to be substantially involved in a common question of fact or law. In the event that more than one claim, dispute, or other matter in question, shall be in existence at the same time, the Owner may at its sole option decide which of such claims, disputes or other matters in question shall be arbitrated and which shall not be arbitrated. Such decision shall be final and unappealable, and no arbitration shall be authorized to consider, decide, or make any award on any claim or matter which Owner has determined shall not be arbitrated.

In the event that the Design/Builder wishes to request arbitration of any claim, dispute or other matter in question, the Design/Builder shall file a notice of demand for arbitration in writing with the Owner specifically describing the claims, disputes and other matters in question which the Design/Builder wishes to submit to arbitration. The Design/Builder may not unilaterally elect arbitration or cause arbitration to occur. The Owner has the sole discretion to decide whether or not any such claims, disputes, and other matters shall be submitted for arbitration. If the Owner wishes to submit any claim, dispute or other matter in question, whether or not it is the subject of a request for arbitration by the Design/Builder, the Owner shall file a notice of demand for arbitration with the American Arbitration Association and with the Design/Builder.

The Owner shall have the right, but not the obligation, by so electing in its arbitration demand, to invoke the following method of selection of arbitrators in lieu of that otherwise provided by the American Arbitration Association rules. If the Owner so elects in its notice of demand for arbitration, the Owner may appoint one party-appointed arbitrator in its notice of demand for arbitration. If the Owner does so, the Design/Builder may, within ten (10) days, appoint a second party-appointed arbitrator. These two party-appointed arbitrators shall, within thirty (30) days, or such further time as may be agreed upon between the Owner and the Design/Builder, appoint a third party-appointed arbitrator. If the party-appointed arbitrators fail to appoint a third arbitrator, the third arbitrator shall be appointed in accordance with the Construction Industry Arbitration Rules of the American Arbitration Association.

The Owner may elect, in its notice of demand for arbitration, to have the discovery rights and procedures provided by the Federal Rules of Civil Procedure to be available and enforceable within the arbitration proceeding.

In any case in which the Owner elects to submit a claim, dispute, or other matter in question to arbitration as provided herein, the Owner shall, in its sole discretion, select the locale for the arbitration. Any request or demand for arbitration hereunder shall be made before the date when institution of legal or equitable proceedings based on such claim, dispute or other matter in question would be barred by the applicable statute of limitations.

This agreement to arbitrate shall be specifically enforceable by the Owner under the prevailing arbitration law. Any award rendered by arbitrators shall be final and enforceable by any party to the arbitration, and judgment may be rendered upon it in accordance with applicable law in any court having jurisdiction thereof.

The Design/Builder and Owner mutually agree to arbitrate under the terms and conditions outlined above in this paragraph. The Design/Builder has included in the contract price to be paid on this contract a sum of not less than ten dollars ($10.00) as compensation and consideration for irrevocably offering the foregoing options and arbitration rights to Owner. In further consideration for such irrevocable offer and grant of the foregoing options and arbitration rights to it, Owner agrees that, notwithstanding its right and discretion not to do so, it shall arbitrate, after the final completion of the Work, any claims which Design/Builder selects which total, in the aggregate, up to one thousand dollars ($1,000.00). Owner's obligation to arbitrate such claims totalling up to one thousand dollars ($1,000.00) shall be specifically enforceable by Design/Builder under the prevailing arbitration law and any award rendered by the arbitrator(s) shall be final and enforceable by any party to the arbitration, and judgment may be rendered upon it in accordance with applicable law in any court having jurisdiction thereof.

Unless otherwise agreed in writing, and notwithstanding any other rights or obligations of either of the parties under any Contract Documents or agreements, Design/Builder shall carry on with the performance of its services and duties hereunder during the pendency of any claim, dispute, other matter in question or arbitration or other proceeding to resolve any claim, dispute or other matter in question, and the Owner shall continue to make payments in accordance with the Contract Documents, but the Owner shall be under no obligation to make payments on or against such claims, disputes, or other matters in question, during the pendency of any arbitration or other proceeding to resolve such claims, disputes or other matters in question.

Commentary: This modified arbitration clause gives the owner considerable control over whether the disputes will be arbitrated and what procedures will be employed. This clause gives the owner the flexibility to litigate disputes, if arbitration is not desired. Further, this clause allows the owner to consolidate or join other parties into an arbitration, use discovery procedures at its discretion, choose the site for the arbitration and modify the selection procedure for arbitrators. Although an attempt is made in this arbitration clause to ensure mutuality of obligation in connection with the owner's option to arbitrate, a court could sustain an attack on an owner's option arbitration clause.

Therefore, owners that are willing to agree to compulsory arbitration of disputes can exercise the owner option features of this proposed amendment, while maintaining the other rights established in the arbitration clause.

Of course, some owners will not want to participate in arbitration in any circumstance. If so, Article 6 should simply be deleted.

§ 10.9 Article 7—Miscellaneous Provisions

Article 7 of A191 provides a series of paragraphs for possible incorporation into the contract. The standard provisions need to be modified for each contract according to the project and the interests of the owner.

7.1

Paragraph 7.1 is deleted in its entirety and the following is added in lieu thereof:

7.1 This Part 1 shall be governed by the law of the place of the project.

or

7.1 This Part 1 shall be governed by the laws of (state a particular jurisdiction).

Commentary: There is no sound reason to favor the design-builder with the application of its home state law. For consistency of resolution, the better course is to apply the law of the project site, since that law will apply by statute to many aspects of the design and construction, ranging from licensing requirements to lien rights to warranty claims. Application of the law of another jurisdiction is also an option, but that state should have some reasonable relationship to the project.

7.4.1

Delete the second sentence of Paragraph 7.4.1 and substitute in lieu thereof the following:

The Design/Builder shall not assign, sublet or transfer an interest in Part 1 without written consent of the Owner.

Commentary: An owner may wish to have the right to sell, syndicate, or otherwise transfer its interest in the project. It should not be necessary to obtain the design-builder's consent for such a change in ownership structure or transfer, since the first sentence of this paragraph protects the design-builder's expectation interest by making the provisions of Part 1 binding on the owner's successors and assigns.

§ 10.10 Article 8—Termination of the Agreement

Article 8 sets out a procedure to be employed for termination of the agreement. The owner needs to have the ability to terminate the work of the design-builder when the design-builder is not performing or when the owner has decided not to proceed with the project using the design-builder. In either instance, it is necessary to have procedures in place and an ability to limit owner exposure. The following set of suggested modifications strengthens the owner's position:

8.1

Delete Paragraph 8.1 in its entirety and add the following in lieu thereof:

8.1 Part 1 may be terminated by the Owner upon three days written notice at the Owner's election. In the event of termination at the Owner's election and not the fault of the design/builder, the design/builder shall be compensated for services performed to termination date, together with reimbursable expenses then due.

8.2

Delete Paragraph 8.2 in its entirety and add the following in lieu thereof:

8.2 If the Design/Builder defaults or persistently fails or neglects to carry out the work in accordance with the contract documents or fails to perform the provisions of Part 1, the Owner may give written notice that the Owner intends to terminate Part 1. If the Design/Builder fails to correct the defaults, failure or neglect within three days after being given notice, the Owner may without prejudice to any other remedy make good such deficiencies and may deduct the cost thereof from the payment due the Design/Builder or, at the Owner's option, may terminate the employment of the Design/Builder and take possession of the site and of all materials, equipment, tools and construction equipment and machinery thereon owed by the Design/Builder as well as all drawings, plans, and specifications and finish the Work by whatever means the Owner may deem expedient. If the unpaid balance of the contract sum exceeds the expense of finishing the Work, the excess shall be paid to the Design/Builder, but if the expense exceeds the unpaid balance, the Design/Builder shall pay the difference to the Owner.

8.3

Delete Paragraph 8.3 in its entirety and add the following in lieu thereof:

8.3 If the Owner fails to make payment when due, the Design/Builder may give written notice of the Design/Builder's intention to terminate Part 1. If the Design/Builder fails to receive payment within fourteen days after receipt of such notice by the Owner, the Design/Builder may give a second written notice and, fourteen days after receipt of such second written notice by the Owner, may terminate Part 1 and recover from the Owner payment for the cost of the Work executed.

Commentary: The owner should retain the ability to stop the design-builder at any point in the design and construction of the project with the minimum possible exposure to the design-builder. A termination for convenience clause, such as outlined above, is one method of minimizing the owner's exposure should the project be abandoned or should the owner choose to proceed using services other than the design-builder's. It is important to set out the total scope of the owner's exposure in terms of a limitation of possible damages to the actual cost of the work performed. Further, the owner needs to have the ability to quickly remove a nonperforming design-builder. The default termination paragraph set out above allows the owner to move expeditiously to keep its project on line in the event of design-builder default.

§ 10.11 Article 9—Basis of Compensation

A191's Article 9 sets out one possible outline of providing compensation to the design-builder. Obviously the possible methods of compensation for the design-builder are virtually limitless. However, the following are suggested modifications to the scheme set out in A191. The important points in negotiating the basis of compensation for the design-builder are going to revolve around mark ups, multipliers and reimbursable expenses. It is important in working with Article 9 that the owner establish clear definitions and perimeters of its obligations.

9.3.1

Delete Paragraph 9.3.1 in its entirety and add the following in lieu thereof:

9.3.1 Reimbursable expenses include the actual verifiable expenditures made by the Design/Builder at the Owner's request in addition to compensation for basic and additional services and are limited to the following:

9.5.1

Add the specific interest rate applicable for the contract.

Commentary: As previously noted, it is desirable for the owner to limit its obligation to pay interest on past due payments contractually. In the absence of a specific contractual limitation, the owner could be subject to significantly higher interest rates.

9.6

Delete Paragraph 9.6 in its entirety.

Commentary: Deletion of this paragraph is necessary in order to prevent the owner from being subjected to claims as a result of a change in the nature or scope of the project. Obviously the design-builder can still request an equitable adjustment of its contract price should there be significant changes in the scope and nature of its work, but deletion of the clause eliminates an easy contractual vehicle for claims.

9.7

Delete Paragraph 9.7 in its entirety.

Commentary: This paragraph also exposes the owner to claims. Deletion of it reduces the design-builder's basis for delay claims. This deletion should be accompanied by a no damage for delay clause to further solidify the owner's position.

§ 10.12 Article 10—Other Provisions

10.1.1

New paragraph:

10.1.1 If the Design/Builder is delayed in the performance of the Project by any acts of or neglect of the Owner, or by an employee, agent or representative of the Owner, or by changes ordered in the Work by the Owner, and not required to correct design problems or discrepancies, or by the combined action of the Owner and any of its employees, agents or representatives and is in no way caused by or resulting from default or collusion on the part of the Design/Builder or by any other cause which the Design/Builder could not reasonably control or circumvent, then the Scheduled Completion Date shall be extended for a period equal to the length of such delay if within ten (10) days after the beginning of any such delay the Design/Builder delivers to the Owner a request for extension for such delay and such request is approved by the Owner.

Extension of time shall be the Design/Builder's sole remedy for any such delay unless the same shall have been caused by acts constituting intentional interference by the Owner with the Design/Builder's performance of the Work when such acts continue after the Design/Builder's written notice to the

Owner of such interference. The Owner's exercise of any of its rights under the Contract Documents regarding changes in the Work, regardless of the extent or number of such changes, or the Owner's exercise of any of its remedies of suspension of the Work or requirement of correction or re-execution of any defective Work shall not under any circumstances be construed as intentional interference with the Design/Builder's performance of the Work.

Commentary: This is one form of a no damage for delay clause. By providing that owner changes and suspensions of the work do not constitute intentional interference, this clause is designed to eliminate a common end run around the other no damage for delay clauses.

PART 2—FINAL DESIGN AND CONSTRUCTION

§ 10.13 Part 2—Terms and Conditions

In the Part 2 agreement to A191, the owner has moved from preliminary design to a much more specific project definition and outline of the scope of work. It is important to maintain consistency between Part 1 and Part 2 in order to avoid ambiguity and unanticipated interpretations. By the time of execution of Part 2, the scope of work, performance criteria, and major components should be set out in the plans and specifications in sufficient detail that the owner is satisfied that the completed project meets its needs and project criteria.

§ 10.14 Article 1—General Provisions

Certain modifications are recommended to clarify the general provisions and a good deal of caution must be exercised by the owner when agreeing to any of the provisions of Article 1. The major potential stumbling block is the inclusion of the design-builder's proposal as a contract document. The following addresses a method of handling this potential problem.

1.1.1

Delete the language "the Design-Builder's Proposal identified in Article 14," in Paragraph 1.1.1.

Commentary: The incorporation of the design-builder's proposal into the contract invites trouble. Oftentimes the proposal will contain language contrary to other parts of the contract documents, or exclusions and scope limitations not wanted by the owner. The better course is to use Article 14 to set out the scope of work within the Part 2 agreement. This reduces the possibility of ambiguity, arguments over scope of work, and conflict between a proposal and other portions of the contract.

If the design-builder proposal is made part of the contract documents, scrutinize every clause of the proposal in order to ensure that the scope of work is set out accurately, without undesired exclusions or limitations, and that there is an internal consistency among the various documents that make up the contract.

1.1.4

New paragraph:

1.1.4 The Design/Builder accepts the relationship of trust and confidence established between it and the Owner by this agreement. The Design/Builder agrees to furnish the architectural, engineering and construction services set forth herein and agrees to furnish efficient business administration and superintendence, and to use its best efforts to complete the Project in the best and soundest way and in the most expeditious and economical manner consistent with the interest of the Owner.

Commentary: This new paragraph reinforces the reliance of the owner on the design-builder for the completion of all phases of the design and construction of the project. Also, it amplifies the design-builder's obligation to complete the project efficiently and in the most expeditious and economical manner possible. Although it may be argued that such a clause is unnecessary, it does strengthen the owner's position in the event that the owner is forced to prosecute any claims for delay or excess costs.

1.3.1

Delete the language "for additions to this Project or," in line 7 of Paragraph 1.3.1.

Commentary: Although the design-builder has an understandable interest in preserving its ownership interests in the drawings, specifications and other documents furnished by it, the owner should not be precluded from using these documents for additions to the project. The deletion recommended allows the owner to use the design-builder's documents for subsequent additions or modifications to the project. If an owner subsequently decides to alter, modify, or rehabilitate its project, it should not be precluded from using the project documents.

§ 10.15 Article 2—Design-Builder

2.1.1

Delete the words "any professional obligation or" in line 9 of Paragraph 2.1.1, and add after the word "Owner" in line 11:

except it is understood and agreed that the Owner is an intended third party beneficiary of all contracts with design professionals, subcontracts, purchase orders and other agreements between the Design/Builder and third parties. The Design/Builder shall incorporate the obligations of this contract with the Owner in its respective contracts with design professionals, subcontracts, supply agreements, purchase orders and other agreements.

Commentary: As noted in Paragraph 1.2.2, the amendment proposed strengthens the owner's legal standing and rights vis-a-vis the designers, subcontractors and suppliers of the design-builder. As written, A191's Paragraph 2.1.1 states that nothing contained in the contract documents creates a professional obligation or contractual relationship between the owner and any third parties. Unless amended, the architect and consulting engineers could argue that they have no professional obligation to the owner. Although the owner perceives the design-builder as the single entity responsible for design and construction of the project, additional security is available if the design professionals and their errors and omissions insurance carriers are also liable for any design defects. This also reiterates that the purchase of design and construction services as a package includes design services in accordance with the appropriate professional standard of care.

Also, by establishing that the owner is the intended beneficiary of the design-builder's subcontracts and purchase orders, the owner is in a stronger position to enforce warranties or guarantees and is in a better position to terminate the design-builder and take over completion of the project if such a course of action becomes necessary. Although the defense of privity of contract has eroded, it still remains an obstacle in certain circumstances. This proposed modification attempts to avoid that obstacle by use of third party beneficiary law permitting the owner to proceed directly, if it desires, against the third parties employed by the design-builder.

2.2.2

Delete the first clause of Paragraph 2.2.2, "Based on the Design/Builder's Proposal."

Commentary: As noted in conjunction with Paragraph 1.1.1, the better practice is to set out the work as part of the contract rather than incorporate the design-builder's proposal. If the proposal is incorporated, this paragraph can remain unchanged.

2.2.2.1

Delete this paragraph in its entirety and add in lieu thereof at the end of 2.2.2 "establish the scope of the work in greater detail;"

Commentary: For consistency purposes, if the scope of work is set out as an explicit part of Article 14, there is no need for reference to the design-builder's proposal.

2.2.2.2

Delete the word "customarily" in line one of Paragraph 2.2.2.2.

Commentary: There is no reason for the owner to get involved in whether the design-builder has provided the building trades with the information customarily necessary. The design-builder is hired to design and construct the project. If information is required, the design-builder is obligated to provide it.

2.2.2.3

Delete the word "customarily" in line one of Paragraph 2.2.2.3.

Commentary: Similarly, by the time of execution of Part 2, the design-builder should know what documents are required for regulatory approval. Use of the word "customarily" gives the design-builder an out and a possible basis for claims and cost overruns. The burden should properly be placed on the design-builder to determine and assemble whatever documents are required for the regulatory agency approvals.

2.2.3

Delete Paragraph 2.2.3 in its entirety and add the following in lieu thereof:

2.2.3 The Design/Builder shall file the documents required to obtain necessary approvals of governmental authorities having jurisdiction over the project.

Commentary: As worded, Paragraph 2.2.3 when read in conjunction with Paragraph 2.2.2.3 is unclear as to preparation of documents for governmental authorities. These modifications squarely place the responsibility with the design-builder. If it is necessary to alter this scheme due to particular governmental authorities, then those particular responsibilities can be specifically allocated to the owner with a requirement that the design-builder assist the owner in obtaining approvals and filing documents.

2.2.7

Delete Paragraph 2.2.7 in its entirety.

Commentary: There is no logical reason to set up the design-builder as the initial arbitrator for interpretation of the requirements of the contract documents. If there is a dispute as to performance, the design-builder is going to have already communicated its position to the owner. Giving any additional validity to the design-builder's position by establishing it as the initial interpreter of the contract documents is simply unwarranted.

2.2.12

Insert a period after the word "thereof" in line four and delete the rest of Paragraph 2.2.12.

Commentary: This modification removes any ambiguity as to the responsibility of the design-builder to pay royalties and license fees and to defend and indemnify the owner from claims relating to infringement of patent rights. If the design-builder cannot use a process without violating patent rights it should not be scoped by the design-builder and incorporated into the contract documents.

2.2.13

Add the following to the current end of Paragraph 2.2.13:

The Design/Builder shall also be responsible to the Owner for acts and omissions of the subcontractors, suppliers, agents and employees of those in privity with the Design/Builder.

Commentary: This modification emphasizes the design-builder's role as the single responsible party. The intent is to lessen the possibility that the owner will be responsible for the acts or omissions of any party in the design-builder's chain of privity.

2.2.16

Delete Paragraph 2.2.16 in its entirety and add in lieu thereof:

2.2.16 The Owner shall notify the Design/Builder when the Work or an agreed portion thereof is substantially completed by issuing a Certificate of Substantial Completion which will establish the Date of Substantial Completion, shall state the responsibility of each party for security, maintenance, heat, utilities, damage to the Work, and insurance, shall include a list of items to be completed or corrected and shall fix a time within which the Design/Builder shall complete items listed therein. Disputes between the Owner and Design/Builder regarding the Certificate of Substantial Completion may, at the Owner's election, be resolved by arbitration in accordance with Article 10.

Commentary: Paragraph 2.2.16 gives the design-builder the power to decide when the project is substantially complete. The date of substantial completion materially affects the liability of both parties for delay damages. The owner will prefer to control this decision, which determines when the project is sufficiently complete to be used for its intended purpose. This modification lets the owner control this determination.

§ 10.16 Article 3—Owner

A191's Article 3, Part 2, sets out a very brief and general description of the owner's responsibilities to render decisions and provide services for the project. The owner and its attorney must carefully examine the obligations and services set out in order to tailor desired obligations to the particular project. It is important for the owner to maintain consistency between its Part 1 and Part 2 responsibilities, particularly in regard to an obligation to respond with reasonable promptness to questions and notification to the design-builder of any observed defects in the work. Also, Article 3, Part 2, obligates the owner to provide all geotechnical services.

These responsibilities increase the owner's exposure. Some owners may wish to delete significant portions of Article 3 as set forth below. Each project, however, will have different owner requirements.

3.1

End Paragraph 3.1 with the word "project" in line three and delete the remainder.

Commentary: The deleted portion of the paragraph imposes an affirmative obligation on the owner to examine documents submitted by the design-builder and to render a decision promptly to avoid delay in the progress of the work. This provides the design-builder with strong contractual ammunition for the recovery of delay damages, e.g., extended jobsite costs and extended home office overhead. Any implied obligations similar to that set out in the deleted language should be limited or avoided by the use of a "no damage for delay" clause as set out in Part 2, Article 4 below.

3.2

Insert a period after the word "Work" in line two of Paragraph 3.2 and delete the remainder.

Commentary: If the owner is going to have an on-site representative, any duties or responsibilities should be specifically set out. The owner must recognize that to the extent it gives duties and responsibilities to any on-site representative an increased potential of liability and exposure to claims exists. Accordingly, any duties or responsibilities assigned to the on-site representative should be kept to a minimum to ensure that the on-site representative does not affect or attempt to change the design-builder's quality, quantity, means, methods, techniques, sequences and procedures.

3.3

Delete Paragraph 3.3 in its entirety and add in lieu thereof:

3.3 The Design/Builder shall secure all building and other permits, licenses and inspections and shall pay the fees for such permits, licenses and inspections as part of its contract price.

Commentary: The assignment of the responsibility to obtain building and other permits, licenses and inspections is appropriately with the design-builder. The design-builder is the experienced entity responsible for the overall design and construction of the project and is in the best position to obtain all necessary permits, licenses and inspections. However, it is recognized that for certain projects, or for certain permits or licenses, the owner's cooperation will be necessary. Even in those circumstances, the owner's obligations regarding specific permits, licenses and inspections should be set out clearly.

3.4

Delete Paragraph 3.4 in its entirety.

3.5

Delete Paragraph 3.5 in its entirety.

3.6

Delete Paragraph 3.6 in its entirety.

Commentary: Paragraphs 3.4, 3.5, and 3.6 assign the responsibility for site investigation to the owner and allow the design-builder to rely upon the accuracy and completeness of the owner generated information. These paragraphs provide the design-builder with a good vehicle for claims. The better way to approach site conditions is to assign the responsibility for investigation, reports, testing and interpretation of tests to the design-builder. Although reasonable site investigations by the design-builder will be necessary, these modifications require the design-builder to assume the risk of faulty tests, incomplete data or inaccurate information.

3.7

Delete Paragraph 3.7 in its entirety.

Commentary: The owner has contracted with the design-builder for the design and construction of the project. The owner should not have to act as a quality control inspector and should not have to respond to later allegations that if it knew the work was defective, it should have told the design-builder. This paragraph allows the design-builder to argue that the owner's silence was acceptance of deviating work. Accordingly, it is recommended that this paragraph be deleted.

3.8

Delete Paragraph 3.8 in its entirety.

Commentary: The owner should avoid affirmative obligations to avoid delay, such as that contained in this paragraph. Such obligations run counter to the intent of the no damage for delay clause set out in Part 2, Article 4 and could be interpreted as either ambiguous or as specific exceptions to the no damage for delay clause.

3.9

Delete Paragraph 3.9 in its entirety.

Commentary: This paragraph serves no owner interest and should be deleted. If the design-builder requires information regarding the project funding, it can easily be provided in a different means than that set out in this paragraph.

3.10

Delete the word "only" and add "or with the Design/Builder's knowledge" at the end of the paragraph.

Commentary: If the owner can foresee circumstances which are going to require direct communication or coordination with the design-builder's contractors, it is preferable to establish that right, rather than to operate in the face of the preclusion established in Paragraph 3.10. However, it is better practice to follow the mandate of Paragraph 3.10 and channel all communications through the design-builder. Every direct contact and communication between the owner and a contractor of the design-builder is a possible source of claims or excuses for nonperformance by the design-builder.

§ 10.17 Article 4—Time

4.1

Delete the phrase "as expeditiously as is" from Paragraph 4.1.

Commentary: The deleted language vitiates the owner's desired intent. The owner wants the services completed with reasonable skill and care and on time. As originally worded, the paragraph has an internal conflict between the concept of timeliness and that of as expeditiously as is possible, given the restraint of reasonable skill and care. Reasonable skill and care is a contract requirement that must be exercised during the specific time of contract performance.

4.4

Delete Paragraph 4.4 in its entirety and add in lieu thereof the following:

4.4 Not more than seven days after the execution of this Part 2 agreement, the Design/Builder shall submit a progress schedule indicating each major category or unit of general work to be performed at site, properly sequenced and intermeshed and showing completion of the Work consistent with the time period established in Article 14. The Design/Builder shall provide the Owner with monthly updates of the progress schedule indicating completed activities and any changes in sequencing or activity durations.

Commentary: Although it is important that the owner obtain complete scheduling information at the outset of the job, that information is of no utility if it is not updated on a regular and periodic basis. This amended scheduling requirement provides for the necessary updating of the owner to allow for its coordination and completion of related project activities.

4.5

Delete Paragraph 4.5 in its entirety and add the following in lieu thereof:

4.5 If the Design/Builder is delayed in the performance of the Project by any acts of or neglect of the Owner, or by an employee, agent or representative of the Owner, or by changes ordered in the Work by the Owner, and not required to correct design problems or discrepancies, or by the combined action of the Owner and any of its employees, agents or representatives and is in no way caused by or resulting from default or collusion on the part of the Design/Builder or by any other cause which the Design/Builder could not reasonably control or circumvent, then the Scheduled Completion Date shall be extended for a period equal to the length of such delay if within ten (10) days after the beginning of any such delay the Design/Builder delivers to the Owner a request for extension for such delay and such request is approved by the Owner.

Extension of time shall be the Design/Builder's sole remedy for any such delay unless the same shall have been caused by acts constituting intentional interference by the Owner with the Design/Builder's performance of the Work where such acts continue after the Design/Builder's written notice to the Owner of such interference. The Owner's exercise of any of its rights under the Contract Documents regarding changes in the Work, regardless of the extent or number of such changes, or the Owner's exercise of any of its remedies of suspension of the Work or requirement of correction or re-execution of any defective Work shall not under any circumstances be construed as intentional interference with the Design/Builder's performance of the Work.

Commentary: This no damage for delay clause is designed to limit the potential liability of the owner for project delays. It is important to consult with your attorney to determine any requirements or limitations in the use of a no damage for delay clause. Often the largest claims arising from a project are the result of extended home office overhead costs and extended jobsite costs. Through the use of this clause the owner can reduce its exposure to the risk of project delay.

§ 10.18 Article 5—Payments

Article 5 of A191 sets out a payment scheme that may be appropriate and desirable for some projects. Owners should examine this proposed scheme and timetable to determine whether it should be employed on a particular project.

5.1.2

Change "ten" to "thirty" in line one of Paragraph 5.1.2.

Commentary: Ten days for the receipt, verification, processing and funding of an application for payment is unrealistic for many projects. Evaluate the particular project, the complexity of measuring and verifying work-in-place, the administrative procedures that will be employed and any time lags or constraints that will result from the involvement of financial institutions or lenders before agreeing to the ten day timetable suggested in Paragraph 5.1.2. Be realistic in the assessment of the necessary time for payments and alter the contract language accordingly. Otherwise, the owner will not meet the payment schedule and will be liable for interest and possibly work stoppages.

5.1.3

Delete the clause "to the best of the Design/Builder's knowledge, information and belief," which starts on line two and ends on line four.

Commentary: This qualification of the work performed by the design-builder is an escape clause for the design-builder, which leaves the owner vulnerable to overpayment and deficient work. The design-builder should properly inspect its work, qualitatively and quantitatively, before presenting an application for payment. This deletion is intended to put the design-builder on notice that its applications are representations of both the quality and quantity of work performed.

5.1.5

Insert a period on line three after the word "Design/Builder" and delete the rest of Paragraph 5.1.5.

Commentary: The proposed deletion slightly lessens the position of the contractors of the design-builder. However, the incorporation of a no lien clause into the design-builder's agreement and its subcontracts may not be enforceable in the applicable jurisdiction. If a contractor has a statutory right, an owner is limited in its protection. The intent of the deletion is to reduce the possibility of a contractor successfully employing any non-statutory, extra-contractual theories of recovery.

5.2.4

Insert a period after "Design/Builder" on line two and delete the remainder of Paragraph 5.2.4.

Commentary: At the time of final payment, the owner should not have any contingent liability to the design-builder. Final payment should be final, and acceptance of that payment constitutes a waiver of all claims by the design-builder.

5.3.1

Insert a period after "Article 13" on line three and delete the remainder of Paragraph 5.3.1.

Commentary: The owner should limit by express contract terms its obligation to pay interest on past due payments. In the absence of a specific contractual limitation, the owner could be subject to significantly higher interest rates.

§ 10.19 Article 6—Protection of Persons and Property

Article 6 of A191 generally establishes that the design-builder is the responsible entity for site safety. Modify or delete any clause herein which does not apply to your particular project.

6.1

Insert the word "solely" before the word "responsible" in line one of Paragraph 6.1.

Commentary: This modification simply emphasizes the design-builder's responsibility for site safety.

6.4

Delete the parenthetical clause starting on line two and continuing until line four of Paragraph 6.4; insert a period after the word "liable" in line eight and delete the remainder of Paragraph 6.4.

Commentary: This modification is recommended when the design-builder is providing project insurance. The intent of the modification is to prevent third parties from looking to the owner for coverage. The last deleted clause of this paragraph is an unnecessary clarification of the prior language.

§ 10.20 Article 7—Insurance and Bonds

Article 7 of A191 sets out one possible scheme for the division of insurance responsibilities. Because insurance is written in well defined categories, the owner often must purchase coverage in addition to that provided by the design-builder. The owner's insurable interest is oftentimes distinct from the design-builder's and the owner policy is necessary to prevent gaps in coverage. The owner should work with its insurance brokers to outline the possible risks and the necessary policies. Article 7 should then be modified accordingly.

7.1.4

Delete the clause "if requested" in lines one and two of Paragraph 7.1.4.

Commentary: The owner should obtain copies of the design-builder's policies of insurance for review by its insurance adviser and for its permanent project records. The summary certificate of insurance does not provide any details as to coverage or exclusions, which are necessary to determine the adequacy of the project insurance.

7.3.1

Substitute "Design/Builder" for "Owner" in line two, insert the word "mortgages" in line seven after the word "Owner," and delete the next three sentences, starting with the sentence beginning with "If the Owner . . ." in line twelve to the sentence ending with "costs property attributable thereto" in lines twenty-three and twenty-four.

Commentary: One approach is to require the design-builder to obtain as much of the insurance as possible. If the design-builder's insurance company is providing liability coverage, contractual liability coverage, property insurance, and the builder's risk policy, there is less chance of delay in insurance settlements as different insurance companies argue about coverage and subrogation rights. If the design-builder is providing the builder's risk policy, make sure the mortgagee, and any other party with an interest, is named as a separate insured.

Often, however, the owner does purchase the property and-or builder's risk policies. In those circumstances, this paragraph may be left intact, or modified to be consistent with the particular project insurance purchased.

7.3.2

Substitute "Design/Builder" for "Owner" in line two and insert the words "lenders, mortgagees" after the word "Owner" in line seven.

Commentary: The owner should consistently seek to establish the design-builder as the single responsible party for design, construction and installation, and for insuring those processes. Also, make sure no ambiguity exists as to the provision of insurance coverage for any financing entities.

7.3.3

Substitute "Design/Builder" for "Owner" in line one and insert the words "Design/Builder and" before the word "Owner" in line two.

Commentary: Make sure this clause tracks the provision of the property insurance. Also, require the adjustment to be with the owner and design-builder, so the owner can ensure adequate adjustment and appropriate distribution.

7.3.4

Delete Paragraph 7.3.4 in its entirety.

Commentary: This deletion is made for consistency with the rest of Paragraph 7.3.

7.3.7

Delete Paragraph 7.3.7 in its entirety.

Commentary: The requirement that the owner post a bond if requested by another insured is an unwarranted imposition on the owner. The procedure established in this paragraph is an unnecessary and burdensome manner for the distribution of insurance proceeds.

7.3.8

Substitute the words “agreed to” for “required” in line eight.

Commentary: Do not weaken the owner elective arbitration clause by allowing inconsistent provisions in other parts of the contract.

7.4.1

Delete Paragraph 7.4.1 in its entirety.

Commentary: This deletion is necessary to prevent any ambiguity as to the design-builder’s liability due to loss of use of the project. This modification is intended to prevent an argument by the design-builder that the owner should look to the insurance company, rather than the design-builder for its consequential damages due to fire and other hazards. Unambiguous single point responsibility is the goal of the recommended modifications.

7.5.1

Delete Paragraph 7.5.1 in its entirety and substitute the following in lieu thereof:

7.5.1 The Design/Builder shall provide performance and payment bonds covering the faithful performance of the Contract and the payment of all obligations arising thereunder, in a form approved by the Owner, with a surety acceptable to the Owner and in an amount set out in Article 14.

Commentary: The most effective way for an owner to manage the risk of design-builder default is to investigate the prospective design-builder to determine its experience, capability and capacity to undertake the project at the time of the project. Once satisfied as to the selection of the design-builder, added assurance and protection is available by requiring payment and performance bonds. However, it should be noted that some design-builders will be unable to bond the full contract price, including the design portion, so either the bondable amount will have to exclude the design fee or a different design-builder, with full bondability, will have to be selected.

7.6

New paragraph:

7.6 Professional Liability Insurance:

7.6.1 The Design/Builder shall provide a project policy for the design services on the project or a professional liability endorsement in a form and in an amount acceptable to the Owner.

Commentary: Particularly if the design services portion of the contract are excluded from the bond provided, it is important that costs and damages attributable to design errors or omissions are separately covered. Check the type of professional liability policies that the designers have as well as the amount. A project policy is recommended because it guarantees a source of funds for the particular project if there is a claim. If the designer has a claims made policy with a limit of coverage (which is normal), there could be no coverage by the time of the owner's claim.

§ 10.21 Article 8—Changes in the Work

Article 8 of A191 exists in recognition of the inevitable occurrence of change orders, even on design-build projects. Change orders can be minimized by complete initial project definition and timely decision-making by the owner. The following modifications are recommended to improve the procedure established in Article 8.

8.1.1

Add after the last sentence in Paragraph 8.1.1 the following:

No action, conduct, omission, prior failure or course of dealing by the Owner shall act to waive, modify, change, or alter the requirement that Change Orders must be in writing signed by the Owner and Design/Builder, and that such written change orders are the exclusive method for effecting any change to the contract sum or contract time. The Design/Builder understands and agrees that the contract sum and contract time cannot be changed by implication, oral agreements, actions, inactions, course of conduct, or constructive change order.

Commentary: The requirement that change orders must be in writing is oftentimes modified by the conduct of the parties and recovery is allowed by application of principles of waiver, estoppel and constructive change order. The purpose of this amendment is to further strengthen the owner's position. It must be stressed that the owner should administer the contract consistent with its language to avoid any possibility that the protection of the contract language will be lost. Use written change orders in every instance of change to the contract involving money and/or time, otherwise a court could find waiver even in the face of this stronger language.

8.1.3

Delete Paragraph 8.1.3 in its entirety.

Commentary: Eliminate this source of potential liability. The design-builder should expect to get requests for proposal from the owner and should respond without the owner becoming obligated for costs. The design-builder is going to obtain its fee and markups if the proposal is accepted, so it is not too much for the owner to ask for the preparation of proposals without cost when the owner elects to proceed without the change.

8.1.5

Delete the words "reasonable allowance" and substitute "10% allowance" (or other appropriate amount) in line ten of Paragraph 8.1.5. Delete the word "value" and substitute "cost" in line twenty. Delete "additional costs of suspension and field office personnel directly attributable to the change" in lines twenty-one and twenty-two. Delete "Pending final determination of cost to the Owner, payments on account shall be made on the Application for Payment." in lines twenty-four through twenty-six.

Commentary: Control the project costs. Eliminate future arguments as to what a "reasonable allowance" is for overhead and profit. Do not become vulnerable to internal rental rates. Specify that equipment costs be reimbursed at "cost" not "value."

The allowance for overhead and profit should cover any additional costs of supervision and field office personnel. The owner should not have to pay those costs in addition to the allowance. Finally, the owner should not be obligated to make any payment for work not made definite by change order. The suggestion of payment on account runs contrary to a procedure requiring a written change order for any adjustment in time or price.

8.1.6

Delete Paragraph 8.1.6 in its entirety.

Commentary: This paragraph adds nothing to the contract and is so vague as to create more problems than solutions. Paragraph 8.1.4.2 already suggests the use of original or subsequently agreed upon unit prices as a method of pricing a change in the work. Clauses that revolve around allegations of substantial inequity are useful only as vehicles for claims.

8.2.1

Delete Paragraph 8.2.1 in its entirety.

Commentary: The design-builder has control over testing, inspection, borings and obtaining the necessary reports to design and construct the project. The design-builder establishes the scope of work to meet the performance criteria after performing the necessary testing on the site. In these circumstances, a differing site condition or concealed conditions clause does not seem appropriate. If the owner and design-builder agree to such a clause being included in the contract, it should be limited to particular portions or areas of the work where reasonable testing or investigation is either impossible or too costly.

8.3.1

Delete "the submission of the Design/Builder's Proposal under Part 1" and substitute in lieu thereof "the execution of Part 2 of this Agreement."

Commentary: Because final pricing of the project is established in Part 2, it does not make sense to compensate the design-builder for changes subsequent to its submission of a proposal under Part 1. The regulatory changes of relevance to pricing are only those which occur after execution of Part 2 of the agreement.

§ 10.22 Article 9—Correction of Work

9.4

Change "seven" to "three" in line three. Delete the phrase "give a second written notice to the Design/Builder and seven days following receipt by the Design/Builder of that second written notice and" in lines six through eight. Change "shall" to "may" in the last line of Paragraph 9.4 and insert a comma after the word "arbitration" in the last line and add the following language "in accordance with Article 10."

Commentary: The owner needs to be able to move decisively in case of the design-builder's default or failure to carry out corrections of defective work. The two seven-day notices unnecessarily prolong the doldrums of a project when the design-builder is not prosecuting the work.

The modification to the part of the paragraph pertaining to arbitration is for consistency.

§ 10.23 Article 10—Arbitration

Article 10 of A191 sets out the standard arbitration clause providing for binding arbitration in accordance with the Construction Industry Arbitration Rules of the American Arbitration Association. A discussion of the merits of arbitration versus litigation is beyond the scope of this work and the inclusion of an arbitration clause is a matter of preference and tactics.

The following proposed arbitration clause contains features intended to give the owner greater flexibility and control over the arbitration of disputes.

10

Article 10, including paragraphs 10.1, 10.2, 10.3, 10.4, and 10.5, is deleted in its entirety and the following Article 10 is substituted in lieu thereof:

10.1 All claims, disputes and other matters in question between the Design/Builder and the Owner arising out of, or relating to this Agreement, the Project, the Work, the Contract Documents or the breach thereof may, at the Owner's sole option, and only upon the exercise of that sole option by the Owner, together or separately as the Owner sees fit, be decided by arbitration in accordance with the Construction Industry Arbitration Rules of the American Arbitration Association then obtaining as modified hereby.

Any arbitration arising out of or relating to this Agreement, the Project, the Work, the Contract Documents, or the breach thereof may include by consolidation, joinder or in any other manner, at the Owner's sole option, any other entities or persons whom the Owner believes to be substantially involved in a common question of fact or law. In the event that more than one claim, dispute, or other matter in question, shall be in existence at the same time, the Owner may at its sole option decide which of such claims, disputes or other matters in question shall be arbitrated and which shall not be arbitrated. Such decision shall be final and unappealable, and no arbitration shall be authorized to consider, decide, or make any award on any claim or matter which the Owner has determined shall not be arbitrated.

In the event that the Design/Builder wishes to request arbitration of any claim, dispute or other matter in question, the Design/Builder shall file a notice of demand for arbitration in writing with the Owner specifically describing the claims, disputes and other matters in question which the Design/Builder wishes to submit to arbitration. The Design/Builder may not unilaterally elect arbitration or cause arbitration to occur. The Owner has the sole discretion to decide whether or not any such claims, disputes, and other matters shall be submitted for arbitration. If the Owner wishes to submit any claim, dispute or other matter in question, whether or not it is the subject of a request for arbitration by the Design/Builder, the Owner shall file a notice of demand for arbitration with the American Arbitration Association and with the Design/Builder.

The Owner shall have the right, but not the obligation, by so electing in its arbitration demand, to invoke the following method of selection of arbitrators in lieu of that otherwise provided by the American Arbitration Association rules. If the Owner so elects in its notice of demand for arbitration, the Owner may appoint one party-appointed arbitrator in its notice of demand for arbitration. If the Owner does so, the Design/Builder may, within ten (10) days, appoint a second party-appointed arbitrator. These two party-appointed arbitrators shall, within thirty (30) days, or such further time as may be agreed upon between the Owner and the Design/Builder, appoint a third party-appointed arbitrator. If the party-appointed arbitrators fail to appoint a third arbitrator, the third arbitrator shall be appointed in accordance with the Construction Industry Arbitration Rules of the American Arbitration Association.

The Owner may elect in its notice of demand for arbitration, to have the discovery rights and procedures provided by the Federal Rules of Civil Procedure to be available and enforceable within the arbitration proceeding.

In any case in which the Owner elects to submit a claim, dispute, or other matter in question to arbitration as provided herein, the Owner shall, in its sole discretion, select the locale for the arbitration. Any request or demand for arbitration hereunder shall be made before the date when institution of legal or equitable proceedings based on such claim, dispute or other matter in question would be barred by the applicable statute of limitations.

This agreement to arbitrate shall be specifically enforceable by the Owner under the prevailing arbitration law. Any award rendered by arbitrators shall be final and enforceable by any party to the arbitration, and judgment may be rendered upon it in accordance with applicable law in any court having jurisdiction thereof.

The Design/Builder and Owner mutually agree to arbitrate under the terms and conditions outlined above in this paragraph. The Design/Builder has included in the contract price to be paid on this contract a sum of not less than ten dollars ($10.00) as compensation and consideration for irrevocably offering the foregoing options and arbitration rights to Owner. In further consideration for such irrevocable offer and grant of the foregoing options and arbitration rights to it, Owner agrees that, notwithstanding its right and discretion not to do so, it shall arbitrate, after the final completion of the Work, any claims which Design/Builder selects which total, in the aggregate, up to one thousand dollars ($1,000.00). Owner's obligation to arbitrate such claims totalling up to one thousand dollars ($1,000.00) shall be specifically enforceable by Design/Builder under the prevailing arbitration law and any award rendered by the arbitrator(s) shall be final and enforceable by any party to the arbitration, and judgment may be rendered upon it in accordance with applicable law in any court having jurisdiction thereof.

Unless otherwise agreed in writing, and notwithstanding any other rights or obligations of either of the parties under any Contract Documents or agreements, Design/Builder shall carry on with the performance of its services and duties hereunder during the pendency of any claim, dispute, other matter in question or arbitration or other proceeding to resolve any claim, dispute or other matter in question, and the Owner shall continue to make payments in accordance with the Contract Documents, but the Owner shall be under no obligation to make payments on or against such claims, disputes, or other matters in question, during the pendency of any arbitration or other proceeding to resolve such claims, disputes or other matters in question.

Commentary: This modified arbitration clause gives the owner considerable control over whether the disputes will be arbitrated and what procedures will be employed. This clause gives the owner the flexibility to litigate disputes, if arbitration is not desired. Further, this clause allows the owner to consolidate or join other parties into an arbitration, use discovery procedures at its discretion, choose the site for the arbitration and modify the selection procedure for arbitrators. Although an attempt is made in this arbitration clause to ensure mutuality of obligation in connection with the owner's option to arbitrate, a court could sustain an attack on an owner's option arbitration clause.

Therefore, owners that are willing to agree to compulsory arbitration of disputes can exercise the owner option features of this proposed amendment, while maintaining the other rights established in the arbitration clause.

Of course, some owners will not want to participate in arbitration in any circumstance. If so, Article 10 should simply be deleted.

§ 10.24 Article 11—Miscellaneous Provisions

11.4.2

Delete Paragraph 11.4.2 in its entirety.

Commentary: The clause is duplicative of Paragraph 2.1.1, which, when modified as suggested, establishes that the owner is an intended third-party beneficiary of the design-builder's contract.

11.5.1

Delete the last sentence of Paragraph 11.5.1.

Commentary: This deletion gives meaning to the owner having the "right" to perform work at the site. The deleted language emasculates the rights of the owner and if allowed to remain in the contract could be interpreted as an exception to the "no damage for delay" clause.

11.6

Delete Paragraph 11.6.1 in its entirety and add the following in lieu thereof:

11.6.1 If the Design/Builder suffers any injury or damage to person or property because of an act or omission of the Owner, the Owner's employees or agents, or another for whose acts the Owner is legally liable, any claim shall be made in writing in the form of a Request for Change Order within ten (10) days after such injury or damage is or should have been first observed. Any and all claims not made within ten (10) days are barred, waived, released and discharged. The decision of the Owner shall be final and binding on both parties unless the Design/Builder files a Demand for Arbitration within ten (10) days of the Owner's decision. If the Owner elects, the claim will be arbitrated in accordance with Article 10. Otherwise, the Demand for Arbitration shall only preserve the claim for the Design/Builder.

Commentary: Article 8 establishes that change orders are the only basis for a change in the contract sum, while Article 10 provides for arbitration of all disputes, at the owner's election. Together they establish an adequate mechanism for the submission of requests for additional compensation or claims, obviating the need for the paragraph. In addition, by limiting the submission period to ten days, the owner is better able to avoid the post-project deluge of change orders.

11.8.1

Delete the second sentence of Paragraph 11.8.1 and substitute in lieu thereof the following:

The Design/Builder shall not assign, sublet or transfer an interest in Part 2 without written consent of the Owner.

Commentary: An owner may wish to have the right to sell, syndicate, or otherwise transfer its interest in the project. It should not be necessary to obtain the design-builder's consent for such a change in ownership structure or transfer because the first sentence of this paragraph protects the design-builder's interest by making the provisions of Part 2 binding on the owner's successors and assigns.

§ 10.25 Article 12—Termination of the Agreement

Article 12 sets out a procedure for termination of the agreement. The owner needs to have the ability to terminate the work of the design-builder when the design-builder is not performing or when the owner has decided not to proceed with the project using the design-builder. In either instance, it is necessary to have procedures in place and an ability to limit owner exposure. The following suggested modifications strengthen the owner's position:

12.1

Delete Paragraph 12.1 in its entirety and add the following in lieu thereof:

12.1 Part 2 may be terminated by the Owner upon three days written notice at the Owner's election. In the event of termination at the Owner's election and not due to the fault of the Design/Builder, the Design/Builder shall be compensated for services performed to termination date, together with reimbursable expenses then due.

12.2

Delete Paragraph 12.2 in its entirety and add the following in lieu thereof:

12.2 If the Design/Builder defaults or persistently fails or neglects to carry out the Work in accordance with the contract documents or fails to perform the provisions of Part 2, the Owner may give written notice that the Owner intends to terminate Part 2. If the Design/Builder fails to correct the defaults within three days after being given notice, the Owner may without prejudice to any other remedy make good such deficiencies and may deduct the cost thereof from the payment due the Design/Builder or, at the Owner's option, may terminate the employment of the Design/Builder and take possession of the site and of all materials, equipment, tools and construction equipment and machinery thereon owned by the Design/Builder as well as all drawings, plans, and specifications and finish the Work by whatever means the Owner may deem expedient. If the unpaid balance of the contract sum exceeds the expense of finishing the Work, the excess shall be paid to the Design/Builder, but if the expense exceeds the unpaid balance, the Design/Builder shall pay the difference to the Owner.

12.3

Delete Paragraph 12.3 in its entirety and add the following in lieu thereof:

12.3 If the Owner fails to make payment when due, the Design/Builder may give written notice of the Design/Builder's intention to terminate Part 2. If the

Design/Builder fails to receive payment within fourteen days after receipt of such notice by the Owner, the Design/Builder may give a second written notice and, fourteen days after receipt of such second written notice by the Owner, may terminate Part 2 and recover from the Owner payment for the cost of the Work executed.

Commentary: The owner should retain the ability to stop the design-builder at any point in the design and construction of the project with the minimum possible exposure to the design-builder. A termination for convenience clause, such as outlined above, is one method of minimizing the owner's exposure if the project is abandoned or if the owner chooses to proceed using the services other than those provided by the design-builder. It is important to set out the total scope of the owner's exposure in terms of a limitation of possible damages to the actual cost of the work performed. Further, the owner needs to have the ability to remove a nonperforming design-builder quickly. The default termination paragraph set out allows the owner to move expeditiously to keep its project on line in the event of design-builder default.

§ 10.26 Article 13—Basis of Compensation

Article 13 of A191 provides a general outline for compensation of the design-builder with provision for payment for basic services and reimbursable expenses. The owner should specify a compensation scheme timetable that its lenders or financiers can meet and should provide for adequate retainage for additional protection until the work is complete and accepted.

Reimbursable expenses should be limited to the absolute minimum amount feasible in order to keep the project within its budget. The design-builder should be required to include everything possible within basic services.

13.2.2

Add "1.1" to the parenthesis in Paragraph 13.2.2.

Commentary: After minimizing reimbursables, a mark up of 10% or no mark up at all should be negotiated with the design-builder.

13.3.1

Commentary: Add the specific interest rate applicable for the contract. It is desirable for the owner to limit by the contract its obligation to pay interest on past due payments. In the absence of a specific contractual limitation, the owner could be subjected to significantly higher interest rates.

§ 10.27 Article 14—Other Provisions

14.1

Delete the language "authorized adjustments and to delays not caused by the Design/Builder" and substitute the following in lieu thereof: "executed change orders granting extensions of time."

Commentary: The contract provides a change order process that should be strictly enforced. The deleted language invites post project arguments about delays justifying extensions of time.

14.2

Commentary: Set out an all encompassing description of the project to include all necessary or reasonably implied components. Do not use the design-builder's proposal if it contains project-essential exclusions or is vague. The owner should set a scope of work in the description of basic services that is as complete, detailed and all inclusive as possible.

14.4

Delete Paragraph 14.4 in its entirety and add the following in lieu thereof: "The Contract Documents include . . ."

Commentary: Use A191 as the operative contract document and list incorporated supplementary and other conditions, the technical specifications, the drawings (including sheet numbers and dates), any addenda or modifications and other documents which define the scope of work. Again, avoid incorporation of the design-builder's proposal in order to avoid the possibility of ambiguity or conflict with the other contract documents.

§ 10.28 Owner's Design-Build Contract Checklist

The goal of the design-build contract is to set out the risks and responsibilities assumed by the owner and design-builder. For the owner to obtain true single source responsibility from its design-builder, the contract should establish clearly the full scope of the design-builder's undertaking. Regardless of proposed contract form, the following subjects should be reviewed by the owner to verify the clarity of the contract and the appropriate allocation of risks:

____ Is there a clear project definition?
____ Are all major elements of the project set out in the project program?
____ Are the performance specifications sufficiently comprehensive that the owner's goals are clearly spelled out?
____ How will the scope of work be definitized?
____ What is the owner's role or responsibility regarding design approvals, shop drawings, and submittals?
____ What are the consequences of late delivery, nondelivery, or nonperformance?
____ Has the design-builder attempted to limit its liability for late delivery or nonperformance?
____ Does the contract address a partial failure to meet performance criteria?
____ Are there any disclaimers of guarantees or warranties?
____ Are there provisions for contingencies or allowances?
____ Is the use of the contingency fund controlled by the owner?
____ What is the project payment scheme?
____ Who will verify percent complete for periodic pay requests?
____ What are the preconditions for final payment?
____ Does the design-builder share in any savings in project costs?
____ Are there any costs that are to be paid outside the lump sum or GMP?
____ How is the lump sum or GMP to be adjusted?
____ Does the owner have the right to audit project costs?
____ Who is responsible for payment of audit costs?
____ Is there a limitation on markups for change orders or additional work?
____ Is the owner's risk set out if the project is canceled or the design-builder is terminated?
____ What is the owner's exposure if the work is suspended or stopped?
____ Will there be a resident engineer?
____ Will design professionals be conducting construction inspections?
____ Is there a quality control program proposed?
____ Does the owner have the right to communicate directly with the design-builder's design professionals?
____ Are the design professionals required to have any errors or omissions insurance?

____ Is the owner a third-party beneficiary of the design-builder's subcontracts?
____ Does the owner have the right to reject the design-builder's subcontractors, suppliers, and employees?
____ Are payment and performance bonds required?
____ Who is providing the builders' risk insurance?
____ Is the owner an additional named insured on any policies?
____ Who bears the risk of the site?
____ Is there a changed condition or differing site conditions clause?
____ How will the changes clause operate?
____ What are the notice requirements for changes?
____ Does the owner have the right to accelerate performance?
____ What are the project scheduling requirements?
____ What schedule submittals must be made?
____ Are there any critical milestone dates or any requirements for phased completion of the project?
____ How is substantial completion defined?
____ Does the owner control the use of project float?
____ What is the time extension process?
____ Has the design-builder waived its lien rights?
____ Is the design-builder required to bond off any subcontractor or supplier liens?
____ Is there any choice of law provision?
____ Is the design-builder's proposal a contract document?
____ Is any part of the proposal inconsistent with the other contract language?
____ What is the disputes resolution process and is the design-builder required to continue work during a dispute?
____ What role or responsibility does the owner have during each phase of the project?

The design-build method of project delivery works when owners have a clear idea of what they want, carefully choose their design-builder, and draft a contract consistent with the sole source responsibility of the design-builder. Suggestions made in this chapter are intended to assist owners to obtain the single source responsibility characteristic of the design-build method. However, because any significant shifting of risks has significant costs, each proposed risk-shifting provision should be addressed during negotiations to determine whether the associated cost is appropriate for the given project.

CHAPTER 11

PROTECTING DESIGN-BUILDER WITH APPROPRIATE CONTRACT CLAUSES

Susan R. Brooke*

Susan R. Brooke is a member of the firm Dutton & Overman, P.C., an Indianapolis, Indiana, firm with a national construction practice. She graduated from the University of Delaware with distinction and highest honors and from Indiana University-Indianapolis, summa cum laude. Ms. Brooke primarily represents contractors and construction managers, negotiating numerous contracts with owners, subcontractors, and trade contractors. She is a member of the American Bar Association Construction Industry Forum, and has served on the steering committee for its Construction Management and Design Build Division.

*The author wishes to thank Alan H. Goldstein, Dutton Overman Goldstein Pinkus, P.C., and Bruce W. Bennett, Huber, Hunt & Nichols, Inc., for their encouragement and support, without which the author would not have entered the practice of construction law. The author also wishes to thank Robert F. Cushman for his many efforts to educate construction lawyers through his seminars and books such as this one.

§ 11.1 Introduction

An owner has made a decision to go forward on a project using design-build as the project delivery method in lieu of the more traditional method of construction that utilizes an architect and a general contractor. Furthermore, the owner has selected a general contractor to serve as the design-builder. This chapter focuses on design-build from the perspective of a general contractor who does not have in-house the necessary design professionals and who will enter into separate contracts for design services. No apologies are offered to those who believe that design-build must be an architect-driven activity.

This chapter analyses AIA Document A191 and proposes modifications to that document that will turn the contract into one that will protect the contractor who is the design-builder. Many of the suggested modifications would also strengthen a contract between the owner and architect-driven design-builder.

§ 11.2 Contract Forms

The owner and the design-builder do not want to go forward into this design-build project using only a handshake. Although there would be nothing to prevent that from happening, prudence dictates that a written contract be entered into between the owner and the design-builder.

Owners with experience in construction are familiar with documents promulgated by the American Institute of Architects (AIA). AIA Document A191 is the Standard Form of Agreement Between Owner and Design/Builder.[1] Any biases that are reflected in the document originate in the concept of an architect's serving as the head of design-build. Accordingly, for purposes of this chapter, the focus will be on modifications that a prudent design-builder (general contractor) may wish to consider when an owner insists upon the use of AIA Document A191.

The Associated General Contractors (AGC) have issued AGC Document 410, Standard Form of Design-Build Agreement and General Conditions Between Owner and Contractor. The AGC acknowledges that certain provisions of its design-build contract have been derived from AIA documents, although not from A191.[2] Any biases reflected in the AGC documents, of course, will mirror those of the general contractors.

AIA Document A191 is divided into two portions. The first portion is titled "Part 1 Agreement-Preliminary Design and Budgeting." The second portion of A191 is "Part Two Agreement-Final Design and Construction." Part 1 allows the owner to decide in an orderly fashion whether or not it wants to go forward with a design-build project. If the owner decides to go forward, then part 2 sets forth the actual construction arrangements. For purposes of this chapter, a general familiarity with AIA Document A191 is presumed.

Sections 11.4 through **11.27** present suggested modifications to the AIA Document A191 to make the contract applicable to the contractor-driven design-build entity. These modifications are followed by an explanation for the change to the AIA language. No two construction projects, design-build included, are exactly the same; no two design-build contracts should be exactly the same, either. The interrelationship of terms between part 1 and part 2 as well as the interdependence of terms within each of the parts requires that each change be carefully analyzed and addressed. A

---

[1] The 1985 edition of A191 is the basis of all offered changes.

[2] The AGC states "certain provisions of this document have been derived, with modifications, from the following documents published by The American Institute of Architects: AIA Document A111, Owner-Contractor Agreement, c. 1978; AIA Document A201, General Conditions, c. 1976 by the American Institute of Architects." AGC Document 410, page 1.

design-builder should strongly consider the use of knowledgeable attorneys skilled in the construction field before attempting this adventure without such assistance.

The proposed modifications to A191 do not defeat the integrity of the document. Many of the provisions suggested would be important to a design-builder regardless of whether the design-builder were an architect, contractor, or single entity combining architectural and construction services. Just as design-build is not for every project, the contractor-driven design-builder is not appropriate 100 percent of the time. Because each project is unique, these modifications cannot simply be adopted without careful thought about their application to the contemplated project.

§ 11.3 The Errors and Omissions Dilemma

The design-builder's expertise and reputation in construction, including the ability to budget and to complete projects in a timely, economical manner, presumably contributed to the owner's decision to select the contractor-driven design-builder in lieu of one architect-driven. For the design-build project, however, the general contractor now must contract with the architect/engineers. A general contractor can procure builder's risk insurance for the project and commercial general liability insurance but may not be able to procure professional liability insurance (errors and omissions insurance), which the architect and engineers will be able to procure. Perhaps the single largest risk for the general contractor serving as the design-builder is that of design liability. It is in the design-builder's best interest to shift as much risk for design to the architect/engineers in the owner/design-builder agreement.

This problem is not solely that of the design-builder. The owner also has a strong interest to see that the project is protected with professional liability insurance. Usually the insurance company providing the professional liability insurance will not include the owner or the contractor as additional or named insureds.[3] The owner may be willing to accept this proposal if the design-builder can offer the owner certainty on costs. Under the modifications to AIA Document A191 which follow, the design-builder develops a guaranteed maximum price during the orderly design and budgeting process of part 1 for use in part 2.

---

[3] Hum & O'Brien, *Insuring and Bonding Design/Build Projects, in* Design/Build: Issues for the 90's and Beyond, A.B.A. Forum on Construction Industry (1990).

AIA DOCUMENT A191, PART 1

§ 11.4 Definition of the Scope of Work

Page 1 of AIA Document A191 Part 1 calls upon the owner and design-builder to designate not only their identities and the identity of the licensed architect, but also has them provide a "detailed description" of the scope of the project. The key to success in a design-build project is a complete and thorough understanding of the scope of work. Understanding the scope of work goes well beyond bricks and mortar. Is this a "spec" building for which there is a prototype that the owner can visit so the owner knows exactly what the design-builder will deliver? Is this a turnkey project which leaves great discretion to the design-builder? Is this going to be a fast-track project with design on an ongoing basis, which demands as much timely input from the owner as any non-design-build, fast-track project? The difficulty in providing a detailed scope for part 1 is that the owner and the design-builder are in a preliminary design phase. Too narrow a scope could unwittingly cause a positive option or opportunity to be ignored; too broad a scope leaves too many choices to be explored, increasing the period devoted to design. The design-builder must craft an appropriate scope description.

§ 11.5 Article 1: General Provisions

Delete subparagraph 1.2.2 in its entirety and substitute for it the following:

The Owner shall be a third-party beneficiary of the contract between the Design-Builder and the Architect and any other design professional under the Contract who shall owe to the Owner a professional standard of care. Nothing contained in the Design-Builder Contract Documents shall create a professional obligation or contractual relationship with any other third party.

Explanatory remarks. The owner must have a direct route to the design professional. In the event the architect fails to perform to the professional standard of care, then the owner has a direct cause of action against the architect. Obviously, this right of the owner has meaning only if the contract between the design-builder and the architect includes the same provision. In view of the nature of the risk to the design-builder who has no other way to protect itself from catastrophic loss, it would be better practice to restate this obligation in the contract between the design-builder and the architect rather than simply using a flow-down clause incorporating all of the terms of A191 into the contract between the design-builder and the architect.

§ 11.6 Article 2: Design-Builder

The last sentence in subparagraph 2.1.1 is deleted and the following is substituted for it:

Nothing contained in Part 1 shall create any contractual relationship between qualified construction contractors and suppliers and the Owner.

Explanatory remarks. Now that subparagraph 1.2.2 has been changed, several part 1 provisions are affected. Revisions to subparagraph 2.1.1. resolve the conflict.

At the end of subparagraph 2.1.2, add the following clause:

[except as provided in Subparagraph 2.1.3;]

and add a new subparagraph 2.1.3.:

The Owner agrees that the liability of the Design-Builder for any claims, damages, errors, or omissions arising out of the professional services to be performed by the Architect (as defined in the Contract) under the Contract, whether through indemnity or otherwise, shall be limited to the amounts of insurance to be carried by the Architect. Owner agrees that the liability of the Design-Builder for any claims, damages, errors, or omissions arising out of the professional services to be performed by other design professionals under the Contract, whether through indemnity or otherwise, shall be limited to the amounts of insurance to be carried by such other design professionals. The Design-Builder will provide to the Owner satisfactory evidence of professional liability insurance under this Part 1.

Explanatory remarks. If the design-builder intends to have the owner look solely to the architect for ultimate design liability and limit the liability of the design-builder, the design-builder must incorporate those provisions into AIA Document A191. The design-builder can anticipate that the owner will want to see evidence of the architect's insurance before agreeing to this provision. Later, article 7 of part 2 sets forth specific limits of insurance for the architect's errors and omissions insurance. Part 1 makes no provision for insurance of any type.

Add a new subparagraph 2.1.4:

Design-Builder is not licensed as an architect or engineer in the State of the Project and not authorized by law to perform design services. Accordingly, Design-Builder will not perform design services pursuant to this Contract, but will furnish and warrant such services as otherwise herein provided. Design-Builder is a licensed contractor in the State of the Project.

Explanatory remarks. Presumably, the owner already knows these facts. In context, it explains the reluctance of the design-builder to acquire a liability for which the design-builder cannot procure insurance.

§ 11.7 Article 3: Owner

Add a new subparagraph 3.6.1:

Should the reports prepared under Paragraph 3.6 or any other report or test result conducted by any governmental agency reveal contamination, pollution, or hazardous material requiring abatement or other remedial work, the Owner and the Design-Builder shall promptly meet and confer to determine the continued feasibility of the Project. The Owner may terminate this Part 1 as a result of such on-site contamination, pollution, or hazardous material pursuant to Paragraph 8.2. The Design-Builder may terminate this Part 1 as a result of such on-site contamination, pollution, or hazardous material pursuant to Paragraph 8.4.

Explanatory remarks. Soils information may show contamination, which must be addressed under a plethora of federal, state, and local pollution laws. The cost of abatement alone may eliminate the owner's ability to pay for the work being contemplated. Furthermore, the design-builder may not be interested in performing the pollution abatement work or waiting until the pollution abatement is completed.

Add a new subparagraph 3.11:

The Owner shall furnish prior to the execution of Part 1 reasonable evidence satisfactory to the Design-Builder that sufficient funds are available and committed for the entire cost of the Project. Furthermore, in the event the Owner is relying in whole or in part on a construction loan, the Owner shall identify the financial institution that is making the loan to the Owner and, if requested by the Design-Builder, the terms and conditions of said loan.

Explanatory remarks. The design-builder needs to establish that funds are available for the project. In a day of great turmoil in the banking industry, the design-builder must not only investigate the financial soundness of the owner, but it should also investigate the financial soundness of the owner's lender.

§ 11.8 Article 5: Payments

Add a new paragraph 5.5:

There shall be no retainage held on payments to the Design-Builder under this Part 1.

Explanatory remarks. Payments from the owner are for services and out-of-pocket expenses, such as direct personnel expenses. Retainage should be used only when construction activities are underway, which in A191 occurs under part 2.

§ 11.9 Article 6: Arbitration

Delete the title ARBITRATION and replace it with DISPUTE RESOLUTION.

Explanatory remarks. Under part 1, disputes under $50,000 will be arbitrated and disputes $50,000 or over will be litigated. Part 2 will completely abandon arbitration. The size and nature of the disputes arising under part 1 are far more amenable to arbitration inasmuch as no construction has begun and the parties fundamentally are the owner, the design-builder, and the design professionals.

In paragraph 6.1, at the end of line 2 after the words "Part 1," add the following:

[the value of which shall not exceed Fifty Thousand Dollars ($50,000.00)]

; and add a new sentence at the end of paragraph 6.1:

Claims, disputes and other matters in question between the parties to Part 1 arising out of or relating to Part 1 the value of which exceed Fifty Thousand Dollars ($50,000.00), shall not be subject to arbitration under this Subparagraph and may be litigated in any court of competent jurisdiction in the State of the Project.

Explanatory remarks. AIA Document A191 assumes that arbitration will resolve all disputes. The modification to paragraph 6.1 reserves smaller disputes for arbitration. Larger disputes which could be "bet the company" disputes are not included under the arbitration clause of paragraph 6.1.

In paragraph 6.4, in line 3 after "any arbitration," add:

[or legal.]

Explanatory remarks. The design-builder wants to be paid regardless or whether the matter is in arbitration or litigation. This change simply conforms the language of paragraph 6.4 to the modifications of paragraph 6.1.

Add new subparagraph 6.1.1:

Claims, disputes, and other matters in question between the parties to Part 1 arising out of or relating to Part 1 and the design services provided by the Architect or any other design professional under Clause 2.1.1.1 shall be decided in litigation regardless of the size of the claim by the Owner.

§ 11.10 Article 7: Miscellaneous Provisions

In subparagraph 7.4.1, add the following at the end of the second sentence:

[which consent will not be unreasonably withheld.]

Explanatory remarks. It is not uncommon for the owner to need a consent to assignment from the design-builder for the benefit of the owner's financial institution. Similarly, there may be reasons that the design-builder needs to assign an interest under part 1. This prevents either party from possessing an unreasonable veto in this regard.

§ 11.11 Article 8: Termination of the Agreement

Add a new paragraph 8.4:

Part 1 may be terminated by the Design-Builder upon at least seven days' written notice to the Owner in the event that contamination, pollution, or hazardous material requiring abatement or remedial work is encountered as set forth in Paragraph 3.6 and results in the work's being stopped in whole or substantial part for a period of thirty days under an order of any court or other public authority having jurisdiction, or in the event the abatement or remedial work causes the work under this Part 1 to be stopped in whole or substantial part for a period of thirty days or more. The Owner shall compensate the Design-Builder as set forth in Paragraph 8.3.

Explanatory remarks. If contamination, pollution, or hazardous material is encountered, an owner may be unable to admit that the project must be abandoned. The period of 30 days gives the design-builder the opportunity to assess the feasibility of the project. The design-builder will have a much better grasp of the impact in terms of overall cost that abatement or remedial work will have on the project and its continued viability.

§ 11.12 Article 10: Other Provisions

Add a new paragraph 10.3:

All notices pursuant to the Contract shall be in writing and shall be deemed to be given when personally delivered, or when mailed by registered or certified mail, postage prepaid, return receipt requested, in each case at the respective addresses set forth on Page 1 of this Part 1 or at such other address as a party may specify by subsequent notice in accordance with this paragraph. Notices may also be delivered by telecopy, with a copy to be delivered by regular mail, postage prepaid, provided that the burden is upon the sending party to verify that such telecopy has in fact been received by the intended recipient.

Explanatory remarks. Notice provisions must be carefully followed. Many parties are already using telecopy transmissions (faxes) to communicate notices, even though the contracts do not provide that a telecopy is sufficient notice. The sender needs to verify that the telecopy was received, which can be done in several ways. First, the telecopy machine should generate a transmission report showing a date, phone number of the receiving machine (or some other identification), and the number of pages transmitted. Second, the sender should call the recipient to verify that the telecopy was received.

AIA DOCUMENT A191, PART 2

§ 11.13 Article 1: General Provisions

Delete subparagraph 1.2.2 in its entirety and add the following in its place:

The Owner shall be a third-party beneficiary of the contract between the Design-Builder and the Architect and any other design professional under the Contract who shall owe to the Owner a professional standard of care. Nothing contained in the Design-Builder Contract Documents shall create a professional obligation or contractual relationship between any other third party and the Owner.

Explanatory remarks. The first step in shifting the risk of design liability from the design-builder to the architect is to give the owner status as a third-party beneficiary to the architect's contract.

§ 11.14 Article 2: Design-Builder

Delete the last sentence in subparagraph 2.1.1 and substitute the following for it:

Nothing contained in Part 2 shall create any contractual relationship between qualified construction contractors and suppliers and the Owner.

Explanatory remarks. With the modification in subparagraph 1.2.2, this subparagraph must be changed to conform to the owner's status vis-à-vis the architect.

Add a new clause 2.1.1.1:

The Owner agrees that the liability of the Design-Builder for any claims, damages, errors, or omissions arising out of the professional services to be performed by the Architect (as defined in the Contract) under the Contract, whether through indemnity or otherwise, shall be limited to the amounts of insurance to be carried by the Architect pursuant to Paragraph 7.6 of the Contract or otherwise. The Owner agrees that the liability of any other design professional with a contract with the Design-Builder for the Project for any claims, damages, errors, or omissions arising out of the professional services to be performed by the design professional under the Contract whether through indemnity or otherwise, shall be limited to the amounts of insurance to be carried by such design professional pursuant to Paragraph 7.7 of the Contract or otherwise.

Explanatory remarks. For the design-builder who must contract with an architectural firm to provide the architectural services for the project, the liability of the design professional is a great risk for the design-builder to assume. Unlike the architect who can obtain professional errors and omissions insurance coverage, the design-builder may not be able to obtain such insurance at commercially reasonable rates, if at all.

Add a new subparagraph 2.1.2:

Design-Builder is not licensed as an architect or engineer in the State of the Project and not authorized by law to perform design services. Accordingly, Design-Builder will not perform design services pursuant to this Contract but will furnish and warrant such services as otherwise herein provided. Design-Builder is a licensed contractor in the State of the Project.

Explanatory remarks. The design-builder wants no misunderstanding on this point. This change dovetails with subparagraph 2.1.1 and clause 2.1.1.1 and unequivocally provides that the architect will be the design professional.

Add a new subparagraph 2.1.3:

The Design-Builder shall be responsible to the Owner for acts and omissions of the Design-Builder's employees and parties in privity of contract with the Design-Builder to perform a portion of the Work, including their agents and employees, as limited by Clause 2.1.1.1 with regard to the professional obligations of the Architect and other design professionals.

Explanatory remarks. This change tracks the concept embodied in clause 2.1.1.1 that limits the liability of the design-builder.

In subparagraph 2.2.7, delete from line 5 at the beginning of the line the phrase ", subject to demand for arbitration," and delete from line 10 at the beginning of the line the words "arbitrator(s) or the".

Explanatory remarks. The AIA documents always assume arbitration is the dispute resolution method of choice. Arbitration of disputes under part 2 will be discussed in article 10 (see **§ 11.23**). The modification to subparagraph 2.2.7 presumes the design-builder will not select arbitration to settle disputes but will rather litigate the disputes.

In subparagraph 2.2.11, add the following:

Where laws, ordinances, rules, regulations, and lawful orders of public authorities conflict, the Design-Builder shall be entitled to rely on the regulations of the State of the Project.

Explanatory remarks. Bureaucracy at all levels can promulgate a maze of conflicting ordinances, rules, and regulations. This is particularly acute in the health care industry, and design-build is a popular choice for the construction of health care facilities. The design-builder is not relieved from the obligation to harmonize the rules when possible. The design-builder must know which rules govern if a true conflict appears.

In subparagraph 2.2.13, add to line 5 after the word "employees" the following:

, provided that Design-Builder shall have a limited liability for acts and omissions of the Architect or other design professional pursuant to Clause 2.1.1.1.

Explanatory remarks. This conforms to the change at clause 2.1.1.1.

In subparagraph 2.2.16, delete the word "arbitration" at the end of the second sentence and add the following:

[litigation in any court of competent jurisdiction in the State of the Project.]

Explanatory remarks. Again, part 2 assumes arbitration will solve disputes. These changes remove the arbitration references and substitute litigation.

§ 11.15 Article 3: Owner

In subparagraph 3.10, add to line 1 after the word "contractors" the words:

[Architect and design professionals.]

Explanatory remarks. The design-builder does not want the owner unilaterally communicating with the architect. The owner may be conditioned from non-design-build projects to contacting the architect directly. However, if the owner balks at this proposal, the design-builder should propose that any communications between the owner and architect be in writing, with a copy to the design-builder.

Add a new subparagraph 3.11:

The Owner shall furnish prior to the execution of Part 2 reasonable evidence satisfactory to the Design-Builder that sufficient funds are available and committed for the entire cost of the Project. Furthermore, in the event the Owner is relying in whole or in part on a construction loan, the Owner shall identify the financial institution that is making the loan to the Owner and, if requested by the Design-Builder, the terms and conditions of said loan.

Explanatory remarks. Now that the project has moved to the construction phase, part 2, it is imperative that the design-builder investigate the continued soundness of the owner and the owner's financing before the design-builder commits to separate contracts with various trade contractors or subcontractors. Even if the design-builder conducted that investigation in part 1, it should update that information. If the owner balks at updating the information, then perhaps the design-builder has a problem, not a project.

§ 11.16 Article 4: Time

To paragraph 4.3, add to line 4 after the word "can" the words:

[or does.]

Explanatory remarks. If the owner does in fact occupy the premises, such occupation demonstrates that the owner can occupy the premises for their intended purposes. After all, the owner cannot occupy the premises until the appropriate authority issues a certificate of occupancy.

From paragraph 4.5, delete from lines 8 and 9 the words "or by delay authorized by the Owner's pending arbitration".

Explanatory remarks. More references to arbitration are deleted.

§ 11.17 Article 5: Payments

Add new clause 5.1.2.1:

The Owner shall be entitled to withhold ten percent (10%) of each Application for Payment as retainage until the Project is fifty percent (50%) complete, at which time no additional retainage will be withheld. Retainage shall be paid pursuant to Subparagraph 5.1.8.

Explanatory remarks. The design-builder may as well anticipate that the owner will insist upon holding retainage. This clause contains a standard feature of many construction contracts in that it eliminates retainage on pay applications for the last half of the project.

In subparagraph 5.1.8, delete from line 1 the words "If the Contract provides for retainage, then at" and add as the first word:

[At]

Explanatory remarks. With the addition of clause 5.1.2.1, the contract provides for retainage. The deletion simply seeks to avoid confusion.

§ 11.18 Article 6: Protection of Persons and Property

Add a new subparagraph 6.1.1:

The responsibility for the safety of the Design-Builder's contractors and their employees, property, and equipment utilized in the performance of their work rests exclusively with the Design-Builder's contractors. Failure of the Design-Builder to discover safety violations or potentially unsafe conditions in no way creates or establishes any liability of the Owner, unless such violations or conditions were created by the Owner or Owner's separate contractors.

Explanatory remarks. The design-builder does not want to assume the liability for the acts of the owner or the owner's separate contractors. Furthermore, the design-builder does not want its own contractors to claim subparagraph 6.1.1 as an escape from their own jobsite safety obligations.

Add a new subparagraph 6.4.1:

Design-Builder agrees to cooperate fully with Owner in pursuing its rights hereunder and under the contract, including assignment to Owner of any rights or remedies Design-Builder may have against the Architect or other design professional relating to any such claims, damages, errors, or omissions.

Explanatory remarks. Should a malpractice claim against the architect exceed the amounts of the required insurance, the design-builder can assist the owner in attempts to be made whole. The ability to collect against the architect individually is only as valuable as the architect's financial solvency. The architect may be independently wealthy or may be judgment-proof. The key is the professional liability insurance required under paragraph 7.6 of part 2.

Add a new subparagraph 6.4.2:

Other than recourse with respect to claims, damages, errors, and omissions relating to the Architect or other design professionals arising out of the professional services to be performed under the contract, Clause 2.1.1.1 shall not constitute a waiver of any other remedy which the Owner may have against the Design-Builder for any other failure of the Design-Builder to perform in accordance with the Contract or any other agreement between the Owner and the Design-Builder.

Explanatory remarks. The owner may need to be encouraged to accept the risk limitations contained in clause 2.1.1.1. This subparagraph clarifies that no other remedy is impacted.

§ 11.19 Article 7: Insurance and Bonds

Delete subparagraph 7.1.2 in its entirety and substitute for it the following:

The Design-Builder as required by Subparagraph 7.1.1 shall maintain the following insurance coverage for not less than the limits of liability as set forth herein or required by law, whichever is greater.

- .1 Commercial General Liability:
  - .1 General Aggregate $ A
  - .2 Products—Completed Operations Aggregate $ B
  - .3 Personal and Advertising Injury $ C
  - .4 Each Occurrence $ D
  - .5 Fire Damage (any one fire) $ E
  - .6 Medical Expense (any one person) $ F

.2 Automobile Liability:
Combined single limit $ G

.3 Excess Liability:
Other than umbrella form
Each occurrence $ H, aggregate $ I

.4 Workers' Compensation and Employers' Liability:
.1 Statutory Limits
.2 Each Accident $ J
.3 Disease Policy Limit $ K
.4 Disease Each Employee $ L
.5 Excess Umbrella Liability Coverage $ M

Explanatory remarks. The design-builder needs to set out exactly the various insurance limits. Part 2, of AIA Document A191 presumes that such limits will be specified in some form.

Delete from subparagraph 7.3.8 line 7 the words "arbitration as provided in Article 10" and substitute for them:

a Court of competent jurisdiction in the State of the Project

; and delete the last sentence of subparagraph 7.3.8.

Explanatory remarks. Subparagraph 7.3.8 must be conformed to the change in dispute resolution.

Add the following sentence at the end of subparagraph 7.3.9:

The Owner shall provide insurance for the Owner's personal property moved into the premises.

Explanatory remarks. The design-builder should not be the insurer of the owner's personal property. The owner and design-builder can create appropriate security measures in the event of the owner's occupancy under subparagraph 7.3.9.

Add the following clause 7.3.9.1:

The Owner will give at least fourteen (14) days' notice of Owner's intended use and occupancy to the Design-Builder and the insurance company or companies providing property insurance.

Explanatory remarks. The design-builder needs information from the owner in a timely manner to notify the appropriate insurance carrier in order to meet the obligations of subparagraph 7.3.9. The design-builder may also need to revise or rearrange schedules to accommodate the owner's intentions.

Delete from subparagraph 7.4.1 in line 1 the words ", at the Owner's option, may" and substitute for them:

[will.]

Explanatory remarks. Clearly, the design-builder benefits when the owner procures this insurance.

Delete subparagraph 7.5.1 in its entirety and substitute for them the following:

The Owner shall designate the construction contractors of the Design-Builder from whom the Owner desires to furnish payment and performance bonds covering the faithful performance of work under the construction contractors' contracts with the Design-Builder for the Project. The Design-Builder shall be entitled to an increase in the budget and the Guaranteed Maximum Price as established in Paragraph 14.4 of this Part 2 for each such bond required by the Owner if the cost of it is not already included in the budget or cost of the Work.

Explanatory remarks. If the owner has faith in the design-builder, the owner may be better served by requiring bonds only on major or critical systems to be installed by specific contractors. It will be less costly to the owner to bond in this manner. The guaranteed maximum price will be explained in **§ 11.27** below.

§ 11.20 —Professional Liability Insurance

Add the following paragraph 7.6:

[Architect's Professional Liability Insurance,]

and add the following subparagraph 7.6.1:

The Architect shall purchase and maintain in a company or companies authorized to do business in the State of the Project such insurance as will protect the Architect from claims by the Owner or Design-Builder for any claims, damages, errors, or omissions arising out of the professional services to be performed by the Architect under the contract. This insurance shall be written for not less than the following limits of liability:

.1 Each occurrence—$ AA
.2 Aggregate—$ BB

Explanatory remarks. Subparagraph 7.6.1 is the heart of the design-builder's efforts to limit its design liability.

Add a new paragraph 7.7:

[Other Design Professional Liability Insurance]

; and add a new subparagraph 7.7.1:

In the event the Design-Builder directly employs any other design professionals in addition to the Architect, the design professional shall purchase and maintain insurance in the style and manner of the architect, such limits of liability to be determined by the Design-Builder after consultation with Owner.

Explanatory remarks. If the design-builder separately contracts with engineers rather than having the engineers contract be with the architect, the design-builder may seek to shift this risk as well. Better practice is to have the architect responsible for all professional services.

§ 11.21 Article 8: Changes in the Work

At the end of subparagraph 8.1.3, add a new sentence:

In the event it appears to the Design-Builder that the cost of preparing a proposal for change in the Work will exceed $1,000, the Design-Builder shall give the Owner notice of the anticipated cost prior to proceeding to prepare the proposal; the Owner shall have fifteen (15) days in which to advise the Design-Builder whether to proceed or abandon such proposal for change.

Explanatory remarks. When an owner is constantly proposing possible changes to the work, especially at the part 2 stage of the work, the scheduling and completion of the work are impacted. Under subparagraph 8.1.3 as written, the owner pays the costs of design services incurred in making proposals that are rejected. The proposed modification to the subparagraph takes that risk and brings it into focus. Not only is the owner going to reimburse the design-builder for these costs, but the owner also receives a warning before the design services are performed on major changes that the estimated design work costs exceed $1,000. Then it is the owner's decision to proceed with design or abandon this potential change before money is spent on designing it.

Add a new subparagraph 8.2.2:

Should pollution or hazardous material be encountered in concealed and unknown conditions, the Design-Builder shall immediately cause the Work on the

Project to cease and report the discovery to the Owner. It shall be the Owner's sole responsibility to investigate and undertake abatement or remedial work that is required by federal, state, and local regulations. Such abatement and remedial work shall be carried out by the Owner's separate contractors unless otherwise agreed to in writing between the Owner and the Design-Builder. The Design-Builder shall be entitled to a Change Order for any increased costs as a result of any delay to the work or expenses incurred in decontaminating property polluted prior to the discovery of the nature of the problem.

Explanatory remarks. Unless the design-builder regularly performs hazardous waste abatement, the design-builder must analyze the risk under the numerous environmental statutes applicable to hazardous wastes. The design-builder does not want the owner to have the ability to force it to perform the work even with a change order.

§ 11.22 Article 9: Correction of Work

In paragraph 9.4, delete the last sentence, "Such action by the Owner shall be subject to arbitration." and substitute for it:

All disputes arising under Paragraph 9.4 shall be resolved in a court of competent jurisdiction in the State of the Project.

Explanatory remarks. The modified part 2 deletes arbitration in favor of litigation.

§ 11.23 Article 10: Arbitration

Delete article 10 in its entirety.

Explanatory remarks. Arbitration has long been the presumed dispute resolution mechanism under construction contracts, but it has not necessarily resulted in disputes' being settled more quickly or more economically. Construction disputes can be of such size and magnitude that the continued existence of the design-builder is at issue. Further, arbitration does not necessarily permit discovery. Attorneys may abuse discovery rules, but discovery is necessary in complex construction litigation, including design-build issues when the life of the company is on the line. The grounds for overturning an incorrect arbitration award are so limited as to be virtually nonexistent.

Should the owner and design-builder decide to leave arbitration in the contract, they should not leave article 10 of part 2 unmodified. The parties need to specify the location of the arbitration. If the arbitration is to be conducted by one arbitrator, then the parties need to specify the qualifications for that arbitrator (that is, should the arbitrator be a judge, professor, attorney, contractor, owner, or engineer). If there is to be more than one arbitrator, then typically three arbitrators are used. For one form of tripartite panel the parties each select a party advocate arbitrator and the two party advocate arbitrators select a third arbitrator. The alternate method is to designate the qualifications of each of the arbitrators and have the American Arbitration Association select appropriate personnel. Finally, provision should be made for extended arbitrations in terms of the handling of costs and fees and the ability of the parties to request continuances.

§ 11.24 Article 11: Miscellaneous Provisions

In subparagraph 11.4.2, add to line 4 after the word "party" the following:

[except as specifically provided in Clause 2.1.1.1 and Subparagraph 6.4.1.]

Explanatory remarks. This change simply tracks modifications made previously in the document to the relationship between the owner, design-builder, and the architect.

In subparagraph 11.5.2, add to line 7 after the word "Documents" the following:

, provided the Design-Builder shall not be responsible for scheduling the work of the Owner's separate contractors, coordination among Owner's separate contractors, or safety practices of the Owner's separate contractors.

Explanatory remarks. The design-builder may have to coordinate with the owner's separate contractors, but the design-builder wants to make clear to the owner that the owner's separate contractors must perform their own scheduling and coordination and remain primarily responsible for their own safety. If the owner wants the design-builder to schedule and coordinate the owner's separate contractors, then the services need to be detailed as beyond the basic services of paragraph 14.2. The more work that the design-builder performs with the separate contractors, the more likely the design-builder will be held accountable for their safety practices.

In subparagraph 11.7.1, add to line 7 after the word "Work" the following:

except as specifically provided in Clause 2.1.1.1 and Subparagraph 6.4.1 for the claims, damages, errors, and omissions arising out of the professional services to be performed by the Architect or other design professional.

Explanatory remarks. This addition clarifies the risk shifting that is set forth earlier in the document.

Add at the end of subparagraph 11.7.2 the following:

except that the Owner shall be liable for injury incurred by an employee of the Design-Builder, its contractors, anyone directly or indirectly employed by them, or their suppliers and material suppliers for injury arising out of or resulting from the discovery of hazardous materials as described in Subparagraph 8.2.2.

Explanatory remarks. The design-builder should not take on any of the owner's liability for contamination indigenous to the project site. The design-builder is likely to first learn of the potentially hazardous material only after workers have been exposed to the materials. The owner has put everyone at peril, not the design-builder, and should step up to the liability. Many insurance policies have pollution exclusions.

In subparagraph 11.8.1, add to line 5 following the word "other" the words:

[which consent shall not be unreasonably withheld.]

Explanatory remarks. Frequently, the owner wants to assign, sublet, or transfer part or all of its interest prior to the completion of the project. A design-builder may also have that need. A dispute can arise if either the owner or the design-builder has a veto or perceives such an ability. For the owner or design-builder to object under the modified language, there must exist a bona fide objection.

§ 11.25 Article 12: Termination of the Agreement

In subparagraph 12.1.2, delete from lines 13–15 "all materials, equipment, tools and construction equipment and machinery thereon" and substitute:

[all materials to be incorporated into the Work and all tools to be consumed by the Work.]

Explanatory remarks. Under the unmodified language of subparagraph 12.1.2, the owner can lawfully possess not only construction materials and tools but heavy equipment and the like. The modified language allows the design-builder to retrieve bulldozers, cranes, trailers, and the like from the site. Although the owner's use of such equipment potentially reduces the liability of the design-builder, the owner has no incentive nor does any design-builder or contractor who completes the work, to maintain and protect the equipment. To the extent that the design-builder was wrongfully terminated, not only is the design-builder suffering economically from a lack of income from the project, but it also must locate and pay for additional equipment to perform on new work obtained to make up for the lost project. Finally, in the event of injury or death from faulty equipment, the design-builder can expect to be sued by either the injured parties (for the injuries) or the owner (for indemnity arising out of the injuries) or both. This modification eliminates that risk.

Add a new subparagraph 12.2.2:

If the Project is stopped in whole or substantial part for a period of thirty days under an order of any court or any public authority having jurisdiction or as a result of an act of government, such as a declaration of a national emergency making materials unavailable, through no act or fault of the Design-Builder or the Architect, other design professional, qualified construction contractors and suppliers, or any other persons performing any of the work under a contract with the Design-Builder, or if the work should be stopped for a period of thirty days because of contamination, pollution, or hazardous material abatement or remedial work, then the Design-Builder may upon seven days' additional written notice to the Owner terminate the Contract and recover from the Owner payment for all work executed and fees earned to date and for any proven loss sustained upon any materials, equipment, tools, construction equipment, and machinery, including cancellation charges on existing obligations, including reasonable profit and damages of those under contract with the Design-Builder for the Project. The Owner shall also reasonably compensate the Design-Builder for the time incurred in the negotiation of cancellation charges.

Explanatory remarks. Discovery of pollution can be the death knell for a project. Even if the owner is unwilling to admit the project cannot go forward, after a 30-day period the design-builder will have a sense of whether the project is feasible. If it is no longer feasible because of the delay, the design-builder has the option of walking away. The owner may request that if the design-builder elects the remedy of cancellation under this paragraph it will assign all of the subcontracts to the owner so the owner can go forward. If the design-builder agrees to that request, then the subcontracts must be written to allow such assignment.

§ 11.26 Article 14: Other Provisions— Guaranteed Maximum Price

Add to paragraph 14.4 as part of the design-builder's proposal a detailed breakdown of the guaranteed maximum price, including contingency.

Explanatory remarks. Although the contractor-driven design-builder does not have the architectural expertise or insurance to benefit an owner, it has the ability to provide the owner with a guaranteed maximum price (G.M.P.). For the owner, the downside to the risk-shifting provisions proposed by the design-builder may be balanced by the guaranteed maximum price option and make the contractor-driven design management project the owner's best decision.

Add a new paragraph 14.5:

[Guaranteed Maximum Price]

with the following subparagraphs:

Subparagraph 14.5.1: The Design-Builder has established the Guaranteed Maximum Price (G.M.P.) for the Work in Paragraph 14.1. Such G.M.P. will be subject to modification for changes in the Work as provided in Article 8 and for delay caused by the Owner as set forth in Paragraph 4.5. The G.M.P. contains a contingency fund as agreed to by the Design-Builder and Owner. The contingency fund shall be utilized to absorb additional costs (if any) in the following priority sequence:

.1 Additional costs attributable to design changes inherent in the final design plans.
.2 Additional costs attributable to unusual or unseasonal weather conditions.
.3 Owner-requested change orders attributable to building shell up-grades.
.4 Any remaining funds in the contingency line item will be returned to the Owner and will count as part of the first $300,000 of Project savings.

Explanatory remarks. A contingency line item is an important component in any guaranteed maximum price project. By considering unspent contingency funds as a part of savings, the design-builder has an incentive not to spend such funds.

Add a new subparagraph 14.5.2:

If upon completion of all Work hereunder, the total amount of the costs and charges for the Project shall be less than the G.M.P. as adjusted pursuant to 14.5.1, the Owner shall be entitled to the first Three Hundred Thousand Dollars ($300,000) of savings; in the event such savings are greater than Three Hundred Thousand Dollars ($300,000), then the Owner shall pay to the Design-Builder an amount equal to Twenty-Five Percent (25%) of such difference between actual savings and Three Hundred Thousand Dollars ($300,000).

Explanatory remarks. Another incentive the design-builder has to avoid unnecessary expenses is the savings clause. The numbers contained in the savings clause must reflect the size of the project. The savings clause is not a license for the design-builder to vary from the agreed-upon plans and specifications. In any design-build project, be it contractor-driven or architect-driven, the owner must rely upon the design-builder to perform pursuant to the contract documents. The owner has legal recourse to the extent the design-builder fails to build according to the plans and specs.

Add a new subparagraph 14.5.3:

The G.M.P. will only include those taxes in the cost of the Project which are legally enacted at the time the G.M.P. is enacted. Any taxes enacted or effective after the establishment of the G.M.P. shall be borne by the Owner.

Explanatory remarks. If a G.M.P. option is selected, the design-builder is not the guarantor for taxes that are assessed after the G.M.P. is derived. If there is a sales tax of 4 percent in effect at the time the contract is signed and that figure is raised to 5 percent, then the incremental difference would be an additive change to the G.M.P.

Add a new subparagraph 14.5.4:

If, after the establishment of the G.M.P., the Owner, upon review of a proposed Subcontractor of the Design-Builder, objects in writing within seven (7) days to the awarding of a Subcontract to that proposed Subcontractor, the Design-Builder shall be entitled to an increase in the G.M.P. for any increased cost incurred by the Design-Builder in selecting an alternate Subcontractor for the Project.

Explanatory remarks. Under subparagraph 11.4.1, the design-builder informs the owner of the identity of the design-builder's subcontractors. In the event the owner objects to one or more of such contractors, those contractors can be removed from the work, provided that the design-builder is entitled to increase the G.M.P. for additional costs incurred in the change.

Add a new paragraph 14.6:

[Allowances]

with the following Subparagraphs:

14.6.1 The Design-Builder shall include in the G.M.P. all allowances stated in the Contract Documents. Items covered by these allowances shall be supplied for such amounts and by such persons as the Owner may direct, but the Design-Builder will not be required to employ persons against whom it makes a reasonable objection.

14.6.2 Unless otherwise provided in the Contract Documents:

.1 these allowances shall cover the cost to the Design-Builder, less any applicable trade discount, of the materials and equipment required by the allowance delivered at the site, and all applicable taxes;
.2 the Design-Builder's costs for unloading and handling on the site, labor installation costs, overhead, profit, and other expenses contemplated for the original allowance shall be included in the G.M.P. and not in the allowance;
.3 whenever the cost is more than or less than the allowance, the G.M.P. shall be adjusted accordingly by Change Order, the amount of which will recognize changes, if any, in handling costs on the site, labor, installation costs, overhead, profit, and other expenses.

Explanatory remarks. There is no provision in part 2 dealing with allowances. To the extent that a given G.M.P. will generally include allowances, this section defines allowances and adjustments to the G.M.P. based upon actual cost. Even when the contract does not provide for a G.M.P., the design-builder and the owner need a definition of allowances if any of the budgeted items include allowances.

§ 11.27 —Notices

Add a new paragraph 14.7:

All notices pursuant to the Contract shall be in writing and shall be deemed to be given when personally delivered, or when mailed by registered or certified mail, postage prepaid, return receipt requested, in each case at the respective addresses set forth on Page 1 of this Part 2 or at such other address as a party may specify by subsequent notice in accordance with this paragraph. Notices may also be delivered by telecopy, with a copy to be delivered by regular mail, postage prepaid, provided that the burden is upon the sending party to verify that such telecopy has in fact been received by the intended recipient.

Explanatory remarks. Notice provisions are basic to all types of construction contracts. See the explanatory comments to paragraph 10.3 of part 1 in **§ 11.12**.

CHAPTER 12

PROTECTING SUBCONTRACTOR WITH APPROPRIATE CONTRACT CLAUSES

Steven M. Siegfried
Stanley P. Sklar

Steven M. Siegfried is a partner in the firm of Siegfried, Kipnis, Rivera, Lerner, De La Torre & Mocarski, P.A. in Coral Gables, Florida. He received his undergraduate degree in economics from Brooklyn College and his law degree with honors from American University, Washington College of Law. He is a contributing author to *Troubled Construction Loans: Law and Practice* (John Wiley & Sons 1991) and has written many other articles. Mr. Siegfried is chapter counsel to the American Subcontractors Association of South Florida; chairman of Division 9—Specialty Trade Contractors of the American Bar Association's Forum on the Construction Industry; chairman of the Dade County Bar Association's Construction Law Committee; and also teaches construction law as an adjunct professor of law at the University of Miami. He is a founding fellow of the American College of Construction Lawyers, and is a board certified civil trial lawyer.

Stanley P. Sklar is chair of the Construction Practice Group of Pretzel & Stouffer, Chartered, Chicago, Illinois. He graduated from Northwestern University School of Law, is a member of the American College of Real Estate Lawyers and a founding fellow of the American College of Construction Lawyers. He is chair of the Chicago Bar Association Real Property Committee for 1991–92.

§ 12.1 The Subcontractor as Part of the Design-Build Team

During the last 20 years the construction industry has experienced an increasing tendency to depart from the traditional owner/design professional, owner/contractor relationship. One of the variations is the design-build relationship. Perhaps this trend toward the use of design-build contractors is a result of the need for a reduction in construction costs and for faster and more efficient project delivery, as well as a recognition of the owner's economic interest in dealing with one responsible entity to avoid numerous claims and finger-pointing when problems arise. Perhaps it is the result of a desire on the part of contractors to have greater control of the construction projects they undertake and to control costs through design and value engineering and thereby increase profits.

The design-build relationship occurs when a single entity contracts with an owner to perform both design services and construction. Whether this new method has been an improvement to the construction industry has been the subject of many articles.[1]

The single-entity design-build company seems to be particularly well suited to the special use project, such as a specialty warehouse or hospital facilities, or when special mechanical, electrical, or other unique equipment will be utilized to operate a facility. Even though design-build contracts may have had their origins in such special use projects or turnkey government contracts, their use is becoming more widespread in today's construction market.

---

[1] *Construction Management and Design Build/Fast Track Construction,* 46 Law & Contemp. Probs. 1 (Winter 1983).

Traditionally, subcontractors have played a limited but valuable role in the design-build system of project delivery. In its simplest form, we have seen the mechanical or electrical trade contractor review bid plans and provide input by way of *value engineering,* which is the revision to plans and specifications leading to meaningful cost savings in terms of project delivery time, efficiency in operating the end product, and a better product and service to the owner.

This chapter will primarily focus on the use of specialty trade subcontractors, such as electrical, mechanical, fire protection, plumbing, or steel erection subs, in the design-build project. It will also address contract clauses which covertly have the purpose and intent of transferring design responsibility and the risk attendant thereto from the prime contractor to the subcontractor, a new role for the subcontractor that is fraught with extended liability risks.

Because of their experience in their particular trade, their knowledge of available equipment, whether traditional or resulting from new technological advances, in terms of price and efficiency (cost to operate and service), and their special skills required in the installation, specialty trade subcontractors are particularly suited to assist in the design-build team. It may be because of this expertise that these subcontractors have been asked to assume performance obligations (a euphemism for design responsibility) for their subcontracts. The fact is, however, that specialty trades that do not participate in the early design stages of the project often have design responsibility foisted upon them through risk-shifting clauses contained in their subcontracts. As the title of this chapter indicates, there has been an attempt through disclaimers and exculpatory clauses, coupled with flow-down provisions, to covertly transfer from the design professional, the contractor, and owner the risk of project failure due to design defects to the specialty trade contractor.

§ 12.2 Licensing Considerations

An often overlooked consideration is whether the contract contemplating design services complies with the local laws regarding design professionals. While all 50 states, U.S. possessions, and the District of Columbia require that architects and engineers be licensed,[2] such laws do not clearly provide guidance to the design-build contractor and subcontractor. Many states require corporations and partnerships that provide architectural or engineering services to obtain state approval[3] through professional licensing laws.

[2] *See* American Institute of Architects, Architectural Licensing: Summary of State Statutes (July 1981).

[3] Annotation, *Practice of Architecture by Corporation,* 56 A.L.R.2d 726 (1957).

In some states, a contractor who is neither licensed as an architect or professional engineer and who contracts with an owner to perform both design and construction services may very well have entered into an illegal and unenforceable contract.[4] This could have severe repercussions regarding insurance coverage and liabilities. Because the contractor has contracted to perform services for which it is not licensed, the unenforceability of its contract may prove to be a windfall for the owner and financial disaster for the contractor and the subcontractor. The owner may use the illegality of the contract as a defense to paying for the services rendered, and if the contract is not severable into enforceable and nonenforceable parts, payment for all services may be unrecoverable, despite the unjust enrichment to the owner.[5]

Some state statutes and cases allow a nonlicensed contractor to "furnish or provide" design services so long as they are "performed" by a licensed design professional retained by the contractor, either by in-house or independently retained professionals.[6] For example, Florida provides an exemption, in certain instances, from the architect and engineering licensing statutes for contractors that furnish design-build services.[7] Illinois permits such a relationship provided at least two-thirds of the stock ownership of the design-build contractor is owned by licensed design professionals.[8]

Therefore, licensing considerations are crucial and should never be overlooked by the specialty trade contractor considering a design-build project.[9]

§ 12.3 Forms of Agreements

The National Society of Professional Engineers,[10] the Associated General Contractors,[11] and the American Institute of Architects[12] have developed form contracts for the design-build scenario. These contracts may be a

---

[4] *See, e.g.,* Mo. Rev. Stat. § 327.461 (1986); Ark. Code Ann. § 17-14-311(c) (1987).

[5] *See* F.F. Bolinger Co. v. Widmann Brewing Co., 14 A.2d 81 (Pa. 1940); American Store Equip. & Constr. Corp. v. Jack Dempsey's Punch Bowl, 21 N.Y.S.2d 117, *aff'd,* 258 A.D. 794, 16 N.Y.S.2d 702, *appeal denied,* 258 A.D. 876, 17 N.Y.S.2d 220 (1939), *aff'd,* 283 N.Y. 601, 28 N.E.2d 23 (1940). See also **Ch. 3**.

[6] *See* Charlebois v. J.M. Weller Assocs., Inc., 531 N.E.2d 1288 (N.Y. 1988); People *ex rel.* State Bd. of Architects v. Rodgers Co., 115 N.E. 146 (Ill. 1917); Binford v. Boyd, 174 P. 56 (Cal. 1918).

[7] Fla. Stat. Ann. §§ 481.229(3), 489.103(11) (West 1990).

[8] Ill. Rev. Stat. ch. 111, para. 1321(b)(1) (1989).

[9] For a good discussion on the validity of design-build contracts see Halsey & Quatman, *Design/Build Contracts: Valid or Invalid,* 9 Construction Law. 3 (Aug. 1989).

[10] NSPE Document 2802-1 (1977).

[11] AGC Documents No. 400, 410, 415, 420, 450, and 450-1.

[12] AIA Documents A191 and A491.

good starting point, but, as with all form contracts, they should be tailored to fit one's individual needs. None of these organizations has a standard form agreement that is tailored to the design-build subcontractor. Although AIA Document A491 is designed to be used by a subcontractor of the design-build contractor, this document does not contemplate that the subcontractor assume primary design responsibility. In the Document Synopses provided as a guide by the AIA, it is noted that a design-builder will enter into an initial agreement covering management consulting services for the preliminary design and budgeting phase and a second agreement, which the parties are not obligated to enter into, for the actual construction.

§ 12.4 New Forms of Subcontractor Relationships

There is a variety of possible design-build services that specialty trade subcontractors will be asked to perform. The nature of these services may be dictated by the special needs of the owner. But with these new forms of services come many liability questions. Within the design-build team, is the design-build subcontractor part of the architect's team or the contractor's team? What is the role of the engineer who prepares and seals plans and inspects the subcontractor's work? When there is a question of design intent, does the subcontractor who furnished the engineering drawings have the final word, a role traditionally reserved for the design professional?

Many specialty subcontractors, such as mechanical (HVAC), fire protection/sprinkler system, plumbing, electrical, and like contractors, are moving into the design-build arena. The most fertile area for the use of the design-build specialty trade has been in the multiple prime contractor scenario. In this relationship, each specialty subcontractor deals directly with the owner or the owner's agent, often the construction manager, as a prime contractor. As with design-build contractors, the advantages to the design-build subcontractor are many. There is a potential for higher profit, because the sub will be paid by the owner without the intervention of the general contractor as a conduit for payment, with the delays encountered when payments come from the contractor. The specialty trade contractor will not be subject to artificial budget constraints placed upon it by the contractor or the arbitrary backcharges for illusorily defective work. The specialty trade contractor deals directly with the owner and, through design of its own work, it can order materials, schedule delivery of materials, make manpower allocations, and, in general, perform its work more efficiently.

Conversely, the owner can get the most for its money from each trade. In this scenario, the owner must be sophisticated enough to establish a detailed project program in order to convey the project's needs. When the owner uses the multiprime or specialty trade contractor approach, all players must understand their design role. The owner usually has one architectural/engineering firm performing the complete design role and several contractors bidding and performing their work.

In the single point design-build relationship, one firm contracts with the owner to provide the completed project, both designing and building it. The subcontractor then, as in the traditional relationship, simply agrees to perform services for the contractor. The only variation is that the architect is no longer the representative of the owner but rather is part of the contractor's team. This relationship is set forth in AIA Document A491.

Over the years, in the traditional method of construction, the duties and responsibilities of the parties have become somewhat clear.[13] However, in these new forms of relationships, the lines of responsibility have become somewhat blurred.

§ 12.5 Risk-Shifting Clauses

Many of the owner's responsibilities for design in the traditional construction setting (owner/design professional/contractor) may be shifted onto the design-build entity. Some design responsibilities may be covertly shifted to the contractor or subcontractor through warranty, shop drawing, coordination with other trades, and code compliance clauses. Often, these risk-shifting clauses relating to design responsibility may impose upon the subcontractor increased risks without giving it the contractual or practical means to manage these risks.

In the traditional setting, unless specifically agreed upon in the owner/design professional contract, the law does not impose upon a design professional the legal duty to warrant that its drawings and specifications will produce the result that the owner intended.[14] Rather, the design professional is held to a standard of performance.[15] Additionally, as long as the contractor's performance conforms to the prescribed plans and specifications, in the commercial setting it does not warrant that the completed

---

[13] AIA, The Architect's Handbook and Professional Practice (1987); The Associated General Contractors of America, Manual of Contract Documents (1988); Maloney v. Oak Builders, Inc., 224 So. 2d 161 (La. Ct. App. 1969); Miller v. Dewitt, 226 N.E.2d 630 (Ill. 1967).

[14] S.M. Siegfried, Introduction to Construction Law 139 (ALI/ABA 1988); Bayshore Dev. Co. v. Bonfoey, 78 So. 507 (Fla. 1918); Annotation, *Responsibility of One Acting as Architect for Defects or Insufficiency of Work Attributable to Plans,* 25 A.L.R.2d 1085, 1092 (1952).

[15] The design professional is under a duty to exercise such reasonable care, technical skill, ability, and diligence as is ordinarily required of design professionals in the course of their plans, inspections, and supervision to any person who foreseeably, and with reasonable certainty, may be injured by their failure to do so. *See* S.G.M. Stein, 1 Construction Law § 5.04 [6][a] (1986).

structure will be suitable for the intended purpose.[16] In the design-build process, these established legal doctrines will be different.

In the design-build setting, the owner has approached the design-build entity to supply both the design plan and specifications and the subsequent construction, often because of the firm's expertise.

> Accordingly, except where the contract expressly stipulates against the existence of such a warranty, where a person holds himself out as specially qualified to perform work of a particular character, there is an implied warranty that the work he undertakes shall be of proper workmanship and reasonable fitness for its intended use; and in building and construction contracts it is implied that the building shall be erected or the work shall be done in a reasonably good and workmanlike manner and when completed the structure shall be reasonably fit for the intended purpose.[17]

It is an easy step to extend this warranty theory to the design-builder. But is the design-builder providing a product or a service? If services are provided, will the contract determine what warranties are given? Does this entire concept now bring the construction industry under the purview of the Uniform Commercial Code? These are clearly questions which are not easily answered but about which subcontractors should be concerned.

Many subcontractors have been called upon, as specialty trades, to design and construct various aspects of a project. In such cases, the subcontractor will no doubt be asked to expressly warrant its work and, indirectly, the sufficiency of the plans and specifications. There are many times when the subcontractor is called upon to guarantee the plans and specifications prepared by the owner's design professional[18] or is subject to performance specifications which guarantee the same.[19]

Moreover, when a design professional prepares the plans and specifications and also acts as contractor as to the actual construction, it cannot rely on the *Spearin* doctrine, which would relieve the contractor from liability for defects attributable to the design in plans prepared by the owner's design professional. In *Barraque v. Neff,*[20] the court held:

> the doctrine that if a contractor is bound to build according to the plans and specifications prepared by the owner, the contractor will not be responsible

---

[16] United States v. Spearin, 248 U.S. 132 (1918); Annotation, *Construction Contractor's Liability to Contractee for Defects or Insufficiency of Work Attributable to the Latter's Plans and Specifications,* 6 A.L.R.3d 1394, § 2 at 1397 (1966).

[17] 17A C.J.S. *Contracts* § 329 (1963).

[18] *See, e.g.,* Philadelphia Hous. Auth. v. Turner Constr. Co., 343 Pa. 512, 23 A.2d 426 (1942).

[19] *See* City of Orlando v. H.L. Coble Constr. Co., 282 So. 2d 25 (Fla. Dist. Ct. App. 1973).

[20] 11 So. 2d 697 (La. 1942).

for the consequences of defects in the plans and specifications, was not applicable in the present case because the contractor himself had drawn the plans and specifications according to which he prepared the contract for construction of the building.[21]

§ 12.6 —Incorporation by Reference Clauses

The incorporation by reference provision incorporates the general contractor's agreement with the owner by reference into the subcontract between the general contractor and the subcontractor. Frequently, the subcontractor fails to examine the general contract between the owner and the general contractor, and oftentimes the subcontractor does not even ask for this agreement to review prior to signing its subcontract. The danger that a subcontractor faces when dealing with the incorporation by reference provision is that the general contract can have numerous "murder" clauses included, which the subcontractor never reviews and which impact upon the purported design responsibility of the subcontractor.[22]

The subcontractor must be certain to review all documents included in the owner/design-builder agreement in order to determine its duties and obligations under a contract containing an incorporation by reference clause.

§ 12.7 —Scope of Work Clause

The purpose of scope definition of work is to impose upon the subcontractor the obligation of performing the construction called for in the plans, whether shown in the plans or not or whether shown in the specifications or not, and thus the clause imposes the obligation to do whatever is necessary to complete the project so long as it is reasonably inferable from the contract documents. The danger to the subcontractor is that a review of the plans and specifications may not raise issues of additional work required until such time as the construction actually commences. If the subcontractor then requests a change order or an extra at that time, the request is

---

[21] *Id.* at 699. *See also* Baerveldt & Honig Constr. Co. v. Sombathy, 365 Mo. 845, 289 S.W.2d 116 (1956); McConnell v. Gorden Constr. Co., 105 Wash. 659, 178 P. 823 (1919); White v. Mitchell, 123 Wash. 630, 213 P. 10 (1923); Annotation, *Construction Contractor's Liability to Contractee for Defects or Insufficiency of Work Attributable to the Latter's Plans and Specifications*, 6 A.L.R.3d 1394 n.3.; Presnall v. Adams, 214 S.W. 357 (Tx. Civ. App. 1919).

[22] *See* Sklar, *Subcontract Form: Subcontractor's Perspective, in* Construction Subcontracting: A Legal Guide for Industry Professionals § 3.2, at 44 (O. Currie et al. eds., John Wiley & Sons 1991). Copyright © 1991 by John Wiley & Sons, Inc. Used with permission.

denied on the basis that the allegedly extra work is really a part of the original scope of work for the project. Subcontractors should approach such scope of work definitions with great caution and wherever possible should limit them to curtail their liability.

For example, the following clause should protect the subcontractor:

> Subcontractor's scope of work is expressly limited to the plans and specifications specifically identified by subcontractor in writing, which contractor certifies to be true, complete, and sufficient to complete the work to be performed by subcontractor.[23]

§ 12.8 —Flow-Down Clauses

A typical contractor/subcontractor flow-down provision transfers to the subcontractor all obligations that the contractor owes to the owner. The classic flow-down provision is contained in AIA Document A401 ¶ 2.1.

Caution is advised with regard to those clauses, because AIA Document A201 ¶ 3.2.1 imposes a duty upon the contractor (and therefore the subcontractor) to study the contract documents and compare the information contained there with other information furnished by the owner and AIA Document A201 ¶ 2.2.2, which includes surveys, utility easements, and the legal description, and then requires the contractor and, by extension via the incorporation by reference clause, to notify the owner and architect of any error, inconsistency, or omission therein. This is not only tantamount to secondary design review, wherein the subcontractor is required to opine upon the work of the architect, but it also requires the subcontractor to render legal opinions on the sufficiency of surveys, easements, and legal descriptions. The subcontractor should indicate that the opinions rendered by it relate solely to the subcontractor's work and to the standards of its industry only.

§ 12.9 —Responsibility for Uncovering Nonconforming Work

The owner may attempt to shift the risk of design defects by inserting language into the contract by which the contractor and subcontractor impliedly accept the prior work as conforming unless they affirmatively object to the work, specifying the reasons for their refusal to accept the work.[24]

---

[23] *Id.* at 50.

[24] AIA Document A201, ¶ 3.2.1, requires the contractor, and AIA A401, ¶ 2.1 requires the subcontractor, by virtue of flow-down clauses, to pay the cost of correcting defects they should have known were nonconforming.

AIA Document A201 article 12 must be read carefully, as it defines nonconforming work as "work which is contrary to the architect's request or the . . . contract documents" under AIA Document A201 ¶¶ 12.1.1 and 12.2.1. The interrelationships of architect review of shop drawings under AIA Document A201 ¶ 3.12 and the architect's interpretations under AIA Document A201 ¶ 4.2.12 will become critical if the subcontractor is to be charged with the costs associated with the uncovering and repairs.

Subcontractors should specifically disclaim any responsibility for work performed by others that is found to be nonconforming. A subcontractor should accept the responsibility for nonconforming work only if the work is its own and not that of a third party.

§ 12.10 —Shop Drawing Provisions

Shop drawings are the detailed directions that demonstrate how a specific component is to be actually built, fabricated, or constructed. They are prepared by the specialty subcontractor to comply with design drawings and specifications, and to elaborate upon fabrication, assembly, and installation details that are customarily omitted from the architectural plans. According to some studies, there can be as many as 15 shop drawings to one contract drawing.[25] It is in the shop drawing process that the subcontractor often has the greatest exposure for design liability. Architects claim that their "review" is solely for the purpose of determining compliance with the "design concept" of the project and not for the purpose of compliance with performance standards or construction. General contractors claim they are merely conduits for passing the shop drawings from the subcontractor to the architect and then back to the subcontractor. Of course, the subcontractor claims it is not a design professional and looks to the design professional for direction. Needless to say, when none of the parties accept responsibility, and each points to the other, a situation ripe for conflict is created and litigation invariably ensues.

Generally, the shop drawing procedure starts when the subcontractor submits shop drawings to the prime contractor, who generally identifies them and logs them for purposes of follow-up.

After the prime contractor identifies the shop drawings and logs them in, it then submits them to the design professional in an orderly, sequential manner.

The design professional receives shop drawings and checks to see if the contractor has properly identified them. The design professional then reviews the shop drawings against design drawings for conformity to design concept and consistency. At this point, it is well to remember that *design concept* has no accepted legal definition.

---

[25] S.G.M. Stein, 2 Construction Law § 8.01 (1986).

The design professional affixes its own stamp—"approved," "reviewed," "approved-as-noted," "rejected," "resubmission required," or other similar stamp. The stamp "approved," without some form exculpation of the architect, is a relic rarely to be found, and today's approval always contains some form of language attempting to shift the responsibility to the subcontractor.

The design professional retains a copy and returns additional copies to the contractor, who then returns it to the subcontractor.

Shop drawings and other design responsibilities are being constantly shifted to the subcontractor and the subcontractor's suppliers, for such things as curtain walls, structural steel, drywall installation for "exotic" designs, equipment design, and even glass suppliers who now have available glass windows with 90-degree corners. In addition, one should be aware of any requirement that the subcontractor advise the architect and owner of any design deficiencies in the architect's plans. The subcontractor is not a licensed design professional and it does not carry errors and omissions insurance for design.

Although there is a continuing debate over the responsibility for shop drawings, unfortunately there is no clear line of responsibility for the liability that would attach for defective shop drawings. The subcontractor may find itself in the design business, especially if there is a clause extolling the virtues of the expertise of the subcontractor and the architect's obligation is only the "review" of shop drawings to verify that they are consistent with the "design concept," a vague notion that defies definition.

With ever-increasing frequency we see engineers requiring subcontractors to design certain elements of a project. Even when the justification exists for such delegation of authority, the transfer of responsibility for design to those without proper qualifications can result in defects in performance or construction catastrophes. A typical method by which such transfer may occur is a contract requirement that the subcontractor's shop drawings be stamped by a licensed design professional before submission to the architect for approval. The Standard Form of Agreement Between Owner and Contractor, AIA Document A201 (1987), ¶ 4.2.7 provides for the architect's review for conformance with the design concept and goes on to state:

> Review of such submittals is not conducted for the purpose of determining the accuracy and completeness of other details such as dimensions and quantities, or for substantiating instructions for installation or performance of equipment or systems, all of which remain the responsibility of the Contractor to the extent required by the Contract Documents. The Architect's review of the Contractor's submittals shall not relieve the contractor of the obligations under Paragraphs 3.3, 3.5 and 3.12. The Architect's review shall not constitute approval of safety precautions or, unless otherwise specifically stated by the Architect, of any construction means, methods, techniques, sequences or procedures. The Architect's approval of a specific item shall not indicate approval of an assembly of which the item is a component.

More stringent language requiring a subcontractor to assume design responsibility could be as follows:

The Subcontractor shall assume full responsibility for the design and detailing of the [description of the work] as shown on the drawings or specified therein. Shop drawings shall be properly sealed by a licensed professional engineer.

The following language, which may be inserted in the agreement with the design-build subcontractor, is suggested to impose a greater duty on the subcontractor:[26]

Architect's approval of shop drawings submitted by subcontractor shall in no way relieve subcontractor from any defects or deficiencies caused by any omission or other statements indicated on the shop drawings; the subcontractor's responsibility being the construction of a complete and workable installation usable and satisfactory for the work included, whether or not shown on the plans or shop drawings, so long as the result to be intended is reasonably inferable therefrom.

From the subcontractor's point of view, the following is more desirable than the prior language:

This shop drawing is submitted solely for purposes of installation of the material herein and subcontractor's liability is limited solely to damages arising out of its failure to properly apply or install the material. Subcontractor is not a licensed architect, structural engineer, or design professional, and renders no opinion regarding the structural integrity or suitability of the material for the project, and specifically disclaims any responsibility therefor. Receipt of a Notice to Proceed or similar directive from the architect shall be conclusive proof that the owner or general contractor has had this shop drawing verified and approved by a qualified structural engineer, architect, or other design professional as to the product's suitability or structural integrity for use in this project.

Depending on the local law, the delegation of such design responsibility to the subcontractor may not be permissible.[27] Nevertheless, it would seem possible that a subcontractor preparing shop drawings, "rubber-stamped" by a licensed professional, would assume design responsibility.[28]

---

[26] Sklar, *Subcontract Form: Subcontractor's Perspective, in* Construction Subcontracting: A Legal Guide for Industry Professionals § 3.8, at 48 (O. Currie et al. eds., John Wiley & Sons 1991). Copyright © 1991 by John Wiley & Sons, Inc. Used with permission.

[27] *See, e.g.*, Charlebois v. J.M. Weller Assocs., Inc., 531 N.E.2d 1288 (N.Y. 1988) (state's licensing statute not violated simply because a nonlicensed design professional may have contracted to provide design services; the distinction, the court held, was in the difference between performing services and providing services).

[28] Halsey & Quatman, *Design/Build Contracts: Valid or Invalid,* 9 Construction Law. 3 (Aug. 1989). As evidenced by the Hyatt Regency disaster, the responsibility for design

In the traditional relationship, the design professional must respond as to whether or not the shop drawings comport with contract documents, which includes the plans, specifications, and addenda but interestingly enough do not include shop drawings. Paragraph 3.2.1 of AIA Document A201 imposes on the contractor the obligation to report any "errors, inconsistencies or omissions discovered." Does this provision transfer design responsibility to the contractor and ultimately to the subcontractor? Does this attempt to shift responsibility serve the needs of the construction industry or interests of society by shifting responsibility not based upon qualification, but based upon the desire to protect one's self by shifting the risk to another?[29]

The subcontractor should be cautioned when using the AIA documents. In view of the definition of *contract documents,* which excludes shop drawings by omission in AIA Document A201 ¶ 1.1.1 and specifically in AIA Document A201 ¶ 3.12.4, a dispute over extras or work beyond the scope of work as bid will often become a significant issue, because it would impact upon the alleged design responsibility of the subcontractor. The subcontractor should strive for the inclusion of shop drawings as a contract document despite their omission in the definition of contract documents in AIA Document A201. However, if the contractor or subcontractor has received a shop drawing from the architect, who has stamped it "approved," it cannot be seriously contended that the contractor or subcontractor has breached its contract for failure of its work to meet the performances expectations of the owner (if the work is performed in accordance with the approved shop drawing).[30]

AIA Document A201 ¶ 3.12.7 states that by its approval of shop drawings, the contractor verifies that it has checked materials and measurements to assure accordance with the contract documents. The requirement for such a representation amounts to a deviation from the normal process of submittal. Even though the specialty trade has the ability to determine the means, methods, and techniques of its own work, it is highly unlikely that it has the skill or expertise to "determine and verify" the data. Does this mean that subcontractors are required to employ testing services to verify the plans of the design professional? If so, has the subcontractor included this cost in its contract price, and, if not, is it a proper extra?

AIA Document A201 ¶ 3.12.11 seems to answer the foregoing questions by imposing an implied duty on the subcontractor to require its own

---

can sometimes be unclear. The design professional may claim that the subcontractor has design responsibility, and the subcontractor may, in fact, assume such responsibility when it submits its shop drawings. This may effectively occur when the shop drawings contain an engineer's seal.

[29] *See* Rubin & Ressler, *To Build a Better Mousetrap; The Search To Define Responsibility For Shop Drawing Review,* 5 Construction Law. No. 4, at 1 (Apr. 1985).

[30] *See* J. Sweet, Sweet on Construction Documents (John Wiley & Sons 1987 and Supp. 1990).

professional engineer to certify performance with its submittal. A subcontractor cannot rely upon the architect's design concept as a standard because no one is clear on the definition of the term.

Shop drawings have always been a problem area, and under AIA Document A201 ¶ 3.12.5 it is the duty of the general contractor to gather all shop drawings and other submittals from the subcontractors and mark them "approved" before submitting them to the architect. Thus, subcontractors and material suppliers do not submit shop drawings to the architect directly, which could further impact upon their ability to perform within the specified time period.

The subcontractor may well have a duty to furnish professional technical certifications of performance criteria for certain portions of the work under AIA Document A201 ¶ 3.12.11, and it should be read with caution.

Material suppliers and, in particular, mechanical contractors should note AIA Document A201 ¶ 3.12.11 deals with performance criteria. It states that the architect is entitled to rely upon the accuracy and completeness of calculations and certifications of performance criteria. Does this require the trade subcontractor to have its own independent testing service? If so, it then becomes the subcontractor's obligation to pay for the service. Further, it is the architect who establishes performance standards in the first instance. The query, then, is whether the failure is due to the standards specified by the architect or the performance standards certified by the subcontractor.

If one were to carry the logic of the shop drawing clauses to their illogical extreme, the architect should be removed from the shop drawing process entirely, which would, of course, be an unmitigated disaster. There can be no doubt that contractors and subcontractors have the ability to prepare shop drawings, but the needs of owners and of society in general require the overall responsibility for such a design review to be placed in the hands of a truly qualified, licensed, third-party professional who has a global view of the project for review, correction, approval, or rejection of shop drawings.

§ 12.11 The Effect of the *Spearin* Doctrine on Design-Build Subcontractors

Numerous decisions have held that a contractor is entitled to rely on the plans and specifications supplied by an owner, and that the contractor and subcontractor are not thereafter liable for loss or damage that results from insufficiencies or defects in those plans. After all, the contractor, in performing its work in accordance with the contract plans and specifications, is merely doing precisely what the owner ordered it to do, and it would be unfair to hold the contractor responsible for additional construction costs if the plans are defective. This principle, sometimes designated the *Spearin* doctrine, finds its firmest foundation in the United States Supreme Court decision, *United States v. Spearin.*[31] In *Spearin,* the Supreme Court ruled that a contractor who is bound to build according to plans and specifications supplied by the owner will not be responsible for the consequences of defects in the plans and specifications. *Spearin* involved the allocation between contractor and owner of the responsibility for damages to a sewer project. The Supreme Court held that the articles of the owner-supplied contract documents which prescribe the character, dimensions, and location of the sewer imparted a warranty that if so constructed, the sewer would be adequate. That warranty was not preempted by clauses requiring the contractor to examine the site, check the plans, and assume responsibility for the work until completion and acceptance. The contractor was entitled to his proper expenditures for the additional, changed work and to the profits that he would have earned if allowed to fully perform.

Generally, this rule has found favor in modern case law involving private contracts as well as public contracts.[32] A showing of greater knowledge on the part of the owner than the contractor is not necessary, and it is not necessary to demonstrate negligence in drafting the defective contract documents when the rule is involved.

A contractor can bid with confidence that the bidding documents have been examined for errors, and while the contractor is responsible for bringing obvious errors to the attention of the owner (for which it would be entitled to additional compensation), it is not required to analyze the plans and specifications for obscure errors.[33]

Now, after 72 years, some courts appear willing to shift this responsibility to contractors. For example, in *Don Sieboth Pontiac, Inc. v. Asphalt Road Building & Resurfacing, Inc.,*[34] under the terms of its contract, the highway contractor was not required to perform any work on the existing sub-base of a parking lot which it was to resurface. Naturally, the existing sub-base caused the new surface to crack. The court held the highway contractor responsible because it should have used its "expert knowledge" to call the owner's attention to the shortcomings of the design.

Similarly, in *Bethesda Lutheran Church v. Twin City Construction Co.,*[35] the roofing contractor was held liable for roof leaks based upon the

---

[31] 248 U.S. 132 (1918).

[32] *See* McGovner & McKee, Inc. v. City of Berea, 444 F. Supp. 1049, 1056 (E.D. Ky. 1978), *aff'd,* 627 F.2d 1091 (6th Cir. 1980). *See also* S.G.M. Stein, 1 Construction Law ¶ 5.07(i) (1986).

[33] *See* S.G.M. Stein, 1 Construction Law (1986); Harrington, *The Owner's Warranty of the Plans and Specifications For A Construction Project,* 14 Pub. Cont. L.J. 1240 (1984); and Centex Constr. Co. v. James, 374 F.2d 921 (8th Cir. 1967).

[34] 407 So. 2d 42 (La. Ct. App. 1982).

[35] 356 N.W.2d 344 (Minn. Ct. App. 1984).

innovative design of the architect. The rationale of the court was that the numerous peaks and valleys were a design flaw that made construction impractical, and the roofing contractor should have so advised the owner.

Merely by analyzing the foregoing cases as examples, one can see an erosion of the *Spearin* doctrine and a gradual expansion of the contractor's principal role of building to one requiring some design responsibility. It is easy for a court, using the prior cases, to make the leap from design flaws to design responsibility for shop drawings, thus eroding even further the *Spearin* doctrine.

Some owners have attempted to avoid liability for design errors and contractors have attempted to pass on such liability to subcontractors by asserting that the *Spearin* warranty of the drawings is overcome by the express warranty in the AIA contract documents. In *Atlantic National Bank of Jacksonville v. Modular Aoe, Inc.,*[36] the Florida District Court of Appeal affirmed that the implied warranty of the drawings and specifications is not overcome by the express guarantee in the standard AIA contract documents. The contractor was found to have installed modular wall panels substantially as specified. Therefore, he was not liable for its failure to function. The failure was based upon the wall's failure to achieve certain fire rating required by the Southern Standard Building Code. The applicable building agency ordered a different and more expensive wall panel. Even though the contractor warranted its work, the implied warranty of the plans and specifications from *Spearin* superseded the contract warranty and relieved the contractor of any responsibility for compliance with code. The court rejected the owner's argument that it was the contractor's responsibility to comply with code even when the design violated code and stated that "[t]his duty . . . cannot be avoided by delegating the responsibility of insuring that the parties of this design comport with applicable laws and regulation [and] the contractor is not liable if the item's failure to function properly is due to its design being improper for the intended use."[37]

§ 12.12 Insurance

The design-builder's role as both design professional and contractor carries with it an increased assumption of risk which demands that the design-builder be made "aware of the various methods by which potential monetary liabilities can be foreseen and handled through the use of a carefully maintained package of insurance coverage."[38] When purchasing an

[36] 363 So. 2d 1152 (Fla. Dist. Ct. App. 1978).

[37] *Id.* at 1155. *See also* St. Joseph Hosp. v. Corbetta Constr. Co., 316 N.E.2d 51 (Ill. App. Ct. 1974).

[38] Block, *Design-Build Insurance Protection, in* Legal Handbook for Architects, Engineers and Contractors 63 (A. Dib et al. eds., 1985) [hereinafter Block].

insurance package, the design-builder specialty contractor must be knowledgeable concerning the different types of insurance policies available and the existing gaps in coverage.

Generally, a design-builder specialty trade contractor needs to acquire both professional liability insurance to cover his liability as a design professional and business liability insurance to cover his liability as a contractor.[39] Professional liability insurance, "which defends and indemnifies the insured against malpractice suits arising from either faulty services rendered or the failure to perform services expected under the circumstances,"[40] is the most common type carried by a design professional. Indemnification exists for damages which an individual is legally obligated to pay and arising out of "the performance of professional services as a result of an act, error, or omission."[41] The most common policy is written on a claims-made basis, which covers the insured for any claims made against him during the policy period.[42] Less frequently, the policy will be written on an occurrence basis, which protects the insured indefinitely against any claim brought against it for an occurrence that took place within the policy period.[43] But professional liability coverage only protects the specialty trade subcontractor for its acts arising out of its design professional duties, because a "contractor's portion of a design build project is a standard exclusion."[44] Thus, for protection against claims arising from the subcontractor's design responsibility, the subcontractor must purchase business liability insurance.

Commercial General Liability insurance (CGL), a form of business liability insurance that protects subcontractors against claims for tangible property damage[45] and bodily injury arising out of their work, is the broadest coverage available for a subcontractor.[46] Most commonly, CGL is written on an occurrence basis.[47] There are gaps in CGL coverage that do not protect the design-builder from liability. First, protection under the CGL

---

[39] *See generally id.*

[40] *Id.* at 65.

[41] *Id.*

[42] *Id.; see* Williamson & Vollmer Eng'g, Inc. v. Sequoia Ins. Co., 64 Cal. App. 3d 261, 134 Cal. Rptr. 427 (1976).

[43] Block at 65. *See also* R. Mehr & E. Cammack, Principles of Insurance 285, 296 (7th ed. 1980) for a discussion of occurrence and claims-made policies.

[44] Block at 66.

[45] The 1973 Standard Form basic policy defines stated that *property damage* is "physical injury to or destruction of tangible property which occurs during the policy period including (1) the loss of use thereof at any time resulting therefrom, or (ii) loss of use of tangible property which has not been physically injured or destroyed provided such loss of use is caused during the policy period." Block at 66.

[46] Block at 66.

[47] *Id.*

policy does not exist for claims brought against the subcontractor for poor workmanship and defective materials.[48] Secondly, recent case law supports the proposition that claims for economic loss are barred because they are not property damage.[49] As an example, "if a contractor builds a wall that falls down, the CGL coverage would pay for the damage the wall caused, but not for the replacement of the wall itself."[50] Thus, any damage to the work product would not be covered. Lastly, a possible gap in coverage exists when the design-subcontractor has identified a problem that is yet to cause damage. This situation presents a double-edged quandary. First, under CGL, an occurrence has not taken place since there is no property damage or bodily injury, so no coverage yet exists. Secondly, if the design-subcontractor waits for the damage to occur it will be denied coverage because of its knowledge of the defect. The contractor's only option is to personally make the repair to the defect.[51]

The design-subcontractor can further protect itself by purchasing additional insurance above and beyond professional and CGL. A common addition is the builder's special risk insurance. This policy provides protection during the course of construction, alteration, or repair for such things as fire, vandalism, windstorm, hail, explosion, riot, civil commotion, and smoke damage.[52] The design-subcontractor can designate whether it prefers the policy on a named-peril or all-risk basis.[53] This type of coverage typically terminates once the project is occupied.

The design-subcontractor assumes a great amount of risk. This increased risk makes it imperative that it purchase the correct insurance package to protect against claims arising out of its dual role as design professional and contractor, and factor in this additional cost when it bids on the project. Lastly, the design-subcontractor should consult with a qualified insurance agent who can put together an insurance package that will adequately protect it from all potential future liability arising out of the design-build project.

---

[48] This bar exists because of the CGL's exclusions, which include the business risk, insured product, and work performed exclusions.

[49] *See, e.g.*, Dreis & Krump Mfg. Co. v. Phoenix Ins. Co., 548 F.2d 681 (7th Cir. 1977) (loss of use of special structure not considered tangible property damage); Stone & Webster Eng'g Corp. v. American Motorist Ins. Co., 458 F. Supp. 792 (E.D. Va. 1978), *aff'd mem.*, 628 F.2d 1351 (4th Cir. 1980) (replacement of defective supports is not property damage).

[50] Block at 68.

[51] *Id.* at 70.

[52] Pierce, *The Contractor's Claims Against Its Insurance Carrier, in* Construction Litigation 457, 471–82 (Practicing Law Institute 1981).

[53] Block at 66.

CHAPTER 13

PERFORMANCE GUARANTEES AND TESTING; INTELLECTUAL PROPERTY AND TECHNOLOGY TRANSFER ISSUES

Jeffrey S. Roehl
Jesse B. Grove III*

Jeffrey S. Roehl is a partner in the Washington, D.C., office of Thelen, Marrin, Johnson & Bridges, concentrating on construction law and project financing. He received his law degree from the University of California, Berkeley, in 1975, and is a member of the Order of the Coif and Phi Beta Kappa.

*C. Reade Williams, William F. Hughes, and Scott A. Harvey provided invaluable help in writing this chapter.

Jesse B. Grove III is a trial lawyer specializing in construction, antitrust, and commercial litigation for Thelen, Marrin, Johnson & Bridges in San Francisco, California. He received a B.A. from Washington and Lee University and his J.D. from the University of Virginia Law School. Mr. Grove is a speaker and instructor on construction-related matters, and is a contributing author to many John Wiley & Sons books including *Construction Failures* (1989) and *Proving and Pricing Construction Claims* (1990). He is a member of the California and American Bar Associations, a charter member of the American College of Construction Lawyers, and is admitted to practice before the United States Court of Claims, the Ninth Circuit Court of Appeals, and the United States Supreme Court.

INTRODUCTION

§ 13.1 Performance Guarantees in Design-Build Contracts

This chapter briefly discusses guarantees of performance that are given or implied in design and construction projects. The following sections discuss the nature of performance guarantees that are implied in law or that arise from the nature of the contracting relationship (see §§ **13.4** through **13.7**), give advice on describing performance guarantees in the design-build contract (see §§ **13.8** through **13.11**), and describe insurance that may be available to mitigate the risk inherent in performance guarantees (see §§ **13.12** through **13.14**).

As shown in the cases discussed in §§ **13.4** and **13.5**, performance guarantees are not unique to design-build contracts; they can arise in any contracting situation. But, as those cases also show, a discussion of performance guarantees is particularly appropriate in a book on design-build contracts. The nature of the design-build contract is such that it is frequently chosen as the contracting model when the project owner is interested in obtaining performance guarantees. In addition, the nature of the design-build relationship may lead a court to infer a performance guarantee, even if it is not specifically provided for in the contract. It is important, therefore, that the parties to a design-build contract be familiar with the law concerning performance guarantees and with the drafting issues that such guarantees raise.

A brief word about definitions. *Performance guarantee* is used to mean any obligation by a party to a construction project that any part of the project, or the project as a whole, will perform in a certain way. Performance guarantees are nothing new. They can be as basic as a guarantee that a wall will perform properly by continuing to stand up, or as complex as guarantees covering the output and operations of entire power plants, refineries, or factories.

§ 13.2 Intellectual Property and Technology Transfer Issues

This chapter also briefly discusses the key issues in the laws of copyright (§§ **13.15** through **13.17**), technology transfer (§ **13.18**), and patent (§ **13.19**) that affect design-build projects. These issues are not essentially related to either design-build projects or performance guarantees and should be considered whenever architectural or engineering plans are prepared, confidential information is used, or patented materials or processes are employed.

Nonetheless, owners and contractors are using the design-build approach more and more often when a high tech design is involved, and intellectual property issues are especially important in such cases. Also, in a complex design-build project, a number of different firms may participate in the design process, which may make it difficult to tell who owns the intellectual property rights to the design. This chapter will focus on contract drafting issues that will help avoid this and other intellectual property problems.

§ 13.3 Joint Ventures and Teaming Arrangements

While large engineer-contractors can undertake the work of a design-build contract alone, many architect/engineers and construction companies cannot. For these companies, some form of teaming agreement or subcontracting arrangement is needed under which an architect/engineer and a construction company combine to provide the owner with the full range of design-build services. It is not the purpose of this chapter to discuss the details of these teaming arrangements but only to note briefly the potential responsibility of team members for achieving performance guarantees. A team member may be liable to the owner in damages for a failure to achieve performance guarantees, even if the failure did not arise from the work performed by the team member and even if the team member has no contract directly with the owner.

A common teaming arrangement is the joint venture. In this approach, an architect/engineer and a construction company enter into a joint venture, and the joint venture then enters into the design-build contract with the owner. A joint venture is usually treated like a general partnership that is entered into for a particular purpose.[1] For our purposes, the most important consequence of entering into a design-build contract as a member of a joint venture is that each of the joint venturers is jointly and severally liable for the obligations and liabilities of the joint venture. For example, a joint venturer may bind the joint venture to a contract, thereby exposing other venturers to joint and several liability for damages caused by a breach.[2] A joint venturer may also expose other venturers to joint and several tort liability by negligently injuring third parties while acting within the scope of the joint venture.[3]

---

[1] *See, e.g.,* Pritchett v. Kimberling Cove, Inc., 568 F.2d 570, 579–80 (8th Cir. 1977), *cert. denied sub nom.* Dando Enters., Ltd. v. Pritchett, 436 U.S. 922 (1978); Stone v. First Wyoming Bank, 625 F.2d 332, 340 (10th Cir. 1980); Moran v. H.W.S. Lumber Co., 538 F.2d 238, 242 (9th Cir. 1976).

[2] Singer Hous. Co. v. Seven Lakes Venture, 466 F. Supp. 369, 376 (D. Colo. 1979).

[3] Woolard v. Mobile Pipeline Co., 479 F.2d 557, 561–62 (5th Cir. 1973), *cert. denied sub nom.* Mobile Oil Corp. v. Woolard, 414 U.S. 1025 (1973) (each joint venturer is an agent

Another common arrangement is that used in the Standard Form of Design-Build Agreement and General Conditions Between Owner and Contractor published by the Associated General Contractors of America.[4] In this approach, the construction company contracts directly with the owner to provide both the design and construction services required, but, as noted in the contract, the services of a named architect/engineer are to be provided pursuant to an agreement between the construction company and the architect/engineer.[5]

This is essentially a subcontracting arrangement, and the owner may sue the construction company directly and recover damages for failures made by the architect/engineer, because the architect/engineer is a subcontractor.[6] Furthermore, case law suggests that the owner, as a third-party beneficiary of the architect/engineer's agreement with the construction company, may sue the architect/engineer directly to recover damages resulting from its failure to provide the design services specified in its contract.[7]

Because the construction company and the architect/engineer risk direct liability to the owner and third parties as a result of joint ventures and teaming arrangements, the parties must draft their joint venture and subcontracting agreements carefully to ensure that they are adequately compensated for the risks they assume. Participants who wish to limit their risks should obtain agreements from the other parties to indemnify them for the costs of litigation and judgments that result from events for which they are not directly responsible. Team members should also make sure that they carry sufficient insurance to cover the risks associated with their involvement in particular projects.

---

of the other for purposes of tort liability. When facts show a joint interest in the purpose of the enterprise and an equal right to control its conduct, the doctrine of joint venture imposes vicarious liability upon one venturer for the other's negligence.); Pritchett v. Kimberling Cove, Inc., 568 F.2d 570, 580 (8th Cir. 1980), *cert. denied sub nom.* Dando Enters., Ltd. v. Pritchett, 436 U.S. 922 (1978) (when negligence of a member of a joint enterprise acting within the scope of the enterprise causes harm to a third person, such negligence is imputed to all members, who become mutually liable).

[4] Associated General Contractors of America (AGC) Document No. 410 (1982).

[5] *Id.* at art. 1.

[6] Brooks v. Hayes, 395 N.W.2d 167 (Wis. 1986) (general contractor is liable to owner for negligent work performed by a subcontractor).

[7] *See* Charlebois v. J.M. Weller Assocs., Inc., 526 N.Y.S.2d 648, 648–50 (App. Div.), *aff'd,* 535 N.Y.S.2d 356, 531 N.E.2d 1288 (N.Y. 1988) (dictum) (pursuant to a "design-build" contract under which a contractor agreed to be responsible for furnishing a design and requiring that all architectural and engineering services be provided by a licensed professional engineer, owners were third-party beneficiaries of a contract between contractor and licensed professional engineer).

CONTRACTORS' LIABILITY FOR PERFORMANCE GUARANTEES

§ 13.4 Design and Performance Specifications

Under what has become known in the construction industry as the *Spearin* doctrine, an owner is deemed to warrant that the specifications and other design information it provides to the contractor are accurate and suitable for use on the project.[8] Accordingly, if a contractor performs the work in compliance with the owner's plans and specifications, the contractor cannot be held responsible if the design proves defective.

In *Spearin,* a contractor contracted with the government (owner) to build a sewer and dry-dock according to the owner's detailed design specifications. During the course of construction, a dam in a connecting sewer on the property caused the newly constructed dam to burst, causing the contractor to incur additional costs in completing the project. The court awarded damages to the contractor on the grounds that the owner had warranted that work done in accordance with its detailed design specifications would produce a sewer and dry-dock capable of serving its intended purpose. According to the court, an integral part of the owner's design warranty was that the conditions at the site were as the owner had stated in the specifications, that is, that there was no other dam. Because this had not in fact been the case, the *Spearin* court awarded the contractor damages.

The owner's *Spearin* warranty for its design specifications does not apply to design details created by the contractor pursuant to a design-build contract. Instead, as the following case discussions illustrate, a contractor assumes the responsibility of providing its own detailed design when the owner sets forth in the contract general performance specifications, that is, specifications that merely set forth the owner's performance objectives for the project. In those cases, the contractor, not the owner, warrants the sufficiency and accuracy of the specifications and the performance of the completed project.

Many design-build jobs require preparation of the design documents in phases, with commencement of construction of each stage of the project occurring as each phase of the design is completed. In those instances, there is generally a great deal of interaction between the owner and contractor concerning the design and construction of the project, and the parties may assume liability for the design on an item-by-item basis according to their respective design roles. To allocate liability for design

[8] United States v. Spearin, 248 U.S. 132 (1918). *See also* Stuyvesant Dredging Co. v. United States, 834 F.2d 1576, 1582 (Fed. Cir. 1987) ("Detailed design specifications contain an implied warranty that if they are followed, an acceptable result will be produced.").

defects in this context, courts often refer to the contract specifications as *design specifications* when the owner has dictated the details of the contractor's performance, and as *performance specifications* when the details are left to the contractor's discretion.[9] As the case of *Aleutian Constructors v. United States*[10] illustrates, however, contracts often do not contain pure design or performance specifications.

In the *Aleutian Constructors* case, the U.S. Army Corps of Engineers (owner) hired a contractor to construct a $12.8 million airplane hangar and dormitory at the Shemya Air Force Base in Alaska. During the course of construction, high winds partially destroyed a portion of a watertight membrane in the hangar roof. In an effort to repair the damage, the contractor worked with the roofing manufacturer to redesign the membrane and eventually rebuilt the hangar roof at its own expense. Upon final acceptance of the project by the owner, the contractor filed a claim for an equitable adjustment to the contract price to reflect the cost of repair. In doing so, the contractor contended that the roofing failure had resulted from the owner's faulty design specifications, that is, that the owner had breached its implied warranty that the specifications, if followed, would create a conforming structure. Rejecting the contractor's claim, the owner argued that the contract had instead dictated performance specifications for the roof and that the contractor had thereby assumed full responsibility for the faulty design.

In determining the nature of the roofing specifications, the court explained that design specifications typically "set forth in precise detail the materials to be employed and the manner in which the work is to be performed," which the contractor is required to follow as one would a "road map."[11] Conversely, performance specifications state "an objective or standard to be achieved . . . requiring the contractor to exercise its ingenuity in achieving the standard of performance, in selecting the means, and in assuming a corresponding responsibility for that selection."[12]

Pointing out that construction contracts often contain both types of specifications, the court concluded that the specifications concerning the roofing membrane had in fact been performance requirements. Although the contract contained detailed design specifications for numerous aspects of the project, the court found that the owner had delegated certain crucial elements of the project design to the contractor's expertise and ingenuity. In particular, the contract specified merely that the roofing materials should meet an 80 p.s.f. test requirement, and that the contractor should work with one of its subcontractors (the roofing manufacturer) to design the roofing

---

[9] *See, e.g.,* Stuyvesant Dredging Co. v. United States, 834 F.2d 1576 (Fed. Cir. 1987); J.L. Simmons Co. v. United States, 188 Ct. Cl. 684 (1969).

[10] 24 Cl. Ct. 372 (1991).

[11] *Id.* at 378.

[12] *Id.*

system and determine how the contractor would install it. Accordingly, the court dismissed the contractor's claim on grounds that the contractor had accepted a performance specification and had therefore warranted that the roofing membrane would perform as intended.

Aleutian Constructors illustrates how a single design-build contract may contain both design and performance specifications. Thus, it is imperative that parties to such contracts recognize how different language pertaining to project specifications creates different duties among the parties. Significantly, when the contract delegates discretion to the contractor for even a small percentage of the overall design, the contractor may be liable for all design deficiencies related to that element of the project. Perhaps even more importantly, dictum in the *Aleutian Constructors* decision indicates that a contractor may inadvertently transform a design specification into a performance requirement during the course of a project by persuading the owner to substitute a new design feature, or by otherwise modifying the owner's original design specification.

Like the *Aleutian Constructors* case, the United States Claims Court's decision in *Utility Contractors, Inc. v. United States*[13] illustrates the type of liabilities a contractor may incur when it fails to determine accurately the nature of the specifications in a given contract. In *Utility Contractors,* the project owner hired a contractor to design and build a flood control system to collect all rainwater along a two and one-half mile section of a creek in Tulsa, Oklahoma. The system was supposed to channel water through the city into the Arkansas River without causing flood damage. The contract required the contractor to perform channel and drainage excavation and to construct a concrete transition section in order to lower the overall elevation of the channel.

During the course of the project, heavy rainstorms caused the creek to overflow temporary cofferdams installed by the contractor to keep the construction area dry, as required by the terms of the contract. The overflow significantly damaged the permanent concrete work. The contractor sued in court for an equitable adjustment to the contract price to reflect the costs of repair, claiming that the damage occurred because the owner's design of the transition section was faulty. In particular, the contractor alleged that the owner had failed to include detailed specifications and procedures in the contract for the protection of the permanent work during the construction phase.

As in *Aleutian Constructors,* the contract in *Utility Contractors* contained both performance and design specifications. Consistently with *Aleutian Constructors,* the court analyzed the various design specifications in the contract separately and concluded that the provisions requiring the owner to protect the construction project merely set performance standards. The

[13] 8 Cl. Ct. 42 (1985), *aff'd,* 790 F.2d 90 (11th Cir.), *cert. denied,* 479 U.S. 827 (1986).

court observed that the plans failed to specify how the contractor should build or protect the channel improvements, and instead set forth a number of acceptable construction procedures from which the contractor could select. Although the court found that the contract "was replete with examples . . . which stated, in detail, how the concrete was to be mixed, its contents, proportioning, production, etc.,"[14] it noted that, "at almost every step, the contractor was to use its own judgment and experience in deciding how, when, where, under what conditions, and which proportion would be best for which project section."[15] The court found that when viewed as a whole, the contract required the contractor to possess sufficient hydrological expertise and construction skills to protect its unfinished work and to complete the project. Accordingly, the court denied the contractor's claim for an equitable adjustment for costs it incurred in replacing the damaged concrete.

Above all, the *Utility Contractors* case illustrates the willingness of the judiciary to classify particular contract requirements as performance specifications unless the owner has left very little or no discretion to the contractor concerning the manner in which design features are to be constructed. If a court concludes that a contract provision sets performance objectives rather than design specifications, the contractor must do whatever is necessary to complete the project and bear full responsibility for any precompletion losses that may occur.

Finally, a decision of the Utah Supreme Court in *Allen Steel Co. v. Crossroads Plaza Associates*[16] further illustrates the different liabilities contractors and owners assume in a design-build project, depending on whether specifications are found to be of performance or of design. In *Allen Steel,* the owner solicited design-build proposals on the structural steel work for a mall/office building project in Salt Lake City, Utah. One contractor retained a structural engineer to prepare a preliminary design for its proposal, which set forth three structural design alternatives for the project and contained the following provision limiting its responsibility for design:

> This proposal is offered for the design, fabrication, and erection of the Structural Elements only for the tower and mall. The following design parameters have been used for the structural steel design . . . *Owner's engineer is to check this design and make changes if necessary to enable him to accept overall responsibility for design.*[17]

---

[14] *Id.* at 51.

[15] *Id.*

[16] 119 Utah Adv. Rep. 6 1989 Utah LEXIS 124 (Utah 1989), *withdrawn,* 1991 Utah LEXIS 30 (Utah 1991).

[17] *Id.* (emphasis added).

The owner accepted the contractor's proposal, authorizing the contractor to prepare detailed plans for the fabrication of the structural steel and to proceed with fabrication based on those plans. During the course of performance, however, Salt Lake City halted construction of the project due to inadequacies and defects it believed existed in the building's structural design. The owner then retained its own engineer to provide a remedial engineering design to correct the defect, and directed the contractor to perform the remedial work and to finish the project as set forth in the contract. The owner continued regular progress payments to the contractor until performance of the project had been completed, but withheld the final $579,294 payment for the three previously erected stories of reinforced steel that had to be torn down and replaced. The owner also asserted a back-charge of over $2 million for costs stemming from redesign and delay.

The parties stipulated that a design flaw caused the damages at issue, and the sole issue before the court in *Allen Steel* was whether the contractor "was liable for the basic design of the project under the terms of its design-build contract with [the owner], notwithstanding a disclaimer of its liability."[18] Although the court found that the owner had provided the contractor only with general design parameters for the structural steel (that is, that they were straightforward performance specifications), it held that the contractor had effectively disclaimed all responsibility for the design flaws in the structure as well as the implied warranties that its performance would meet any particular design parameters. By virtue of the disclaimer in its proposal, the contractor had promised merely to provide a working design for purposes of the bid itself. Notwithstanding the fact that the owner's solicitation for proposals had clearly sought a design-build contractor for the entire project, the language cited above effectively transferred all design responsibilities (and liability for all resulting losses) back to the owner.

§ 13.5 Traditional Warranties and Performance Guarantees

Design-build contracting can alter some fundamental warranty expectations established in more traditional construction situations. In addition to assuming an obligation to build a project, the design-build contractor assumes the obligations and liabilities of a design professional, including express and implied warranties and performance guarantees.

The distinctive characteristic of design-build contracting is its consolidation of responsibility for both design and construction in the design-build contractor. This contracting approach is especially useful when the owner has a general idea of the building it wants but has not had a detailed design

---

[18] *Id.*

prepared. The owner may describe the general parameters of the finished product and its performance requirements in the contract, and the design-build contractor then undertakes the project to fulfill these requirements in whatever way it deems best. In this case, the owner has, in effect, issued a performance specification[19] for the entire project.

Unlike traditional reliance on detailed specifications and enumerated construction processes in the bid documents, the design-build owner can avoid, or at least limit, its potential warranties under the *Spearin* doctrine[20] by leaving almost all of the design and construction details to the contractor. *Arkansas Rice Growers Cooperative Ass'n v. Alchemy Industries, Inc.*[21] is an example of a project in which the performance specification concerned performance of the project as a whole. In *Arkansas Rice,* the dispute involved a construction contract for a pollution-free rice hull combustion plant that generated steam and marketable ash from the rice hull fuel. Rice hulls were required to be the sole fuel for the plant furnace. In the contract, the designers agreed to provide:

> the necessary engineering plant layout and equipment design and the onsite engineering supervision and start up engineering services necessary for the construction of a hull by-product facility capable of reducing a minimum of 7-1/2 tons of rice hulls per hour to an ash and producing a minimum of 48 million BTU's per hour of steam at 200 pounds pressure.[22]

The plant never performed as expected. The plant was plagued by shutdowns from blockages, excessive pollution emissions, and inadequate furnace combustion, and the plant closed less than three years after completion of construction.

The owner filed suit against the design contractors for more than $3 million in damages for breach of contract and the negligent design of the facility. The district court held that the design contractors had breached their contractual warranty in failing to design a plant capable of meeting the contractual performance requirements. Although the designers argued, and the court agreed, that faulty pollution control equipment added by the owner had contributed to the failures of the plant, the court found that even without such problems the furnace as designed, assuming ideal operation, could not have met the contract performance criteria. Additionally, the court found that the design contractor had adopted certain defective designs offered by the owner's pollution control contractor so as to include them in the plant design.[23]

---

[19] See § **13.4**.

[20] See § **13.4**.

[21] 797 F.2d 565 (8th Cir. 1986).

[22] *Id.* at 566.

[23] *Id.* at 568–69.

In affirming the breach of warranty claim, the Eighth Circuit found that the contractual provision cited above established a warranty that the design would meet the stated performance requirements.[24] The designers had materially breached the contract by providing defective design plans and had excused owner from further performance under the contract.[25] The district court calculated the damages as the cost of plant construction less the costs associated with the defective pollution equipment not provided or approved by the design contractors, but did not include the costs of plant operation.[26]

Although applying a somewhat limited legal analysis, the court in *Arkansas Rice* had no difficulty finding a performance warranty in the contractual language requiring the engineering, design, and on-site supervision and start-up necessary to construct the rice hull plant. The factual and legal determination that the furnace failed to perform as specified seemed a sufficient justification for the verdict. Unlike the ordinary negligence standard for design professionals, this court's approach demonstrates that a greater warranty may be applied, and this warranty relates to the performance of the product.

Like the *Arkansas Rice* project, the *Omaha Pollution Control Corp.* project never achieved the expected performance levels.[27] The design-build contract called for the construction of a special treatment plant to complete an elaborate sewage treatment system for the filtration and processing of packing house wastes including animal carcasses. The system utilized more than five miles of collector sewers, eight gravity and flotation basins, and a processing plant capable of extracting grease and dry solids for resale. Under § 1.4 of the amended agreement, Carver-Greenfield Corporation (contractor) agreed to design, engineer, and construct a processing plant that would be sufficient to process the packing house wastes. Omaha Pollution Control Corporation's (owner's) acceptance of the completed project would hinge on continuous "commercial operation level" performance of the processing plant for a period of five days.

In its recitation of the facts, the court allocated responsibility for the failures of the packing house waste disposal system. Although the contractor was excused from some of the responsibility for the failures due to the weather, acts of God, and the errors by the owner or its agents, the court found that the primary responsibility was borne by the contractor for its "inadequately designed, engineered and constructed" processing plant,

---

[24] *Id.* at 569 (citing U.S. v. Spearin, 248 U.S. 132 (1918); Centex Constr. Co. v. James, 374 F.2d 921 (8th Cir. 1967)).

[25] *Id.* at 570.

[26] *Id.* at 570–71.

[27] Omaha Pollution Control Corp. v. Carver-Greenfield Corp., 413 F. Supp. 1069 (D. Neb. 1976).

which failed to deliver a plant capable of meeting the five-day continuous operation performance requirement for completion specified in the amended agreement.[28] The court awarded the owner contract damages in excess of $3.3 million.[29]

§ 13.6 UCC Warranties for the Supply of Goods

Courts are generally reluctant to apply the Uniform Commercial Code (UCC)[30] to the services rendered by design professionals and construction contractors, but some courts have demonstrated a willingness to relax this restraint. Courts have adopted several different approaches to applying the UCC to construction contracts and the contracting parties: some courts never apply the UCC to construction contracts;[31] some balance the amount of goods and services to be provided and apply the UCC if the supply of goods is the predominant element;[32] and some apply the UCC by analogy, or apply the UCC if the parties treat the contract as a sale of goods, with incidental services.[33] Several courts have applied the UCC to construction subcontracts, when the subcontractor designs, produces, and installs a discrete element of the overall project.[34]

At least one court has ventured further and applied UCC warranties to a design-build contractor so as to create a performance guarantee.[35] Courts

---

[28] *Id.* at 1084.

[29] *Id.* at 1086.

[30] Every state except Louisiana has adopted some form of the Uniform Commercial Code. Article 2 of the UCC regulates the sale of goods in situations when buyers and sellers have failed to include express provisions in their contracts. For example, it sets forth certain implied warranties of merchantability and fitness for particular use that automatically become part of sales contracts. *See* UCC §§ 2-314, 2-315 (1977).

[31] *See, e.g.,* Vernali v. Centrella, 28 Conn. Supp. 476, 266 A.2d 200 (Super. Ct. 1970) (denying UCC application to construction services case).

[32] Bonebrake v. Cox, 499 F.2d 951 (8th Cir. 1974) (services incidental to primary goods contract; UCC applied); Aluminum Co. of Am. v. Electro Flo Corp., 451 F.2d 1115 (10th Cir. 1971) (flooring contractor's design services incidental to construction of flooring system; UCC warranties applied); DeGroft v. Lancaster Silo Co., 527 A.2d 1316 (Md. Ct. Spec. App. 1987) (UCC applied under predominant purpose test).

[33] Wellmore Coal Co. v. Powell Constr. Co., 600 F. Supp. 1042 (D. Va. 1984) (UCC applied because contracting parties described transaction as sale of goods).

[34] *See* Bonebrake v. Cox, 499 F.2d 951 (8th Cir. 1974) (services incidental to primary goods contract; UCC applied); Aluminum Co. of Am. v. Electro Flo Corp., 451 F.2d 1115 (10th Cir. 1971) (flooring contractor's design services incidental to construction of flooring system; UCC warranties applied); Port City Constr. Co. v. Henderson, 266 So. 2d 896 (Ala. Civ. App. 1972).

[35] *See* Omaha Pollution Control Corp. v. Carver-Greenfield Corp., 413 F. Supp. 1069 (D. Neb. 1976).

may be more willing to deem a completed construction project a good or product when the design-build contractor is asked to design and provide a project that meets performance specifications, as compared with a contractor asked to build the same project in strict compliance with the owner's detailed design specifications.

In its legal analysis, the *Omaha Pollution* court demonstrated the possible UCC warranty implications of a design-build contract. Having found the contractor responsible for the failure of the project to perform as the owner had specified, the court analyzed the legal aspects of its failings by applying article 2 of the Nebraska Uniform Commercial Code.[36] After justifying its use of the UCC by reference to Fifth[37] and Tenth Circuit cases,[38] the court stated:

> Here, as in those cases, the buyer relied on the seller and the seller's expertise to examine a problem, recommend, design, and manufacture a product which, it was represented, would afford a solution. . . . Then, [Contractor] . . . undertook to design, construct, and deliver a product, the processing plant, which would afford a solution, the production of marketable product from sewerage.[39]

Given these obligations and representations, the court found that contractor's design and construction of the processing plant had included an implied warranty of merchantability for fitness for ordinary use as well as an implied warranty of fitness for the particular intended use of the product.[40] Having found no contractual alterations to or exclusions of these warranties, and determining that the owner had relied on the contractor's expertise and its knowledge of the particular purpose of the project, the court awarded the owner contract damages in excess of $3.3 million.[41]

The court's analysis is particularly interesting in its ready application of the UCC warranties to a construction contract. Rather than weigh the goods and services portions of the contract to determine the predominant factor, the court analyzed the contract as one for the delivery of a product, the processing plant. Although the contract required design and construction services, the court's focus was on the finished building's conformance to the contract. Rather than emphasizing the design-build contractor's exercise of due care or its workmanlike manner of construction, the court used the UCC to expand the contractor's warranty. When a contract only requires a contractor to build what the architect and owner put in the specifications, the contractor's duty is more limited. As the contractor's ability

---

[36] *Id.*

[37] Sperry Rand Corp. v. Industrial Supply Corp., 337 F.2d 363 (5th Cir. 1964).

[38] Aluminum Co. of Am. v. Electro Flo Corp., 451 F.2d 1115 (10th Cir. 1971).

[39] Omaha Pollution Control Corp. v. Carver-Greenfield Corp., 413 F. Supp. at 1085.

[40] *See* UCC §§ 2-314(2)(c), 2-315.

[41] Omaha Pollution Control Corp. v. Carver-Greenfield Corp., 413 F. Supp. at 1086.

to control the design specifications increases, its obligation to achieve the contractual performance specifications tends to increase as well.

§ 13.7 The Defenses of Impossibility and Impracticability

There has been a fair amount of confusion regarding the proper role of the impossibility and commercial impracticability doctrines in the design-build context. As a general rule, courts recognize that when a contractor agrees to do, for a fixed sum, a thing that is possible to be performed, it will not be excused or entitled to additional compensation for unforeseen difficulties that have been encountered on the project.[42] However, when an owner provides true design specifications in a contract, courts generally conclude that the risk that the contractor's performance will be impossible due to unforeseen circumstances should be placed solely upon the owner.[43] When such a deficiency or defect in an owner's specifications precludes fabrication of an item, it may technically be said that the contractor's performance has been rendered *impossible.* However, the proper analysis in these situations is essentially whether the owner's design specifications were *defective* because, for example, they inaccurately described the site conditions. If they were, responsibility for cost overruns and other losses are shifted to the owner simply because it breached the implied warranty that, if followed, the design specifications would produce a conforming structure. There is simply no need to resort to the doctrine of impossibility here.[44]

When, on the other hand, a design-build contract contains performance-type specifications, most courts will conclude that the contractor assumes responsibility for all damages or increased costs that it may incur if performance of the contract becomes impossible.[45] For example, in the *Aleutian Constructors* case,[46] the Court of Claims found that, by altering the

---

[42] *See, e.g.,* United States v. Spearin, 248 U.S. 132, 136 (1918); Day v. United States, 245 U.S. 159 (1917).

[43] *See, e.g.,* J.W. Hurst & Son Awnings, Inc., ASBCA No. 4167, 59-1 B.C.A. (CCH) ¶ 2,095 (1959); Robert E. McKee Gen. Contractor, Inc., ASBCA No. 5759, 60-1 B.C.A. (CCH) ¶ 2,585 (1960).

[44] *See* Dynalectron Corp.-Pac. Div., ASBCA No. 18057, 77-1 B.C.A. (CCH) ¶ 12,348 (1977) (recognizing the confusion created by characterizing a breach of the owner's implied warranty under the doctrine of impossibility).

[45] *See, e.g.,* Aleutian Constructors v. United States, 24 Cl. Ct. 372 (1991); J.A. Maurer, Inc. v. United States, 485 F.2d 588, 595 (Ct. Cl. 1973) ("[I]f the contractor, from the stance of superior expertise, asks for and obtains leave to perform according to methods defined and stated by him, he impliedly warrants that he is able to overcome the technical difficulties inherent in the project, whatever they are.").

[46] Aleutian Constructors v. United States, 24 Cl. Ct. 372 (1991).

owner's initial design specifications for the design features at issue, the contractor had impliedly "assume[d] the risk that performance under its proposed specifications may be impossible."[47] Accordingly, the contractor's assumption of responsibility for the design of the roofing membrane caused it to assume all liability for losses stemming from the inability of that design to meet the owner's performance goals. Similarly, in *J.A. Maurer, Inc. v. United States,*[48] a government contractor was awarded a contract by the government (owner) to supply the methodology and design for an Air Force test track. Because the contractor had superior expertise and had modified the test methods specified by the owner in the specifications, the court in *Maurer* found that it had warranted its capability to perform the contract and could not rely on the defense of impossibility when it was terminated from the contract for default.

The word *impossibility* may be somewhat of a semantic trap in the context of design-build contracts. As the cases above illustrate, the proper inquiry is to determine which party has assumed responsibility for the design feature at issue. By supplying the design, the owner or contractor assumes liability for all cost overruns and losses caused by flaws in the specifications. Whether the contractor's performance has, in fact, been rendered "impossible" or "impracticable" is simply immaterial.

DRAFTING A DESIGN-BUILD CONTRACT WITH PERFORMANCE GUARANTEES

§ 13.8 Describing the Guarantees

The preceding sections have described the legal consequences, in the absence of specific contract provisions, to the owner and the design-build contractor of performance guarantees in a design-build contract. These consequences have come as an unpleasant shock to many of the parties to the disputes discussed in those sections, and the consequences imposed by the court often may have been far from the intentions of the parties. Prudent owners and design-build contractors may avoid these surprises by drafting explicit provisions concerning the guarantees in their design-build contracts. **Sections 13.9** through **13.11** outline what the provisions should cover.

For the benefit of both the owner and the design-build contractor, the most important drafting job in a contract with performance guarantees is to state exactly the performance that the owner requires, to provide

---

[47] *Id.* at 378.

[48] 485 F.2d 588 (Ct. Cl. 1973).

enforceable guarantees of that performance by the contractor, and to exclude other performance guarantees that might otherwise be inferred.

The details of the performance guarantees, of course, depend on the details of the particular project. In some instances, the guarantee concerns the performance of only a limited part of the design-build project, such as the roof in the *Aleutian Constructors* case, discussed in § **13.4**. In other cases, the guarantee concerns the performance of the entire completed facility, as in the *Arkansas Rice Growers* case, discussed in § **13.5**. In either situation, the performance guarantee generally falls into one of three basic categories: (a) output and consumption guarantees, (b) completion guarantees, and (c) compliance guarantees.

Output and Consumption Guarantees

Output and consumption guarantees are the heart of the matter. They describe what the owner wants from either the specific guaranteed part of the work or the whole completed facility, and they need to be stated as precisely as possible. Guarantees for specific parts of the work are usually unique to each situation and can usually be limited to technical descriptions of the intended performance of the part. Guarantees concerning the completed facility need to be more extensive. Usually they must describe the significant products of the completed facility and the significant materials consumed in the making of those products.

For example, if the owner wants to build a power plant, it will want a plant that produces a certain amount of electric energy at a certain cost. In such a case, the output and consumption guarantees will usually consist of (a) a guarantee of the net electrical output of the plant (the amount of energy the owner can sell to a utility or deliver to the owner's customers); (b) if the facility is also to produce steam, a guarantee of the steam output of the plant, stated as a certain amount of steam per hour at a specified temperature and pressure; and (c) a guarantee of the amount of fuel and other key consumables that the facility will need to burn to produce a specified amount of electricity. A similar level of specificity can be provided whether the project is a refinery, a waste-water treatment plant, an automated factory, or any other design-build project in which a particular level of performance is important.

Completion Guarantees

Completion guarantees are common in construction contracts, whether or not they are design-build or contain performance guarantees. In the ordinary contracting situation, satisfaction of the guarantee is usually measured by the achievement of what is called "substantial completion" or "mechanical completion." These terms refer to the physical completion or assembly of the plant in conformance with the plans. If a design-build contract contains guarantees describing the performance of the completed facility, the completion guarantee needs to be stated differently. What the owner should be concerned about is not so much when the facility will be physically completed, but when the facility will be able to perform its intended functions.

In this case, the completion guarantee is a guarantee of *when* the performance guarantees are to be achieved. Satisfaction of the completion guarantee should be demonstrated not by a physical inspection of the work, as in the case of a guarantee of substantial completion, but by passing a test designed to show that the facility can meet the performance guarantees. Once the test has been passed, the completion guarantee is met.

Compliance Guarantees

Even if the facility is completed within the expected time and produces the expected output at the expected cost, it may nonetheless not be able to perform as expected or to perform at all. The facility must also be in compliance with other requirements for it to operate commercially.

First, the facility must be in compliance with applicable law and permits. With today's complex environmental regulations, applicable permits are likely to impose severe restrictions on any facility subject to performance guarantees. The design-build contractor must carefully review the applicable legal and permit restrictions on the facility's operation to assure itself that the facility can achieve the performance guarantees, while at the same time complying with restrictions on air and water emissions and other requirements.

Second, the facility may not be able to enter commercial operation unless it can operate in compliance with the owner's agreements with third parties concerning essential facility operations. For example, an owner building a power plant will have contracts for the supply of fuel, for operation of the facility, for the sale of electricity, and for the disposal of ash, among others. These agreements need to be carefully reviewed by the owner and the design-build contractor to determine what restrictions these third-party agreements may impose on the facility's operation, and how the restrictions should be incorporated into the contract's performance guarantees.

§ 13.9 Testing

In addition to a clear statement of the performance guarantee, it is important that the design-build contract clearly state how compliance with the guarantee is to be measured and what the consequences will be if the guarantee is not met.

Compliance with a performance guarantee is usually established by a test of performance. The nature of the test can have a substantial effect on how difficult it will be to comply with the performance guarantee, and care needs to be taken to describe the test in detail. To take an example from outside of construction, if the performance guarantee for an automobile is that it can travel at 100 mph, the chances of it meeting the guarantee will be much different if the test is of its speed after 30 seconds from a standing stop on a level road than if the test were of the top speed reached at any time during a day of driving downhill.

Some performance guarantees, especially those of only a part of the work, may not easily be susceptible to testing and in some cases cannot be tested without putting the facility at risk of damage. Even in these cases, however, the parties should consider describing in the contract the actual operating conditions that the guarantee is supposed to meet, so that if the part fails to perform during operation, the parties will have a reference to determine if the performance guarantee has been breached.

In establishing a testing program for a performance guarantee, the following issues should be kept in mind:

A. The timing of the tests should be established, so that the parties agree on: (1) when the tests may be performed (2) how complete the facility needs to be before testing can start (3) whether and how often tests can be reperformed in the event of initial failure (4) which test result will govern in the case of multiple tests (5) how long the design-builder has to demonstrate compliance with the guarantee.

B. Details of the testing can include: (1) the length of the test (2) the measurement of performance over the length of the test (3) the instruments and methods used for measuring performance and the associated testing uncertainty (4) the correction of the test results to account for changes in agreed conditions, such as ambient weather conditions, performance parameters, and fuel specifications (5) the method of operation of the facility during the test period, particularly to see that the facility is run during the test in the same way it will during commercial operation (6) reference to applicable codes and standards, such as those produced by ANSI and ASME.

C. Agreements should be reached on: (1) how and by whom the tests should be monitored (2) what laboratories are acceptable for performing off-site testing (3) what methods should be used for resolving disputes concerning the performance of the tests and the accuracy of test results.

§ 13.10 Remedies

The contract should describe what remedies the owner has if the performance guarantee is not met. In the case of guarantees for only a portion of the work, the best remedy may be that the contractor reperform the defective work so that it satisfies the guarantee. The reperformance remedy is usually also required by the owner for a failure of the facility to comply with one of the compliance guarantees discussed in **§ 13.8**.

However, when performance of the facility as a whole is guaranteed, or in some cases of a guarantee of only a portion of the facility, the reperformance remedy may be a bad idea for both the owner and the contractor. In some cases, satisfaction of the guarantee is simply impossible, and although the owner will have a remedy in damages in such a situation, its legal remedies may not be sufficient. In addition, the reperformance remedy may impose a burden on the design-build contractor that is out of all proportion to the harm suffered by the owner.

Take the case of an owner who has contracted for the construction of an automated manufacturing facility and has obtained a performance guarantee from the design-build contractor that the facility will be able to produce a specified number of units of the end product per hour. In setting the performance guarantee, the owner has, among other things, determined that its revenue from the expected production of the facility will cover the costs of operation of the facility and the costs of financing its construction, as well as return a profit. If there is a slight shortfall in expected production, the owner may lose some expected return on its investment. But the owner might have difficulty in demonstrating that loss in a breach of contract action, and the net present value of the owner's lost return may be far less than the cost to the design-build contractor of making the necessary repairs.

In this situation, it may be in the interest of both the owner and the design-build contractor to agree to liquidate the owner's damages. A common approach is for the parties to agree on a specific amount of damages to be paid to the owner for each increment of shortfall in performance from the level guaranteed. When liquidated damages are agreed to, the design-build contract usually provides that the contractor will attempt, through repairs and reperformance, to make the project fulfill the guarantees but that, after an agreed level of effort, the contractor has the option of ceasing further repair efforts and paying the owner liquidated damages based on the final tested level of performance.

§ 13.11 Controlling the Risk

In addition to careful descriptions of the performance guarantee, the testing of performance, and the remedies for failure to achieve the guarantee, there are a number of important steps the design-build contractor can take to mitigate the risks of failing to meet the performance guarantee. Several of these steps are briefly described in this section. The contractor should note, however, that some of the following steps will not be available to it in contracts with the government and that some may be firmly resisted by some private owners.

Once the owner and the design-build contractor have provided in their contract the performance guarantees that are being given, they should provide the guarantees that are *not* being given. Absent an express waiver, the courts may imply performance guarantees in addition to those provided in the contract.[49] Assuming that the contract has a traditional contractor's warranty in addition to the performance guarantee, the safest course for the contractor is to add to the contract an express waiver by the owner of all warranties and guarantees not expressly stated in the contract. The wording of such a waiver should be checked against the relevant state law to make sure it is effective. The following is a general example:

CONTRACTOR DISCLAIMS, AND OWNER WAIVES, ANY OTHER OR FURTHER EXPRESS, IMPLIED, OR STATUTORY STANDARDS, WARRANTIES, OR GUARANTEES, INCLUDING WITHOUT LIMITATION ANY IMPLIED WARRANTY AS TO MERCHANTABILITY OR FITNESS FOR A PARTICULAR PURPOSE OR ARISING FROM A COURSE OF DEALING OR USAGE OF TRADE AS TO ANY EQUIPMENT, MATERIALS, OR WORK FURNISHED UNDER THIS CONTRACT.

The ability of the contractor's work to comply with the performance guarantee usually depends on factors outside of the design-build contractor's control. The contractor needs to identify as many of these factors as it can and to expressly condition its obligation to achieve the performance guarantee on their occurrence.

For example, in a project in which the owner has issued both design and performance specifications,[50] the design-build contractor may be held to guarantee the performance of some parts of the work but not others. But the success of the work whose performance the contractor guarantees may depend on the work it does not. In these cases, it is important for the contractor to identify those parts of the project over which it does not have design control but which can affect the successful performance of its portion.

When the design-build contractor guarantees the performance of the entire facility, its success still depends on services and goods provided by the owner and the owner's contractors, such as fuel, operations services, and interconnections with suppliers of feed stocks and with customers of the

[49] See §§ **13.4, 13.5**.

[50] See the discussion of the difference between these two types of specifications in § **13.4**.

facility's products. It is important that each of these services and goods be identified as conditions of the performance guarantee, so that, if a failure by any prevents achievement of the performance guarantee, the design-builder may have an excuse.

As was discussed in §§ **13.4** through **13.7**, the contractor may be liable for breach of a performance guarantee even if successful performance is impossible or commercially impracticable. However, this does not mean that the contractor must take the risk that unforeseen circumstances will render performance impossible. Just as in the case of more traditional warranties, circumstances such as owner changes, events of force majeure, changes in law, and differing site conditions can excuse the achievement of a performance guarantee. But these excuses should be expressly stated in the design-build contract Thus, care must be exercised in drafting such exculpatory clauses to make clear that the occurrence of an excusing event can result in relief from the requirement of the performance guarantee. Generally, the contract should be drafted so that the occurrence of the excusing event does not relieve the contractor entirely from the guarantee obligation but requires an equitable adjustment to the terms of the guarantee to take account of the occurrence.

Finally, the design-build contractor should consider adding specific limitations to its liability for failure to achieve a performance guarantee. The failure of a project to perform as intended can significantly reduce the revenue that the owner expected to receive from the project. The net present value of lost revenues over the expected life of a large project can be enormous, and can grow even larger if the owner incurs other expenses to make up for shortfalls in the project's performance. When the size of these consequential damages is out of proportion to the benefits to the contractor from the design-build contract, the contractor should consider proposing waivers by the owner of its right to claim consequential damages. If an outright waiver of all consequential damages is not appropriate, the contractor can propose a limitation on such damages to an agreed set of liquidated damages, as discussed in § **13.10**.

INSURANCE

§ 13.12 Insurance and Performance Guarantees

Most insurance issues that arise in design-build projects are treated elsewhere in this book. This chapter will discuss two specialized types of insurance that can be used to mitigate the exposure of a design-build contractor to damages for failure to meet a performance guarantee. *Delayed completion insurance* provides limited protection if the project is not completed when promised. So-called *efficacy insurance* can provide protection if the completed project does not perform as expected.

§ 13.13 Delayed Completion Insurance

Every project insures against damage during construction by obtaining what is commonly called builder's risk insurance. An endorsement to the builder's risk insurance is often available that provides limited coverage to the design-build contractor for liquidated damages due for late completion of the project. What is often called delayed opening or delayed completion insurance provides coverage for delay in the completion of the facility due to the occurrence of a peril covered under the builder's risk policy. Proceeds from the insurance policy are often in the amount of the debt service due under the construction financing for the period of the delay, with a deductible (usually 30 to 45 days) and a maximum period of coverage (often 12 months). Because the contractor's liquidated damages for delayed completion are often tied to debt service, the design-build contractor should provide in its contract that it receives a credit against its liability for delay damages in the amount of any proceeds from the delayed completion insurance.

Keep in mind, however, that delayed completion insurance only pays if the loss is due to the occurrence of a peril covered under the builder's risk policy, which usually means physical loss or damage. Delayed completion insurance usually will not respond when the job is late simply because the contractor is having difficulty making the completed project perform as guaranteed. For that, the design-build contractor needs to turn to efficacy insurance.

§ 13.14 Efficacy Insurance

Efficacy insurance, sometimes called contractor's performance insurance, may be available to insure against a failure to achieve a performance guarantee. In essence, this insurance responds if the facility fails to operate as guaranteed. This section describes two policies of efficacy insurance that may be available. The requirements for obtaining efficacy insurance are high and the market volatile. There can be no assurance that either coverage will be available for a particular project at an affordable price.

Coverage

One policy that may be available provides coverage for liquidated damage liabilities payable by the contractor under the construction contract for failure to achieve performance guarantees (as defined in the construction contract) and for failure to meet the guaranteed completion date (again, as defined in the construction contract), which liabilities, in either case, arise directly as a result of fault, neglect, error, or omission in the design or construction of the project.

Another policy provides coverage for liquidated damage liabilities for failure to meet the insured technical performance (as specified in an endorsement to the policy) and for delays beyond the insured completion date (again, as specified in the policy), which liabilities, in either case, arise solely as a result of deficiencies in the design, materials or construction of the project. With respect to the delay damages, the deficiencies must "manifest themselves after installation at the Project site." Under this policy, with respect to performance losses, loss is measured according to a policy endorsement which sets forth a schedule of payments to be made if performance does not reach specified levels during testing. With respect to delay damages, an established daily indemnity is provided.

Deductible and Contribution

Efficacy insurance often provides that the contractor assumes a percentage of the first liquidated damages. In addition, the insured completion date is often 30 days later than the guaranteed completion date set forth in the construction contract. The contractor may also have to contribute an additional percentage of further losses.

Exclusions

Efficacy insurance usually excludes losses resulting from:

1. War
2. Nuclear radiation and radioactive contamination
3. Costs of rectification and/or improvement
4. Laws not in effect at the commencement of the policy
5. Insolvency of the contractor
6. Events that could reasonably be remedied by the insured.

Efficacy insurance may also exclude losses resulting from:

1. The enforcement of any law
2. Failure of pollution control equipment associated with the system
3. Failure to obtain governmental licenses or permits

4. Vandalism, riot, sabotage, malicious mischief, labor slowdown, strike, or lock-out
5. Physical damage to the system, however caused
6. Failure to take appropriate action in response to a written recommendation by the insurer
7. Any other event or circumstance excluded from the construction contract
8. Any delay occasioned by a dispute between the contractor and the owner which is not related to the ability of the system to pass performance tests
9. Contractor's failure to abide by the terms of the construction contract.

Experimental Technology

Efficacy insurance coverage often excludes losses resulting from use of any experimental equipment, technology, or method of construction. A common condition to coverage is that design of the project is consistent with standard engineering practice and incorporates no experimental items of equipment, technology, or method of construction.

INTELLECTUAL PROPERTY AND TECHNOLOGY TRANSFER ISSUES

§ 13.15 Copyright Protection

Copyright is a federal scheme of intellectual property protection that protects the form in which a party expresses ideas and information, once that expression is fixed in a tangible means of expression, and, among other things, copyright affords protection for computer software, architectural drawings and plans, and even finished buildings.[51] Recent developments have broadened copyright coverage of software and the computer codes in that software, and although the physical architectural drawings and plans have long been afforded copyright protection, copyright has only recently been extended to the actual buildings produced from those plans. These developments highlight the importance of copyright to the design-build arena. Whether the design-build contractor, the architect, or the owner

---

[51] Copyright protection extends to any original work of authorship fixed in a tangible medium of expression, which includes books, sound recordings, computer programs, and a number of other types of works. 17 U.S.C. § 102(a) (1988).

holds the copyright to a plan or design could determine if that design can be reused in another project or used by someone other than the copyright owner for purposes of operating, repairing, or modifying the building. The fundamental factors addressed in **§§ 13.16** and **13.17** include what can be protected by copyright, who owns those rights, and how those rights and parties affect the design-build process.

§ 13.16 —The Subject Matter of Copyright

Among other things, copyright protection extends to "pictorial, graphic, and sculptural works."[52] Following the 1988 amendment of the Copyright Act,[53] "pictorial, graphic, and sculptural works" are more clearly defined to include, among other things, two-dimensional and three-dimensional models and also technical drawings, such as architectural plans.[54] However, the definition still contains a limitation that the copyright protection extends only to those portions of the work, such as decorative embellishments, that are separate from the utilitarian nature of the work.[55] It appears that architectural plans should not be affected by this *useful article limitation,* because they exist to convey the information necessary to build or analyze a structure rather than serve a utilitarian function.[56]

The enactment of the Architectural Works Copyright Protection Act,[57] which became effective in December 1990, clarified the application of copyright protection to architectural plans and extended such protection to the actual buildings produced from such plans. Bypassing the uncertainty of the pictorial, graphic, and sculptural useful article limitation, *architectural works* are now defined to include:

> the design of a building as embodied in any tangible medium of expression, including a building, architectural plans, or drawings. The work includes

---

[52] 17 U.S.C. § 102(a)(5) (1988).

[53] Berne Convention Implementation Act of 1988, Pub. L. No. 100-568, 102 Stat. 2853 (1988) (effective Mar. 1, 1989).

[54] 17 U.S.C. § 102(a)(5) (1988).

[55] *Id.* § 101.

[56] *Id. See* M. Nimmer, 1 Nimmer on Copyright § 2.08[D](2) (1991). Intellectual property protection of utilitarian or useful articles is left to patent law. *See* Baker v. Selden, 101 U.S. 99 (1879). *See also* DeSilva Constr. Co. v. Herrald, 213 F. Supp. 184 (M.D. Fla. 1962) (building resulting from use of copyrighted plan held not infringement); Muller v. Triborough Bridge Auth., 43 F. Supp. 298 (S.D.N.Y. 1942) (use of copyrighted plan to build bridge approach held not to infringe).

[57] *See* Architectural Works Copyright Protection Act, Title VII of Judicial Improvements Act of 1990, Pub. L. No. 101-650, 104 Stat. 5089.

> the overall form as well as the arrangement and composition of spaces and elements in the design, but does not include individual standard features.[58]

The provision applies only to architectural works created after the effective date and unconstructed works in unpublished plans created before the effective date.[59] Although the definition does not appear to include utilitarian structures such as bridges, highway ramps, and pedestrian crosswalks, clearer protection is afforded buildings such as homes, offices, and industrial structures. Clearly, such protection is relevant to the construction process if the author (or copyright owner) holds exclusive rights to architectural plans or the finished building constructed using those plans.

Although broad, the scope of the exclusive rights of the architectural copyright owner are not absolute. If the work is in a public place, pictures or other representations of the work may be made, copied, and distributed without infringing the copyright.[60] Also, the building owner may alter the building, demolish, or order the destruction of the copyrighted work without the authorization of either the copyright owner or the author.[61] Although these two limitations are worthy of note, they do not affect the remaining exclusive rights of the copyright owner.

Computer software is protected by copyright law as well. Not only can computer programs be copyrighted, the copyright protection can extend to the structure and organization of the program in addition to the literal computer codes.[62] Whether used in the project, developed during the project, or integrated into building or plant, copyright formalities should be observed, and parties should be aware of the need to safeguard their copyright interests and avoid possible copyright infringement complications and liabilities. Design-build contractors should be especially careful to protect any software developed to aid in design or construction of a project.

---

[58] 17 U.S.C. § 101.

[59] As for covered works created before the effective date, copyright protection will cease Dec. 31, 2002, unless the work is actually constructed. Plans and drawings made prior to the effective date can still be protected as pictorial, graphic, or sculptural works, but the copyright protection will not extend to construction of buildings described in those plans or drawings.

[60] 17 U.S.C. § 120(a).

[61] *Id.* § 120(b).

[62] *See* Whelen Assocs., Inc. v. Jaslow Dental Lab., Inc., 797 F.2d 1222 (3d Cir. 1986), *cert. denied,* 479 U.S. 1031 (1987); Apple Computer, Inc. v. Formula Int'l, Inc., 725 F.2d 521 (9th Cir. 1984).

§ 13.17 —Ownership of the Copyright

Regardless of the subject matter covered by the copyright, the next step is to determine who owns the copyright, because the owner is the one permitted to exploit the copyrighted work. The copyright owner has the exclusive right to reproduce the work, prepare derivative works, and distribute, publish, or display the copyrighted work, and the right to authorize others to do so.[63] Also, the copyright owner has the right to transfer any or all of its rights of ownership.[64] The copyright owner is entitled to enjoin infringement, seize infringing items, and receive damages from any infringement of its exclusive ownership rights.[65]

Generally, the author (or creator) of the work owns the copyright. In the construction context, an architect ordinarily creates the plans and therefore owns the copyright for those plans, absent an agreement to the contrary. The copyright vests in the author at the time of creation of the work.[66] The copyright is effective for the life of the author plus 50 years.[67]

If the architect drafting the plans is an employee of an architectural firm or a design-build firm, the firm would be the author under the *work for hire doctrine.*[68] Under this doctrine and in the absence of an agreement to the contrary, if the work is produced by an employee within the scope of his or her employment, the employer or the person requesting the work is deemed the author rather than the individual employee(s) who personally created the work.[69] The copyright for a work for hire is valid for 75 years from publication or 100 years from creation, whichever is shorter.[70] Although the doctrine is limited to the employment context, there is still some uncertainty attached to this factor. The uncertainty rests upon the required factual determination of whether a party is an employee or an independent contractor.[71]

The discussion so far assumes that there is a single author (either individual or company) of the architectural plans. In design-build projects, of course, several companies may be involved in the design. Each of the

---

[63] 17 U.S.C. § 106 (1988).

[64] *Id.* § 201(d).

[65] *Id.* §§ 501–510.

[66] *Id.* § 201(a).

[67] *Id.* § 302(a).

[68] *Id.* § 101.

[69] 17 U.S.C. § 101. *See, e.g.,* Aitken, Hazen, Hoffman, Miller, PC v. Empire Constr. Co., 542 F. Supp. 252 (D. Neb. 1982) (former law applied to joint work and work for hire analysis).

[70] 17 U.S.C. § 302(c).

[71] *See* Community for Creative Non-Violence v. Reid, 490 U.S. 730 (1989) (sculptor/designer commissioned for work held to be independent contractor).

companies involved may be a joint author and have a joint undivided co-ownership of the copyright. Although joint works require more than de minimus contribution or participation, they do not require any particular degree of co-authorship. Subject to accountability to co-authors, any of the co-authors may license, distribute, or use the copyrighted work. A joint work copyright is valid until the death of the last surviving author.[72] The number of parties involved in a design-build project and the potential uncertainty of ownership highlight the wisdom of contractual resolution of copyright issues.[73] The resolution of the ownership question could have serious repercussions later in the construction process and may require licensing or other permission be granted others wishing to copy, modify, or use the plans and drawings.

§ 13.18 Technology Transfers

Rather than relying solely upon the protections provided by patent and copyright laws, the parties should include express provisions in the design-build contract addressing the ownership and use of intellectual property rights commonly associated with a project design. In the typical design-build project, any architect, engineer, or design consultant who plays a role in the design process may in fact obtain a copyright interest in the design documents. Thus, in light of the potential for co-ownership of the rights and the uncertainty in many cases concerning the identity of the individuals who in fact may have obtained such interests, it is imperative that the parties address these concerns in the contract.

The parties should designate whether the owner, contractor, or other third parties own the drawings, specifications, and other design documents that have been provided for the project, and specify any conditions or limitations they may have placed on such ownership. For example, although either party may assume ownership of the plans, the standard design-build agreement prepared by the AIA provides that the contractor retains all rights in the design documents and the owner can claim no rights to them.[74] Similar agreements can be reached concerning computer software, models of the project, and the copyright on the completed building itself.

Once ownership of the plans and other matters subject to copyright has been established, the owner of those documents can grant a license to the other party for certain uses enumerated in the contract. The licensing clause should clearly and unambiguously identify the licensed subject matter (that is, specify the documents) and should state whether the license is

---

[72] 17 U.S.C. § 302(b).

[73] See **§ 13.18**.

[74] AIA A191-1985, art. 1, ¶ 1.3.1.

limited only to the named licensee or whether that party may transfer its rights to other entities. Thus, having designated ownership of the plans, the parties should specify whether the project owner and/or the contractor may use them on subsequent projects, and whether the owner or third party may use them for improvements, additions, and repairs to the current project. Similarly, if the contractor were to retain ownership of the design documents, it may consider including a provision that the project owner's right to use the plans will expire in the event the contractor is improperly terminated from the project.

The parties are free to proscribe subsequent use of the design documents in any manner they may choose, but the AIA standard form agreement illustrates an approach the contractor may take to limit the scope of an owner's license. The AIA form design-build contract states that:

> [d]rawings, specifications and other documents furnished by the Design/Builder shall not be used by the Owner on other projects, for additions to this Project or, unless the Design/Builder is in default under Part 1, for completion of this Project by others, except by written agreement relating to use, liability and compensation.[75]

Agreements concerning the use of the design documents in design-build contracts generally are *nonexclusive licenses,* for use by the licensee solely in connection with the current project. These usually are not commercial licenses, which typically provide for the payment of royalties by the licensee based on the nature and extent of its use of the licensed subject matter. Nonetheless, the owner of the design rights may want to specify in the contract how and under what circumstances it would be compensated for the licensee's use of the design plans beyond the scope of the immediate contract. Although its ability to do so may be limited in certain jurisdictions,[76] the design-builder should also consider requiring the licensee to indemnify it for losses or damages caused by defects or flaws in the licensed plans. Finally, and perhaps most importantly, the owner of the design documents may want to specify in the contract that submission or distribution of the documents to meet certain regulatory requirements will not constitute "publication" in derogation of that party's copyrights or other reserved rights.[77]

In addition to licensing arrangements concerning the use of the design documents themselves, the owner and contractor may want to include a

---

[75] *Id.*

[76] *See, e.g.,* Md. Cts. & Jud. Proc. Code Ann. § 5-305 (1989) (prohibiting parties to construction agreements from requiring others to indemnify them for damages caused by their own negligent acts); N.Y. Gen. Oblig. Law § 5-322.1 (McKinney 1991); Va. Code Ann. § 11-4.1 (1989).

[77] *See id.* ¶ 1.3.2.

confidentiality agreement in the contract regarding trade secrets and other proprietary information not otherwise protected by the copyright and patent laws. Indeed, although techniques which are generally known in an industry are usually not trade secrets, certain construction processes, such as a particular method of performing structural analyses, for example, and hidden structural features used on a project may be protected if proper measures have been taken to prevent disclosure of this information to the public. In addition, certain nontechnical trade secrets such as customer lists, supplier lists, financial data, and business plans may also warrant protection in the contract.

Confidentiality agreements should be broadly worded so as to restrict the use and disclosure of all trade secrets and other information designated in writing as confidential by the parties, absent written consent from the disclosing party. For example, the agreement should obligate the parties to disclose trade secrets to their employees, agents, and subcontractors on a need-to-know basis, requiring the receiving party to obtain signed agreements from those persons promising to keep the information confidential. Similarly, the contract may delineate specific safeguards to be followed by the parties during construction, such as the construction of a temporary wall, to inhibit access to the site by persons not obligated to protect the trade secret. These subsidiary agreements should be made enforceable by the disclosing party, and the receiving party should be made responsible for damages caused by a breach of those agreements.

Confidentiality provisions often contain exemptions for circumstances in which disclosure by the receiving party would be permitted, as, for example, when the information is in the public domain or when the receiving party has obtained the information through another source without violating any rights of the disclosing party. In addition, these provisions often allow the owner or contractor to disclose proprietary information to their subcontractors and consultants if those parties in turn execute similar confidentiality agreements. Finally, the contract may authorize the receiving party to disclose the subject information to certain governmental bodies, provided the owner of the rights is given notice and an opportunity to propose restrictions upon subsequent disclosure by the agency.

As with the patents and copyrights related to the design documents, the owner and contractor might also consider licensing certain "inventions" that have been based on or derived from proprietary information received from either party, or that have been first reduced to practice during performance of the contract. Such a provision should limit the receiving party's use of the invention to the project itself and might read:

Contractor hereby grants to Owner an irrevocable, non-exclusive license, for use solely in connection with the operation, maintenance, repair, or alteration of the Facility, with respect to any invention based wholly or in part on or derived from proprietary information received from Owner and conceived or first reduced to practice by Contractor, its employees, or agents during the course of the Work.

Further, the parties should specify how much and what type of copying (if any) is permitted of the licensed design drawings and/or trade secrets. It is important that the contract provide that each copy bear an appropriate notice that the item is copyrighted or otherwise subject to a proprietary interest.

Finally, the contract should set forth the disposition of all licensed materials at the termination of the license agreement.

§ 13.19 Patents

In design-build projects, as with any other complex construction project, the completed building or facility will likely contain materials and machinery, or employ technical procedures, that are covered by patents. Buildings typically incorporate special alloys, glass, and other patentable materials directly into their structure. Plants and other working facilities typically contain patented component parts or are designed to employ patented processes to produce goods or provide services.

Parties to complicated construction transactions risk the possibility that the facilities they own and construct contain patented inventions or employ patented procedures that have not been licensed for such use by the rightful patent holders. The fact that particular parties may lack any involvement in procuring or installing infringing parts, equipment, or other technology does not limit their liability for patent infringement. Federal law expressly provides that "whoever without authority makes, uses, or sells any patented invention infringes the patent."[78]

The Supreme Court has expressly held that the unauthorized use of a patented invention, without more, constitutes patent infringement.[79] In particular, the Court held that persons who purchase patented inventions from a source that is not properly licensed to make or sell them are liable for patent infringement if they use the inventions.[80] Furthermore, courts have consistently held that liability for patent infringement is strict, and it is

---

[78] 35 U.S.C. § 271(a) (1988).

[79] Aro Mfg. Co. v. Convertible Top Replacement Co., 377 U.S. 476, 484 (1964). *See* Reynolds Metals Co. v. Aluminum Co. of Am., 457 F. Supp. 482, 509 (N.D. Ind. 1978), *rev'd on other grounds,* 609 F.2d 1218 (7th Cir.), *cert. denied,* 446 U.S. 989 (1980) (infringement of a patent may consist of any one, two or all three of the acts in the making, using or selling the patented invention without the authority of the patent owner).

[80] *See* Aro Mfg. Co. v. Convertible Top Replacement Co., 377 U.S. 476 (1964).

irrelevant whether the purchaser or user of an infringing invention lacks any intent to infringe a patentholder's rights.[81]

Under prevailing principles of patent law, project owners are liable as *users* of infringing inventions that contractors and subcontractors incorporate into finished projects.[82] Likewise, courts have held general contractors liable as users of patents that their subcontractors infringe.[83] Patent infringers are liable for money damages, and courts may enjoin them from continuing to use infringing inventions.[84] The remedies for patent infringement, particularly that of injunction, can be devastating to projects that rely on patented technology for continued, profitable operation.

Project owners and design-build contractors are particularly vulnerable to patent infringement claims, because they rely on a diverse group of subcontractors and suppliers to provide technology, component parts, and materials that become incorporated into completed projects. Owners and design-build contractors cannot contract out of liability for patent infringement, but they can employ various contracting strategies to minimize the risk that they will actually suffer damages attributable to instances of infringement for which they are not directly responsible.

For example, the owner of a project may obtain an agreement from the design-build contractor to ensure that only licensed patented inventions are incorporated into the project and to indemnify the owner for the costs of litigation and damages suffered or paid out as a result of liability for patent infringement arising from the contractor's, subcontractors', and/or suppliers' use of designs and materials during the construction of the project. In addition, the owner may require the contractor to remedy instances of infringement by purchasing appropriate licenses or redesigning the facility to avoid infringement. The owner can further reduce its risks by requiring

---

[81] *See* Blair v. Westinghouse Elec. Corp., 291 F. Supp. 664, 670 (D.D.C. 1968) (infringement may be entirely inadvertent and unintentional and without knowledge of patent); Ames Shower Curtain Co. v. Heinz Nathanson, Inc., 285 F. Supp. 640, 645 (S.D.N.Y. 1968) (neither knowledge of the patent nor intent to infringe is relevant to the issue of infringement) (citing Thurber Corp. v. Fairchild Motor Corp., 269 F.2d 841, 845, 849 (5th Cir. 1959)); Baut v. Pethick Constr. Co., 262 F. Supp. 350, 360 (M.D. Pa. 1966) (knowledge and intent are not material to issue of infringement of patents) (citing Freedman v. Friedman, 242 F.2d 364 (4th Cir. 1957)).

[82] *See, e.g.,* Cheney Co. v. City of Medford, 5 F. Supp. 262 (D. Mass. 1933), *rev'd on other grounds sub nom.* E. Van Noorden Co. v. Cheney Co., 75 F.2d 298 (1st Cir. 1934) (holding owner of school building liable for infringement of patented invention incorporated into the structure by contractor); Blumcraft of Pittsburg v. Citizens & S. Nat'l Bank, 286 F. Supp. 448 (D.S.C. 1968), *rev'd on other grounds,* 407 F.2d 557 (4th Cir.), *cert. denied,* 395 U.S. 961 (1969) (holding owner of building liable for infringement of patented railing components incorporated into structure by contractor).

[83] Baut v. Pethick Constr. Co., 262 F. Supp. 350, 360 (M.D. Penn. 1966) (citing Jackson v. Nagle, 47 F. 980 (C.C.N.D. Cal. 1891)).

[84] 35 U.S.C. §§ 283, 284 (1988).

the design-build contractor to obtain indemnity agreements in favor of the owner in all subcontracts and purchase orders submitted to suppliers in connection with the project. Finally, the owner should take care to ensure that the design-build contractor, subcontractors, and suppliers are sufficiently credit-worthy to fulfill their indemnity and other infringement-related obligations pursuant to the terms of their contracts.

The design-build contractor will similarly benefit by obtaining indemnity agreements in its favor from subcontractors and suppliers, and it should also require subcontractors and suppliers to purchase licenses and redesign equipment to the extent necessary to remedy instances of patent infringement attributable to their involvement in the project. Again, it is important for the design-build contractor to ensure that its subcontractors and suppliers are financially capable of satisfying such obligations.

The design-build contractor can also reduce its exposure to liability by limiting the extent of its indemnity obligations to the owner. For example, the design-builder may agree to obtain indemnity agreements from subcontractors and suppliers in favor of the owner, in exchange for the owner's promise to limit the design-builder's liability to the owner to instances in which the design-builder knew or had reason to know an infringement was occurring in connection with the project. The design-builder may also expressly refuse to indemnify the owner for patent infringement that arises from the contractor's efforts to comply with particular design specifications provided by the owner in the contract.

Of course, there is no single correct way to allocate the risks of patent infringement liability among parties to a construction contract. Parties involved in such transactions, however, should be aware that such liability is shared among all those who use infringing inventions and is not limited to parties who knowingly engage in infringing activity. With that in mind, project owners, contractors, and subcontractors should make use of contractual devices, including indemnity and insurance provisions,[85] to adjust their risks to acceptable levels.

---

[85] Litigation costs and damages sustained as a result of patent infringement may be covered by a party's commercial general liability (CGL) policy. Prior to entering into a contract, it would be prudent for each party to check with its CGL carrier to see if it is covered and arrange for alternative or additional coverage, if necessary.

TABLE OF CASES

Case	*Book §*
Day v. United States, 245 U.S. 159 (1917)	§ 13.7
Day v. West Coast Holdings, Inc., 699 P.2d 1067 (Nev. 1985)	§ 3.5
Dayton, University of, Research Inst., B-2271115, 87-2 CPD ¶ 178 (Aug. 19, 1987)	§ 7.5
Degroft v. Lancaster Silo Co., 527 A.2d 1316 (Md. Ct. Spec. App. 1987)	§ 13.6
Del Mar Beach Club v. Imperial Contracting Co., 176 Cal. Rptr. 886 (Ct. App. 1981)	§ 1.25
Design Dev., Inc. v. Brignole, 570 A.2d 221 (Conn. App. Ct. 1990)	§ 3.5
DeSilva Constr. Co. v. Herrald, 213 F. Supp. 184 (M.D. Fla. 1962)	§ 13.16
Diamond v. Commissioner, 56 T.C. 530 (1971), *aff'd,* 492 F.2d 286 (7th Cir. 1974)	§ 4.16
Don Sieboth Pontiac, Inc. v. Asphalt Rd. & Bldg. & Resurfacing, Inc., 407 So. 2d 42 (La. Ct. App. 1982)	§ 12.22
Dow v. Holley, 154 F.2d 707 (10th Cir. 1946)	§ 3.5
Dreis & Krump Mfg. Co. v. Phoenix Ins. Co., 548 F.2d 681 (7th Cir. 1977)	§ 12.12
Duncan v. Cameron, 244 S.E.2d 217 (S.C. 1978)	§ 3.5
Dunn v. Finlayson, 104 A.2d 830 (D.C. 1954)	§ 3.5
Dynalectron Corp.-Pac. Div., ASBCA No. 18057, 77-1 B.C.A. (CCH) ¶ 12,348 (1977)	§ 13.7
Dyson & Co. v. Flood Eng'rs, Architects, Planners, Inc., 523 So. 2d 756 (Fla. Dist. Ct. App. 1988)	§ 6.10
Ebasco Servs., Inc. v. Pennsylvania Power & Light Co., 460 F. Supp. 163 (E.D. Pa. 1078)	§§ 1.8, 1.22, 1.25
Ecodyne v. Shah, 718 F. Supp. 1454 (N.D. Cal. 1989)	§ 8.3
Edward Hines Lumber Co. v. Vulcan Materials Co., 861 F.2d 155 (7th Cir. 1988)	§ 8.3
Electro-Methods, Inc. v. United States, 3 Cl. Ct. 500 (1983), *aff'd in part, rev'd in part,* 728 F.2d 1471 (Fed. Cir. 1984)	§ 7.6
Elephant Lumber Co. v. Johnson, 202 N.E.2d 189 (Ohio Ct. App. 1964)	§ 3.5
Essex Electro Eng'rs, Inc. v. United States, 3 Cl. Ct. 277 (1983)	§ 7.6
Fanning v. College of Steubenville, 197 N.E.2d 422 (Ohio Ct. C.P. 1961), *appeal dismissed,* 189 N.E.2d 72 (Ohio 1965)	§ 3.5
Federal Elec. Corp. v. Fasi, 527 P.2d 1284 (Haw. 1974)	§ 7.10
Federal Ins. Co. v. P.A.T. Homes, Inc., 547 P.2d 1050 (Ariz. 1976)	§ 6.9
Ferrite Eng'g Labs, B-222972, 86-2 CPD ¶ 122 (July 28, 1986)	§ 7.5
F.F. Bollinger Co. v. Widmann Brewing Corp., 14 A.2d 81 (Pa. 1940)	§§ 3.5, 12.2

Case	*Book §*
Hawaiian Tel. Co. v. Microform Data Sys., 829 F.2d 919 (9th Cir. 1987)	§ 1.22
Haworth v. Montgomery, 18 S.W. 399 (Tenn. 1891)	§ 3.5
Heyer Prods. Co. v. United States, 140 F. Supp. 409 (Ct. Cl. 1956)	§§ 7.4, 7.6
Helda v. McCool, 476 F.2d 1223 (9th Cir. 1973)	§ 3.5
Hickey v. Sutton, 210 N.W. 704 (Wis. 1926)	§ 3.5
Hillside Sec. Co. v. Minter, 254 S.W. 188 (Mo. 1923)	§ 7.12
Honig Constr. Co. v. Szombathy, 345 S.W.2d 111 (Mo. 1961)	§ 3.5
Hospital Dev. Corp. v. Park Lane Land Co., 813 S.W.2d 904 (Mo. Ct. App. 1991)	§ 3.5
Hydrotech Sys., Ltd. v. Oasis Waterpark, 803 P.2d 370 (Cal. 1991)	§ 3.5
INA v. Radiant Elec. Co., 222 N.W.2d 323 (Mich. 1974)	§ 1.26
Indiana & Mich. Elec. Co. v. Terre Haute Indus., Inc., 507 N.E.2d 588 (Ind. 1987)	§ 9.9
Inglewood, City of v. Superior Court, 500 P.2d 601 (Cal. 1972)	§ 7.10
J. Ray McDermott & Co. v. Vessell Morning Star, 431 F.2d 714 (5th Cir. 1979)	§ 1.12
J.A. Croson v. City of Richmond, 822 F.2d 1355 (4th Cir. 1987), *aff'd,* 488 U.S. 469 (1989)	§ 7.9
J.A. Maurer, Inc. v. United States, 485 F.2d 588 (Ct. Cl. 1973), *aff'g* ASBCA No. 12071, 69-2 B.C.A. (CCH) ¶ 7,884 (1969)	§§ 2.8, 13.7
Jackling v. Snyder, 411 P.2d 822 (Ariz. 1966)	§ 3.5
Jackson v. Nagle, 47 F. 980 (C.C.N.D. Cal. 1891)	§ 13.19
Jary v. Emmett, 234 So. 2d 530 (La. Ct. App. 1970)	§ 3.5
J.C. Penney Co. v. Davis & Davis, Inc., 279 S.E.2d 461 (Ga. Ct. App. 1981)	§ 1.28
J.F. Ahern Co. v. Wisconsin State Bldg. Comm'n, 336 N.W.2d 679 (Wis. Ct. App. 1983)	§§ 7.10, 7.12
J.L. Simmons Co. v. United States, 188 Ct. Cl. 684 (1969)	§ 13.4
J&M Indus. v. Huguley Oil Co., 546 So. 2d 369 (Ala. 1989)	§ 3.5
Johnson v. Delane, 290 P.2d 213 (Idaho 1955)	§ 3.5
Joseph v. Drew, 225 P.2d 504 (Cal. 1950)	§ 3.5
Juneau, City & Borough of v. Breck, 706 P.2d 313 (Alaska 1985)	§§ 7.10, 7.12
J.W. Hurst & Son Awnings, Inc., ASBCA No. 4167, 59-1 B.C.A. (CCH) ¶ 2,095 (1959)	§ 13.7
Kansas City Community Ctr. v. Heritage Indus., 773 F. Supp. 181 (W.D. Mo. 1991)	§ 3.5
Keco Indus. v. United States, 428 F.2d 1233 (Ct. Cl. 1970)	§ 2.4

Case	*Book §*
Metropolitan Paving Co. v. United States, 163 Ct. Cl. 241 (1963)	§ 9.9
Miller v. Dewitt, 226 N.E.2d 630 (Ill. 1967)	§ 12.4
Miller Constr. Co. v. First Indus. Technology Corp., 576 So. 2d 748 (Fla. Dist. Ct. App. 1991)	§§ 1.12, 1.15, 3.5
Mobile Hous. Env't v. Barton & Barton, 432 F. Supp. 1343 (D. Colo. 1977)	§§ 1.12, 3.5
Moran v. H.W.S. Lumber Co., 538 F.2d 238 (9th Cir. 1976)	§ 13.3
Mounds View, City of v. Walijarvi, 263 N.W.2d 420 (Minn. 1978)	§ 9.13
Mudgett v. Marshall, 574 A.2d 867 (Me. 1990)	§ 1.12
Mueller v. Birchfield, 218 S.W.2d 180 (Mo. Ct. App. 1949)	§ 3.5
Muller v. Triborough Bridge Auth., 43 F. Supp. 298 (S.D.N.Y. 1942)	§ 13.16
N. Fiorito Co. v. United States, 416 F.2d 1284 (Ct. Cl.), *aff'g* ASBCA Nos. 10037, 10041, 66-1 B.C.A. (CCH) ¶ 5,381 (1965)	§ 2.7
Negley v. Lebanon Community Sch. Corp., 362 N.E.2d 178 (Ind. Ct. App. 1977)	§ 3.5
Neilsen & Co. v. Cassia & Twin Falls County Joint Class A Sch. Dist., 647 P.2d 773 (Idaho Ct. App. 1982)	§ 7.9
Nelson Erection Co., B-217556, 85-1 CPD ¶ 482 (Apr. 29, 1985)	§ 3.3
North Broward Hosp. Dist. v. Fornes, 476 So. 2d 154 (Fla. 1985)	§ 7.12
North Country Div. Corp. v. Massena Hous. Auth., 316 N.Y.S.2d 894 (1970)	§ 7.10
Northern v. Elledge, 232 P.2d 111 (Ariz. 1951)	§ 3.5
Oakson v. Lebanon Valley Uranium Co., 154 F. Supp. 692 (D. Utah 1957)	§ 3.5
O'Kon & Co. v. Reidel, 540 So. 2d 836 (Fla. Dist. Ct. App. 1988)	§ 3.5
Olympia USA, Inc. v. United States, 6 Cl. Ct. 550 (1984)	§ 7.5
Omaha Pollution Control Corp. v. Carver-Greenfield, 413 F. Supp. 1069 (D. Neb. 1976)	§§ 1.26, 6.5, 13.5, 13.6
Orlando, City of v. H.L. Coble Constr. Co., 282 So. 2d 25 (Fla. Dist. Ct. App. 1973)	§ 12.5
Pacific Chromaloc Div. v. Irey, 787 P.2d 1319 (Utah Ct. App.), *cert. denied,* 800 P.2d 1105 (Utah 1990)	§ 4.13
Paul Sardella Constr. Co v. Braintree Hous. Auth., 329 N.E.2d 762 (Mass. App. Ct. 1975)	§ 7.10
Paxson Elec. Co. v. United States, 14 Cl. Ct. 634 (1988)	§§ 2.4, 7.7
People *ex rel.* State Bd. of Architects v. Rodgers Co., 115 N.E. 146 (Ill. 19 7)	§ 12.2

Case	*Book §*
Philadelphia Hous. Auth. v. Turner Constr. Co., 23 A.2d 426 (Pa. 1942)	§ 12.5
Phoenix, City of v. Wittman Contracting Co., 509 P.2d 1038 (Ariz. Ct. App. 1973)	§ 7.10
Pierce Assoc., Inc., GSBCA No. 4163, 77-2 B.C.A. (CCH) ¶ 12,476 (1977)	§ 1.24
Playskool, Inc. v. Elsa Benson, Inc., 497 N.E.2d 1199 (Ill. App. Ct. 1986)	§§ 4.7, 4.9
Port City Constr. Co. v. Henderson, 266 So. 2d 896 (Ala. Civ. App. 1972)	§ 13.6
PRB Uniforms, Inc., ASBCA Nos. 21504-21506, 21743, 21957, 80-2 B.C.A. (CCH) ¶ 14,602 (1980)	§ 2.8
Presnall v. Adams, 214 S.W. 357 (Tex. Civ. App. 1919)	§ 12.5
Pritchett v. Kinberling Cove, Inc., 568 F.2d 570 (8th Cir. 1977), *cert. denied sub nom.* Dando Enters., Ltd. v. Pritchett, 436 U.S. 922 (1978)	§ 13.3
Progressive Survey, Inc. v. Pearson, 410 A.2d 1123 (N.H. 1980)	§ 1.20
Reynolds Metals Co. v. Aluminum Co. of Am., 457 F. Supp. 482 (N.D. Ind. 1978), *rev'd on other grounds,* 609 F.2d 1218 (7th Cir.), *cert. denied,* 446 U.S. 989 (1980)	§ 13.19
RFI Shield-Rooms, ASBCA Nos. 19005, 19038, 10163, 77-1 B.C.A. (CCH) ¶ 12,237 (1977)	§ 2.7
Riney v. City of Hannibal, 712 S.W.2d 49 (Mo. Ct. App. 1986)	§ 7.12
Robert E. McKee Gen. Contractor, Inc., ASBCA No. 5759, 60-1 B.C.A. (CCH) ¶ 2,585 (1960)	§ 13.7
Rodgers v. Kelley, 259 A.2d 784 (Vt. 1969)	§ 3.5
Rosell v. Silver Crest Enters., 436 P.2d 915 (Ariz. 1968)	§§ 1.12, 1.26
Rubin v. Douglas, 59 A.2d 690 (D.C. 1948)	§ 3.5
St. John Farms, Inc. v. D.J. Irvin Co., 609 P.2d 970 (Wash. Ct. App. 1980)	§ 3.5
St. Joseph Hosp. v. Corbetta Constr. Co., 316 N.E.2d 51 (Ill. App. Ct. 1974)	§ 12.11
St. Luke's Hosp. v. Midwest Mechanical Contractors, Inc., 681 S.W.2d 482 (Mo. Ct. App. 1984)	§ 7.2
St. Paul Fire & Marine Ins. Co. v. Freeman-White Assocs., Inc., 366 S.E.2d 480 (N.C. 1988)	§ 6.10
Sarkco, Inc. v. Edwards, 482 S.W.2d 623 (Ark. 1972)	§ 3.5
Scanwell Lab., Inc. v. Shaffer, 424 F.2d 859 (D.C. Cir. 1970)	§§ 7.4, 7.6
Scott-Daniels Properties, Inc. v. Dresser, 160 S.W.2d 675 (Minn. 1968)	§ 3.5
Seaview Hosp., Inc. v. Medicenters of Am., Inc., 570 S.W.2d 35 (Tex. Ct. App. 1978)	§§ 1.31, 3.5, 4.13, 4.25

Case	*Book §*
Securities & Exch. Comm'n v. Senex Corp., 399 F. Supp. 497 (E.D. Ky. 1975), *aff'd,* 534 F.2d 1240 (6th Cir. 1976)	§ 1.6
Shaw v. Aetna Casualty & Sur. Co., 407 F.2d 813 (7th Cir. 1969)	§ 6.9
Sherwood v. Wise, 232 P.2d 309 (Wash. 1929)	§ 3.5
Shipper v. Levitt & Sons, Inc., 207 A.2d 314 (N.J. 1965)	§§ 6.5, 9.13
Shirley Constr. Co., 70 Comp. Gen. 62 (1990)	§ 7.5
Singer Hous. Co. v. Seven Lakes Venture, 466 F. Supp. 369 (D. Colo. 1979)	§ 13.3
Smith v. Tyonek Timber, Inc., 680 P.2d 1148 (Alaska 1984)	§ 3.5
Snodgrass v. Immler, 194 A.2d 103 (Md. 1963)	§ 3.5
South Dakota Bldg. Auth. v. Geiger-Berger Assocs., P.C., 414 N.W.2d 15 (S.D. 1987)	§ 3.5
Southern Metal Treating Co. v. Goodner, 125 So. 2d 268 (Ala. 1960)	§ 3.5
Spanish Trails Lanes, *In re,* 16 B.R. 304 (Bankr. D. Ariz. 1981)	§ 3.5
Spencer, White & Prentis, Inc. v. Southwest Sewer Dist., 477 N.Y.S.2d 681 (App. Div. 1984)	§ 7.8
Sperry Rand Corp. v. Industrial Supply Corp., 337 F.2d 363 (5th Cir. 1964)	§ 13.6
State *ex rel.* Love v. Howell, 328 S.E.2d 77 (S.C. 1985)	§ 3.5
State Mechanical Contractors, Inc. v. Village of Pleasant Hill, 477 N.E.2d 509 (Ill. Ct. App. 1985)	§ 7.9
Stone v. First Wyo. Bank, 625 F.2d 332 (10th Cir. 1980)	§ 13.3
Stone & Webster Eng'g Corp. v. American Motorist Ins. Co., 458 F. Supp. 792 (E.D. Va. 1978), *aff'd mem.,* 628 F.2d 1351 (4th Cir. 1980)	§ 12.12
Stuyvesant Dredging Co. v. United States, 834 F.2d 1576 (Fed. Cir. 1987)	§ 13.4
Sutter Bros. Constr. Co. v. City of Leavenworth, 708 P.2d 190 (Kan. 1985)	§ 7.10
Swinerton & Wallberg Co. v. City of Inglewood, 114 Cal. Rptr. 834 (Ct. App. 1974)	§ 7.10
Tanglewood E. Homeowners v. Charles-Thomas, Inc., 849 F.2d 1568 (5th Cir. 1988)	§ 8.3
Tectonics, Inc. v. Castle Constr. Co., 496 So. 2d 704 (Ala. 1986)	§ 7.9
Telephone Assocs., Inc. v. St. Louis County Bd., 364 N.W.2d 378 (Minn. 1985)	§ 7.9
Thomas v. Lundgren, 449 P.2d 628 (Ariz. 1969)	§ 3.5
Thurber Corp. v. Fairchild Motor Corp., 269 F.2d 841 (5th Cir. 1959)	§ 13.19
Tichenor v. State Lottery Comm'n, 742 S.W.2d 170 (Mo. 1989)	§ 7.10
Titan Pac. Constr. v. United States, 17 Cl. Ct. 630 (1989)	§ 9.9

Case	*Book §*
Whittaker Corp., Power Sources Div., ASBCA Nos. 14191, 14722, 14740, 15005, 15628, 79-1 B.C.A. (CCH) ¶ 13,805 (1979)	§ 2.8
William Coltin & Co. v. Manchester Sav. Bank, 197 A.2d 208 (N.H. 1964)	§ 3.5
William Graham, Inc. v. City of Cave City, 709 S.W. 94 (Ark. 1986)	§ 1.22
Williamson & Vollmer Eng'g, Inc. v. Sequoia Ins. Co., 134 Cal. Rptr. 427 (Ct. App. 1976)	§ 12.12
Wilson v. Kealakekua Ranch, Ltd., 551 P.2d 525 (Haw. 1976)	§ 3.5
Wilson v. United States, 376 F.2d 280 (Ct. Cl. 1967)	§ 4.21
Wise v. State Bd. for Qualification & Registration of Architects, 274 S.E.2d 544 (Ga. 1981)	§§ 3.5, 4.1
Woodhaven Homes, Inc. v. Kennedy Sheet Metal Co., 803 S.W.2d 508 (1991)	§ 3.5
Woolard v. Mobile Pipeline Co., 479 F.2d 557 (5th Cir.), *cert. denied sub nom.* Mobile Oil Corp. v. Woolard, 414 U.S. 1025 (1973)	§ 13.3

INDEX